**NIEUWE ZIJDE**
*Pages 70–85*

**OUDE ZIJDE**
*Pages 56–69*

Nieuwe
Zijde

Oude Zijde

Plantage

Eastern
Canal Ring

**EASTERN CANAL RING**
*Page 114–123*

**PLANTAGE**
*Pages 138–147*

metres          500

yards          500

# EYEWITNESS TRAVEL GUIDES

# AMSTERDAM

EYEWITNESS TRAVEL GUIDES

# AMSTERDAM

*Main contributors:*
ROBIN PASCOE
CHRISTOPHER CATLING

DK

LONDON, NEW YORK,
MELBOURNE, MUNICH AND DELHI
www.dk.com

PROJECT EDITOR Heather Jones
ART EDITOR Vanessa Hamilton
EDITORS Peter Adams, Sasha Heseltine,
Fiona Morgan, Alice Peebles, Nichola Tyrrell
US EDITOR Mary Sutherland
DESIGNERS Emma Hutton, Erika Lang, Malcolm Parchment

CONTRIBUTORS
Paul Andrews, Hedda Archbold, Marlene Edmunds, Adam
Hopkins, David Lindsey (Restaurants), Fred Mawer, Alison Melvin,
Catherine Stebbings, Richard Widdows

PHOTOGRAPHERS
Max Alexander, Rupert Horrox, Kim Sayer

ILLUSTRATORS
Nick Gibbard, Maltings Partnership,
Derrick Stone, Martin Woodward

Film outputting bureau Cooling Brown, London
Reproduced by Colourscan, Singapore
Printed and bound by L. Rex Printing Company, China

First American edition 1995
04 05 10 9

Published in the United States by DK Publishing, Inc.,
375 Hudson Street, New York, New York 10014
**Reprinted with revisions 1997, 1998, 1999, 2000,
2001, 2002, 2003, 2004**

Copyright 1995, 2004 © Dorling Kindersley Limited, London

Published in Great Britain by Dorling Kindersley Limited.

ISSN 1542-1554
ISBN 0-7894-9558-9

THROUGHOUT THIS BOOK, FLOORS ARE REFERRED TO IN ACCORDANCE
WITH EUROPEAN USAGE, I.E., THE "FIRST FLOOR" IS THE FLOOR
ABOVE GROUND LEVEL.

---

**The information in this
Dorling Kindersley Travel Guide is checked annually**.
Every effort has been made to ensure that this book is as up-to-date
as possible at the time of going to press. Some details, however,
such as telephone numbers, opening hours, prices, gallery hanging
arrangements and travel information are liable to change. The
publishers cannot accept responsibility for any consequences arising
from the use of this book, nor for any material on third party
websites, and cannot guarantee that any website address in this
book will be a suitable source of travel information. We value the
views and suggestions of our readers very highly. Please write to:
Publisher, DK Eyewitness Travel Guides,
Dorling Kindersley, 80 Strand, London WC2R 0RL, Great Britain.

# CONTENTS

Model boat at Scheepvaart Museum

# INTRODUCING
AMSTERDAM

# AMSTERDAM AREA
BY AREA

Traditional drawbridge

Children in Dutch costume outside a church in the Zuiderzee Museum

Café terrace in Artis zoo

Façade of the Rijksmuseum

Wheels of Gouda cheese

Dutch Renaissance canal house and details of cornices and gables

# HOW TO USE THIS GUIDE

THIS GUIDE helps you get the most from your stay in Amsterdam. It provides expert recommendations as well as detailed practical information. *Introducing Amsterdam* maps the city and sets it in its historical and cultural context. *Amsterdam Area by Area* describes the important sights, with maps, pictures and illustrations. *Further Afield* looks at sights outside the city centre and *Beyond Amsterdam* explores other places near Amsterdam. Suggestions on food, drink, where to stay and what to do are made in *Travellers' Needs,* and *Survival Guide* has tips on everything from travel to Dutch telephones.

## AMSTERDAM AREA BY AREA

The centre of the city has been divided into seven sightseeing areas. Each area has its own chapter, which opens with a list of the sights described. All the sights are numbered and plotted on an *Area Map.* The detailed information for each sight is presented in numerical order, making it easy to locate within the chapter.

**Sights at a Glance** lists the chapter's sights by category: Churches, Museums and Galleries, Historic Buildings, Streets and Canals.

**2 Street-by-Street Map**
This gives a bird's-eye view of the heart of each sightseeing area.

**A suggested route** for a walk covers the more interesting streets in the area.

**Each area** of central Amsterdam has colour-coded thumb tabs.

**A locator map** shows where you are in relation to other areas of the city centre.

**1 Area Map**
*For easy reference, the sights are numbered and located on a map. The sights are also shown on the* Amsterdam Street Finder *on pages 280–87.*

**Stars** indicate the sights that no visitor should miss.

**3 Detailed information on each sight**
*All the sights in Amsterdam are described individually. Addresses and practical information are provided. The key to the symbols used in the information block is shown on the back flap.*

## 4 Introduction to Beyond Amsterdam

Beyond Amsterdam *has its own introduction, which provides an overview of the history and character of the region around Amsterdam and outlines what the region has to offer the visitor today. The area covered by this section is highlighted on the map of the Netherlands shown on page 165. It covers important cities, such as Den Haag, as well as attractive towns and places of interest in the Dutch countryside.*

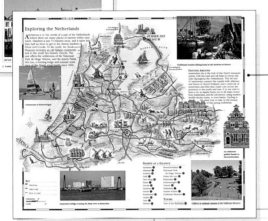

## 5 Pictorial Map

*This gives an illustrated overview of the whole region. All the sights covered in this section are numbered, and the network of major roads is marked. There are also useful tips on getting around the region by bus and train.*

## 6 Detailed information on each sight

*All the important cities, towns and other places to visit are described individually. They are listed in order, following the numbering given on the Pictorial Map. Within each town or city, there is detailed information on important buildings and other sights.*

**Stars** indicate the best features and works of art.

**The Visitors' Checklist** provides a summary of the practical information you will need to plan your visit.

## 7 The top sights

*These are given two or more full pages. Historic buildings are dissected to reveal their interiors; museums and galleries have colour-coded floorplans to help you locate the most interesting exhibits.*

# INTRODUCING
# AMSTERDAM

# Putting Amsterdam on the Map

Although the Netherlands' seat of government is at Den Haag, Amsterdam is the nominal capital. It is the country's largest city, with a population of almost 750,000, and the most visited, receiving over 3.5 million foreign visitors a year. It stands on precariously low-lying ground at the confluence of the Amstel and IJ rivers near the IJsselmeer and, like much of the Netherlands, would flood frequently but for land reclamation and sea defences. This position places Amsterdam at the heart of the Randstad, a term used to describe the crescent-shaped conurbation covering much of the provinces of Noord Holland, Zuid Holland and Utrecht, and encompassing the cities of Utrecht, Rotterdam, Den Haag, Leiden and Haarlem.

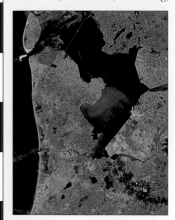

**Satellite photograph showing the north-west Netherlands and the IJsselmeer**

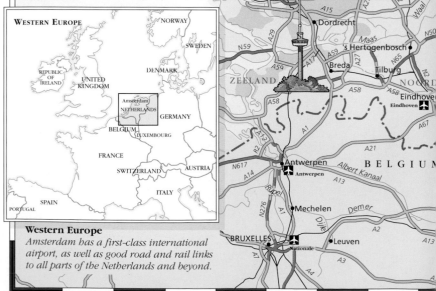

## Western Europe
*Amsterdam has a first-class international airport, as well as good road and rail links to all parts of the Netherlands and beyond.*

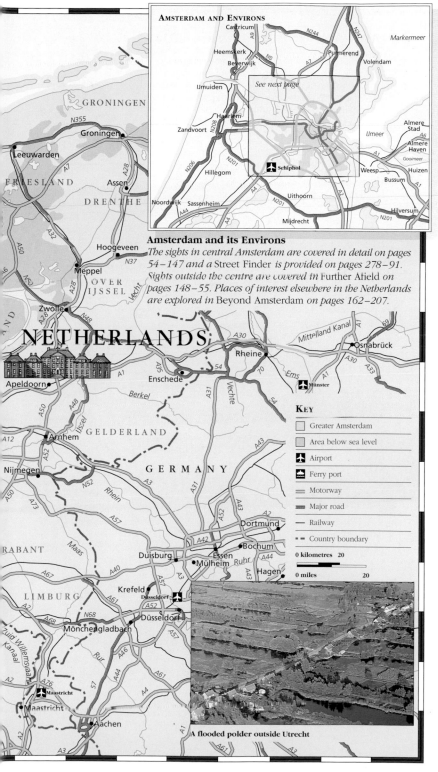

**AMSTERDAM AND ENVIRONS**

Castricum

Heemskerk

Beverwijk

IJmuiden

*See next page*

Haarlem

Zandvoort

Hillegom

Noordwijk    Sassenheim

Mijdrecht

N244

Purmerend

Volendam

*Markermeer*

Almere
Stad

Almere
Haven

*Gooimeer*

*IJmeer*

Schiphol

Weesp

Bussum

Uithoorn

Huizen

Hilversum

## Amsterdam and its Environs

*The sights in central Amsterdam are covered in detail on pages 54–147 and a* Street Finder *is provided on pages 278–91. Sights outside the centre are covered in* Further Afield *on pages 148–55. Places of interest elsewhere in the Netherlands are explored in* Beyond Amsterdam *on pages 162–207.*

Groningen

GRONINGEN

Leeuwarden

FRIESLAND

Assen

DRENTHE

Hoogeveen

Meppel

OVER
IJSSEL

Zwolle

# NETHERLANDS

Apeldoorn

Enschede

Berkel

Rheine

Mittelland Kanal

Osnabrück

Ems

Münster

Arnhem

GELDERLAND

Nijmegen

GERMANY

Dortmund

RABANT

Maas

Duisburg

Mülheim

Essen

Ruhr

Bochum

Hagen

LIMBURG

Krefeld

Mönchengladbach

Düsseldorf

Maastricht

Aachen

### KEY

| | Greater Amsterdam |
| | Area below sea level |
| ✈ | Airport |
| ⛴ | Ferry port |
| | Motorway |
| | Major road |
| | Railway |
| | Country boundary |

0 kilometres    20

0 miles    20

**A flooded polder outside Utrecht**

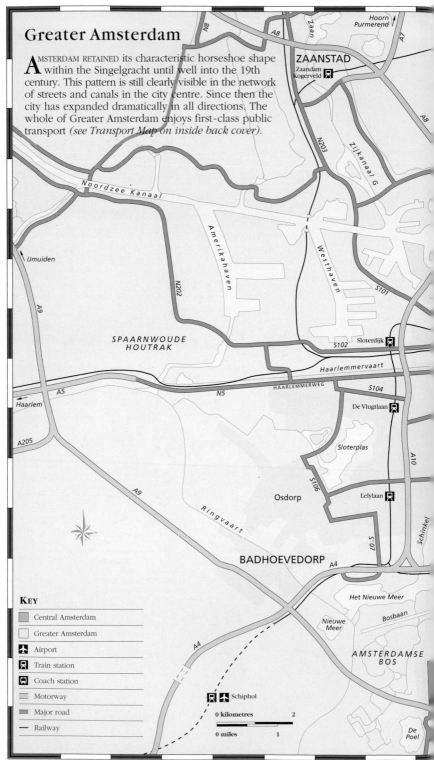

# Greater Amsterdam

AMSTERDAM RETAINED its characteristic horseshoe shape within the Singelgracht until well into the 19th century. This pattern is still clearly visible in the network of streets and canals in the city centre. Since then the city has expanded dramatically in all directions. The whole of Greater Amsterdam enjoys first-class public transport *(see Transport Map on inside back cover).*

**ZAANSTAD**

Zaandam
Kogerveld

Hoorn
Purmerend

*Noordzee Kanaal*

*Amerikahaven*

*Westhaven*

IJmuiden

*SPAARNWOUDE HOUTRAK*

Sloterdijk

Haarlemmervaart

HAARLEMMERWEG

Haarlem

De Vlugtlaan

Sloterplas

Osdorp

Lelylaan

**BADHOEVEDORP**

Ringvaart

Het Nieuwe Meer

Bosbaan

Nieuwe Meer

*AMSTERDAMSE BOS*

Schiphol

De Poel

## KEY

| | |
|---|---|
| | Central Amsterdam |
| | Greater Amsterdam |
| ✈ | Airport |
| 🚉 | Train station |
| 🚌 | Coach station |
| | Motorway |
| | Major road |
| | Railway |

0 kilometres          2

0 miles          1

Volendam

Het
Twiske

De Leek

Noordhollands Kanaal

N247

A10

WATERLAND

A10

S118

Holysloter
Die

Ransdorper
Die

S116

Kinselmeer

Het IJ

S115

S101

A10

See next page

Centraal
Station

IJ Tunnel

Het IJ

S103

Prinsengracht

Singel

S114

Buiten IJ

Dam

AMSTERDAM

IJmeer

Oostvlorenvaart

S100

Singelgracht

Amstel

Nieuwe Diep

S106

Muiderpoort

Amsterdam-Rijnkanaal

ONDELPARK

Rijksmuseum

S108

S112

Amstel

Amstel

A10

Diemen

De
Diemen

BEATRIXPARK

S109

S112

DIEMEN

A1

A10

Diemen-
Zuid

S211

Hilversum
Amersfoort

Zuid
WTC

RAI

AMSTERDAM
ZUIDOOST

Gaasp

Duivendrecht

BIJLMERMEER

S112

MSTELVEEN

A2

Bijlmer

A9

Gaasperplas

Gein

A9

OUDERKERK
AAN DE AMSTEL

Bullewijk

Utrecht

# Central Amsterdam

**A street musician on Waterlooplein**

THIS GUIDE divides central Amsterdam into seven distinct areas, each of which has its own chapter. Most city sights are contained in these areas. The Oude Zijde and Nieuwe Zijde make up the two halves of medieval Amsterdam, while the Museum Quarter was developed in the 19th century and has the three most important national museums. In between lies the Canal Ring, which retains many fine buildings from Amsterdam's Golden Age, while the Plantage *(see pp138–47)*, once an area of green space outside the city, is today best known for the zoological and botanical gardens.

**Anti-war Barge on the Singel**
*The Singel was the first concentric canal to be cut in Amsterdam. It forms the border between the medieval centre and the newer Western and Central Canal Rings (see pp86–113).*

**Vondelpark**
*This attractive park in the Museum Quarter (see pp124–37) is a good place to relax after a visit to one of Amsterdam's museums.*

0 metres          500

0 yards          500

**Spires of Nieuwe Kerk and the Magna Plaza**
*The Nieuwe Zijde's skyline (see pp70–85) is pierced by the Neo-Gothic spire of Magna Plaza (the former Postkantoor), the steeples of the Nieuwe Kerk and the statues on the Koninklijk Paleis.*

**House on the Oudezijds Voorburgwal**
*This attractive residential canal, which now runs through the Red Light District, was first cut in front of the ramparts protecting the Oude Zijde (see pp56–69).*

**Flowers at the Bloemenmarkt**
*A fragrant, floating flower market, the Bloemenmarkt is situated beside the Munttoren on the Singel in the Eastern Canal Ring (see pp114–23).*

**KEY**

| | |
|---|---|
| | Major sight |
| | Place of interest |
| | Other building |
| **P** | Parking |
| | Tourist information |
| | Police station |
| | Church |
| | Synagogue |
| **C** | Mosque |

# THE HISTORY OF AMSTERDAM

AMSTERDAM, the greatest planned city of northern Europe, is today one in which beauty and serenity co-exist happily with a slightly seamy underside. Both parts of this split personality continue to draw visitors. Most of the racier aspects of Amsterdam spring directly from the city's long and honourable tradition of religious, philosophical and political tolerance. Developing at a time when many countries were riven by conflict, a precedent for freedom of speech was established early in Amsterdam. The notion of individual freedom of conscience was fought for, long and hard, during the struggles against Spanish domination in the 16th century. This belief stands firm today, with the caveat that no-one should be harmed by the actions of others – a factor which sparked off the riots involving squatters in the 1970s.

Amsterdam's coat of arms on the Munttoren

The city was founded as a small fishing village in an improbable position on marsh at the mouth of the Amstel river. The waters around the village were controlled by a system of dykes and polders, and the young township expanded prodigiously to become the chief trading city of northern Europe, and ultimately, in the 17th century, the centre of a massive empire stretching across the world. The construction of the canals and gabled houses in the 16th and 17th centuries – the hallmark Amsterdam – coincided with a period of fine domestic architecture. The glorious result is a city centre of unusually consistent visual beauty. By the 18th century, Amsterdam was a major financial centre, but internal unrest and restrictions imposed under Napoleonic rule led to a decline in her fortunes.

The city quietly slipped into a period of obscurity, and industrialization came late. In the 20th century, however, the city entered the European mainstream again. Its international airport, expanded in 1993, provides access for the world, and tourists pour in to see the stunning art museums and sample the delights of a modern, vibrant city.

Plan of Amsterdam (c. 1725) showing the Grachtengordel *(see pp44–5)* and Plantage *(see pp138–47)*

◁ *The Maid of Amsterdam Receiving the Homage of her People* (c. 1685) by Gerard de Lairesse

# The Origins of Amsterdam

**A**MSTERDAM emerged from the mists of the Low Countries in about 1200, on a watery site at the mouth of the Amstel river. It was a settlement of fisherfolk before turning to trade. The first permanent dwellings were built on terps, man-made mounds high enough to provide protection from flood water. As the settlement grew, it was fashioned by dynastic and religious combat, with feudal struggles between the Lords van Amstel and the counts of Holland, who had the backing of the all-powerful bishops of Utrecht *(see p202)*. This rivalry continued into the next century.

**Windmills drained the land**

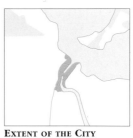

**EXTENT OF THE CITY**

▨ 1100        ▢ Today

**Farming on polders outside the village walls**

**Dam**

**Cooking Pot**
*Sturdy earthenware pots were used for cooking communal meals over an open fire in the kitchen area of 13th-century houses.*

**Wooden defence walls**

**Lord Gijsbrecht**
*The 19th-century etching shows Gijsbrecht van Amstel IV being marched into Utrecht as a prisoner by Guy of Hainaut, brother of the Count of Holland, in 1298.*

**Livestock** grazed on reclaimed land called polder.

## THE VILLAGE OF AMSTERDAM IN 1300
This medieval artist's impression shows the first tiny settlement on polders along the Damrak. The village was protected by wooden walls, and it is thought that the castle of the Van Amstels may have been located in the area around today's Dam square *(see pp72–3)*.

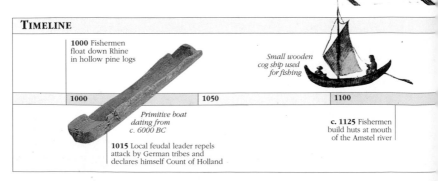

**TIMELINE**

**1000** Fishermen float down Rhine in hollow pine logs

*Small wooden cog ship used for fishing*

| 1000 | 1050 | 1100 |
|---|---|---|

*Primitive boat dating from c. 6000 BC*

**c. 1125** Fishermen build huts at mouth of the Amstel river

**1015** Local feudal leader repels attack by German tribes and declares himself Count of Holland

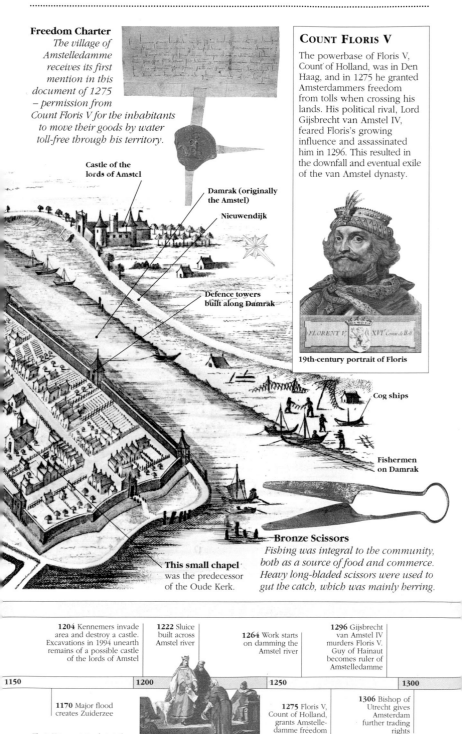

**Freedom Charter**
*The village of Amstelledamme receives its first mention in this document of 1275 – permission from Count Floris V for the inhabitants to move their goods by water toll-free through his territory.*

## COUNT FLORIS V

The powerbase of Floris V, Count of Holland, was in Den Haag, and in 1275 he granted Amsterdammers freedom from tolls when crossing his lands. His political rival, Lord Gijsbrecht van Amstel IV, feared Floris's growing influence and assassinated him in 1296. This resulted in the downfall and eventual exile of the van Amstel dynasty.

19th-century portrait of Floris

Castle of the lords of Amstel

Damrak (originally the Amstel)

Nieuwendijk

Defence towers built along Damrak

Cog ships

Fishermen on Damrak

**Bronze Scissors**
*Fishing was integral to the community, both as a source of food and commerce. Heavy long-bladed scissors were used to gut the catch, which was mainly herring.*

**This small chapel** was the predecessor of the Oude Kerk.

**1204** Kennemers invade area and destroy a castle. Excavations in 1994 unearth remains of a possible castle of the lords of Amstel

**1222** Sluice built across Amstel river

**1264** Work starts on damming the Amstel river

**1296** Gijsbrecht van Amstel IV murders Floris V. Guy of Hainaut becomes ruler of Amstelledamme

1150     1200     1250     1300

**1170** Major flood creates Zuiderzee

*Floris V presents trade privilege to village of Amstelledamme*

**1275** Floris V, Count of Holland, grants Amstelledamme freedom from tolls

**1306** Bishop of Utrecht gives Amsterdam further trading rights

# Medieval Amsterdam

THE LITTLE TOWN at the mouth of the Amstel fortified itself against both its enemies and the surrounding water. Amsterdam grew rich quickly after the discovery of a method of curing herring in 1385, which preserved the fish longer, enabling it to be exported. The town became a port for handling beer from Hamburg. Elaborate waterside houses with warehouses attached were used to service the trade. The Low Countries were under the rule of the Dukes of Burgundy, and control passed by marriage to the Austrian Habsburgs.

**Medieval leather boot (c. 1500)**

**EXTENT OF THE CITY**
🟦 *1300*    ⬜ *Today*

**Miracle of Amsterdam**
*This tapestry cushion depicts a miraculous event. A dying man was given the Sacrament which he regurgitated. Thrown on the fire, the Host would not burn.*

## CANALSIDE HOUSE

Early canal houses were simple structures, built of wood with a thatched roof. From a single-storey design with the front and back on different levels, the layouts grew more complex. At the front, side rooms became separated off from the main room, and the back house was similarly divided up. The family slept on the first floor and goods were stored under the roof.

**The wooden façades** had simple spout gables *(see pp96–7).*

**Flour, beer** and other foodstuffs were stored under the sloping roof.

**Philip of Burgundy and Isabella of Portugal**
*Philip ruled the Low Countries after 1419. His wedding to Isabella in 1430 led to the Habsburg dynasty ruling the Netherlands.*

**Timber structure**

# TIMELINE

**1304** Lord Gijsbrecht van Amstel exiled

**Early 1300s** Work starts on Oude Kerk *(see pp68–9)*

*Misericord in the Oude Kerk*

**c. 1380** Work begins on Nieuwe Kerk *(see pp76–7)*

**1385** Willem Beukelszoon discovers method of curing herring

| 1300 | 1325 | 1350 | 1375 | 1400 |
|---|---|---|---|---|

**1301** Guy of Hainaut made Bishop of Utrecht

**1323** Count of Holland designates Amsterdam a toll port for beer

**1345** Miracle of Amsterdam

**1350** Amsterdam becomes a beer and grain entrepôt

*Stained-glass window in the Nieuwe Kerk*

## Making Beer

*The brewing industry expanded after 1323, when the Count of Holland permitted Amsterdam to become a toll port for beer. Hops were introduced early in the century.*

Thatched roof

### The Great Fire of 1452

*After Amsterdam's second devastating blaze, which destroyed the Nieuwe Kerk, legislation was passed preventing the use of wood as a building material.*

Access to canal at rear

Stone side walls

**Wooden support piles** were driven into the first stable layer of sand.

Warehouse space

### Amsterdam's Seal

*The seal shows the diagonal crosses of St Andrew, the coat of arms of the Habsburgs and the cog ship that brought wealth through trade.*

## WHERE TO SEE MEDIEVAL AMSTERDAM

Few buildings remain from this period, as fire destroyed two-thirds of the city. The Oude Kerk *(see pp68–9)* dates from the early 14th century and the Nieuwe Kerk *(pp76–7)* from 1380. The Agnietenkapel *(p61)* was built in 1470 and is one of very few Gothic chapels to survive the Alteration of 1578 *(pp22–3)*.

**The Waag** (p60)
*Built in 1488, this was originally a gateway in the city wall.*

**No. 34 Begijnhof** (p75)
*The oldest wooden house in the city, it dates from about 1420.*

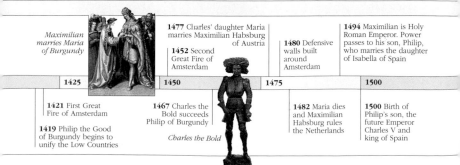

*Maximilian marries Maria of Burgundy*

**1477** Charles' daughter Maria marries Maximilian Habsburg of Austria

**1452** Second Great Fire of Amsterdam

**1480** Defensive walls built around Amsterdam

**1494** Maximilian is Holy Roman Emperor. Power passes to his son, Philip, who marries the daughter of Isabella of Spain

| 1425 | 1450 | 1475 | 1500 |

**1421** First Great Fire of Amsterdam

**1419** Philip the Good of Burgundy begins to unify the Low Countries

**1467** Charles the Bold succeeds Philip of Burgundy

*Charles the Bold*

**1482** Maria dies and Maximilian Habsburg rules the Netherlands

**1500** Birth of Philip's son, the future Emperor Charles V and king of Spain

# The Age of Intolerance

**B**Y 1500, AMSTERDAM had outpaced rivals to become the main power in the province of Holland. Trade in the Baltic provided wealth and the city grew rapidly. Spain's Habsburg rulers tried to halt the Protestant Reformation sweeping northern Europe. Dutch resistance to Philip II of Spain resulted in 80 years of civil war and religious strife. Amsterdam sided with Spain but switched loyalties in 1578 – an event known as the Alteration – to become the fiercely Protestant capital of an infant Dutch Republic.

**EXTENT OF THE CITY**

■ *1500*      □ *Today*

Nieuwe Kerk (1395)

Rokin

Dam square

Oudezijds Voorburgwal

**Anabaptists' Uprising** *(1535)*
*An extremist Protestant cult of Anabaptists seized the Stadhuis. Many were executed after eviction.*

Oude Kerk (1306)

## PERSPECTIVE OF AMSTERDAM
This painted woodcut is a bird's-eye view of Amsterdam by Cornelis Anthonisz (1538). It is a critically important, detailed and precise map, heralding a centuries-long tradition of world-class map making in the city *(see p146).*

Schreiers-toren

**Much of the farmland** in the Netherlands is below sea level.

**William of Orange**
*William, portrayed in 1555 by Anthonius Mor, led the Dutch against the Spanish until his assassination in Delft* (see p195).

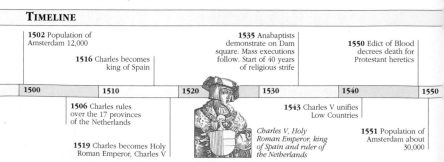

## TIMELINE

**1502** Population of Amsterdam 12,000

**1516** Charles becomes king of Spain

**1535** Anabaptists demonstrate on Dam square. Mass executions follow. Start of 40 years of religious strife

**1550** Edict of Blood decrees death for Protestant heretics

| 1500 | 1510 | 1520 | 1530 | 1540 | 1550 |
|------|------|------|------|------|------|

**1506** Charles rules over the 17 provinces of the Netherlands

**1519** Charles becomes Holy Roman Emperor, Charles V

*Charles V, Holy Roman Emperor, king of Spain and ruler of the Netherlands*

**1543** Charles V unifies Low Countries

**1551** Population of Amsterdam about 30,000

**The Guild of St George** *(1533)*
*Guilds set up to keep order in the growing city later formed the Civic Guard (see pp82–3). Map-maker Cornelis Anthonisz painted this guild at supper.*

## WHERE TO SEE 16TH-CENTURY AMSTERDAM

Few buildings of early 16th-century provenance remain, but No. 1 Zeedijk *(see p67)* was built mid-century as a hostel for sailors. The Civic Guards' Gallery at the Amsterdams Historisch Museum *(pp80–83)* contains a series of splendid group portraits of 16th-century militia companies and guilds.

Nieuwezijds Voorburgwal

Singel

**The Third Expedition**
*Gerrit de Veer's copper engraving (1597) shows Willem Barentsz on his search for a passage to the Arctic Sea.*

Damrak

**Montelbaanstoren**
*The lower section of the tower was built in 1512 (see p66), forming part of the city defences.*

**Silver Drinking Horn**
*As the guilds grew richer, ceremony played a larger part in their lives. This ornate drinking horn shows St George defending the hapless maiden against the dragon.*

Wind-powered pump

Sea

**Draining the Polders**
*"Gangs" of windmills were built to drain the low-lying land. Each mill scooped water up, stage by stage, until it drained away into the sea (see p173).*

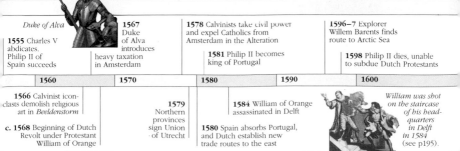

*Duke of Alva*

**1555** Charles V abdicates. Philip II of Spain succeeds

**1567** Duke of Alva introduces heavy taxation in Amsterdam

**1578** Calvinists take civil power and expel Catholics from Amsterdam in the Alteration

**1581** Philip II becomes king of Portugal

**1596–7** Explorer Willem Barents finds route to Arctic Sea

**1598** Philip II dies, unable to subdue Dutch Protestants

| 1560 | 1570 | 1580 | 1590 | 1600 |
|---|---|---|---|---|

**1566** Calvinist iconoclasts demolish religious art in *Beeldenstorm*

**c. 1568** Beginning of Dutch Revolt under Protestant William of Orange

**1579** Northern provinces sign Union of Utrecht

**1584** William of Orange assassinated in Delft

**1580** Spain absorbs Portugal, and Dutch establish new trade routes to the east

*William was shot on the staircase of his headquarters in Delft in 1584 (see p195).*

# The Golden Age of Amsterdam

THE 17TH CENTURY was truly a Golden Age for Amsterdam. The population soared, three great canals *(see pp44–5)*, bordered by splendid houses, were built in a triple ring round the city and scores of painters and architects were at work. Fortunes were made and lost, and this early capitalism produced paupers who were cared for by charitable institutions – a radical idea for the time. In 1648, an uneasy peace was formalized with Catholic Spain, causing tension between Amsterdam's Calvinist burgomasters and the less religious House of Orange, dominant elsewhere in the country.

**EXTENT OF THE CITY**

■ *1600*    ☐ *Today*

Livestock and grain trading

**Self-Portrait as the Apostle Paul** *(1661)*
*Rembrandt* (see p62) *was one of many artists working in Amsterdam in the mid-17th century.*

**Nieuwe Kerk (1395)**

**The new Stadhuis**
(now the Koninklijk Paleis) was being constructed behind wooden scaffolding.

**The Love Letter** *(1666)*
*Genre painting* (see p194), *such as this calm domestic interior by Jan Vermeer, became popular as society grew more sophisticated.*

## DAM SQUARE IN 1656

Money poured into Amsterdam at this time of civic expansion. Jan Lingelbach (c. 1624–74) painted Dam square as a busy, thriving and cosmopolitan market, full of traders and wealthy merchants.

**Delft Tiles**
*Delicate flower paintings were popular themes on 17th-century Delft tiles* (see p195), *used as decoration in wealthy households.*

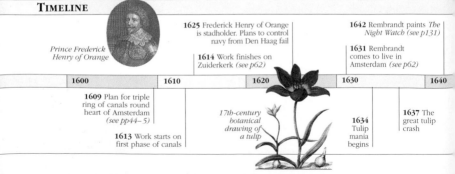

**TIMELINE**

*Prince Frederick Henry of Orange*

**1625** Frederick Henry of Orange is stadholder. Plans to control navy from Den Haag fail

**1642** Rembrandt paints *The Night Watch* (see p131)

**1614** Work finishes on Zuiderkerk *(see p62)*

**1631** Rembrandt comes to live in Amsterdam *(see p62)*

| 1600 | 1610 | 1620 | 1630 | 1640 |
|---|---|---|---|---|

**1609** Plan for triple ring of canals round heart of Amsterdam *(see pp44–5)*

*17th-century botanical drawing of a tulip*

**1634** Tulip mania begins

**1637** The great tulip crash

**1613** Work starts on first phase of canals

**Flora's Bandwagon** *(1636)*
*Many allegories were painted during "tulip mania". This satirical oil by HG Pot symbolizes the idiocy of investors who paid for rare bulbs with their weight in gold, forcing prices up until the market collapsed.*

**Commodities weighed at the Waag** *(see p60)*

**Ships sailing up the Damrak**

Cargo unloaded by cranes    Turkish traders

**Giving the Bread**
*The painting by Willem van Valckert shows the needy receiving alms. A rudimentary welfare system was introduced in the 1640s.*

## WHERE TO SEE 17TH-CENTURY AMSTERDAM

Many public buildings sprang up as Amsterdam grew more wealthy. The Westerkerk *(see p90)* was designed by Hendrick de Keyser in 1620, the Lutherse Kerk *(p78)* by Adriaan Dortsman in 1671. Elias Bouman built the Portugese Synagoge *(p66)* in 1675 for members of the immigrant Sephardic Jewish community *(p64)*.

**Apollo** *(c. 1648)*
*Artus Quellien's statue is in the South Gallery of the Koninklijk Paleis (see p74).*

**Rembrandthuis** *(1606)*
*Jacob van Campen added the pediment in 1633 (see p66).*

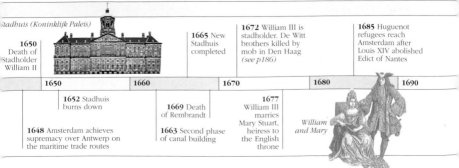

Stadhuis (Koninklijk Paleis)

**1650** Death of Stadholder William II

**1652** Stadhuis burns down

**1648** Amsterdam achieves supremacy over Antwerp on the maritime trade routes

**1665** New Stadhuis completed

**1669** Death of Rembrandt

**1663** Second phase of canal building

**1672** William III is stadholder. De Witt brothers killed by mob in Den Haag *(see p186)*

**1677** William III marries Mary Stuart, heiress to the English throne

**1685** Huguenot refugees reach Amsterdam after Louis XIV abolished Edict of Nantes

| 1650 | 1660 | 1670 | 1680 | 1690 |

*William and Mary*

# The Golden Age Overseas

Coat of arms of the VOC

SUPREMACY IN THE NETHERLANDS led to success overseas for Amsterdam. The Dutch colonized the Indonesian Archipelago, establishing a profitable empire based on spice trading in the East. The Dutch East India Company (VOC) thrived, using vast wooden ships called East Indiamen. In the New World, the Dutch ruled large parts of Brazil and bought Manhattan from its native owners, naming it New Amsterdam. However, war with England radically trimmed Dutch sea-power by the end of the 17th century.

**Purchase of Manhattan**
*In 1626, explorer Pieter Minuit bought the island of Manhattan from the Native Americans for $24.*

**Salvaged Silverware**
*The* Batavia *sank off the coast of western Australia in 1629. This bedknob, ewer and plate were salvaged in 1972.*

Main mast          Steering stand

Officers' cabin

Mizzen mast

Poop deck

**World Map** *(1676)*
*Joan Blaeu's map charted the known world, with parts of Asia and Australia missing.*

## THE BATAVIA
Owned by the VOC, the *Batavia* was an East Indiaman, with three main masts. She was 45 m (148 ft) in length and carried a complement of about 350, including crew, soldiers and families.

## TIMELINE OF EXPLORATION

*Peter Stuyvesant*

**1602** Dutch East India Company (VOC) founded

**1620** Pilgrim Fathers depart for the New World *(see p185)*

**1642** Abel Tasman discovers Tasmania

| 1600 | 1610 | 1620 | 1630 | 1640 |
|------|------|------|------|------|

**1595** First voyage to Indonesia via Cape of Good Hope

*VOC logo*

**1609** Hugo Grotius advocates freedom of trade at sea

**1626** Peter Minuit buys Manhattan and founds New Amsterdam

**1621** Dutch West India Company founded

**Dutch Battle Ships** *(1683)*
*Ludolf Backhuysen (1631–1708) painted the Dutch battle fleet routing the rival Portuguese navy off the coast of northern Spain.*

## THE DUTCH EAST INDIA COMPANY

Founded in 1602, the VOC had a monopoly on all profits from trade east of the Cape of Good Hope. It became a public company and many a Dutch merchant's fortune was made. By 1611, it was the leading importer of spices into Europe, with ships ranging as far as China, Japan and Indonesia. For nearly 200 years the VOC ran a commercial empire more powerful than some countries.

*The Nederlands Scheepvaart Museum (see pp146–7) has a hall devoted to the VOC. A replica of the East Indiaman, the Amsterdam, is moored outside.*

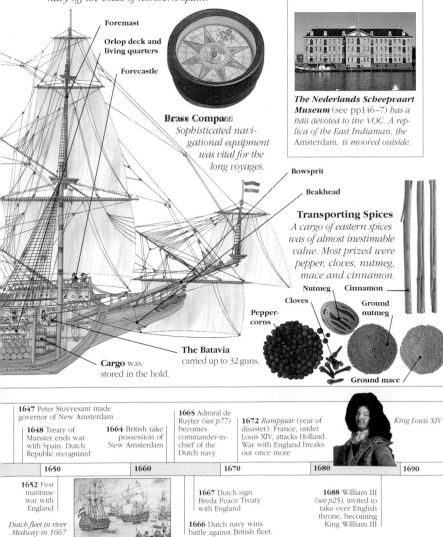

Foremast

Orlop deck and living quarters

Forecastle

**Brass Compass**
*Sophisticated navigational equipment was vital for the long voyages.*

Bowsprit

Beakhead

**Transporting Spices**
*A cargo of eastern spices was of almost inestimable value. Most prized were pepper, cloves, nutmeg, mace and cinnamon.*

Nutmeg     Cinnamon

Cloves     Ground nutmeg

Pepper-corns

**The Batavia**
carried up to 32 guns.

**Cargo** was stored in the hold.

Ground mace

| | | | | |
|---|---|---|---|---|
| **1647** Peter Stuyvesant made governor of New Amsterdam | | **1665** Admiral de Ruyter *(see p77)* becomes commander-in-chief of the Dutch navy | **1672** *Rampjaar* (year of disaster). France, under Louis XIV, attacks Holland. War with England breaks out once more | *King Louis XIV* |
| **1648** Treaty of Munster ends war with Spain. Dutch Republic recognized | **1664** British take possession of New Amsterdam | | | |
| **1650** | **1660** | **1670** | **1680** | **1690** |
| **1652** First maritime war with England | | **1667** Dutch sign Breda Peace Treaty with England | **1688** William III *(see p25)*, invited to take over English throne, becoming King William III | |
| *Dutch fleet in river Medway in 1667* | | **1666** Dutch navy wins battle against British fleet | | |

# The Age of Consolidation

THOUGH THE DUTCH EMPIRE declined, the Netherlands remained wealthy. Amsterdam's ships became commercial cargo carriers and by the mid-18th century, the city was the world's financial capital. Tolerance prevailed and the city was flooded with immigrants, including Jews from all across Europe. Dissatisfaction with the ruling House of Orange intensified; although Prussian troops crushed a Patriot uprising in 1787, the Patriots established a short-lived republic, with French backing, only to see Napoleon take over, making his brother Louis king of the Netherlands.

**Silver Torah finials** *(see p64)*

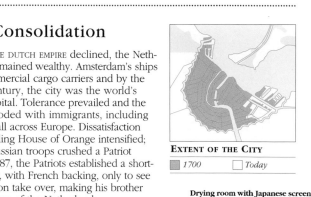

**EXTENT OF THE CITY**

■ *1700*      □ *Today*

Drying room with Japanese screen

Bathroom

**Receiving Visitors** *(c. 1713)*
*Amsterdam was cosmopolitan and decadent; in Cornelis Troost's satire, the ladies of a brothel parade before Prince Eugène of Savoy.*

**Wintertime in Amsterdam** *(c. 1763)*
*Petrus Schenk's print shows people skating on the frozen canals. The ice-breaking barges in the background are bringing fresh water to the city.*

Drawing room

## DOLLS' HOUSE

Costly dolls' houses were designed for show rather than play, and are a fitting symbol of the extravagance of the age. This example is a miniature replica of the house of an Amsterdam merchant. Now in the Frans Hals Museum in Haarlem *(see pp178–9)*, it was made around 1750 for Sara Rothé.

## TIMELINE

**1702** Death of William III. Second stadholderless period begins in the Netherlands

**1713** Treaty of Utrecht signed. Dutch Republic becomes isolated

*French musketeer*

**1748** Tax collector riots

**1744** France invades Southern Provinces

| 1700 | 1710 | 1720 | 1730 | 1740 | 175 |

**1697** Tsar Peter the Great of Russia visits Amsterdam to study shipbuilding

*Portrait of Tsar Peter the Great (1727) on gold snuff box*

**1716** Second meeting of the Grand Assembly meets in Den Haag *(see p186)*. Radical government reforms imposed

**1747** Stadholdership becomes hereditary under William IV

**1751** Death of William IV. Start of 40 years of political strife

**Prussian Troops Enter Amsterdam** *(1787)*
*A lithograph by an unknown artist shows Prussian troops entering the city on 10 October 1787, coming to the aid of the House of Orange after pro-French Patriot upheavals.*

## WHERE TO SEE 18TH-CENTURY AMSTERDAM

De Gooyer windmill *(see p144)* produced corn for the growing city from 1725. A clandestine church was opened in 1735 in today's Museum Amstelkring *(pp84–5)*, in response to the Alteration *(pp22–3)*. Fine canal houses include No. 465 Herengracht *(p112)* and the Felix Meritis Building *(p113)*, designed by Jacob Otten Husly in 1787. Museum van Loon was renovated in 1752 *(p122)*.

Pavilioned bed with green canopy

Lying-in room

Library

**Florin** *(1781)*
*By 1750, Amsterdam possessed the most sophisticated and successful banking and broking system in the world.*

**Museum Willet-Holthuysen**
*The elaborate, gilded staircase (see p121) was built in 1740.*

**Tax Collector Riots** *(1748)*
*This print by Simonsz Fokke shows an angry mob raiding the house of a tax collector in June 1748.*

**Porcelain Plate** *(c. 1780)*
*The wealthy lived in great style, sparing no expense. This hand-painted plate is decorated with mythological figures and ornate gold leaf.*

**1763** Freezing winter

**1791** VOC *(see pp26–7)* goes into liquidation

**1795** Provinces unite briefly into republic, ruled jointly by Patriots and French

**1806** Napoleon Bonaparte takes over republic

| 1760 | 1770 | 1780 | 1790 | 1800 | 1810 |
|---|---|---|---|---|---|

**1766** William V comes of age

**1768** William V marries Wilhelmina of Prussia

**1780–84** War with England, whose navy destroys Dutch fleet

**1787** Patriots' upheaval ends with Prussian army entering Amsterdam

*Louis Napoleon (1778–1846)*

**1808** Louis Napoleon crowned king of the Netherlands

# The Age of Industrialization

B Y THE END of Louis Napoleon's rule, Amsterdam had stagnated. The decline continued, with little sign of enterprise and scant investment. Industrialization came late and attempts to revive the city's fortunes by digging a canal to the North Sea were less than effective. Politically, the country regrouped round the House of Orange, bringing the family back from exile and declaring a monarchy in 1813. The mid-century saw growth of the liberal constitution; by 1900 the Socialist tradition was well established.

**EXTENT OF THE CITY**

| | |
|---|---|
| 1800 | Today |

## CENTRAAL STATION

The station *(see p79)* was completed in 1889. It became a symbol of the emergent industrial age – a sign that Amsterdam was finally moving towards the future rather than looking back to the Golden Age.

**Cocoa Trading**
*Cocoa was one of Amsterdam's main exports in the 1890s.*

**Dutch Renaissance-style façade**

**The gilded "clock"** shows the wind direction, acknowledging Amsterdam's earlier reliance on the wind to power her sailing ships.

**Main concourse**

**The Sweatshop by H Wolter**
*As industrialization increased, sweatshops, with their attendant poverty, became commonplace.*

**Diamond Cutting**
*The diamond trade thrived in the late 19th century, when precious stones were imported from South Africa.*

**TIMELINE**

**1813** House of Orange returns from exile

**1824** Noordhollands-kanaal is dug but proves ineffective

**1839** Amsterdam-to-Haarlem railway opens *(see p177)*

**1845** Rioters in Amsterdam call for social reform

**1850** Population 245,000

*Johan Rudolf Thorbecke*

| 1820 | 1830 | 1840 | 1850 | 1860 |
|---|---|---|---|---|

**1815** William becomes king of the Netherlands

**1831** Low Countries split into north and south. Southern provinces become Belgium

*King William I at Waterloo (1815)*

**1840** William I abdicates. Succeeded by William II

**1848** New constitution devised by Thorbecke

**1860s** Jews begin to arrive in Amsterdam from Antwerp

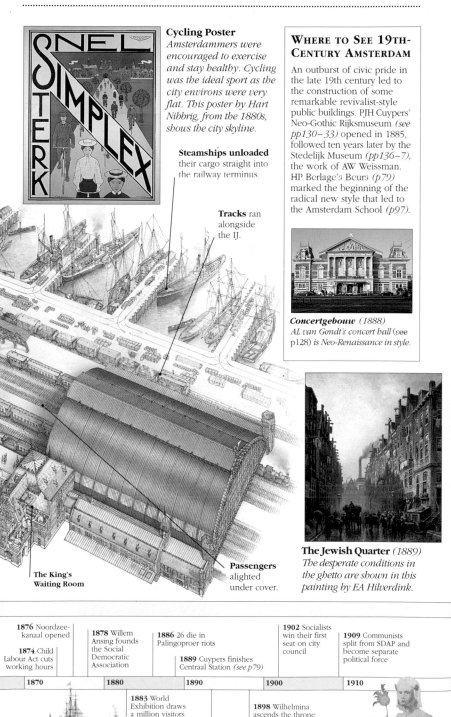

**Cycling Poster**
*Amsterdammers were encouraged to exercise and stay healthy. Cycling was the ideal sport as the city environs were very flat. This poster by Hart Nibbrig, from the 1880s, shows the city skyline.*

**Steamships unloaded** their cargo straight into the railway terminus.

**Tracks** ran alongside the IJ.

## WHERE TO SEE 19TH-CENTURY AMSTERDAM

An outburst of civic pride in the late 19th century led to the construction of some remarkable revivalist-style public buildings. PJH Cuypers' Neo-Gothic Rijksmuseum *(see pp130–33)* opened in 1885, followed ten years later by the Stedelijk Museum *(pp136–7)*, the work of AW Weissman. HP Berlage's Beurs *(p79)* marked the beginning of the radical new style that led to the Amsterdam School *(p97)*.

**Concertgebouw** *(1888)*
*AL van Gendt's concert hall (see p128) is Neo-Renaissance in style.*

**The Jewish Quarter** *(1889)*
*The desperate conditions in the ghetto are shown in this painting by EA Hilverdink.*

**The King's Waiting Room**

**Passengers** alighted under cover.

1876 Noordzee-kanaal opened

1874 Child Labour Act cuts working hours

1878 Willem Ansing founds the Social Democratic Association

1886 26 die in Palingoproer riots

1889 Cuypers finishes Centraal Station *(see p79)*

1902 Socialists win their first seat on city council

1909 Communists split from SDAP and become separate political force

| 1870 | 1880 | 1890 | 1900 | 1910 |
|------|------|------|------|------|

*Noordzee-kanaal*

1883 World Exhibition draws a million visitors

1894 Foundation of Social Democratic Workers' Party (SDAP)

1898 Wilhelmina ascends the throne

*Queen Wilhelmina (c. 1900) by Jean Veber*

# Amsterdam at War

THE NETHERLANDS remained neutral in World War I. After the war, political unrest was rife and the city council embarked on a programme of new housing projects and, in the 1930s, the Amsterdamse Bos was created to counter unemployment. When World War II broke out, the Netherlands again opted for neutrality – only to be invaded by Germany. The early 1940s were bitter years, and many died of starvation in the winter of '44–5. During this time, most of the Jewish population was deported; many, like Anne Frank, tried to avoid detection by going into hiding.

**EXTENT OF THE CITY**
▨ 1945          ☐ Today

**"Vote Red" Poster** *(1918)*
*The Social Democrats (Labour Party) were responsible for the introduction of a welfare state after World War II.*

Attic

The Van Daans' room

**Anne's bedroom**

**The Franks' bedroom**

**Bathroom**

**Revolving bookcase (entrance to hideout)**

## ANNE FRANK'S HOUSE

In July 1942, Anne Frank, her family and the Van Daans went into hiding at the rear of this house *(see p90)*. Anne was 13 and had already begun her diary. She made her last entry in August 1944, three days before her family was arrested. She died in Bergen-Belsen concentration camp in March 1945.

**Potato Riots** *(1917)*
*Daan Bout's drawing shows desperate women fighting for vegetables during World War I. Rioting followed and the army was brought in to quell the uprising.*

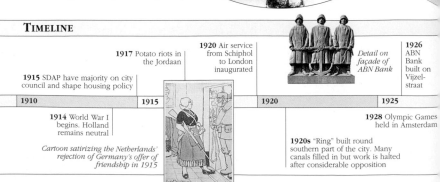

## TIMELINE

**1917** Potato riots in the Jordaan

**1920** Air service from Schiphol to London inaugurated

*Detail on façade of ABN Bank*

**1926** ABN Bank built on Vijzelstraat

**1915** SDAP have majority on city council and shape housing policy

| 1910 | 1915 | 1920 | 1925 |
|------|------|------|------|

**1914** World War I begins. Holland remains neutral

*Cartoon satirizing the Netherlands' rejection of Germany's offer of friendship in 1915*

**1928** Olympic Games held in Amsterdam

**1920s** "Ring" built round southern part of the city. Many canals filled in but work is halted after considerable opposition

**Het Schip by Michel de Klerk**
*At the end of World War I, Amsterdam School architects (see p97) designed new housing projects such as "the ship", to replace the slums in the south of the city.*

(see p97)

## WHERE TO SEE EARLY-20TH-CENTURY AMSTERDAM

Innovative Amsterdam School architecture is found to the south of the city. HP Berlage, PL Kramer and Michel de Klerk collaborated on De Dageraad *(see p151)* and were largely responsible for the Nieuw Zuid *(p154)*. Much of this was built in the run up to the 1928 Olympics; it boasts spectacular housing developments and civic buildings.

**Amsterdamse Bos**
*In 1930, as part of a job-creation scheme, 5,000 unemployed Dutch citizens were drafted in to help develop a woodland and leisure area to the southwest of the city.*

***Tuschinski Theater*** *(1921)*
*The interior of this exotic complex is awash with colour.*

Offices at the front of the building

Façade of No. 263 Prinsengracht

**Dockworker Statue**
*The statue (see p53) by Mari Andriessen commemorates the February 1941 protest by dockers and transport workers against the Nazis' treatment of Jews.*

**The Deportation of Jews**
*Pamphlets were distributed by the Resistance vilifying those who stood by and let the Nazis round up the Jews.*

**1930** Population 750,000. Unemployment worsens. Work on public project of Amsterdamse Bos begins

**1939** Outbreak of World War II. The Netherlands chooses neutrality

**1935** Work parties sent to Germany

**1942** Deportation of Jews begins

**1944** D-Day Landings. "Hunger Winter"

**1945** Germany surrenders and western part of the Netherlands finally liberated

| 1930 | 1935 | 1940 | 1945 |
|------|------|------|------|

**1934** Riots in Jordaan over reduction in social security. Seven die

**1932–7** Rise of Dutch Nazi Party under Anton Mussert

**1940** Germany bombs Rotterdam. The Dutch surrender

**1941** 450 Jews arrested. Dockworkers strike

*Yellow Star of David, which Jews had to wear during Nazi Occupation*

# Amsterdam Today

**Amsterdam tram**

AFTER THE END of World War II, Amsterdam suffered a series of social problems – the city's traditional tolerance made it a haven for the hippy culture of the 1960s, it became a centre of drug use and trafficking, and the left-wing Provos challenged social order. By the mid-1980s, families were moving out in droves. A series of riots over squatting and redevelopment of the city led to measures which alleviated the social problems, and Amsterdam is once more a tranquil and beautiful city for all to visit.

**EXTENT OF THE CITY**

☐ 1950  ☐ Today

**Football**
*The fans were ecstatic when the Dutch national team beat England 3:1 in 1988 in the European Championships.*

**Het Lieverdje**
*The statue of the Little Urchin by Carel Kneulman is in Spui. It became a symbol for the Provos in the 1960s.*

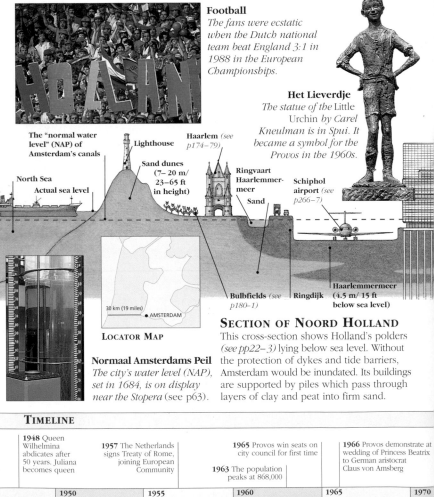

The "normal water level" (NAP) of Amsterdam's canals

**Lighthouse**

**Haarlem** *(see p174–79)*

North Sea

**Actual sea level**

Sand dunes (7– 20 m/ 23–65 ft in height)

**Ringvaart Haarlemmer-meer**

Sand

**Schiphol airport** *(see p266–7)*

**Bulbfields** *(see p180–1)*

**Ringdijk**

**Haarlemmermeer** (4.5 m/ 15 ft below sea level)

30 km (19 miles) • AMSTERDAM

**LOCATOR MAP**

**Normaal Amsterdams Peil**
*The city's water level (NAP), set in 1684, is on display near the Stopera (see p63).*

## SECTION OF NOORD HOLLAND

This cross-section shows Holland's polders *(see pp22–3)* lying below sea level. Without the protection of dykes and tide barriers, Amsterdam would be inundated. Its buildings are supported by piles which pass through layers of clay and peat into firm sand.

## TIMELINE

| | | | |
|---|---|---|---|
| **1948** Queen Wilhelmina abdicates after 50 years. Juliana becomes queen | **1957** The Netherlands signs Treaty of Rome, joining European Community | **1965** Provos win seats on city council for first time<br><br>**1963** The population peaks at 868,000 | **1966** Provos demonstrate at wedding of Princess Beatrix to German aristocrat Claus von Amsberg |
| **1950** | **1955** | **1960** | **1965** | **1970** |
| | **1952** Completion of the Amsterdam-Rhine Canal allows increased trade | **1967** Hippies arrive in Amsterdam | |
| **1949** Indonesia officially independent from the Netherlands | | **1968** First residents move to the vast Bijlmermeer housing estate | **1971** Ajax wins European Cup |

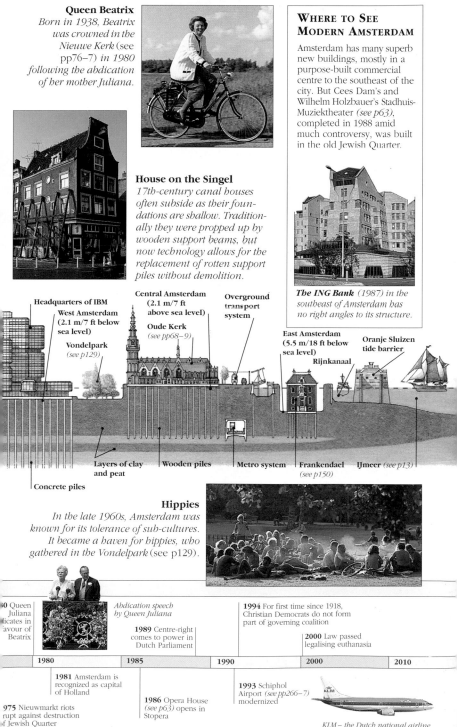

**Queen Beatrix**
*Born in 1938, Beatrix was crowned in the Nieuwe Kerk* (see pp76–7) *in 1980 following the abdication of her mother Juliana.*

**House on the Singel**
*17th-century canal houses often subside as their foundations are shallow. Traditionally they were propped up by wooden support beams, but now technology allows for the replacement of rotten support piles without demolition.*

### WHERE TO SEE MODERN AMSTERDAM

Amsterdam has many superb new buildings, mostly in a purpose-built commercial centre to the southeast of the city. But Cees Dam's and Wilhelm Holzbauer's Stadhuis-Muziektheater *(see p63),* completed in 1988 amid much controversy, was built in the old Jewish Quarter.

*The ING Bank* (1987) *in the southeast of Amsterdam has no right angles to its structure.*

Headquarters of IBM
West Amsterdam (2.1 m/7 ft below sea level)
Vondelpark *(see p129)*
Central Amsterdam (2.1 m/7 ft above sea level)
Oude Kerk *(see pp68–9)*
Overground transport system
East Amsterdam (5.5 m/18 ft below sea level)
Rijnkanaal
Oranje Sluizen tide barrier

Concrete piles
Layers of clay and peat
Wooden piles
Metro system
Frankendael *(see p150)*
IJmeer *(see p13)*

**Hippies**
*In the late 1960s, Amsterdam was known for its tolerance of sub-cultures. It became a haven for hippies, who gathered in the Vondelpark (see p129).*

*Abdication speech by Queen Juliana*

80 Queen Juliana dicates in avour of Beatrix

**1994** For first time since 1918, Christian Democrats do not form part of governing coalition

**1989** Centre-right comes to power in Dutch Parliament

**2000** Law passed legalising euthanasia

| 1980 | 1985 | 1990 | 2000 | 2010 |
|------|------|------|------|------|

**1981** Amsterdam is recognized as capital of Holland

975 Nieuwmarkt rupt against destruction f Jewish Quarter

**1986** Opera House *(see p63)* opens in Stopera

**1993** Schiphol Airport *(see pp266–7)* modernized

*KLM – the Dutch national airline*

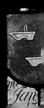

# AMSTERDAM AT A GLANCE

THERE ARE MORE THAN 100 places of interest described in the *Area by Area* section of this book. The broad spectrum of entries covers recreational as well as cultural sights and ranges from sublime buildings, such as the Oude Kerk, to oddities like the Hash Marihuana Museum *(see p61)*. The Golden Bend *(see p112)* and other impressive canalscapes also feature, along with suggested walks past some of Amsterdam's finest architecture and notable sights, such as Anne Frankhuis. To help you make the most of your stay, the following 12 pages are a time-saving guide to the best Amsterdam has to offer. Museums, canals and bridges, and cafés and bars all have their own sections. Below is a selection of attractions that no visitor should miss.

## AMSTERDAM'S TOP TEN ATTRACTIONS

**Nederlands Scheepvaartmuseum**
*See pp146–7*

**Van Gogh Museum**
*See pp134–5*

**Oude Kerk**
*See pp68–9*

**Begijnhof**
*See p75*

**Koninklijk Paleis**
*See p74*

**Rijksmuseum**
*See pp130–33*

**Stedelijk Museum**
*See pp136–7*

**Museum Amstel-
kring** *See pp84–5*

**Magere Brug**
*See p119*

**Anne Frankhuis**
*See pp32–3 & 90–91*

◁ **Stained-glass coats of arms in the Lady Chapel of the Oude Kerk**

# Amsterdam's Best: Museums

F OR A FAIRLY SMALL CITY, Amsterdam has a surprisingly large number of museums and galleries. The quality and variety of the collections are impressive and many are housed in buildings of historical or architectural interest. The Rijksmuseum, with its Gothic façade, is a city landmark, and Rembrandt's work is exhibited in his original home. For more information on museums see pages 40–41.

**Anne Frankhuis**
*Anne Frank's photo is exhibited in the house where she hid during World War II.*

*Western Canal Ring*

**Amsterdams Historisch Museum**
*A wealth of historical information is on display here. Once an orphanage, it is depicted in* Governesses at the Burgher Orphanage *(1683) by Adriaen Backer.*

**Rijksmuseum**
*An extensive collection of paintings by Dutch masters can be seen in the country's largest national museum. Jan van Huysum's* Still Life with Flowers and Fruit, *dating from about 1730, is a fine example.*

*Central Canal Ring*

*Museum Quarter*

**Van Gogh Museum**
*Van Gogh's* Self-portrait with Straw Hat *(1870) hangs in this large, stark museum, built in 1973 to house the bulk of his work.*

**Stedelijk Museum**
*Gerrit Rietveld's simple Steltman chair (1963) is one of many exhibits at this ever-changing contemporary art museum.*

### Museum Amstelkring

Three 17th-century merchant's houses conceal in their attics Amsterdam's only remaining clandestine church. The buildings have been restored as the Museum Amstelkring.

### Nederlands Scheepvaartmuseum

*This national maritime museum is decorated with reliefs relating to the city's maritime history. Moored alongside is a replica of the East Indiaman,* Amsterdam.

### Tropenmuseum

*On display here are exhibits from former Dutch colonies in the tropics, including this wooden Nigerian fertility mask portraying a mother and twins.*

*Nieuwe Zijde*

*Oude Zijde*

*Eastern Canal Ring*

*Plantage*

| 0 metres | 500 |
| 0 yards | 500 |

### Museum Willet-Holthuysen

*An impressive collection of furniture, silverware and paintings is housed in this beautifully preserved 17th-century canalside mansion.*

### Joods Historisch Museum

*Four adjoining synagogues are linked to form this museum. The Holy Ark in the Grote Synagoge is the centrepiece of an exhibition on Judaism in the Netherlands.*

# Exploring Amsterdam's Museums

**Wall plaque in St Luciensteeg**

THE RICHNESS of Amsterdam's history and culture is reflected by its wide range of museums, which cover everything from bibles, beer and African masks to ship-building and space travel. Its national art galleries house some of the world's most famous paintings, including Rembrandt's *The Night Watch*. The Nederlands Scheep-vaart Museum has the largest collection of model ships in the world, while the Anne Frankhuis is a stark reminder of the horrors of World War II.

View of a French-style garden from the Museum van Loon

## PAINTING AND DECORATIVE ARTS

THE WORLD'S most important collection of Dutch art is on display at the **Rijksmuseum**. This vast museum contains approximately 5,000 paintings, including works by Rembrandt, Vermeer, Frans Hals and Albert Cuyp as well as a significant collection of sculptures, prints, artifacts and Asiatic art.

A short stroll across Museum-plein will bring you to the **Van Gogh Museum**. Besides a large collection of Van Gogh's paintings and drawings, which traces his entire career, you can see hundreds of his original letters to his brother Theo and the artist's private collection of Japanese prints. Works by other 19th-century Dutch painters are also displayed here.

Modern art in all its forms is the focus of the **Stedelijk Museum**. While the collection features works by artists such as Henri Matisse and Vassily Kandinsky, the emphasis is on paintings, sculptures, drawings, graphics and photographs completed after 1945. Andy Warhol, Edward Kienholz and the Dutch Cobra artist Karel Appel are all represented.

The three-storey house where Rembrandt lived for 20 years opened as the **Museum Het Rembrandthuis** in 1911. As well as providing an insight into the artist's life, it contains an important collection of his etchings and drawings, including a fascinating series of self-portraits.

The **Museum van Loon**, housed in a beautiful 17th-century mansion, is based on the out-standing private collections of the wealthy van Loon family of Amsterdam.

Other wonderful collections of art can also be enjoyed by travelling from Amsterdam to the **Frans Hals Museum** in Haarlem, the **Mauritshuis** in Den Haag and the **Museum Boijmans Van Beuningen Rotterdam**.

Rembrandt's *The Jewish Bride* (1663) in the Rijksmuseum

**Indonesian mask at the Tropenmuseum**

## HISTORY

VARIOUS ASPECTS of Amster-dam's absorbing history is documented in several of the city's museums. The **Amster-dams Historisch Museum** covers the growth of Amsterdam from its origins as a fishing village in the 13th century, by means of maps, paintings and archaeological objects. The city's glorious maritime history is recalled at the **Nederlands Scheep-vaartmuseum**. Its vast collection of model ships includes a life-size replica of an 18th-century sailing ship. The mechanics of more mod-ern boats is the focus of the **Museum 't Kromhout**, which is housed in one of the few working shipyards left in the city. In the **Museum Willet-Holthuysen**, the richly decor-ated rooms and collection of Dutch paintings, Venetian glass, silverware and furniture reflects the wealth of Amster-dam in the Golden Age. Cath-olic ingenuity is revealed at the **Museum Amstelkring**, where a secret church is preserved in the attic of a 17th-century merchant's home. The history of the Dutch trade unions is documented at the **De Burcht (Vakbondsmuseum)**.

Jewish life in the city is re-membered in the fascinating **Joods Historisch Museum**. The famous **Anne Frankhuis** provides a poignant reminder that Amsterdam's Jewish community was almost wiped out in World War II, and its secret annexe shows what life was like for those living in hiding. Displays on the activities of the Dutch Resistance at the **Verzetsmuseum Amsterdam** provide more fascinating insights on life in the Netherlands during the Nazi occupation.

Outside the city, the **Zuiderzee Museum** recreates the life and traditions of the people who once fished these waters.

## SPECIALIST MUSEUMS

Mummies, sarcophagi and bronze effigies of ancient Egyptian gods are just a few of the archaeological displays at the **Allard Pierson Museum**. The **Bijbels Museum**, in adjoining canal houses, also focuses on the archaeology of Egypt and the Middle East, and contains the oldest Bible ever printed in the Netherlands.

The **Theatermuseum** traces the history of Dutch theatre through costumes, posters and props, while the **Nederlands Filmmuseum** screens more than 1,000 films a year.

The **Heineken Experience** offers a history of beer-making as part of a tour of this former brewery and free samples at the end. More facts can be absorbed at the **Hash Marijuana Hemp Museum**, which shows the many uses this product has had through the ages.

The sounds and sights of anything from a North African village to an Indonesian rainforest are recreated at the **Tropenmuseum** by way of an introduction to cultures from around the world.

The open-air reconstruction village at the Zuiderzee Museum

Model showing the process of precipitation in the Geologisch Museum at Artis

## TECHNOLOGY AND NATURAL HISTORY

A hands-on approach is encouraged by **Nemo** to explain, for instance, how houses are built, how photography works or how computers process information. The history of aviation and space travel is the focus of the **Nationaal Luchtvaartmuseum Aviodome**, which has over 30 historic aircraft on display, including a 1903 Wright Flyer, a Spitfire and a model of Saturn 5. There are also flight simulators on which to try out your flying skills. Along with hundreds of live animals, the **Artis** complex contains a variety of museums. Rock collectors will be tempted by a huge range of minerals, rocks, fossils and helpful models in the Geologisch Museum. There is also a collection of skulls, skeletons and stuffed animals in the Zoölogisch Museum, which is housed in the zoo's Aquarium.

## FINDING THE MUSEUMS

# Amsterdam's Best: Canals and Waterways

FROM THE GRACE and elegance of the waterside mansions along the *Grachtengordel* (Canal Ring) to the rows of converted warehouses on Brouwersgracht and the charming houses on Reguliersgracht, the city's canals and waterways embody the very spirit of Amsterdam. They are spanned by many beautiful bridges, including the famous Magere Brug *(see p119)*, a traditionally styled lift bridge. You can also relax at one of the many canalside cafés or bars and watch an array of boats float by.

**Brouwersgracht**
*The banks of this charming canal are lined with house- boats, cosy cafés and warehouses.*

**Bloemgracht**
*There is a great variety of archi- tecture along this lovely, tree- lined canal in the Jordaan, including a row of houses with step gables* (see p91).

Western Canal Ring

**Prinsengracht**
*The best way to see all the beautiful buildings along Amsterdam's longest 17th-century canal is by bicycle.*

Central Canal Ring

Museum Quarter

**Leidsegracht**
*Relax at a pavement café along the exclusive Leidse- gracht* (see p111).

**Keizersgracht**
*A view of this canal can be had from any of its bridges. For an overview of the Canal Ring go to Metz & Co at Leidsestraat 34–36 (see p112).*

## Singel

*The* Poezenboot, *a boat for stray cats, is just one of the many sights to be found along the Singel, whose distinctive, curved shape established the horseshoe contours of the Canal Ring.*

## Entrepotdok

*The warehouses on the Entrepotdok (see p144) were redeveloped in the 1980s. The quayside is now lined in summer with lively café terraces that overlook an array of houseboats and pleasure craft.*

Nieuwe Zijde

0 metres 500

0 yards 500

Oude Zijde

Plantage

Eastern Canal Ring

## Herengracht

*Known as "the twin brothers", these matching neck-gabled houses at Nos. 409–411 are two of the prettiest houses on the city's grandest canal.*

## Reguliersgracht

*Many crooked, brick buildings line this pretty canal, which was cut in 1664. The statue of a stork, located at No. 92, is symbolic of parental responsibility and commemorates a 1571 by-law protecting this bird.*

## Amstel

*This river is still a busy commercial thoroughfare, with barges carrying grain and coal to the city's port.*

# Exploring Canals and Waterways

IT IS IMPOSSIBLE to explore Amsterdam's canals and waterways without gaining a sense of the city's rich history. Many are crossed by charming bridges and lined with magnificent buildings, such as the ancient Oude Kerk *(see pp68–9)*, which overlooks the city's oldest canal, the Oudezijds Voorburgwal. First-time visitors are advised to take a cruise *(see pp276–7)* to familiarize themselves with the complex network of waterways. Once you have got your bearings, it is fun to explore them independently. The Street Finder on pages 280–87 of this guide locates all the waterways highlighted here.

**Ornate lamps on Blauwbrug**

**View of the Waag and lift bridge along Kloveniersburgwal**

Painting of the Oudezijds Voorburgwal by Cornelis Springer (1817–91)

## FIRST WATERWAYS

PEOPLE ARE THOUGHT to have settled near the mouth of the **Amstel** river as early as AD 1200. In about 1264, the river was dammed and the reaches north and south of the dam later became known as **Damrak** and **Rokin**. Although sea dykes, like the **Zeedijk** *(see p67)*, were built in the 13th century, the city's first canals were not cut until the early 14th century. You can still stroll along the **Oudezijds Voorburgwal** and **Grimburgwal**, which were dug on the town's eastern and southern borders.

## EARLY EXPANSIONS

AS AMSTERDAM expanded, new canals were added to the city's defence, drainage and transport network. The first expansion occurred at the end of the 14th century, when the **Oudezijds Achterburgwal** was cut east of the centre and **Nieuwezijds Achterburgwal** to the west (now Spuistraat).

This pattern was repeated in the 15th century when the **Kloveniersburgwal** and the **Geldersekade** were dug to the east and the **Singel** was cut to the west and south. In 1481, work began on fortifying the new outer canals with the city's first stone defences. Remnants include the Waag *(see p60)*, the city's oldest gatehouse, the Munttoren *(see p123)* and the Schreierstoren *(see p67)*.

A major influx of refugees in the 1580s led to the expansion of Amsterdam eastward to the **Oude Schans**. Today, the network of pretty canals in this area is very peaceful.

## AMSTERDAM'S BRIDGES

Amsterdam has nearly 1,300 bridges crisscrossing its canals and waterways. At night, the bridges in the city centre are lit up by strings of lights, making an evening canal-boat tour a magical experience. One of the prettiest views is found along **Reguliersgracht**, where seven bridges cross the water in quick succession. The most famous bridge is the Magere Brug *(see p119)*, a narrow, wooden drawbridge over the Amstel. Downstream stands Amsterdam's most ornate bridge, the Blauwbrug *(see p118)*. The widest bridge is the Torensluis *(see p78)*, which spans the Singel.

**The Torensluis, Amsterdam's widest bridge, overlooked by some of the Singel's finest canal houses**

## THE GRACHTENGORDEL

SPURRED BY a rapidly growing population, an ambitious plan was drawn up by the city planner, Hendrick Staets, at the beginning of the 17th century to quadruple the size of Amsterdam. In 1614, work began on cutting three new residential canals, collectively known as the *Grachtengordel* (Canal Ring), from **Brouwersgracht** in the west, to encircle the existing city. The land along these canals was settled by wealthy citizens and named after the city's ruling factions. The grandest was the **Herengracht** (Gentleman's Canal), named after the commercial patrician class. The **Keizersgracht** (Emperor's Canal) honoured the Holy Roman Emperor and the **Prinsengracht** (Prince's Canal) referred to Amsterdam's links with the House of Orange.

Beyond the *Grachtengordel*, workers' houses were put up along the drainage ditches in the Jordaan, and the expanded city was protected by a fortified canal, the **Singelgracht**.

**Boats moored in the Waalseilandsgracht**

## THE INDUSTRIAL AGE

IN THE 19th century, Amsterdam's prosperity was under threat, as the approaches to its harbour were too shallow for a new generation of larger ships. In an attempt to revive maritime trade, the harbour was dredged and the **Noordzeekanaal**, completed in 1876, was cut to provide access to the North Sea. The city's shipbuilding industry was also modernized and docks, such as Werf 't Kromhout *(see p145)*, were adapted from building sailing ships to steamships.

A rapid increase in population in the latter half of the century caused a demand for housing. New streets, such as Jacob van Lennepkade, were built in the western suburbs along canals, to reflect the character of the rest of the city. At the same time, many of the oldest canals in the city centre, such as the Nieuwezijds Voorburgwal and much of the Damrak, were filled in to improve road access to Centraal Station *(see p79)*.

## CANALS' MODERN USAGE

AFTER THE ARRIVAL of road and rail links, the commercial importance of Amsterdam's 75 km (47 miles) of canals declined, although barges still ply the waters of the Amstel river. Canals do, however, play a crucial role in the city's tourist industry, as well as providing Amsterdammers with transport routes and a place to live.

In 1994, the city council drew up a series of bylaws aimed at reducing pleasure-boat traffic and imposing stricter rules on houseboats. Despite this, the canals can get very clogged in summer and there are still around 2,500 houseboats officially moored within the city's boundaries. Many of them can be found along the *Grachtengordel* and the Amstel, as well as clustered in the docks near Centraal Station *(see p79)* and the Western Islands *(see p93)*.

**Map (1876) of Amsterdam's network of canals and the Noordzeekanaal**

# Amsterdam's Best: Cafés and Bars

AMSTERDAM IS A CITY of cafés and bars, about 1,500 in all. Each area has something to offer, from friendly and relaxed brown cafés to lively and crowded designer bars. The cafés and bars vary and each has some special attraction: a large range of beers, live music, canalside terraces, art exhibitions, board games and pool tables or simply a brand of *gezelligheid*, the unique Dutch concept of "cosiness". Further details of Amsterdam's cafés and bars are given on pages 48–9. Addresses are given in the directory on page 237.

**De Tuin**
*This large brown café in the Jordaan is always crowded with regular customers, often local artists.*

Western Canal Ring

Central Canal Ring

**Van Puffelen**
*A smart and fashionable clientele is attracted to this intimate canalside café, with its impressive 19th-century interior, reading room and restaurant.*

**Vertigo**
*The café terrace of the Nederlands Filmmuseum has a splendid view across Vondelpark.*

Museum Quarter

**Café Americain**
*The American Hotel's grand café has a beautiful Art Deco interior, and is the place to go to be seen.*

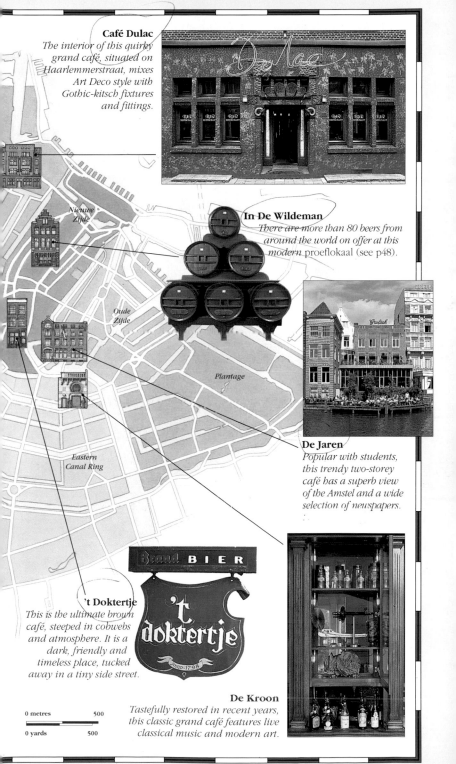

**Café Dulac**
The interior of this quirky grand café, situated on Haarlemmerstraat, mixes Art Deco style with Gothic-kitsch fixtures and fittings.

Nieuwe Zijde

**In De Wildeman**
There are more than 80 beers from around the world on offer at this modern proeflokaal (see p48).

Oude Zijde

Plantage

**De Jaren**
Popular with students, this trendy two-storey café has a superb view of the Amstel and a wide selection of newspapers.

Eastern Canal Ring

**'t Doktertje**
This is the ultimate brown café, steeped in cobwebs and atmosphere. It is a dark, friendly and timeless place, tucked away in a tiny side street.

**De Kroon**
Tastefully restored in recent years, this classic grand café features live classical music and modern art.

0 metres 500
0 yards 500

# Exploring Amsterdam's Cafés and Bars

WHEREVER YOU GO in this vibrant city, you are never far from a café or bar. Amsterdammers are at their most friendly over a beer or a Dutch gin, so exploring the city's drinking establishments is an easy way to meet the locals. Table service is standard in most cafés and bars, though not universal. Instead of paying for each drink, bars keep a running total which you settle as you leave. The exception is outdoor terraces, where you are expected to pay as you order. Most places are open from about 11am until 1am, though some around the Leidseplein stay open until 4 or 5am at the weekends.

**Sportcafé Ajax-Arena, decorated with football memorabilia**

## BROWN CAFÉS

THE TRADITIONAL Dutch "local pub", the brown café, is characterized by dark wooden panelling and furniture, low ceilings, dim lighting and a fog of tobacco smoke. It is a warm and friendly place and

often a social focus for the neighbourhood. Some of the best brown cafés are found in old 17th-century canal houses or tucked away on side streets. The tiny and characterful **'t Doktertje**, just off the Kalverstraat shopping street, is worth a visit, as is the cheap and cheerful **Pieper**, close

to Leidseplein. **De Tuin,** in the heart of the Jordaan, is popular with the local artistic community. Most brown cafés are more than just places to drink at and many serve good, reasonably priced food (see pp236–7).

## PROEFLOKALEN AND MODERN TASTING BARS

LITERALLY MEANING "tasting houses", proeflokalen go back to the Dutch Golden Age of the 17th century. In order to increase sales, wine and spirit importers would invite merchants to taste their wares. Today, proeflokalen denote bars specializing in either wine, spirits or beer. One of the oldest tasting bars, **De Drie Fleschjes**, dates from 1650, and jenever (Dutch gin) is its speciality. **Henri Prouvin** offers a superb range of more than 500 vintage wines and **In De Wildeman** serves beers from around the world, many of them on draught. See the directory on page 237 for other good proeflokalen.

**Sampling the wide range of beers in the popular modern tasting bar, Gollem**

## WHAT TO DRINK

The Dutch national drink is beer. A standard pils (a lager-like beer) is served in bars and cafés – the main brands are Heineken and Grolsch. Darker beers like De Koninck have a stronger flavour, and the wheat-brewed witbiers like Hoegaarden are white and cloudy. Beers from Amsterdam's 't IJ brewery, such as Columbus, are widely available. The most popular spirit, jenever, is the slightly oily Dutch gin. There is either the sharp tasting jonge (young), or the smoother oude (old) variety. For the complete Dutch experience, drink jenever in a single gulp or order a refreshing pils with a jenever chaser.

**Bottle of jonge jenever**

**Traditional oude jenever**

**Hoegaarden, brewed in Belgium**

**Tarwebok, a strong type of Heineken**

## GRAND CAFÉS AND DESIGNER BARS

GRAND CAFÉS first emerged in the 19th century. Today, these large and opulent venues are the haunts of the upwardly mobile and fashion-conscious. **Café Luxembourg** has a street terrace for people-watching, while **Café Schiller** is more intimate and has a beautiful Art Deco interior. Designer bars cater for a similar clientele, but they are modern, stark and bright in style. Some of the best are the chic **Het Land Van Walem**, **De Balie**, **Vertigo** and the trendy **De Jaren**.

The beautifully restored De Jaren

Café Schiller, one of Amsterdam's Art Deco grand cafés

## SMOKING COFFEESHOPS

SMOKING COFFEESHOPS are ones where cannabis is openly sold and smoked. Although technically illegal, the sale of soft drugs is tolerated by the Dutch authorities if it remains discreet *(see p259)*. Many of these cafés are recognizable by their loud music and often psychedelic decor. Smoking coffeeshops appeal to a surprising range of people – old and young alike (under 16s are not permitted) from every social and professional background. **Rusland** and **Siberië** are two of the smaller, more relaxed places, while **The Bulldog Palace** is commercial and tourist-filled. As well as coffee, soft drinks and snacks are generally available. **Chocolata** even specializes in hash confectionery, such as hash cakes. If tempted to smoke, ask for the menu listing what is on sale. The cannabis is strong, especially the local "skunk". Be wary of hash cakes and cookies as there is no way to gauge their strength. See the directory on page 237 for other good smoking coffeeshops.

## COFFEESHOPS AND SALONS DE THÉ

THE MORE CONVENTIONAL type of coffeeshop is where well-to-do ladies go for a chat over coffee and cake. A number of these places use the Dutch spelling, *koffieshop*, or the French *salons de thé* to distinguish themselves from the many smoking coffeeshops, although the differences are obvious. Many, such as **Arnold Cornelis** and **Pompadour**, are attached to confectioners, patisseries or delicatessens, and have a tempting range of cakes and sweets on offer. Several of the city's larger stores and hotels also have tearooms, ideal places to sit down in comfort and relax after a busy day sightseeing or shopping. **Metz & Co** has a comfortable sixth-floor café that offers one of the most impressive canal views in Amsterdam *(see p112)*. Another canalside experience not to be missed is **Reibach**, which has delicious German specialities. For something slightly different, try **Back Stage**, a wonderfully offbeat café run by an eccentric former cabaret artist called Mr. Christmas.

(see p112)

## WHERE TO FIND THE BEST CAFÉS

All the cafés and bars described on these pages are listed in the directory on page 237. The best, as shown on pages 46–7, are also listed below.

**Café Americain**
American Hotel, Leidsekade 97.
**Map** 4 D1.
📞 556 3232.

**Café Dulac**
Haarlemmerstraat 118. **Map** 1 C3.
📞 624 4265.

**'t Doktertje**
Rozenboomsteeg 4. **Map** 7 B4.
📞 626 4427.

**In de Wildeman**
Kolksteeg 3. **Map** 7 C1.
📞 638 2348.

**De Jaren**
Nieuwe Doelenstraat 20.
**Map** 7 C4.
📞 625 5771.

**De Kroon**
Rembrandtplein 17. **Map** 7 C5.
📞 625 2011.

**De Tuin**
2e Tuindwarsstraat 13 (near Anjeliersstraat). **Map** 1 B3.
📞 624 4559.

**Van Puffelen**
Prinsengracht 377. **Map** 4 E1.
📞 624 6270.

**Vertigo**
Nederlands Filmmuseum, Vondelpark 3. **Map** 4 D2.
📞 612 3021.

De Koninck, a dark Belgian beer

Amstel Bockbier, a dark winter beer

Columbus, brewed in Amsterdam

# AMSTERDAM THROUGH THE YEAR

ALTHOUGH there is no guarantee of good weather in Amsterdam, the cosmopolitan ambience of this 700-year-old city and the congeniality of the Dutch make it an appealing place to visit whatever time of year you go. Most tourists flock into the city from April to September, when temperatures are mild. Amsterdammers, however, are undaunted by the weather and maintain

**Herons nest on the canals**

an active programme of festivals and outdoor pursuits throughout the year. Crisp autumn days invite long walks along the city's stately canals, followed by a cosy chat in one of Amsterdam's brown cafés. About twice a decade, the winter temperatures drop so low that the canals freeze over. When this occurs a skating race is held between 11 Dutch cities.

## SPRING

SPRING BEGINS in late March when daffodils and crocuses blossom overnight all over the city. Flower lovers descend on Amsterdam, using it as a base for day trips to Keukenhof, the Netherlands' 28-hectare (69-acre) showcase for Dutch bulb growers *(see pp180–81).*

## MARCH

**Stille Omgang** *(second or third Sat)*, Rokin. Silent night-time procession celebrating the Miracle of Amsterdam *(see p20).*

**Opening of Keukenhof** *(21 Mar)*. One of the world's largest flower gardens *(see p181).*

## APRIL

**National Museum Weekend** *(second weekend of Apr)*. Cut-price or free admission to many state-run museums.
**Koninginnedag** *(30 Apr)*. Amsterdam becomes the world's biggest flea market-cum-street party as the Dutch celebrate Queen Beatrix's official birthday. Transport grinds to a halt as more than 2 million people throng the streets during the day and dance the night away.

**Revellers celebrating in the streets to commemorate Koninginnedag**

**World Press Photo** *(end Apr–early Jun)*, Oude Kerk. Exhibition of the very best press photographs from around the world.

## MAY

**Herdenkingsdag** *(4 May)*. Commemorations throughout the city for the victims of World War II. Largest in Dam square.
**Bevrijdingsdag** *(5 May)*. Concerts and speeches around the city celebrate the end of the German occupation.
**Kunst RAI** *(see p151) (second week)*. A massive exhibition of contemporary art held in Amsterdam RAI.
**Nationale Molendag** *(second Sat)*. Windmills all over the Netherlands are opened to the public and their sails unfurled.
**Boeken op de Dam** *(third or fourth Sun of May, second or third Sun of Jul)*. Dam square fills with book stalls,
**Open Air Theatre in Vondel-park** *(early Jun–end Aug)*. Theatre, music and children's shows *(see p128).*

**Tulip fields in bloom near Alkmaar**

## AVERAGE DAILY HOURS OF SUNSHINE

Hours
10
8
6
4
2
0

Jan  Feb  Mar  Apr  May  Jun  Jul  Aug  Sep  Oct  Nov  Dec

### Sunshine Chart
*The summer months are the sunniest, but this is no guarantee of good weather. Amsterdammers will often carry an umbrella even on the hottest of July days as summer rain in the morning often precedes the arrival of bright sunshine later.*

## SUMMER

SUMMER, which starts with the three week-long Holland Festival, is a hectic cultural roller-coaster ride. As well as the events listed below, classic European drama is staged in the Amsterdamse Bos *(p155)*, and open-air concerts are held in the Vondelpark *(pp128–9)*. This is the best time for people-watching in one of Amsterdam's street-side cafés and bars.

**A rower training on the Bosbaan in the Amsterdamse Bos**

## JUNE

**Grachtenloop** *(last Sun May or first Sun June)*. A choice of 18-, 9- and 5-km runs (11-, 5.5- and 3-mile)

around the city's canals. A treasure hunt takes place on the shortest run.
**Holland Festival** *(3 weeks of June)*. In venues throughout Amsterdam and in other major cities in the Netherlands, a varied programme of concerts, plays, operas and ballets is presented. Famous performers from all over the world take part in this prestigious festival.
**Amsterdam Roots Festival** *(late June)*, De Melkweg *(pp110–11)*, Tropenmuseum *(pp152–3)*, Oosterpark, and Concertgebouw *(p128)*. An ethnic programme of music, dance, film and theatre from Africa and other non-Western countries.

## JULY

**North Sea Jazz Festival** *(mid-Jul)*, the Netherlands Congress Centre. Weekend of jazz ranging from Dixieland to jazz rock a short train ride away in Den Haag.
**Summer Concerts** *(Jul–Aug)*, Concertgebouw *(see p128)*. Annual showcase of classical music.

**Orchestral performance at the Prinsengracht Concert**

## AUGUST

**Grachtenfestival** *(Wed–Sun, around third Sat)*. Classical concerts on Herengracht, Keizersgracht and Prinsengracht. The main concert is on Saturday on a barge in front of the Pulitzer Hotel. *(see p221)*.
**Uitmarkt** *(last weekend, incl. Fri)*. Previews new shows and stages music, dance and drama. Venue changes annually.

**Café-goers relaxing and soaking up the sun at de Jaren Terrace**

## AVERAGE MONTHLY RAINFALL

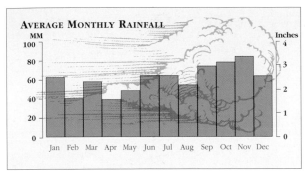

**Rainfall Chart**
*Expect rain all year
round in Amsterdam.
The pattern, however,
is broadly seasonal.
Visit the city in spring
to enjoy the driest
weather of the year.
The heaviest rainfall
occurs in autumn,
reaching a peak in
the windy and wet
month of November.*

## AUTUMN

Temperatures drop quickly at the end of August, but the cultural heat is maintained with the diary of music, dance, opera and drama promoted in the Uitmarkt *(see p51)*. The Autumn is also a busy time for more sporting types. There is a range of spectator sports to watch, and it is a good time of year to enjoy brisk walks in one of the city's many parks or along the Amstel. By November, many Amsterdammers retreat indoors on rainy evenings to cafés like Schaakcafé Het Hok in the Lange Leidsedwarsstraat.

## SEPTEMBER

**Jordaan Festival** *(third weekend, including Fri)*.
Neighbourhood festivals are held in the southern part of this picturesque district, with fairs, street parties, talent contests and music.
**Kano Toertocht door de Grachten** *(first weekend)*.
Some 500 illuminated canoes and kayaks take part in an evening tour of Amsterdam's canals.
**Bloemen Corso** *(first Sat)*. Crowds gather to watch a parade of flower-laden floats around Amsterdam. In the evening, there is an illuminated floral procession through the southern suburb of Aalsmeer.
**Open Monumentendagen** *(first or second weekend)*. A chance to see inside some historic, listed buildings which are normally closed to the public.

**Barges moored along an Amsterdam waterfront in autumn**

## OCTOBER

**Roeisloepengrachtentocht** *(second Sat)*, Oosterdok. One of many rowing competitions.
**PAN** *(mid-Oct)*. Art and antiques fair in RAI *(see p151)*.
**Delta Lloyd Amsterdam Marathon** *(third Sun)*. Some 1,500 runners circle the city before converging on the newly restored Olympic stadium in this 42-km (26-mile) run. A further 10,000 people join in for a 10-km (6-mile) stretch of the race.
**Camping and Caravan RAI** *(end Oct)*, Amsterdam RAI *(p151)*. Annual fair for open-air holiday enthusiasts selling the latest outdoor equipment.

## NOVEMBER

**Jumping Amsterdam** *(Nov/ Dec)*, Amsterdam RAI *(p151)*. International indoor show-jumping competitions.
**Sinterklaas' Parade** *(second or third Sat)*. The Dutch equivalent of Santa Claus arrives by boat near St Nicholaaskerk *(see p79)* with *Zwarte Piet* (Black Peter) and distributes sweets to the children of Amsterdam.

**Sinterklaas parading through Amsterdam**

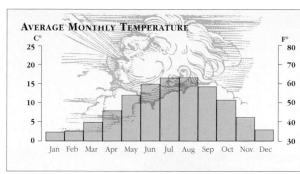

**Temperature Chart**
*The chart shows the average temperature for each month in Amsterdam. Summer is often cooled by the North Sea wind, both spring and autumn can be chilly, and temperatures in winter are frequently freezing.*

## WINTER

CHRISTMAS is a busy tourist season, with visitors and residents thronging to watch Christmas trees being hawked from barges on the main canals. Barrows appear throughout the city, tantalizing passers-by with the smell of freshly fried *oliebollen* and *appelflappen*, two sugary treats not to be missed. After Christmas, the talk of the town is whether or not it will be cold enough for the city authorities to permit skating on the city's canals. If the green light is given – which is rare – whole neighbourhoods turn out to skate under the stars.

### DECEMBER

**Sinterklaasavond** *(5 Dec).* The traditional Dutch gift-giving day when Sinterklaas and his Moorish helpers visit Dutch children to leave a sack of presents. Friends give poems caricaturing each other.

**The Dokwerker Monument in JD Meijerplein**

**Amsterdammers ice skating on the Keizersgracht**

**Christmas Day** *(25 Dec).* Increasingly accepted as the main gift-giving day.
**New Year's Eve** *(31 Dec).* Firework celebrations throughout the city with an organized display over the Amstel.

### JANUARY

**Chinese New Year** *(Jan or Feb),* Nieuwmarkt. Traditional lion dance, fireworks, Chinese exhibitions and stage art.

### FEBRUARY

**Februaristaking** *(25 Feb),* JD Meijerplein. Commemoration of dockworkers' action against deportation of Jewish residents during World War II.

**Carnival** *(end Feb).* Parade, mainly through the city provinces of Limburg and Brabant, designed to shake off the winter blues.

### PUBLIC HOLIDAYS

**New Year's Day** (1 Jan)
**Eerste Paasdag (Easter Monday)** *
**Koninginnedag** (30 April)
**Bevrijdingsdag** (5 May)
**Hemelvaartsdag (Ascension Day)** *
**Pinksteren (Whitsun)** *
**Eerste Kerstdag (Christmas Day)** (25 Dec)
**Tweede Kerstdag** (26 Dec)
\* Dates change in accordance with church calendar.

# AMSTERDAM AREA BY AREA

# OUDE ZIJDE

THE EASTERN HALF of Amsterdam became known as the Oude Zijde (Old Side). Originally it occupied a narrow strip on the east bank of the Amstel river, running between Damrak and the Oudezijds Voorburgwal *(see pp42–5)*. At its heart was built the Oude Kerk, the oldest church in the city. In the early 1400s the Oude Zijde began an eastward expansion which continued into the 17th century. This growth was

**Aäron from Mozes en Aäronkerk**

fuelled by an influx of Jewish refugees from Portugal. The oldest of the four synagogues, now containing the Joods Historisch Museum, dates from this period. These were central to Jewish life in the city for centuries. During the Golden Age *(see pp24–7)*, the Oude Zijde was an important commercial centre. Boats could sail up the Geldersekade to Nieuwmarkt, where goods were weighed at the Waag before being sold at the market.

## SIGHTS AT A GLANCE

### Historic Buildings and Monuments
Waag **2**
Agnietenkapel **3**
Oudemanhuispoort **6**
Oostindisch Huis **7**
Trippenhuis **8**
Pintohuis **16**
Montelbaanstoren **17**
Scheepvaarthuis **18**
Schreierstoren **19**

### Opera Houses
Stadhuis-Muziektheater **11**

### Museums
Hash Marijuana Hemp Museum **4**
Museum Het Rembrandthuis **10**
*Joods Historisch Museum pp64–5* **14**

### Churches and Synagogues
Zuiderkerk **9**
Mozes en Aäronkerk **13**
Portugees-Israëlitische Synagoge **15**
*Oude Kerk pp68–9* **21**

### Streets and Markets
Red Light District **1**
Nieuwmarkt **5**
Waterlooplein **12**
Zeedijk **20**

### GETTING THERE
The best way to reach the Oude Zijde is to get a tram to the Dam (trams 4, 9, 14, 16, 24 and 25) and then walk along Damstraat. Alternatively, take tram 9, 14 or 20 directly to Waterlooplein, or the metro to Nieuwmarkt.

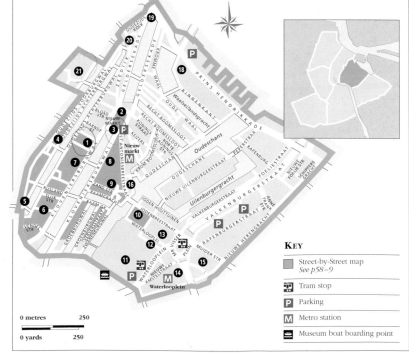

### KEY
Street-by-Street map *See p58–9*
Tram stop
Parking
Metro station
Museum boat boarding point

0 metres 250
0 yards 250

◁ **Some of the many exotic items to be found at the Waterlooplein flea market**

# Street-by-Street: University District

T HE UNIVERSITY OF AMSTERDAM, founded
in 1877, is predominantly located in
the peaceful, southwestern part of the
Oude Zijde. The university's roots lie
in the former Atheneum Illustre, which
was founded in 1632 in the Agnietenkapel. Beyond Damstraat, the bustling
Red Light District meets the Nieuwmarkt, where the 15th-century Waag
evokes a medieval air. South of the
Nieuwmarkt, Museum Het Rembrandthuis gives a fascinating insight into the
life of the city's most famous artist.

**★ Red Light District**
*The sex industry brings
billions of guilders to
Amsterdam every year* ❶

**Hash
Marijuana
Hemp
Museum**
*Marijuana
through
the ages*
❹

**Agnietenkapel**
*Like many buildings in
this area, the cloisters,
which house a museum,
belong to the University
of Amsterdam* ❺

**House (1610), unusually,
facing three canals**

VOORBURGWAL

ACHTERBURGWAL

OUDE ZIJDS

OUDEZIJDS

RUSLAND

**Oudemanhuispoort**
*Spectacles on the
gateway into this
18th-century alms-
house for elderly men
symbolize old age* ❻

**STAR SIGHTS**

★ **Red Light District**

★ **Museum Het
Rembrandthuis**

**Lift bridge over
Groenburgwal**

## Trippenhuis

*Although it appears to be a single 17th-century mansion, this building is in fact two houses, the middle windows being false to preserve the symmetry* **8**

## Nieuwmarkt

*Despite redevelopment southeast of this once-important market square, the Nieuwmarkt itself is still bordered by many fine 17th- and 18th-century gabled houses* **3**

**LOCATOR MAP**
*See Street Finder maps 7 and 8*

## Waag

*Amsterdam's only remaining medieval gatehouse now houses a restaurant* **2**

## Oostindisch Huis

*Now part of the University of Amsterdam, this former Dutch East India Company (VOC) building has a fine example of an early 17th-century façade* **7**

## Zuiderkerk

*This prominent city landmark now houses the city's planning information centre* **9**

0 metres        50

0 yards         50

**KEY**

– – – –   Suggested route

## ★ Museum Het Rembrandthuis

*Hundreds of Rembrandt's etchings, including many self-portraits, are on display in the artist's former home* **10**

# Red Light District ❶

**Map** 8 D2. 🚊 *4, 9, 14, 16, 24, 25.*

**B**ARELY CLAD prostitutes bathed in a red neon glow and touting for business at their windows is one of the defining images of modern Amsterdam. The city's Red Light District, referred to locally as de Walletjes (the little walls), is concentrated on the Oude Kerk (*see pp68–9*), although it extends as far as Warmoesstraat to the west, the Zeedijk to the north, the Kloveniersburgwal to the east and then along the line of Damstraat to the south.

Prostitution in Amsterdam dates back to the city's emergence as a port in the 13th century. By 1478, prostitution had become so widespread, with increasing numbers of sea-weary sailors flooding into the city, that attempts were made to contain it. Prostitutes straying outside their designated area were marched back to the sound of pipe and drum.

A century later, following the Alteration (*see pp22–3*), the Calvinists tried to outlaw prostitution altogether. Their attempts were half-hearted, and by the mid-17th century prostitution was openly tolerated. In 1850, Amsterdam had a

**Entrance to one of the clubs in the Red Light District**

population of 200,000, and more than 200 brothels. The most famous of these, like the luxurious Madame Traese's, catered for rich clients.

Today, the whole area is criss-crossed by a network of narrow lanes, dominated by garish sex shops and seedy clubs, and peppered with junkies, dealers and pickpockets. At night, the little alleys assume a somewhat sinister aspect, and it is not wise to wander away from the main streets. But by day, hordes of visitors crowding in generate a festive buzz, and among the sleaze there are interesting cafés, bars, restaurants and beautiful canalside houses to be discovered.

# Waag ❷

Nieuwmarkt 4. **Map** 8 D3. **(** *422 7772.* 🚊 *9, 14.* **Ⓜ** *Nieuwmarkt.*

**T**HE MULTI-TURRETED Waag is Amsterdam's oldest surviving gatehouse. Built in 1488, it was then, and often still is, called St Antoniespoort. Public executions were held here, and condemned prisoners awaited their fate in the "little gallows room". In 1617, the building became the public weigh house (*waaggebouw*). Peasants had their produce weighed here and paid tax accordingly. Various guilds moved into the upper rooms of each tower. From 1619 the Guild of Surgeons had their meeting room and anatomy theatre here. They added the central octagonal tower in 1691. Rembrandt's *Anatomy Lesson of Dr Tulp*, now in the Mauritshuis (*see pp188–9*), and *The Anatomy Lesson of Dr Jan Deijman*, in the Amsterdams Historisch Museum (*see pp80–1*), were commissioned by guild members and hung here.

The weigh house closed in the early 19th century and the Waag has since served as a fire station, two city museums, and is now home to the restaurant In de Waag (*see p230*).

The 15th-century Waag dominating the Nieuwmarkt, with an antique market on the left

**Part of the commemorative photo display in Nieuwmarkt metro**

# Nieuwmarkt ❸

**Map** 8 D3. 🚊 *9, 14.* Ⓜ *Nieuwmarkt.* **Antiques market** ⃝ *May–Sep: 9am–5pm Sun.*

AN OPEN, PAVED square, the Nieuwmarkt is flanked to the west by the Red Light District. With the top end of the Geldersekade, it forms Amsterdam's Chinatown. The Waag dominates the square, and construction of this gateway led to the site's development in the 15th century as a marketplace. When the city expanded in the 17th century *(see pp24–5)*, the square took on its present dimensions and was called the Nieuwmarkt. It retains an array of 17th and 18th-century gabled houses. True to tradition, an antiques market is held on Sundays during the summer.

The old Jewish Quarter leads off the square down St Antoniesbreestraat. In the 1970s, many houses in this area were demolished to make way for the new metro (marijuana). clashes between protesters and police. The action of conservationists persuaded the city council to adopt a policy of renovating rather than redeveloping old buildings. In tribute to them, photographs of their protests decorate the metro.

# Hash Marijuana Hemp Museum ❹

Oudezijds Achterburgwal 148. **Map** 7 C3. 📞 *623 5961.* 🚊 *4, 9, 14, 16, 24, 25.* Ⓜ *Nieuwmarkt.* ⃝ *11am–10pm.* 🖼 ⃝ ♿ 🚻

THIS MUSEUM is the only one in Europe to chart the history of hemp (marijuana). Exhibits refer back 8,000 years to early Asiatic civilizations,

which used the plant for medicines and clothing. It was first used in the Netherlands, according to a herbal manual of 1554, as a cure for earache.

Until the late 19th century, however, hemp was the main source of fibre for rope, and was therefore important in the Dutch shipping industry. Other exhibits relate to the psychoactive properties of this plant. They include an intriguing array of pipes and bongs (smoking devices), along with displays that explain smuggling methods. The museum also has a small cultivation area where plants are grown under artificial light. Police sometimes raid and take away exhibits, so there may be occasional gaps in displays.

# Agnietenkapel ❺

Oudezijds Voorburgwal 231. **Map** 7 C4. 📞 *525 3339.* 🚊 *4, 9, 14, 16, 24, 25.* ⃝ *9am–5pm Mon–Fri.* ● *public hols.*

NOW HOME to the University Museum, the Agnietenkapel was part of the convent of St Agnes until 1578 when it was closed after the Alteration *(see pp22–3)*. In 1632, the Athenaeum Illustre, the precursor of the University of Amsterdam, took it over and by the mid-17th century it was a centre of scientific learning. It also housed the municipal library until the 1830s. While the museum focuses on the history of the University of Amsterdam, the main attraction is the Agnietenkapel itself, dating from 1470. It is one of the few Gothic chapels to have survived the Alteration. During restoration from 1919 to 1921, elements of Amsterdam School architecture were introduced *(see p97)*. Despite these changes and long periods of secular use, the building still has the feel of a Franciscan chapel. The large auditorium on the first

floor is the city's oldest, and is used for university lectures. It has a lovely ceiling, painted with Renaissance motifs and a portrait of Minerva, the Roman goddess of wisdom and the arts. The walls are hung with 40 portraits of European humanist scholars, such as Erasmus (1466–1536).

**Entrance to Agnietenkapel, home to the University Museum**

# Oudemanhuis-poort ❻

Between Oudezijds Achterburgwal and Kloveniersburgwal. **Map** 7 C4. 🚊 *4, 9, 14, 16, 24, 25.* **Book market** ⃝ *10am–6pm Mon–Sat.*

THE OUDEMANHUISPOORT was once the entrance to old people's almshouses (Oudemannenhuis), built in 1754. Today the building is part of the University of Amsterdam. The pediment over the gateway in the Oudezijds Achterburgwal features a pair of spectacles, a symbol of old age. Trading inside this covered walkway dates from 1757 and today there is a market for second-hand books. Although the building is closed to the public, visitors may enter the 18th-century courtyard via the arcade.

**Crest of Amsterdam, Oudemanhuispoort**

**The spire of the Zuiderkerk, a prominent city landmark**

## Oostindisch Huis ❼

Oude Hoogstraat 24. **Map** 7 C3.
🚊 4, 9, 14, 16, 24, 25.
Ⓜ Nieuwmarkt. ⬤ to the public.

THE OOSTINDISCH HUIS, former
headquarters of the Dutch
East India Company or VOC
(see pp26–7), is now part of
the University of Amsterdam.
Built in 1605, it is attributed
to Hendrick de Keyser (see
p90). The premises have been
expanded several times, in
1606, 1634 and 1661, to house
spices, pepper, porcelain and
silk from the East Indies.

The VOC was dissolved in
1800 (see p29), and for a while
the Oostindisch Huis was taken
over by the customs authorities.
Later, the state tax offices also
moved in, and the VOC med-
allion carved in the stone gate
was removed and replaced
with a lion, which was the
traditional heraldic symbol
of the Netherlands.

Major restyling in the
1890s destroyed much
of the interior dec-
oration, although the
façade has remained
largely intact. The

ornate scrolling on the balustrade that crowns the roof
contrasts with the austerity of
the rest of the building.

## Trippenhuis ❽

Kloveniersburgwal 29. **Map** 8 D3.
🚊 4, 9, 14, 16, 24, 25. Ⓜ Nieuwmarkt. ⬤ to the public.

JUSTUS VINGBOONS designed this
ornate Classical mansion,
completed in 1662. It appears
to be one house: it is in fact
two. The façade, outlined by
eight Corinthian columns, features false middle windows.
The house was designed for
the wealthy arms merchants
Lodewijk and Hendrick Trip,
and hence the chimneys look
like cannons. The city's art
collection was housed here

**Ornate balustrade of the Oostindisch Huis**

from 1817 to 1885, when it
moved to the Rijksmuseum
(see pp130–33). The Trippenhuis now houses the Dutch
Academy. Opposite at No. 26
is the Kleine Trippenhuis, built
in 1698. It is only 2.5 m (7 ft)
wide and has very detailed
cornicing, which includes two
carved sphinxes.

## Zuiderkerk ❾

Zuiderkerkhof 72. **Map** 8 D4. 📞 680
6806. 🚊 9, 14. Ⓜ Nieuwmarkt.
◯ 11am–4pm Mon, 9am–4pm Tue,
Wed & Fri, 9am–8pm Thu. 📷 ♿
**Tower** 🎫 🚶 Jun–Sep: 2pm, 3pm &
4pm Wed–Sat; Oct– May: phone 689
2565 to arrange.

DESIGNED BY Hendrick de
Keyser in 1603, the Ren-
aissance-style Zuiderkerk was
the first Calvinist church to
open in Amsterdam after the
Alteration (see pp22–3). The
spire, with its columns, decorative clocks and onion dome,
is a prominent city landmark.

The Zuiderkerk ceased to
function as a church in 1929.
Restored in 1988, it is now a
public housing exhibiton
centre. The surrounding community housing includes
Theo Bosch's modern apartment building, the "Pentagon",
completed in the mid-1980s.

## Museum Het Rembrandthuis ❿

Jodenbreestraat 4 . **Map** 8 D4. 📞
520 0400. 🖥 www.rembrandthuis.nl
🚊 9, 14. Ⓜ Nieuwmarkt.
◯ 10am–5pm Mon–Sat, 1–5pm
Sun and public hols. ⬤ 1 Jan. 🎫
📷 📄 💻 🚶

REMBRANDT worked and
taught in this house from
1639 until 1660. He lived in the
ground-floor rooms with his
wife, Saskia, who died here in
1642, leaving the artist with a
baby son, Titus (see p200).
Many of Rembrandt's most
famous paintings were
created in the first-floor
studio. Lessons were
conducted in the attic.
A fine collection of
Rembrandt's draw-
ings includes various
self-portraits in

**Façade of Museum Het Rembrandthuis**

different moods and guises. There are also landscapes, nude studies, religious and crowd scenes and sketches of the artist with his wife. A new wing has recently opened, housing a superb collection of the artist's etchings, plus numerous personal effects.

## Stadhuis-Muziektheater ⓫

Waterlooplein 22. **Map** 8 D4. 🚊 9, 14. Ⓜ *Waterlooplein*. **Stadhuis** 552 9111. ◯ *8:30am–3:30pm Mon–Fri, 8:30am–3:30pm & 5–7pm Thu, 3pm Sat (free concerts 6:30pm Tue Sep–May).* **Muziektheater** 625 5455. See *Entertainment pp246–51.*

FEW BUILDINGS in Amsterdam caused as much controversy as the new Stadhuis (city hall) and Muziektheater (opera house). Nicknamed the "Stopera" by protesters, the scheme required the destruction of dozens of medieval houses, which were virtually all that remained of the original Jewish quarter. This led to running battles between squatters and police *(see pp34–5)*.

The building was completed in 1988, a massive confection of red brick, marble and glass. A mural illustrating the Normaal Amsterdams Peil *(see pp34–5)* is shown on the arcade linking the two parts of the complex. The Stopera has the largest auditorium in the country, with a seating capacity for 1,689 people, and it is now home to the Netherlands' national opera and ballet companies. Visitors can join guided backstage tours of the Muziektheater.

## Waterlooplein ⓬

**Map** 8 D5. 🚊 9, 14. Ⓜ *Waterlooplein*. **Holland Experience** 422 2233. ◯ *10am–6pm daily.* **Market** ◯ *9am–5pm Mon–Fri, 8:30am–5pm Sat.*

THE WATERLOOPLEIN dates from 1882, when two canals were filled in to create a large market square in the heart of the Jewish quarter. The site was originally known as Vlooyenburg, an artificial island built in the 17th century to house the Jewish settlers *(see p64)*.

It is now the setting for the new Holland Experience, a spectacular multi-media show taking visitors on a 25-minute tour of the country.

Despite encroachment by the Stadhuis-Muziektheater, the northern end of the Waterlooplein still operates a lively market, selling anything from bric-a-brac and army-surplus clothing to Balinese carvings.

## Mozes en Aäronkerk ⓭

Waterlooplein 205. **Map** 8 E4. 622 1305. 🚊 9, 14. Ⓜ *Waterlooplein*. ● *to the public except for exhibitions.*

DESIGNED BY the Flemish architect T. Suys the Elder in 1841, Mozes en Aäronkerk was built on the site of a clandestine Catholic church. The later church took its name from the Old Testament figures of Moses and Aaron depicted on the gable stones found on the original building. These are now set into the rear wall.

The church was restored in 1990, when its twin wooden towers were painted to look like sandstone. It is now used for exhibitions, public meetings, concerts and celebrations.

**Clothes on offer at the Waterlooplein market**

# Joods Historisch Museum ⑭

THIS COMPLEX of four synagogues was built by Ashkenazi Jews in the 17th and 18th centuries and opened as a museum in 1987. The synagogues were central to Jewish life in Amsterdam, until the devastation of World War II left them empty. They were restored in the 1980s and connected by internal walkways. Displays of art and religious artifacts depict Jewish culture and the history of Judaism in the Netherlands.

**The Nieuwe Synagoge** was built in 1752.

**The Star of David,** worn by all Jews in the Nazi occupation

**My Father at Morning Prayers** *(1886)*
*Eduard Frankfort (1864–1920) painted this scene showing his father, Solomon Frankfort, wearing his tallit and tefillin at morning prayers.*

**Main entrance**

## JEWS IN AMSTERDAM

The first Jew to gain Dutch citizenship was a member of the Portuguese Sephardic community in 1597. The Ashkenazi Jews from eastern Europe came to Amsterdam later, in the 1630s. They were restricted to working in certain trades, but were granted full civil equality in 1796. With the rise of Zionism in the 19th century, Jewish identity re-emerged, but the Nazi occupation decimated the community *(see pp32–3).*

**18th-century Torah scroll finial in shape of the Westerkerk tower**

**★ Festival Prayer Book**
*Presented to Amsterdam's Jewish community by printer Uri Phoebus ha-Levi in 1669, this Festival Prayer Book was one of the few to survive the late Middle Ages.*

## MUSEUM GUIDE

*Temporary exhibitions are shown in the Nieuwe Synagoge, the upper level of which focuses on children's exhibitions. The Grote Synagoge houses a permanent collection illustrating the religion, culture and history of the Jews in the Netherlands.*

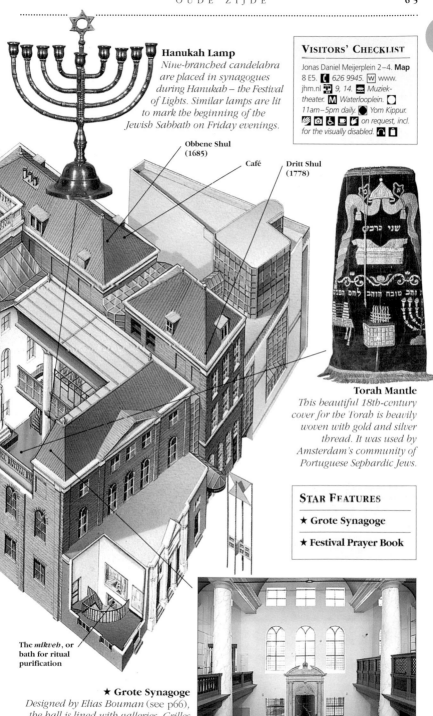

**Hanukah Lamp**
*Nine-branched candelabra are placed in synagogues during Hanukah – the Festival of Lights. Similar lamps are lit to mark the beginning of the Jewish Sabbath on Friday evenings.*

Obbene Shul (1685)

Café

Dritt Shul (1778)

**Torah Mantle**
*This beautiful 18th-century cover for the Torah is heavily woven with gold and silver thread. It was used by Amsterdam's community of Portuguese Sephardic Jews.*

**STAR FEATURES**

★ **Grote Synagoge**

★ **Festival Prayer Book**

The *mikveh*, or bath for ritual purification

**★ Grote Synagoge**
*Designed by Elias Bouman (see p66), the hall is lined with galleries. Grilles screen the women's gallery from the male congregation. The Ark was given to the synagogue by Rabbi Abraham Auerbach when it opened in 1671.*

## Portugees-Israëlitische Synagoge ⓯

Mr Visserplein 3. **Map** 8 E5.
█ 624 5351. 🚏 9, 14.
Ⓜ Waterlooplein. ⏰ 10am–4pm
Sun–Thu, 10am–3pm Fri. ● Jewish
hols. 🖼 ♿ 🚻 ✅ by arrange-
ment at the Joods Historische
Museum (see p64–65).

Elias Bouman's design for
the Portuguese
Israëlitische Synagoge was
inspired by the architecture of
the Temple of Solomon in
Jerusalem. Built for the Portuguese Sephardic community
of Amsterdam *(see p64)* and
inaugurated in 1675, the
huge building has a
rectangular ground plan with
the Holy Ark in the southeast
corner facing Jerusalem, and
the *tebah* (the podium from
which the service is led) at
the opposite end.
   The wooden, barrel-vaulted
ceiling is supported by four
Ionic columns. The interior of
the synagogue is illuminated
by more than 1,000 candles
and 72 windows.

**Italianate façade of the 17th-
century Pintohuis**

## Pintohuis ⓰

Sint Antoniesbreestraat 69. **Map** 8 D4.
█ 624 3184. 🚏 9, 14. Ⓜ Nieuwmarkt. **Library** ⏰ 2–8pm Mon &
Wed, 2–5pm Fri, 11am–4pm Sat
(except summer hols). ● public hols.

Isaac de Pinto, a wealthy
Portuguese merchant, bought
the Pintohuis in 1651 for the
then enormous sum of 30,000

guilders. He had it remodelled
over the next decades to a
design by Elias Bouman, and
it is one of the few private
residences in Amsterdam to
follow an Italianate style. The
exterior design was reworked
from 1675 to 1680. Six imposing pilasters break up the
severe, cream façade into five
recessed sections, and the
cornice is topped by a blind
balustrade concealing the roof.
   In the 1970s, the house was
scheduled for demolition
because it stood in the way of
a newly planned main road.
Concerted protest saved the
building, which now houses a
public library. Visitors can still
admire the original painted
ceiling, which is decorated
with birds and cherubs.

## Montelbaanstoren ⓱

Oude Waal /Oudeschans 2. **Map** 8 E3.
🚏 9, 14. Ⓜ Nieuwmarkt. ● to
the public.

The lower portion of the
Montelbaanstoren was
built in 1512 and formed part
of Amsterdam's medieval fortifications. It lay just beyond
the city wall, protecting the
city's wharves on the newly
built St Antoniesdijk (now the
Oudeschans) from the neighbouring Gelderlanders.
   The octagonal structure and
open-work timber steeple were
both added by Hendrick de
Keyser *(see p90)* in 1606. His
decorative addition bears a
close resemblance to the spire
of the Oude Kerk, designed by
Joost Bilhamer, which was built
40 years earlier *(see pp68–9)*.
In 1611, the tower began to
list, prompting Amsterdammers to attach ropes to the
top and pull it right again.
   Sailors from the VOC *(see
pp26–7)* would gather at the
Montelbaanstoren before
being ferried in small boats
down the IJ to the massive
East Indies-bound sailing
ships, anchored further out in
deep water to the north.
   The building appears in a
number of etchings by Rembrandt, and is still a popular
subject for artists. It now
houses the offices of the
Amsterdam water authority.

**One of many stone carvings on
the Scheepvaarthuis façade**

## Scheepvaarthuis ⓲

Prins Hendrikkade 108. **Map** 8 E2. 🚏
1, 2, 4, 5, 9, 13, 16, 17, 24, 25. Ⓜ
Centraal Station. ● to the public.

Built as an office complex
in 1916, the Scheep-
vaarthuis (Shipping House) is
regarded as the first true example of Amsterdam School
architecture *(see p97)*. It was
designed by Piet Kramer
(1881–1961), Johan van der
May (1878–1949) and Michel
de Klerk (1884–1923) for a
group of shipping companies
which no longer wanted to
conduct business on the quay.
   The imposing triangular
building has a prow-like front
and is crowned by a statue of
Neptune, his wife and four
female figures representing
the four points of the compass.

**The medieval Montelbaanstoren,
with its decorative timber steeple**

No expense was spared on the construction and internal decoration of the building, and local dock workers came to regard the building as a symbol of capitalism. The doors, stairs, window frames and interior walls are festooned with nautical images, such as sea horses, dolphins and anchors. Beautiful stained-glass skylights are also decorated with images of sailing ships, maps and compasses.

The Scheepvaarthuis is now home to the municipal transport department. Although closed to the public, Archivisie (see p270) will arrange architectural tours of the building.

## Schreierstoren ⑲

Prins Hendrikkade 94–95. **Map** 8 E1.
🚊 1, 2, 4, 5, 9, 13, 16, 17, 24, 25.
Ⓜ Centraal Station.
● to the public.

THE SCHREIERSTOREN (Weepers' Tower) was a defensive structure forming part of the medieval city walls, and dates from 1480. It was one of the few fortifications not to be demolished as the city expanded beyond its medieval boundaries in the 17th century. The building now houses a nautical equipment shop.

Popular legend states that the tower derived its name from the weeping (schreien in the original Dutch) of women who came here to wave their men off to sea. It is more likely, however, that the title has a less romantic origin and comes from the tower's position on a sharp (screye or scherpe), 90-degree bend in the old town walls. The earliest of four wall plaques, dated 1569, adds considerably to the confusion by depicting a weeping woman alongside the inscription scrayer hovck, which means sharp corner.

In 1609, Henry Hudson set sail from here in an attempt to discover a new and faster trading route to the East Indies. Instead, he unintentionally "discovered" the river in North America which still bears his name. A bronze plaque, laid in 1927, commemorates his voyage.

The Schreierstoren, part of the original city fortifications

## Zeedijk ⑳

**Map** 8 D2. 🚊 1, 2, 4, 5, 9, 13, 16, 17, 24, 25. Ⓜ Centraal Station.

ALONG WITH the Nieuwendijk and the Haarlemmerdijk, the Zeedijk (sea dyke) formed part of Amsterdam's original fortifications. Built in the early 1300s, some 30 years after Amsterdam had been granted its city charter, these defences took the form of a canal moat with piled-earth ramparts reinforced by wooden palisades. As the city grew in prosperity

Plaque on the Café 't Mandje (Little Basket), a gay bar at No. 63 Zeedijk

and the boundaries expanded, the canals were filled in and the dykes became obsolete. The paths that ran alongside them became the streets and alleys which bear their names today.

One of the two remaining wooden-fronted houses in Amsterdam can be found at No. 1. It was built in the mid-16th century as a hostel for sailors, and is much restored. Opposite is St Olofskapel, built in 1445 and named after the first Christian king of Norway and Denmark.

By the 1600s, the Zeedijk had become a slum, and one part was known as "the rats' nest". The area is on the edge of the city's Red Light District, and in the 1960s and 1970s became notorious as a centre for drug-dealing and street crime. Following a clean-up campaign in the 1980s, the Zeedijk is now much improved.

Plaques on the gables of some of the street's cafés reveal their former use – the red boot at No. 17 indicates that it was once a cobbler's.

# Oude Kerk

THE ORIGINS of the Oude Kerk date from the early 13th century, when a wooden church was built in a burial ground on a sand bank (see pp18–19). The present Gothic structure is 14th-century and it has grown from a single-aisled church into a basilica. As it expanded, the building became a gathering place for traders and a refuge for the poor. Its paintings and statuary were destroyed after the Alteration (see pp22–3) in 1578, but the gilded ceiling and stained-glass windows were undamaged. The Great Organ was added in 1724, and the stark interior has changed little since.

**Carving on 15th-century choir misericord**

**The spire** of the bell tower was built by Joost Bilhamer in 1565. François Hemony added the 47-bell carillon in 1658.

**Tomb of Saskia, first wife of Rembrandt** (see pp62–3)

**The Oude Kerk Today**
*The old church, surrounded by shops, cafés and houses, remains a calm and peaceful haven at the heart of the frenetic Red Light District.*

**Christening Chapel**

**Tomb of Admiral Abraham van der Hulst (1619–66)**

★ **Great Organ** (1724)
*Jan Westerman's oak-encased organ has eight bellows and 54 gilded pipes. Marbled-wood statues of biblical figures surround it.*

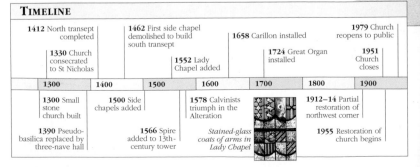

## TIMELINE

| | | | | | | | |
|---|---|---|---|---|---|---|---|
| **1412** North transept completed | **1462** First side chapel demolished to build south transept | | | **1658** Carillon installed | | **1979** Church reopens to public | |
| **1330** Church consecrated to St Nicholas | | **1552** Lady Chapel added | | **1724** Great Organ installed | | **1951** Church closes | |
| 1300 | 1400 | 1500 | 1600 | 1700 | 1800 | 1900 | |
| **1300** Small stone church built | **1500** Side chapels added | **1578** Calvinists triumph in the Alteration | | **1912–14** Partial restoration of northwest corner | |
| **1390** Pseudo-basilica replaced by three-nave hall | **1566** Spire added to 13th-century tower | *Stained-glass coats of arms in Lady Chapel* | **1955** Restoration of church begins | |

★ **Gilded Ceiling**
*The delicate 15th-century vault paintings have a gilded background. They were hidden with layers of blue paint in 1755 and not revealed until 1955.*

**VISITORS' CHECKLIST**

Oudekerksplein 23. **Map** 7 C2.
625 8284. [W] www.oudekerk.nl
4, 9, 16, 24, 25. **Church**
11am–5pm Mon–Sat, 1–5pm
Sun. 11am Sun. **Tower** phone 689 2565 to arrange. 1 Jan, 25 Dec.

**Tomb of Admiral
Jacob van Heemskerk
(1567–1607)**

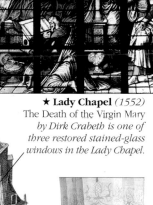

★ **Lady Chapel** *(1552)*
*The Death of the Virgin Mary by Dirk Crabeth is one of three restored stained-glass windows in the Lady Chapel.*

**Brocaded Pillars**
*Decorative pillars originally formed niches holding a series of statues of the Apostles, all destroyed by the iconoclasts in 1578.*

**17th- and 18th-
century houses**

**Former
sacristy**

**The Red Door**
*The inscription on the lintel above the door into the former sacristy warns those about to enter: "Marry in haste, repent at leisure."*

**STAR FEATURES**

★ **Great Organ**

★ **Gilded Ceiling**

★ **Lady Chapel**

# NIEUWE ZIJDE

THE WESTERN SIDE of medieval Amsterdam was known as the Nieuwe Zijde (New Side). Together with the Oude Zijde it formed the heart of the early maritime settlement. Nieuwendijk, now a busy shopping street, was originally one of the earliest sea defences. As Amsterdam grew, it expanded eastwards, leaving large sections of the Nieuwe Zijde, to the west, neglected and in decline. With its many wooden houses, the city was prone to fires and in 1452 much of the area was burnt down. During rebuilding, a broad moat, the Singel, was cut, along which warehouses, rich merchants' homes

"The calf" emblem on a house in the Begijnhof

and fine quays sprang up. The Amsterdams Historisch Museum, which is now housed in a splendid, converted orphanage, has scores of maps and paintings charting the growth of the city from these times to the present day. One room is devoted to the Miracle of Amsterdam *(see p20),* which made the city a place of pilgrimage, and brought commerce to the Nieuwe Zijde. Nearby lies Kalverstraat, Amsterdam's main shopping street, and also the secluded Begijnhof. This pretty courtyard is mostly fringed by narrow 17th-century houses, but it also contains the city's oldest surviving wooden house.

## SIGHTS AT A GLANCE

**Historic Buildings, Monuments and Bridges**
Koninklijk Paleis ❷
Nationaal Monument ❹
Torensluis ❾
Magna Plaza ❿
Centraal Station ⓬
Beurs van Berlage ⓯

**Streets and Squares**
Nes ❺
Begijnhof ❼

**Churches**
*Nieuwe Kerk pp76–7* ❶
Lutherse Kerk ⓫
St Nicolaaskerk ⓭

**Museums**
Madame Tussauds Scenerama ❸
*Amsterdams Historisch Museum pp80–3* ❻
*Allard Pierson Museum* ❽
*Museum Amstelkring pp84–5* ⓮

### GETTING THERE
The Nieuwe Zijde is easily accessible by public transport. Most tram routes terminate at Centraal Station (1, 2, 4, 5, 9, 13, 16, 17, 24 and 25), as does the metro. Or take a tram (4, 9, 14, 16, 24 and 25) to the Dam. Or 1, 2, 5, 13 or 17 to Magna Plaza.

| 0 metres | 250 |
| 0 yards | 250 |

### KEY

| | |
|---|---|
| ▦ | Street-by-Street map *See p72–3* |
| 🚊 | Tram stop |
| **P** | Parking |
| **M** | Metro station |
| 🚉 | Train station |
| 🚤 | Museum boat boarding point |

◁ *The Fatal Fall of Icarus,* one of the many Classical sculptures in the Koninklijk Paleis

# Street-by-Street: Nieuwe Zijde

ALTHOUGH MUCH of the medieval Nieuwe
Zijde has disappeared, the area is still rich
in buildings that relate to the city's past. The
Dam, dominated by the Koninklijk Paleis and
Nieuwe Kerk, provides examples of architecture
from the 15th to the 20th century. Around
Kalverstraat, the narrow streets and alleys
follow the course of some of the earliest
dykes and footpaths. Here, most of the traditional gabled houses have been turned into bustling
shops and cafés. Streets such as Rokin and Nes are
now home to financial institutions, attracted by the
nearby stock and options exchanges. Nes is also
known for its venues which feature alternative theatre.

**Kalverstraat**, now a busy
tourist shopping area, took its
name from the livestock market
which was regularly held here
during the 15th century.

★ **Amsterdams
Historisch Museum**
*Wall plaques and
maps showing the
walled medieval city
are on display in this
converted orphanage
that dates from the
16th century* ⑥

**A pillar** marks the
site of the Miracle
of Amsterdam
*(see p20).*

★ **Begijnhof**
*Two churches and one of
the few remaining wooden
houses in the city nestle in
this secluded, tree-filled
courtyard* ⑦

ST LUCIENSTEEG

KALVERSTRAAT

ROKIN

SPUI

0 metres        50

0 yards        50

**KEY**

- - -    Suggested route

**Café Esprit**
*(see p237)*

★ **Nieuwe Kerk**
*The carved and gilded ceiling above the choir was one of the few sections to survive the great fire of 1645* ❶

WESTERN CANAL RING
NIEUWE ZIJDE
OUDE ZIJDE
CENTRAL CANAL RING

**LOCATOR MAP**
*See Street Finder, maps 7, 1 & 2*

**De Drie Fleschjes bar** *(see p48)*

**St Nicolaas**
wall statue, depicting Amsterdam's patron saint, is thought to date from the 15th century.

SINTER CLAES

**Nationaal Monument**
*Two heraldic stone lions represent the Netherlands on this imposing memorial to the Dutch who lost their lives in World War II* ❹

**Madame Tussauds Scenerama**
*As well as waxworks and animated scenes, there is a fine view of the city from here* ❸

**STAR SIGHTS**

★ **Nieuwe Kerk**

★ **Amsterdams Historisch Museum**

★ **Begijnhof**

**Nes**
*This street is one of Amsterdam's oldest and has been a centre for theatre for 150 years* ❺

**Koninklijk Paleis**
*Built as the town hall, the building's Classical façade and fine sculptures were intended to glorify the city and its government* ❷

**The vast marble-floored Burgerzaal in the Koninklijk Paleis**

## Nieuwe Kerk ❶

*See pp76–7.*

## Koninklijk Paleis ❷

Dam. **Map** 7 B2. 📞 *624 8698.*
🚊 *1, 2, 4, 5, 9, 13, 14, 16, 17, 24,
25.* 🕐 *opening times vary.*
⬤ *phone 620 4060 to check, or
visit the website.* 📷 🚪 🅿 ♿ 🏠
🎫 *2pm Wed & Sun (📞 624 8698 to
reserve a private group tour).*
🌐 *www.kon-paleisamsterdam.nl*

T HE KONINKLIJK PALEIS, still
used occasionally by the
Dutch royal family for official
functions, was built as the
Stadhuis (town hall). Work
began in 1648, after the end of
the 80 Years War with Spain
*(see pp26–7)*. It dominated its
surroundings and more than
13,600 piles were driven into
the ground for the foundations.
The Classically inspired design
by Jacob van Campen (1595–
1657) reflects Amsterdam's
mood of confidence after the
Dutch victory. Civic pride is
also shown in the allegorical
sculptures by Artus Quellien
(1609–68), which decorate
the pediments, and in François
Hemony's statues and carillon.

The full magnificence of the
architecture is best seen in the
vast Burgerzaal (citizen's hall).
Based on the assembly halls
of ancient Rome, this 30-m
(95-ft) high room runs the
length of the building. It
boasts a marble floor inlaid
with maps of the eastern and
western hemispheres, as well
as epic sculptures by Quellien.
  Most of the furniture on
display, including the chandeliers, dates from 1808,
when Louis Napoleon
declared the building his
royal palace *(see pp28–9)*.

## Madame Tussauds Scenerama ❸

Peek & Cloppenburg Building, Dam
20. **Map** 7 B3. 📞 *522 1010.* 🚊 *4,
9, 14, 16, 24, 25.* 🕐 *Sep–Jun:
10am–5:30pm daily; mid Jul–Aug:
9:30am–7:30pm daily.* ⬤ *30 Apr.*
📷 📷 ♿ 🏠

L OCATED ABOVE the Peek &
Cloppenburg department
store, Madame Tussauds
offers an audiovisual tour of
Amsterdam's history, plus
projected future developments.
Some of the displays, such as
the animated 5-m (16-ft)

figure of "Amsterdam Man",
are bizarre, but the wax
models of 17th-century people
give an insight into life in the
Golden Age *(see pp24–5)*.

## Nationaal Monument ❹

Dam. **Map** 7 B3.
🚊 *4, 9, 14, 16, 24, 25.*

S CULPTED BY John Raedecker
and designed by architect
JJP Oud, the 22-m (70-ft) obelisk in the Dam commemorates
Dutch World War II casualties.
It was unveiled in 1956, and is
fronted by two lions, heraldic
symbols of the Netherlands.
Embedded in the wall behind
are urns containing earth from
all the Dutch provinces and
the former colonies of Indonesia, the Antilles and Surinam.

## Nes ❺

**Map** 7 B3. 🚊 *4, 9, 14, 16, 24, 25.*

T HIS QUIET, NARROW street is
home to several theatres. In
1614, Amsterdam's first bank
was opened in a pawnshop at
No. 57. A wall plaque marks
the site, and pawned goods
still clutter the shop window.
At night, Nes can be dangerous
for the unguarded visitor.

**De Engelenbak, one of several
theatres located along Nes**

## Amsterdams Historisch Museum ❻

*See pp80–83.*

# Begijnhof ❼

Spui. **Map** 7 B4. 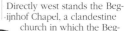 *1, 2, 4, 5, 9, 14,
16, 24, 25.*

THE BEGIJNHOF was originally
built in 1346 as a sanctuary
for the Begijntjes, a lay Catholic sisterhood who lived like
nuns, although they took no
monastic vows. In return for
lodgings within the complex,
these worthy women under-
took to educate the poor and
look after the sick. Nothing survives of the earliest dwellings,
but the Begijnhof, which is cut
off from traffic noise, still retains

a sanctified atmosphere. The
rows of beautiful houses that
overlook its well-kept green
include Amsterdam's old-
est surviving house at
No. 34. On the adjoining
wall, there is a fasci-
nating collection of wall
plaques taken from the
houses. In keeping with
the Begijntjes' religious
outlook, the plaques
have a biblical theme.
    The southern fringe
of the square is domi-
nated by the Engelse
Kerk (English Church), which
dates from the 15th century.

**Plaque on the
Engelse Kerk**

Directly west stands the Begijnhof Chapel, a clandestine
church in which the Beg-
ijntjes and other Catholics
worshipped in secret until
religious tolerance was
restored in 1795. It once
housed relics of the
Miracle of Amsterdam
*(see pp20–21)*. Four
stained-glass windows
and paintings depict
scenes of the Miracle.
Occupants are trying
to close public access
the Begijnhof, and
public tours are not allowed.
It may close in the future.

**The Begijnhof Chapel**, a
clandestine church (Nos. 29–30),
was completed in 1680. It contains
many reminders of Amsterdam's
Catholic past.

**No. 19** has a plaque
depicting the exodus
of the Jews from Egypt.

**Houses** in the Begijnhof are still
occupied by single women.

**Biblical plaques** cover
the wall behind No. 34.

**Spui entrance**

**Arched entrance from
Gedempte Begijnensloot**

**Het Houten Huis** at No. 34 is Amsterdam's oldest house, dating from around
1420. It is one of only two wooden-
fronted houses in the city, as timber
houses were banned in 1521 after a
series of catastrophic fires. Most of the
houses in the Begijnhof were not built
until after the 16th century.

**Engelse Kerk** was built around 1419
for the Begijntjes. The church was
confiscated after the Alteration *(see
pp22–3)* and rented to a group of
English and Scottish Presbyterians in
1607. The Pilgrim Fathers *(see p185)*
may have worshipped here.

# Nieuwe Kerk ❶

DATING FROM the 14th century, Amsterdam's second parish church was built as the population outgrew the Oude Kerk (*see pp68–9*). During its turbulent history, the church has been destroyed several times by fire, rebuilt and then stripped of its finery after the Alteration (*see pp22–3*). It reached its present size in the 1650s. Since 1814 all the Dutch monarchs have been crowned here. Nowadays, it is also a cultural centre.

**Gilded Cherubs**
*Grimacing gilded cherubs struggle to support the corners of the wooden barrel vault above the transept crossing.*

**Baptistry**

**Box pews around the carved pulpit**

**The New Stadhuis, Dam Square**
*The Nieuwe Kerk is in the background, at the corner of Dam square, in this painting by Jan van de Heyden (1637– 1712). It shows the newly completed Stadhuis, which is now the Koninklijk Paleis (see p74).*

**Ornate blind windows**

★ **Great Organ** (*1645*)
*Marbled-wood cherubs and angels adorn the elaborate gilded casing of the Great Organ, which was designed by Jacob van Campen.*

★ **Carved Pulpit** (*1664*)
*It took Albert Vinckenbrinck 15 years to carve the pulpit, which is unusually flamboyant for a Dutch Protestant church.*

| STAR FEATURES |
| --- |
| ★ Great Organ |
| ★ Tomb of De Ruyter |
| ★ Carved Pulpit |

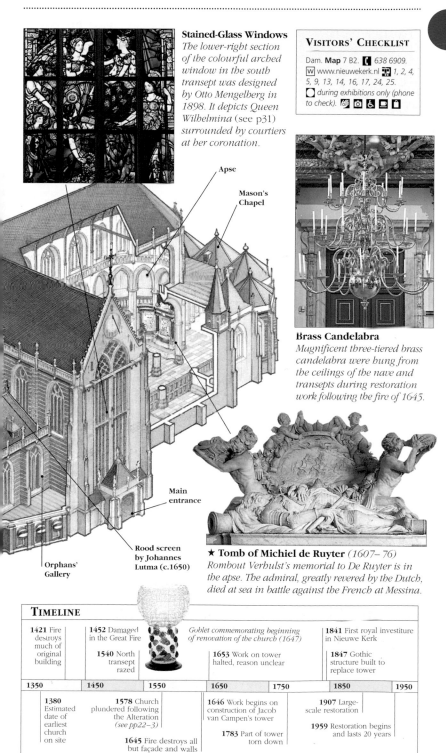

**Stained-Glass Windows**
*The lower-right section of the colourful arched window in the south transept was designed by Otto Mengelberg in 1898. It depicts Queen Wilhelmina (see p31) surrounded by courtiers at her coronation.*

Apse

Mason's Chapel

**Brass Candelabra**
*Magnificent three-tiered brass candelabra were hung from the ceilings of the nave and transepts during restoration work following the fire of 1645.*

Main entrance

Rood screen by Johannes Lutma (c.1650)

Orphans' Gallery

★ **Tomb of Michiel de Ruyter** *(1607– 76)*
*Rombout Verhulst's memorial to De Ruyter is in the apse. The admiral, greatly revered by the Dutch, died at sea in battle against the French at Messina.*

**TIMELINE**

| 1350 | 1450 | 1550 | 1650 | 1750 | 1850 | 1950 |
|---|---|---|---|---|---|---|

**1421** Fire destroys much of original building

**1452** Damaged in the Great Fire

**1540** North transept razed

*Goblet commemorating beginning of renovation of the church (1647)*

**1653** Work on tower halted, reason unclear

**1841** First royal investiture in Nieuwe Kerk

**1847** Gothic structure built to replace tower

**1380** Estimated date of earliest church on site

**1578** Church plundered following the Alteration *(see pp22–3)*

**1645** Fire destroys all but façade and walls

**1646** Work begins on construction of Jacob van Campen's tower

**1783** Part of tower torn down

**1907** Large-scale restoration

**1959** Restoration begins and lasts 20 years

## Allard Pierson Museum ⑧

Oude Turfmarkt 127. **Map** 7 B4. ☎
525 2556. 🔲 www.uba.uva.nl/apm
🚋 4, 9, 14, 16, 24, 25. ⬤
10am–5pm Tue–Fri, 1–5pm Sat,
Sun & public hols. ⬤ 1 Jan, Easter
Sun, 30 Apr, 1 May, Whitsun,
25 Dec. 📷 🔲 ♿ ✔

**Allard Pierson Museum's Neo-Classical façade
made of Bremer and Bentheimer stone**

AⅿsⅽⅾAⅿ's only specialist
archaeological collection
is named after Allard Pierson
(1831–96), a humanist and
scholar. The collection was
moved into this handsome
Neo-Classical building in 1976.
  The museum contains Cyp-
riot, Greek, Egyptian, Roman,
Etruscan and Coptic artifacts.
Look out for a case of rather
gruesome Egyptian mummy
remains, a computer that en-
ables you to write your name
in hieroglyphics, a jointed
Greek doll from 300 BC and
some fine Roman jewellery.

## Torensluis ⑨

Singel between Torensteeg and Oude
Leliestraat. **Map** 7 B2. 🚋 1, 2, 5, 13,
14, 17.

Tⅼⅼ Tⅼ TORENSLUIS is one of the
widest bridges in Amster-
dam. It was built on the site
of a 17th-century sluice gate

and took its name from two
towers that stood here on each
side of the Singel until they were
demolished in 1829. A lock-up
jail was built in its foundations.
  In summer, visitors can sit
out at café tables on the bridge
and enjoy pleasant views down
the Singel. The statue dominating the bridge is of Multatuli,
the 19th-century Dutch writer
who wrote the well-known
book *Max Havelaar*.

## Magna Plaza ⑩

Nieuwezijds Voorburgwal 182. **Map** 7 B2.
☎ 626 9199. 🚋 1, 2, 5, 13, 14, 17.
⬤ noon–7pm Sun, 11am–7pm Mon,
10am–7pm Tue, Wed, Fri & Sat,
10am–9pm Thu.
⬤ public hols. 📷 ♿

A POST OFFICE building has
been sited here since 1748.
A wall panel on the current
building's façade depicts the
original office, which was taken
out of service in 1854. The

present building was com-
pleted in 1899. CP Peters,
the architect, was ridiculed
for the extravagance of its
Neo-Gothic design. Critics
dubbed the Postkantoor's
elaborately decorated style
and spindly towers "post-
office Gothic". It has been
redeveloped, and in 1990
opened as the city's first shopping mall, the Magna Plaza.
The grand dimensions and
arched galleries of Peters' design have been well preserved.

## Ronde Lutherse Kerk ⑪

Kattengat 2. **Map** 7 C1. ☎ 621 2223.
🚋 1, 2, 5, 13, 17.
⬤ for concerts only.

Tⅼⅼ THE RONDE LUTHERSE KERK was
designed by Adriaan Dortsman (1625–82) and opened in
1671. It is the first Dutch
Reformed church to feature a
circular ground plan and two
upper galleries, giving the
whole congregation a clear
view of the pulpit.
  In 1882 a fire destroyed
everything except the exterior
walls. When the interior and
entrance were rebuilt in 1883,
they were made squarer and
more ornate, in keeping with

**An outdoor café on the Torensluis bridge overlooking the Singel canal**

the church architectural style of that time. A vaulted copper dome replaced the earlier ribbed version. Falling attendances led to the closure of the church in 1935. The building is now used by the Amsterdam Renaissance Hotel *(see p219)* as a business and conference centre and banqueting chamber, and is occasionally open to the public during the winter for concerts on Sunday afternoons.

## Centraal Station ⓬

Stationsplein. **Map** 8 D1. 🄲 0900 9292 🚊 1, 2, 4, 5, 9, 11, 13, 16, 17, 24, 25. Ⓜ Centraal Station.
**Information** ◯ Inland: 24 hrs daily. International: 6:30 am–10:30 pm. 📷 ♿

**Weather vane on Centraal Station**

WHEN THE CENTRAAL STATION opened in 1889, it replaced the old harbour as the symbolic focal point of the city *(see pp30–31)* and effectively curtained Amsterdam off from the sea. The Neo-Renaissance red-brick railway terminus was designed by PJH Cuypers, who was also responsible for the Rijksmuseum *(see pp130–31)* and AL van Gendt, who designed the Concertgebouw *(see p128)*.

Three artificial islands were created, using 8,600 wooden piles to support the structure. In the design of the station's twin towers and imposing central section there are architectural echoes of a triumphal arch, and it certainly makes a grand entry point for visitors to the city. The imposing façade is adorned with elaborate

**Decorative brickwork on the façade of the Beurs van Berlage**

gold and coloured decoration showing allegories of maritime trade – a tribute to the city's past. Today it is a major meeting point as well as the transport hub of the capital, with 1,400 trains operating daily *(see p268)*, and buses and trams terminating here.

## Sint Nicolaaskerk ⓭

Prins Hendrikkade 73. **Map** 8 D1. 🄲 624 8749. 🚊 1, 2, 4, 5, 9, 13, 16, 17, 24, 25. Ⓜ Centraal Station.
◯ Easter–mid-Oct: 11am–4pm daily; mid-Oct–Easter 1–4pm daily. ✝ 5:40pm Tue & Thu, 10:30am, 1pm (in Spanish), 5pm Sun. 📷

SINT NICOLAAS was the patron saint of seafarers, and as such was an important icon in Amsterdam. Many Dutch churches are named after him, and the Netherlands' principal day for the giving of presents, 5 December, is known as Sinterklaasavond *(see p53)*.

The Sint Nicolaaskerk was designed by AC Bleys (1842–1912), and completed in 1887. It replaced some clandestine Catholic churches set up in the city when Amsterdam was officially Protestant *(see p84)*.

The exterior is grim and forbidding, its twin towers dominating the skyline. Inside, the church is of a monumental character, with squared pillars and coffered ceiling arches.

## Museum Amstelkring ⓮

See pp84–5.

## Beurs van Berlage ⓯

Damrak 7. **Map** 7 C2. 🄲 530 4141. 🅆 www.beursvanberlage.nl 🚊 4, 9, 16, 24, 25. ◯ 11am–5pm Tue–Sun. ⬤ 1 Jan. 🎫 🚫 ♿ 🚻

HENDRIK BERLAGE'S stock exchange was completed in 1903. Its clean, functional appearance marked a departure from late 19th-century revivalist architecture. Many of its design features were adopted by the Amsterdam School *(see p97)*. It has an impressive frieze showing the evolution of man from Adam to stockbroker. Now used for concerts and shows, is home to the Nederlands Philharmonic Orchestra. The Beurs houses a variety of changing exhibitions.

**Neo-Renaissance façade of the Sint Nicolaaskerk**

# Amsterdams Historisch Museum **❻**

THE CONVENT OF ST LUCIEN was turned into a civic orphanage two years after the Alteration of 1578 *(see pp22–3)*. The original red brick convent has been enlarged over the years, with new wings added in the 17th century by Hendrick de Keyser *(see p90)* and Jacob van Campen *(see p76)*. The present building is largely as it was in the 18th century. Since 1975 the complex has housed the city's historical museum.

**Lecture Room**

**Museum Attic**

★ **The Anatomy Lesson of Dr Jan Deijman** *(1656)*
*In this Rembrandt depicts the dissection of Black John, a criminal sentenced to death.*

**Second floor**

**Orphans' Relief** *(1581)*
*The crooked relief above the gateway to Kalverstraat is a copy of Joost Bilhamer's original. Its inscription asks people to contribute to the upkeep of the orphans.*

**Library**

## MUSEUM GUIDE
*The permanent exhibitions are housed around the complex's inner courtyards. Clear signposting allows the visitor to either concentrate on a specific period – The Young City, The Mighty City or The Modern City – or to take a Grand Tour through Amsterdam's entire history. A new multimedia map offers a concise overview. There are also temporary exhibitions.*

**Kalverstraat main entrance (to the Begijnhof)**

**Goliath** *(c.1650)*
*This massive statue is one of a trio of biblical figures dominating the museum's café.*

---

### STAR FEATURES

★ **The Flower Market by Gerrit Berckheyde**

★ **Civic Guards' Gallery**

★ **The Anatomy Lesson of Dr Jan Deijman**

---

### KEY TO FLOORPLAN

- ☐ Civic Guards' Gallery
- ☐ Regents' Chamber
- ☐ Introduction & The First Amsterdammers
- ☐ The Young City: 1350-1550
- ☐ The Mighty City: 1550-1815
- ☐ The Modern City: 1815-Today
- ☐ Temporary exhibition space
- ☐ Non-exhibition space

**★ The Flower Market** *(1673)*
*Gerrit Berckheyde (1638–98) painted this scene showing the site of Amsterdam's original flower market on the Nieuwezijds Voorburgwal, which was filled in at the end of the 19th century. In the background is the Koninklijk Paleis (see p74).*

**VISITORS' CHECKLIST**

Kalverstraat 92, Nieuwezijds
Voorburgwal 357, St Luciensteeg
27. **Map** 1 C5. ☎ 523 1822.
🆆 *www.ahm.nl* 🚊 1, 2, 4, 5, 9,
13, 14, 16, 17, 24, 25. ◯
10am–5pm Mon–Fri, 11am–5pm
Sat & Sun. ◯ 1 Jan, 30 Apr, 25
Dec. 🎟 🅾 🚻 ♿ 🖥 🍴 🏛

**Keys to the Town of Amsterdam** *(1810)*
*These two silver keys were presented to Napoleon upon his entry into Amsterdam (see p29).*

First floor

**★ The Regentesses (sitting) and two housemistresses of the Spinhuis**
*This was painted in 1638 by D. D. van Santvoort.*

Ground floor

17th-century red brick façade

Entrance in girls' courtyard

Entrance on Nieuwezijds Voorburgwal

St Luciensteeg entrance

**Little Hearts Day** *(1926)*
*Johan Braakensiek's illustration shows the lively carnival atmosphere in Zeedijk during the celebrations for this day, which took place every Thursday throughout August.*

# Exploring the Amsterdams Historisch Museum

The terracotta figure of the Maid of Amsterdam

THE MUSEUM charts the development of Amsterdam from its humble origins as a fishing village on the Amstel in the Middle Ages to todays cosmopolitan city. The main focus is on trade, commerce and culture in the Golden Age *(see pp24–5)*. A series of Civic Guard group portraits are a highlight of the collection, which has recently been reorganised and a new section on the Modern City added.

## CIVIC GUARDS' GALLERY

THIS COVERED walkway is accessible to all during museum hours. Queen Juliana opened the gallery in 1975 to house the group portraits which were popular during the 16th century. The Civic Guard comprised three guilds of marksmen, which merged in 1580. This is a rare collection as few portraits were commissioned after 1650. Best-known are Rembrandt's works; highlights are by Dirck Barendsz *(see p81)* and Cornelis Anthonisz, such as *The Meal of the 17 Guardsmen of Company H* (1533).

## REGENTS' CHAMBER

BUILT IN 1634, this room was the meeting place of the orphanage's directors (regents). Its fine ceiling, added in 1656, shows the orphans receiving charity. Portraits of the regents hang on

17th-century coats of arms on wooden panel

the walls alongside Abraham de Verwer's two paintings of *The Battle on the Slaak* (1634). The long table and cabinets are 17th-century.

## THE FIRST AMSTERDAMMERS

THE FIRST ROOMS of the museum contain a series of displays explaining the growth of early Amsterdam around the Amstel river. A map of the city illuminates each area in turn to show when it was developed and how the buildings, roads, water and green spaces have combined to form the city as it is today. Visitors can choose to explore a specific period, or can take the 'Grand Tour' of the entire history of Amsterdam.

## THE YOUNG CITY: 1350–1550

AMSTERDAM'S RISE to prominence in trade and commerce began at this time *(see pp20–21)*. Scale models and archeological finds such as a cauldron used to soften tar for shipbuilding, and many household items such as shoes and tools, help to explain what the city was like. In addition, there is a huge map on the ground showing where the important areas in the city were. A fervent religious

revival took place during this period, spurred on by the Miracle of Amsterdam in 1345 *(see p20)*, causing thousands of pilgrims to flock into the city. Many churches were built in the 14th century and one of the paintings on show is *St Agnes's Convent* (c. 1490) by Jacob Cornelisz van Oostanen.

## THE MIGHTY CITY: 1550–1815

BETWEEN 1500 and 1560 the city's population tripled. The Civic Guard became defenders of law and order in the overcrowded city and there is a display of its armour and weaponry shown here. Cornelis Anthonisz's bird's-eye *View of Amsterdam (see pp22–3)* is the oldest city plan to survive, dated 1538. A number of churches and convents are clearly marked. A huge wall-relief shows Warmoesstraat, the oldest street in Amsterdam. It details the people who lived there: craftsmen to one side and merchants on the canalside for easy access to their ships. It is during this time that the inner horseshoe of canals was constructed and the Town Hall on the Dam was built. Hendrick Cornelisz Vroom's oil painting (1615) of the fortified Haarlemmerpoort, shows how the city defended itself against any outside attack from its political rivals.

Bronze dagger (c. 1500)

The Golden Age *(see pp24-7)* and the importance of overseas trade and colonial expansion forms a large part of this exhibition and includes the globe of the famous cartographer Willem Blaeu *(see p146)*. A late 18th-century model of an East Indiaman is shown resting on a primitive floating dock known as a "camel". This enabled heavily laden ships to travel through the very shallow waters of the Zuiderzee.

Portraits and busts of a variety of dignitaries abound, as well as a collection of official silverware and a 1648 model of the town hall, now

*The First Steamship on the IJ* (1816) by Nicolaas Bauo

the Koninklijk Paleis *(see p74)*.

The discrepancy between the rich and poorer inhabitants of the city is shown in a room with walls hung with huge, gloomy canvases depicting the wealthy governors of Amsterdam's poor houses.

Art flourished in the Golden Age and artists flooded into the city. Contemporary paintings, often allegorical, portray rich families and their lives such as Jacob de Wit's *Maid of Amsterdam* (1741). This and other paintings by masters such as Pieter de Hooch and Rembrandt, magnificent sculpture are just a few of the exhibits bringing the rich hstory of Amsterdam to life.

## THE OLD ORPHANAGE

*Girls from the Civic Orphanage* (c. 1880) by Nicolaas van der Waay

The orphanage moved to St Lucien's convent in 1580. It was open only to the children of burghers, excluding the poorest children. As the city grew, so did the number of orphans. In the 17th century, two wings were built to accommodate more children, and a separate entrance for girls was added on St Luciensteeg. The building was used as an orphanage until 1960, but the formal uniform was abandoned in 1919.

## THE MODERN CITY: 1815–TODAY

DECLINE IN TRADE resulted in poverty in the 19th century and charitable institutions grew up to deal with the problem. Art began to reflect the social problems such as the squalour and slum conditions in the city. Melancholic late Hague School works by George Breitner *(see p133)* and sombre black-and-white photographs reflect the city's demise. A series of unrealized plans for the expansion of Amsterdam highlight this stagnation.

A spectacular presentation, including interactive multi-media exhibits, documents more recent history. The museum shows a series of evocative photographs taken during the Depression of the early 1930s and the war years *(see pp32–3)*, when the city was under Nazi occupation.

Photographs, videos and computers allow modern city life to be explored in detail. One of the main themes is the 'Young in Amsterdam'. Temporary exhibitions cover aspects of 20th-century life in Amsterdam from homosexuality to diamond-cutting.

# Museum Amstelkring ⑭

T UCKED AWAY on the edge of the Red Light District is a restored 17th-century canal house, with two smaller houses to the rear. The combined upper storeys conceal a secret Catholic church, known as Ons' Lieve Heer op Solder (Our Dear Lord in the Attic), originally built in 1663. After the Alteration *(see pp22–3)*, when Amsterdam officially became Protestant, many such clandestine churches were built throughout the city. The lower floors of the building became a museum in 1888, and today contain elegantly refurbished and decorated rooms, as well as a fine collection of church silver, religious artifacts and paintings.

**Christ and the Dove of Peace in silver**

**Wooden viewing gallery of church**

**A priest's** tiny box bedroom is hidden off a bend in the stairs. There was a resident priest in the church from 1663.

**Amstelkring Façade**
*The house on the canal has a simple spout gable. Along with two smaller houses behind, it was bought by bourgeois merchant Jan Hartman in 1661.*

**Main entrance**

**House on the canal**

**Reception room in Louis XV style**

**★ The Parlour**
*Restored to its former opulence, the Parlour is an unusually fine example of a living room decorated and furnished in the Dutch Classical style of the 17th century.*

## STAR FEATURES

★ **Ons' Lieve Heer op Solder**

★ **Altar Painting by Jacob de Wit**

★ **The Parlour**

Sacristy

**VISITORS' CHECKLIST**

Oudezijds Voorburgwal 40. **Map** 8
D2. ☎ 624 6604. 🚊 4, 9, 16, 24,
25. ⊙ 10am– 5pm Mon–Sat,
1–5pm Sun and public hols.
⬤ 1 Jan, 30 Apr. 📷 ◎ 🖊 🚻 🎁

**Confessional**
*The landing where the tiny
wooden confessional stands
was formerly the living room
of the rear house.*

**★ Altar Painting**
The Baptism of Christ *(1716) hanging above
the mock marble altar is by Jacob de Wit (1695–
1754). It is one of three altar paintings that
were designed to be interchangeable.*

Rear
house

**19th-Century Kitchen**
*The kitchen was originally part of
the sacristan's secret living quarters.
The Delft tiles, fireplace and black-
and-white floor are all original.*

Middle
house

**★ Ons' Lieve Heer op Solder**
*The original clandestine church was
extended in 1735 to create more
seating space. It served the Catholic
community until St Nicolaaskerk
(see p79) was finished in 1887.*

# WESTERN CANAL RING

At the start of the 17th century, construction of the *Grachten-gordel* began here, just west of the Singel *(see p45)*. At the same time, the city planner, Hendrick Staets, laid out the marshy area beyond these fashionable canals as an area for workers whose industries were banned from the town centre. Its network of narrow streets and oblique canals followed the course of old paths and drainage ditches. Immigrants fleeing

"Writing hand" emblem on Claes Claeszhofje

religious persecution also settled here. It is thought that Huguenot refugees called the district *jardin* (garden), later corrupted to "Jordaan". Historically a poor area, it is famous for its almshouses *(hofjes)*, and the Claes Claesz-hofje is a fine early example. Recently, the Jordaan has taken on a more bohemian air. Further north are the characterful Western Islands, created in the mid-17th century to meet the demand for warehouses.

## SIGHTS AT A GLANCE

**Historic Buildings and Monuments**
Huis met de Hoofden ❹
Haarlemmerpoort ❸

**Museums**
Theatermuseum ❶
Anne Frankhuis ❸
Pianola en Piano Museum ⑪

**Canals and Islands**
Egelantiersgracht ❺
Bloemgracht ❻
Brouwersgracht ⑫
Western Islands ⑭

**Churches**
Westerkerk ❷
Noorder-kerk ❾

**Markets**
Noordermarkt ⑩

**Hofjes**
Claes Claeszhofje ❼
De Star and Zon's Hofje ❽

### GETTING THERE
It is a five-minute walk from the Dam and Central Station to the Jordaan. Trams 13, 14 and 17 go to Rozengracht; 3 follows Marnixstraat to Haarlemmer-poort and 10 goes halfway.

**KEY**

- Street-by-Street map See p88–9
- Tram stop
- Parking
- Museum boat boarding point

◁ **View of Prinsengracht with its densely packed houseboats and the Westerkerk in the distance**

# Street-by-Street: Around the Jordaan

WEST OF THE *Grachtengordel (see p45)*, the Jordaan still retains a network of narrow, characterful streets and delightful canals. Among the 17th-century workers' houses are dozens of quirky shops, which are well worth a browse, selling anything from designer clothes to old sinks, and lively brown cafés and bars, which spill on to the pavements in summer. A stroll along the *Grachtengordel* provides a glimpse into some of the city's grandest canal houses, including the Bartolotti House.

**★ Anne Frankhuis**
*For two years, the Frank family and four others lived in a small upstairs apartment that was hidden behind a revolving bookcase* ❸

**Bloemgracht**
*This quiet, pretty canal was once a centre for makers of paint and dye* ❻

**★ Westerkerk**
*Hendrick de Keyser's church is the site of Rembrandt's unmarked grave, and was the setting for the wedding of Queen Beatrix and Prince Claus in 1966* ❷

**Egelantiersgracht**
*This charming tree-lined Jordaan canal is overlooked by an interesting mixture of old and new architecture. Pretty views are provided from its numerous bridges* ❺

**Huis met de Hoofden**
*The name "House with the Heads"
refers to the six Classical busts at
the entrance, depicting Apollo,
Ceres, Mars, Minerva,
Bacchus and Diana* ❹

**LOCATOR MAP**
*See Street Finder maps 1 & 7*

0 metres 75
0 yards 75

PRINSENGRACHT

KEIZERSGRACHT

LELIEGRACHT

KEIZERSGRACHT

WESTERN
CANAL RING

NIEUWE
ZIJDE

CENTRAL
CANAL RING

★ **Theatermuseum**
*The Bartolotti House, now
home of the Theatermuseum,
was built by Hendrick de
Keyser in 1617 for wealthy
banker Guellelmo Bartolotti,
formerly a brewer* ❶

**The Greenpeace
building**, with its
fine façade, is a rare
example of Dutch
Art Nouveau, de-
signed by Gerrit van
Arkel in 1905. It is
now home to the
environmental group.

**KEY**

– – – Suggested route

**STAR SIGHTS**

★ **Theatermuseum**

★ **Westerkerk**

★ **Anne Frankhuis**

**Theatermuseum interior, with 18th-century staircase and stuccowork**

# Theatermuseum ❶

Herengracht 168. **Map** 7 A2. ☎ 551 3300. ⓦ www.tin.nl ➡ 13, 14, 17. ⚓ Prinsengracht. ◯ 11am–5pm Tue–Fri, 1–5pm Sat & Sun. ● 1 Jan, 30 Ap, 25 Dec. 🈲 ⊘ 🖼 🔊 🛗

Tᴡᴏ ꜰɪɴᴇ ʙᴜɪʟᴅɪɴɢꜱ house the theatre museum, which contains costumes, sets and memorabilia. You can even play with antique sound effects and create your own storm. The museum entrance is in the White House, No. 168, a Neo-Classical house designed by Philips Vingboons *(see p99)* in 1638. The interior was re-styled in about 1730, and has

a magnificent spiral staircase, stuccowork by Van Logteren and rich ceiling paintings by Jacob de Wit *(see p122)*.

The museum extends into Bartolotti House (Nos. 170–172). Built by Hendrick de Keyser (1565–1621) in 1617, its elaborate Renaissance façade contrasts sharply with the austerity of the White House. Its interior decoration was carried out by Jacob de Wit and Isaac de Moucheron.

# Westerkerk ❷

Prinsengracht 281. **Map** 1 B4. ☎ 624 7766. ⓦ www.westerkerk.nl ➡ 13, 14, 17. ◯ Easter–Sep: 11am–3pm Mon–Fri & Sat (Jun–Jul only, except during services). ☎ 629 7766. 📷 **Tower** 🈲 🖼 Apr–Sep: every hour 10am–5pm Mon–Sat. Oct–Mar: phone 689 2565 to arrange.

Bᴜɪʟᴛ ᴀꜱ ᴘᴀʀᴛ of the development of the Canal Ring *(see pp44–5)*, this church has the tallest tower in the city at 85 m (272 ft), and the largest nave of any Dutch Protestant church. It was designed by Hendrick de Keyser, who died in 1621, a year after work began.

Rembrandt was buried here but his grave has never been found. The organ shutters (1686) were painted, by Gerard

de Lairesse, with lively scenes showing King David, the Queen of Sheba and the Evangelists. The spire is topped by the Imperial Crown of Maximilian *(see pp20–21)*. The stunning views justify the climb.

# Anne Frankhuis ❸

Prinsengracht 263. **Map** 1 B4. ☎ 556 7100. ⓦ www.annefrank.nl ➡ 13, 14, 17. ⚓ Prinsengracht. ◯ Apr–Aug: 9am–9pm daily;. Sep–Mar: 9am–7pm daily; 1 Jan, 25 Dec: noon–7pm ● Yom Kippur. 🈲 ⊘ 🛗

**Anne's picture display in her room in the Anne Frankhuis**

Fᴏʀ ᴛᴡᴏ ʏᴇᴀʀꜱ during World War II, the Frank and Van Daan families, both Jewish, hid here until their betrayal to the Nazis. In 1957, the Anne Frank Stichting (foundation) took over the house, to carry out "the ideals set down in

**The Westerkerk in the 18th century, a view by Jan Ekels**

the Diary of Anne Frank". The 13-year-old Anne began her now-famous diary in July 1942. It gives a unique account of growing up under persecution, and of life in confinement *(see pp32–3)*. It was first published in 1947 as *Het Achterhuis (The Annexe)* and since translated into dozens of languages, and made into plays and films.

Visitors to the Anne Frankhuis climb to the second floor and enter the annexe via the revolving bookcase that hid its entrance. Its rooms are now empty, except for the film-star pin-ups in Anne's room, and Otto Frank's model of the annexe as it was during the occupation. The front of the house has exhibitions on World War II and anti-semitism. Get here early – with more than 800,000 visitors a year the museum gets very crowded.

## Huis met de Hoofden **❹**

Keizersgracht 123. **Map** 7 A1.
**[** 552 4888. **🚋** 13, 14, 17.
**●** to the public

**B**UILT IN 1622, the Huis met de Hoofden (house with the heads) is one of the largest double houses of the period. It has a fine step gable and takes its name from the six heads placed on pilasters along the façade. Legend has it that they commemorate a housemaid who, when left alone in the house, surprised six burglars and cut off their heads. The sculptures are in fact portrayals of six Classical deities (from left to right): Apollo, Ceres, Mars, Minerva, Bacchus and Diana.

The design of the building is sometimes attributed to Pieter de Keyser (1595–1676), the son of Hendrick de Keyser. It is now home to the Monument-enzorg, an organization which since 1953 has supervised care of Amsterdam's officially recognized public monuments.

**Head of Apollo on the Huis met de Hoofden**

**Bikes and boats along the tranquil Bloemgracht**

## Egelantiersgracht **❺**

**Map** 1 B4. **🚋** 13, 14, 17.

**M**ANY CANALS in the Jordaan were named after trees or flowers, and this includes the Egelantiersgracht (sweet-brier or eglantine). The canal was cut in the 17th century along a drainage ditch. The houses in this area, built for artisans, are on a more intimate scale than the grand mansions along Heren-gracht, Keizersgracht and Prinsengracht. As a result, demand for canalside residences in the Jordaan has boomed. Despite some development, the Egelantiersgracht retains much of its original character and one of the most charming spots along the canal is the St Andrieshofje at Nos. 107–114. This

*hofje* was built in 1617, and the passage through to its courtyard is decorated with splendid blue-and-white tiles.

## Bloemgracht **❻**

**Map** 1 B4. **🚋** 13, 14, 17.

**T**HE BLOEMGRACHT (flower canal) was a centre for dye and paint manufacture in the 17th century. Today, only one paint maker remains, and this quiet canal is called the Heren-gracht (gentlemen's canal) of the Jordaan, because of the fine gable houses along its banks.

The most beautiful are the three houses at Nos. 87 to 91. Built in 1642 in the traditional "burgher" style of the period, they feature stepped gables and a strong use of glass. Their gable stones, which served as house names until numbering was introduced in the 19th century, depict a farmer, a townsman and a seaman.

Stone plaque on the *hofje* founded
in 1616 by the merchant Anslo

# Claes
Claeszhofje [7]

1e Egelantiersdwarsstraat. **Map** 1 B3.
🚃 3, 10, 13, 14, 17. ◻ on & off.

THIS IS A GROUP of *hofjes*,
the earliest of which was
founded in 1616 by a textile
merchant, Claes Claesz Anslo.
They were renovated by the
Stichting Diogenes, a foundation which now rents out
the houses to art students.

One of the oldest and most
distinctive is the "Huis met de
Schrijvende Hand" (house with
the writing hand), Egelantiersstraat 52. Once the home of a
teacher, it dates from the 1630s.

# De Star Hofje and
Zon's Hofje [8]

De Star Hofje: Prinsengracht 89–133;
Zon's Hofje: Prinsengracht 159–171.
**Map** 1 C3. 🚃 3, 10, 13, 14, 17.
◻ *sporadically.*

THESE TWO CHARMING *hofjes*
are within a short walk of
each other. De Star *hofje* was
built on the site of the Star

Brewery in 1804, and it is officially known as Van Brienen
*hofje*. Legend has it that a
merchant, Jan van Brienen,
founded this almshouse in
gratitude for his release from a
vault in which he had been
accidentally imprisoned.
The peaceful courtyard
has a lovely flower garden
with a fine laburnum tree.
Zon's *hofje* was built on the
site of a clandestine church,
known as Noah's Ark, now indicated by a plaque in the
courtyard. The church's original
name of Kleine Zon (Little
Sun) gave the *hofje* its name.

# Noorderkerk [9]

Noordermarkt 44–48. **Map** 1 C3.
📞 626 6436. 🚃 3, 10, 13, 14, 17.
◻ 10.30am–6.30pm Mon, 11am–
1pm Sat. ✝ 10am & 7pm Sun.

BUILT for poor settlers in the
Jordaan, the recently
renovated North Church was
the first in Amsterdam to be
constructed in the shape of a
Greek cross. Its layout around
a central pulpit allowed everyone in the encircling pews to
see and hear well.

The church was designed
by Hendrick de Keyser (*see
p90*), who died in 1621, a
year after building began. It
was completed in 1623, in time
to hold its inaugural service at
Easter. The church is still well
attended by a widespread
Calvinist congregation, and
bears many reminders of the
working-class origins of the

Jordaan. By the entrance is a
sculpture of three bound
figures, inscribed: "Unity is
Strength". It commemorates
the Jordaanoproer (Jordaan
Riot) of 1934 *(see pp32–3)*.

On the south façade is a
plaque recalling the strike of
February 1941, a protest at the
Nazis' deportation of Jews.

# Noordermarkt [10]

**Map** 1 C3. 🚃 3, 10, 13, 14, 17.
**General Market** ◻ 9am–1pm
Mon; **Boerenmarkt** (fruit and
vegetables) ◻ 9am–5pm Sat.

Visitors to the Saturday morning
fair in Noordermarkt

SINCE 1627, the square that
surrounds the Noorderkerk
has been a market site. At that
time, it sold pots and pans
and *vodden* (old clothes), a
tradition that continues today
with a flea market. Since the
18th century, the area has
been a centre for bed shops,
and bedding, curtains and
fabrics are still sold on Monday
morning along the Wester-
straat. On Saturday mornings,
the *vogel-tjes* (small birds)
market sells various birds and
rabbits. Around 10am, the
*boerenmarkt* takes over, selling health foods, ethnic crafts
and candles.

# Pianola en Piano
Museum [11]

Westerstraat 106. **Map** 1 B3.
📞 627 9624. 🚃 3, 10, 13, 14, 17.
◻ 11.30am–5.30pm Sun (Mon–Sat
by appt only). 📷 📹

FIFTEEN INSTRUMENTS and some
15,000 piano rolls are on
show here, celebrating the
automatic pianos that were
introduced in 1900. Their
popularity was soon eclipsed
by the newly invented radio.

The lush garden in the courtyard of De Star *hofje*

A flower-filled houseboat on Brouwersgracht

# Brouwersgracht ⑫

**Map** 1 B2. 🚊 *3*.

Brouwersgracht (brewers'
canal) was named after the
breweries established here in
the 17th and 18th centuries.
Leather, spices, coffee and
sugar were also processed and
stored here. Today, most of the
warehouses are smart
residences that look out on an
array of houseboats moored
between the canal's picturesque hump-backed bridges.
  Prime examples of these
functional buildings, with their
spout gables *(see pp96 – 7)* and
shutters, can be seen at Nos.
188 to 194. The last distillery in
the area, the Ooievaar, is just
off Brouwersgracht on Drie-
hoekstraat (Triangle street). The
Dutch gin, *jenever*, has been
made here since 1782. Visit
one of the many *proeflokalen*
or tasting houses *(see p48)*
around the city to sample it.

# Haarlemmer-
poort ⑬

Haarlemmerplein 50. **Map** 1 B1.
🚊 *3*. ⬤ *to the public*

Originally a defended gateway into Amsterdam, the
Haarlemmerpoort marked the
beginning of the busy route
to Haarlem. The present gateway, dating from 1840, was
built for King William II's
triumphal entry into the city
*(see pp30 – 31)* and officially
named Willemspoort. However,
as the third gateway to be built
on or close to this site, it is
still referred to as the Haarlemmerpoort by Amsterdammers.
  Designed by Cornelis Alewijn
(1788 – 1839), the Neo-Classical
gatehouse was used as tax
offices in the 19th century and
was made into flats in 1986.
Traffic no longer goes through
the gate, since a bridge has
been built over the adjoining
Westerkanaal. Lying beyond
the Haarlemmerpoort is the
peaceful Westerpark, one
of the city's smaller parks.

# Western Islands ⑭

**Map** 1 C1. 🚊 *3*.

Plaque with shipping motif on a
house in Zandhoek, Realeneiland

This district comprises three
islands built on the IJ in
the early 17th century to provide space for warehouses and
shipyards. Some of these are
still in use and many of the
period houses have survived.
  Bickerseiland was bought in
1631 by the merchant Jan
Bicker, who then developed it.
Today, the island is residential
with a mix of colourful apartment blocks on one side of its
walkway and a jumble of tugs
and houseboats on the other.
  Photogenic Realeneiland
has one of the city's prettiest
spots, the waterside street of
Zandhoek. Here, a row of
17th-century houses built by
the island's founder, Jacobsz
Reaal, overlook the sailboats
moored along Westerdok.
  Prinseneiland, the smallest
island, is dominated by characterful warehouses, many of
which are now apartments.
The walk on pages 158–9 explores the area in more detail.

---

The "house with the writing hand"
(*c. 1630*) in Claes Claeszhofje

## DUTCH HOFJES

Before the Alteration *(see pp22 – 3)*,
the Catholic Church usually provided subsidized housing for the
poor and elderly, partic-
ularly women. During the
17th and 18th centuries,
rich merchants and Prot-
estant organizations took
on this charitable role and
built hundreds of alms-
house complexes, which
were planned around
courtyards and known as
*hofjes*. Behind their street
façades lie pretty houses
and serene gardens.
Visitors are admitted to
some but are asked to
respect the residents'
privacy. Many *hofjes* are
found in the Jordaan and
some still serve their original purpose *(see p75)*.

# A CANAL WALK AND
# GUIDE TO ARCHITECTURE

Wɪᴛʜ ᴛʜᴇ increase in wealth and civic pride in Amsterdam during the 17th century, an ambitious plan was formed to build a splendid ring of canals round the city *(see pp24–5)*. Conceived in 1609, and added to in 1664 by Daniel Stalpaert, the scheme grew

**Wall plaque, No. 1133 Prinsengracht**

to encompass wide canals lined with opulent town houses in a variety of architectural styles *(see pp96–7)*. The houses on the canals of Singel, Keizersgracht, Herengracht, Reguliersgracht and Prinsengracht, illustrated on pp98–105, form a fascinating walk through Golden Age Amsterdam.

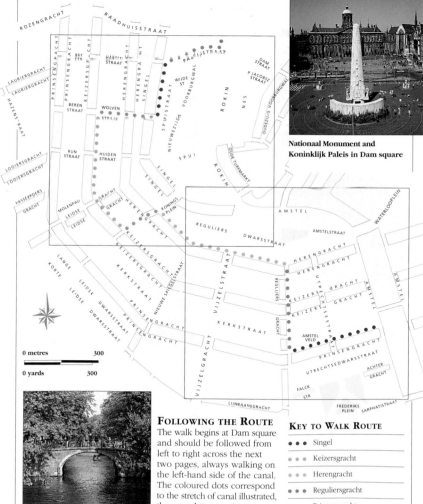

**Nationaal Monument and Koninklijk Paleis in Dam square**

**A picturesque stone hump-back bridge on the Reguliersgracht**

0 metres    300
0 yards     300

## FOLLOWING THE ROUTE
The walk begins at Dam square and should be followed from left to right across the next two pages, always walking on the left-hand side of the canal. The coloured dots correspond to the stretch of canal illustrated, the grey dots trace interconnecting roads forming part of the route, but are not illustrated.

## KEY TO WALK ROUTE
● ● ●   Singel
● ● ●   Keizersgracht
● ● ●   Herengracht
● ● ●   Reguliersgracht
● ● ●   Prinsengracht
● ● ●   Connecting streets

◁ *Keizersgracht* (c. 1750) by Hendrick Keun – a scene of beauty and tranquillity

# A Guide to Canal House Architecture

A MSTERDAM HAS BEEN CALLED a city of "well-mannered" architecture because its charms lie in intimate details rather
than in grand effects. From the 15th century on, planning
laws, plot sizes and the instability of the topsoil dictated that
façades were largely uniform in size and built of lightweight
brick or sandstone, with large windows to reduce the weight.
Canal house owners stamped their own individuality on the
buildings, mainly through the use of decorative gables and
cornices, ornate doorcases and varying window shapes.

**Broken pedi-**
**ment and vase**    **"Broken handle"**
**window surrounds**    **Pediment carvings** symbolize
the arts and sciences.

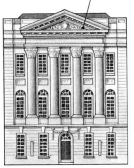

### Bartolotti House (1617)
*The contrasting brick and
stone, flamboyant step gable,
with its marble obelisk and
scrolls, is typical of the Dutch
Renaissance style of Hen-
drick de Keyser (see p90).*

### Felix Meritis Building (1778)
*The Corinthian columns and
triangular pediment are influenced by Classical architecture.
This marks the building (see
p113) by Jacob Otten Husly
as Dutch Classical in style.*

### Ground Plans
*Taxes were levied accord-
ing to width of façade, so
canal houses were often
long and narrow, with an
achterhuis (back annexe)
used for offices and storage.*

## CORNICES
Decorative top moul-
dings, called cornices,
became popular from
1690 onwards when
the fashion for gables
declined. By the 19th
century, they had
become unadorned.

**Louis XV-style with ro-
coco balustrade (1739)**

**19th-century cornice
with mansard roof**

**19th-century dentil
(tooth-shaped) cornice**

## GABLES
The term gable refers to the
front apex of a roof. It
disguised the steepness of
the roof under which
goods were stored
*(see pp20–21)*. In
time, gables became
decorated with
scrolls, crests, and
even coats of arms.

**Warehouse-style
spout gable**

**Simple tri-
angular gable**

**Dutch Renais-
sance style**

**No. 34 Begijnhof** (c. 1420)
is one of few remaining timber houses *(see pp20–21)*.

**The style of gable** on No.
213 Leliegracht (c. 1620)
was used for warehouses.

**Step gables** like the one on
No. 2 Brouwersgracht were
in vogue between 1600–65.

### Leaning Façades

*Canal houses were often built with a deliberate tilt, allowing goods to be winched up to the attic without crashing against the windows. A law dating from 1565 restricted this lean to 1:25, to limit the risk of buildings collapsing into the streets.*

## AMSTERDAM SCHOOL ARCHITECTURE

Members of the Amsterdam School, a loose grouping of like-minded and idealistic architects, built many distinctive housing estates between 1911 and 1923 *(see p151)*. They believed in the ability of unusual architecture to enhance residents' lives, many of whom were rehoused from appalling slums. Michel de Klerk's development, Het Schip (1921), is on

**Michel de Klerk (1884–1923)**

Hembrugstraat in northwest Amsterdam. It is typical of the lively style of the Amsterdam School, with sweeping façades, intricate brickwork and an exotic roofline.

Lateral windows    Needle-shaped spire    Curving façade

**Het Schip (the ship), built to resemble an ocean-going liner**

### Dutch Hofjes

*Almshouses (hofjes) were built throughout the Netherlands by rich benefactors in the 17th and 18th centuries. By providing accommodation for the elderly and infirm (see p93), the hofjes marked the beginning of the Dutch welfare system.*

**Sign of a sailor's hostel**

**Symbol of a dairyman**

**Noah's Ark – a refuge for the poor**

## WALL PLAQUES

Carved and painted stones were used to identify houses before street numbering was introduced in the 19th century. Many reflect the owner's occupation.

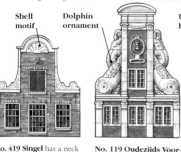

Shell motif    Dolphin ornament    Unadorned bell gable    Stonework with cornucopia decoration

**No. 419 Singel** has a neck gable, a common feature from 1640 to around 1840

**No. 119 Oudezijds Voorburgwal** has an ornate 17th-century neck gable.

**No. 57 Leliegracht** has a plain bell gable, popular from the late 17th century.

**No. 298 Oudezijds Voorburgwal** has a bell gable dating from the 18th century.

# Dam Square to Herengracht 487

THE WALK along Amsterdam's finest canals begins in Dam square *(see pp74)*. Following the grey dots on the map, leave the square past the Koninklijk Paleis *(see p74)*, cross Nieuwezijds Voorburgwal and Spuistraat down Paleisstraat, and turn left along the left bank of Singel, marked by purple dots. Further directions are incorporated into the route below.

**LOCATOR MAP**

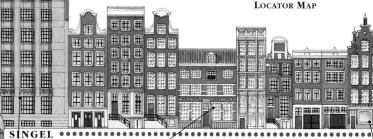

**SINGEL**

### No. 239 Singel
*AL Van Gendt* (see p128) *designed this massive stone office block for trader Julius Carle Bunge. Known as the Bungehuis, it was completed in 1934.*

**The double-fronted** 17th-century canal house at No. 265 Singel has been rebuilt several times since it was first constructed.

**The step gable** at No. 279 Singel dates from the 19th century – most along this canal were built between 1600–65 *(see p96)*.

**The three neck gables** on Nos. 353–7 Keizersgracht date from the early 18th century *(see pp96–7)*.

**Huidenstraat**

### No. 345a Keizersgracht is
a narrow house sharing a cornice with its neighbour.

**In 1708**, No. 333 Keizersgracht was rebuilt for tax collector Jacob de Wilde. It has recently been converted into apartments.

**The Sower at Arles** *(1888)*
*In March 1878, Vincent van Gogh (see pp134–5) visited his uncle, who ran a book-shop and art dealership at No. 453 Keizersgracht.*

**Jan Six II**
*The façade of No. 495 Herengracht was re-built and a balcony added by Jean Coulon in 1739 for burgomaster and art expert Jan Six (see p118).*

**Riots in 1696**
*No. 507 Herengracht was home of mayor Jacob Boreel. His house was looted in retaliation for the burial tax he introduced into the city.*

Vijzelstraat

**Three houses** boasting typical neck gables, at Nos 17, 19 and 21 Reguliersgracht, are now much sought after as prestigious addresses.

**The Nieuwe Amsterdammer**
*A weekly magazine aimed at Amsterdam's Bolshevik intelligentsia was published at No. 19 Reguliersgracht from 1914–20.*

SEVEN BRIDGES

**The spout-gabled** *(see pp96–7)* 16th-century ware-houses at Nos. 11 and 13 Reguliersgracht are called the Sun and the Moon.

**Café Marcella**, at No. 1047a Prinsengracht, is a typical local bar which has seating outside in summer.

**Houseboats on Prinsengracht**
*All registered houseboats have postal addresses and are con-nected to the electricity mains.*

Utrechtsestraat

**Tsar Peter** *(see p101)* stayed at No. 527 Herengracht, home of the Russian ambassador, after a night of drunken revelry at No. 317 Keizersgracht in 1716.

**Herengracht** *(1790)*
*A delicate watercolour by J Prins shows the "gentlemen's canal" from Koningsplein.*

**The asymmetrical building** at Nos. 533–7 Herengracht was built in 1910 on the site of four former houses. From 1968–88 it was the Registry of Births, Marriages and Deaths.

**The façades** of Nos. 37 and 39 Reguliersgracht lean towards the water, showing the danger caused by subsidence when building on marshland.

**Reguliersgracht Bridges**
*Seven arched stone bridges cross the canal which was originally designed to be a street*

**Keizersgracht**

**Nos. 1059 and 1061 Prinsengracht** have tiny basement entrances, rare amid the splendour of the *Grachtengordel* *(see p44)*, where the height of the steps was considered an indication of wealth.

**The sober** spout-gabled building at No. 1075 Prinsengracht was built as a warehouse in 1690.

**My Domestic Companions**
*Society portraitist Thérèse van Duyl Schwartze painted this picture in 1916. She owned Nos. 1087, 1089 and 1091 Prinsengracht, a handsome row of houses where she lived with her extended family.*

### Herengracht *(c. 1670)*
*GA Berckheyde's etching shows one side of the canal bare of trees. Elms were later planted, binding the topsoil, to strengthen the buildings' foundations.*

**No. 543 Herengracht** was built in 1743 under the supervision of owner Sibout Bollard. It has a double-fronted façade with an ornate balustrade and decorated balcony.

**The small houses** at the corner of Herengracht and Thorbeckeplein contrast with the grand neighbouring buildings.

### Isaac Gosschalk
*The architect designed Nos. 57, 59 and 63 Reguliersgracht in 1879. They have ornate stone, brick and woodwork façades.*

### Reguliers Monastery
*This engraving by J Wagenaar (1760) shows the monastery that once stood on the canal.*

### The Amstel
*Turn left and follow the broad sweep of the Amstel river, up past the Magere Brug (see p119) on up okin and back to the Dam, where the walk began.*

# CENTRAL CANAL RING

THE EXTENSION OF Amsterdam's three major canals continued from the early 17th century *(see pp24–5)*, as the merchant classes sought to escape the overcrowding and industrial squalor in the old city, around the Amstel. They bought plots of land along the new extensions to the Herengracht, Keizersgracht and Prinsengracht, and in the 1660s the wealthiest built opulent houses on a stretch of Herengracht known as the

**Pillar decoration on the Felix Meritis Building**

Golden Bend. Designed and decorated by the best architects of the day, such as Philips Vingboons *(see p101)*, the mansions built here were often twice the width of standard canal houses *(see p96)*. Today, many of these grand buildings are owned by institutions. Other architectural landmarks include the Neo-Gothic Krijtberg, with its soaring steeples, the imposing Paleis van Justitie and the Art Nouveau American Hotel overlooking the busy Leidseplein.

## SIGHTS AT A GLANCE

**Historic Buildings and Monuments**
American Hotel ❷
Paleis van Justitie ❺
Metz & Co ❼

**Museums**
Bijbels Museum ❿
Houseboat Museum ⓭

**Canals and Squares**
Leidseplein ❶
Leidsegracht ❻
Golden Bend ❽

**GETTING THERE**
It takes about 15 minutes to walk from the Dam to Leidseplein via the Leidsegracht. Leidseplein can be reached by trams Nos 1, 2 and 5 which terminate at Centraal Station, 6, 7 and 10 also cross the square from the north and west going east towards Plantage.

**Churches**
Krijtberg ❾

**Markets**
Looier Kunst en
    Antiekcentrum ⓫

**Clubs and Theatres**
De Melkweg ❸
Stadsschouwburg ❹
Felix Meritis Building ⓬

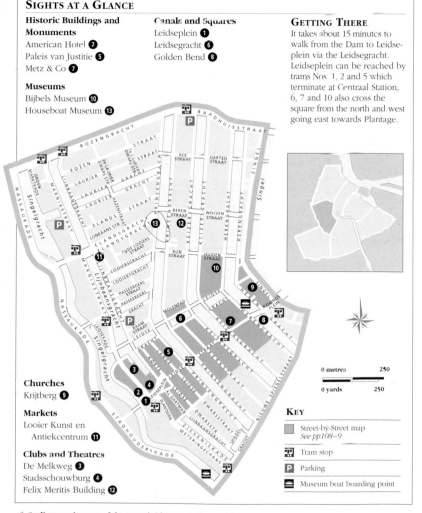

**KEY**

| | |
|---|---|
| ▦ | Street-by-Street map *See pp108–9* |
| 🚉 | Tram stop |
| 🅿 | Parking |
| ⛴ | Museum boat boarding point |

◁ **Cyclist crossing one of the many bridges on Leidsegracht**

# Street-by-Street: Leidsebuurt

THE AREA around Leidseplein is one of Amsterdam's busiest nightspots. There are various films to be seen at the many cinemas, plays at the Stadsschouwburg and lively programmes of music at De Melkweg. In contrast, there is fine architecture to admire around the Canal Ring, such as the imposing Paleis van Justitie on Prinsengracht, the lavish De Krijtberg on the Singel and scores of grand houses on the Golden Bend.

*Leidseplein street-performer*

**Bijbels Museum**
*In addition to bibles, there are several archaeological finds from Egypt and the Middle East on display here* ❿

**Leidsegracht**
*Cut in 1664, this canal was the main waterway for barges heading for Leiden* ❻

**Paleis van Justitie**
*This vast Empire-style building contains Amsterdam's Court of Appeal* ❺

**Stadsschouwburg**
*The city's football team, Ajax, uses the theatre's balcony to greet supporters after winning important games* ❹

**★ American Hotel**
*The hotel's Café Americain has a fine Art Deco interior and is a popular place to while away an afternoon (see p221)* ❷

**De Melkweg**
*This converted milk processing factory and former hippie hang-out survives as one of Amsterdam's key venues for alternative entertainment* ❸

**Leidseplein**
*Young people flock to this square to watch street performances and enjoy the vibrant nightlife* ❶

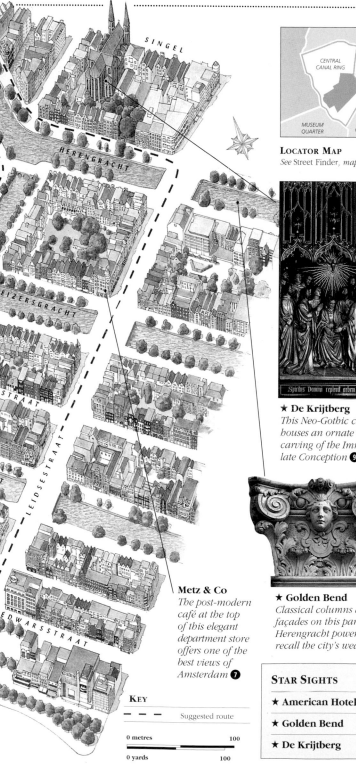

SINGEL

HERENGRACHT

KEIZERSGRACHT

KERKSTRAAT

LEIDSESTRAAT

RACHT

LEIDSEDWARSSTRAAT

**LOCATOR MAP**
See *Street Finder, maps 4 & 7*

NIEUWE ZIJDE

CENTRAL CANAL RING

MUSEUM QUARTER

EASTERN CANAL RING

Spiritus Domini replevit orbem terrarum.

★ **De Krijtberg**
*This Neo-Gothic church houses an ornate wooden carving of the Immaculate Conception* ❾

★ **Golden Bend**
*Classical columns and façades on this part of the Herengracht powerfully recall the city's wealth* ❽

**Metz & Co**
*The post-modern café at the top of this elegant department store offers one of the best views of Amsterdam* ❼

**KEY**

– – – Suggested route

0 metres     100
0 yards      100

---

**STAR SIGHTS**

★ **American Hotel**

★ **Golden Bend**

★ **De Krijtberg**

# Leidseplein ❶

**Map** 4 E2. 🚊 *1, 2, 5, 6, 7, 10.*

A MSTERDAM'S LIVELIEST square,
Leidseplein is also a
busy tram intersection and
centre of night-time transport.

The square developed in
the 17th century as a wagon
park on the outskirts of the
city – farmers and peasants
would leave their carts here
before entering the centre.
It takes its name from the
Leidsepoort, the massive city
gate demolished in 1862,
which marked the beginning
of the route out to Leiden.

During the day, the square
is buzzing with fire-eaters,
buskers and other street performers playing to café aud-
iences. It is also popular with
pickpockets. At night, it is the
focal point for the city's
youth, who hang out in the
many bars, cafés, restaurants,
nightclubs and cinemas in
and around the square.

**Street performer in Leidseplein**

# American Hotel ❷

Leidsekade 97. **Map** 4 E2. 📞 *556
3000.* 🚊 *1, 2, 5, 6, 7, 10.* 🖥 🍴
See **Where to Stay** *p221.*

L EIDSEPLEIN WAS fast becoming
a fashionable entertainment
area when the American
Hotel was built overlooking
it in 1882. The hotel got its
name because its architect,
W Steinigeweg, studied hotel
design in the United States,
and adorned his Neo-Gothic
creation with a bronze eagle,
wooden figures of native
Indians and murals of American landscapes. Within 20
years it was deemed *passé*
and the hotel was demolished.
The present building is by
Willem Kromhout (1864–
1940) and was completed in
1902. His design marked a
radical departure, interpreting
the Art Nouveau style in an
angular Dutch fashion. The
building's turreted exterior
and elaborate brickwork
anticipated the progressive
Amsterdam School *(see p97).*
A carved stone plaque on the
Leidseplein side of the hotel
shows the original building.

The Café Americain *(see
p46),* decorated in Art Deco
style, remains one of the most
elegant in Amsterdam. It retains
its period furnishings and
stained-glass windows. The rest
of the hotel was redecorated in
the 1980s. Samples of the
original furnishings are in the
Rijksmuseum *(see pp130–33).*

# De Melkweg ❸

Lijnbaansgracht 234a. **Map** 4 E2.
📞 *531 8181.* 🌐 www.melkweg.nl
🚊 *1, 2, 5, 6, 7, 10.* **Box office**
🕐 *1–5pm, 7:30–9:30pm Mon–Fri;
4–6pm, 7:30–9:30pm Sat & Sun.*
**Performances**: *9:30pm approx.* 📷
📷 See **Entertainment** *p249.*

D E MELKWEG (Milky Way) is
a multimedia centre situ-
ated in a former dairy behind
the Stadsschouwburg. It
opened in 1970 and soon
gained a dazzling reputation
as an alternative cultural meeting place. Nowadays, it offers
a wide range of entertainment,

**The American Hotel seen from Singelgracht**

including live music, film, video, theatre, dance and a photographic gallery. The theatre has a stage for new international acts, and De Melkweg's annual Amsterdam Roots Festival *(see p51)* promotes the latest in world music.

**De Melkweg's star-lit façade**

## Stadsschouwburg **❹**

Leidseplein 26. **Map** 4 E2. **☎** *624 2311.* 🚊 *1, 2, 5, 6, 7, 10.* **Box office** 🕙 *10am–6pm Mon–Sat. See* **Entertainment** *p246.* 🎭 🚫 ♿ [w] www.stadsschouwburgamsterdam.nl

THIS NEO-RENAISSANCE building is the most recent of three successive municipal theatres in the city, its predecessors having burned down. The theatre was designed by Jan Springer, whose other credits include the Frascati building on Oxford Street in London, and AL van Gendt, who was responsible for the Concertgebouw *(see p128)* and for part of the Centraal Station *(see p79)*. The planned ornamentation of the theatre's redbrick exterior was never carried out because of budget cuts. This, combined with a hostile public reaction to his theatre, forced a disillusioned Springer into virtual retirement. Public

disgust was due, however, to the theatre management's policy of restricting use of the front door to patrons who had bought expensive tickets.

Until the Muziektheater was completed in 1986 *(see p63)*, the Stadsschouwburg was home to the Dutch national ballet and opera companies. Today, the theatre stages plays by local drama groups such as the resident Toneelgroep, and international companies, including many English-language productions. The theatre has now become a favourite venue for Amsterdam's premier football club, Ajax, and their supporters. Whenever this most popular of teams wins an important competition, the players gather on the theatre's balcony to greet their fans, who pack Leidseplein to see their heroes.

## Paleis van Justitie **❺**

Prinsengracht 434–436. **Map** 4 E1. **☎** *541 2111.* 🚊 *1, 2, 5, 6, 7, 10.* 🕙 *with restrictions.*

CONVERSION of the former city orphanage into the Empire-style Palace of Justice, designed by the city architect Jan de Greef, was completed in 1829. Balustrades run along the roofline and the monotony of the imposing Neo-Classical façade is broken up by Corinthian pilasters. The building houses Amsterdam's Court of Appeal, and the courtrooms inside are set around two open yards.

The orphanage opened in 1666 with space for 800 chil-

dren. By 1811, the building housed more than 2,000, over half of the city's orphans. To control their rising numbers, a royal decree was passed permitting the relocation of orphans to other towns. When this act was implemented in 1822, there was widespread protest from local people and accusations that the authorities had stolen children. Once all the children were relocated, the orphanage was closed.

## Leidsegracht **❻**

**Map** 4 E1. 🚊 *1, 2, 5, 6, 7, 10.*

**No. 39 Leidsegracht, on the right**

THE LEIDSEGRACHT was for a few years the main route for barges from Amsterdam to Leiden. It was cut in 1664 to a plan by city architect Daniel Stalpaert, and is now one of the city's smartest addresses.

Cornelis Lely, who drew up the original plans for draining the Zuiderzee *(see p165)*, was born at No. 39 in 1854. A wall plaque shows Lely poised between the Zuiderzee and the newly created IJsselmeer.

**The elongated Neo-Classical façade of the Paleis van Justitie, converted from the city orphanage**

## Metz & Co ❼

Leidsestraat 34–36. **Map** 7 A5.
☎ *520 7020.* 🚊 *1, 2, 5.*
🕐 *11am–6pm Mon, 9:30am– 6pm Tue, Wed, Fri & Sat, 9:30am– 9pm Thu, noon–5pm Sun.* ● *public hols.* ▢ *See* **Cafés** *p49.*

O N ITS COMPLETION in 1891, Metz & Co was the tallest commercial building in Amsterdam, measuring 26 m (85 ft) in height. Designed by J van Looy, it was built for the New York Life Insurance Company. Since 1908, it has housed the luxury store Metz & Co. In 1933, a splendid glass cupola by Gerrit Rietveld *(see p136)* was added. Liberty of London, which bought Metz & Co in 1973, renovated the building and commissioned Cees Dam to design a café on the sixth floor. The views across the city are superb.

**The 1933 cupola of Metz & Co**

## Golden Bend ❽

**Map** 7 A5. 🚊 *1, 2, 4, 5, 9, 14, 16, 24, 25.* **Kattenkabinet** Herengracht 497. ☎ *626 5378.* 🕐 *9am–2pm Mon– Fri, 1pm–5pm Sat & Sun.* ● *public hols.*

T HE STRETCH of the Herengracht between Leidsestraat and Vijzelstraat was first called the Golden Bend in the 17th century, because of the great wealth of the shipbuilders, merchants and politicians who originally lived along here. Most of the mansions have been converted into offices or banks, but their former elegance remains. The majority of the buildings are

**Window decoration on No. 475 Herengracht**

faced with sandstone, which was more expensive than brick and had to be imported. The earliest mansions date from the 1660s. One very fine and largely untouched example, designed by Philips Vingboons in 1664 *(see p99)*, stands at No. 412. Building continued into the 18th century, with the Louis XIV style predominating. No. 475 is typical of this trend. Built in 1730, it is often called the jewel of canal houses. Two sculpted female figures over the front door adorn its monumental sandstone façade. The ornate mansion at No. 452 is a good example of a 19th-century conversion. The Kattenkabinet (cat museum) at No. 497 Herengracht is one of the few houses on the Golden Bend which is accessible to the public. The museum is well worth visiting for its interesting collection of feline artifacts.

## De Krijtberg ❾

Singel 446. **Map** 7 A4. ☎ *623 1923.* 🚊 *1, 2, 5.* 🕐 *half an hour before the services; 2–5pm Tue–Thu.* ⛪ *12:30pm, 5:45pm Mon–Fri; 12:30 pm, 5:15pm, Sat; 9.30am, 11am, 12:30pm, 5:15pm Sun.* ♿

A N IMPRESSIVE Neo-Gothic church, the Krijtberg (or chalk hill) replaced a clandestine Jesuit chapel *(see p84)* in 1884. It is officially known as Franciscus Xaveriuskerk, after St Francis Xavier, one of the founding Jesuit priests.

Designed by Alfred Tepe, the church was constructed on the site of three houses; the presbytery beside the church is on the site of two other houses, one of which had belonged to a chalk merchant – hence the church's nickname. The back of the church is wider than the front, extending into the space once occupied by the original gardens. The narrowness of the façade

is redeemed by its two magnificent, soaring, steepled towers.

The ornate interior of the building contains some good examples of Neo-Gothic design. The stained-glass windows, walls painted in bright colours and liberal use of gold are in striking contrast to the city's austere Protestant churches. A statue of St Francis Xavier stands in front and to the left of the high altar; one of St Ignatius, founder of the Jesuits, stands to the right.

Near the pulpit is an 18th-century wooden statue of the Immaculate Conception, showing Mary trampling the serpent. It used to be housed in the original hidden chapel.

**The twin-steepled façade of the Neo-Gothic Krijtberg**

## Bijbels Museum ❿

Herengracht 366. **Map** 7 A4. ☎ *624 2436.* 🆆 *www.bijbelsmuseum.nl* 🚊 *1, 2, 5.* 🚊 *Herengracht/Leidsegracht.* 🕐 *10am–5pm Mon–Sat, 1–5pm Sun & public hols.* ● *1 Jan, 30 Apr.* 📷 ♿

R EVEREND Leendert Schouten founded the Bijbels Museum in 1860, when he first put his private collection of biblical artifacts on public display. In 1975, the museum moved to its present site, two 17th-century houses in a group of four designed by Philips Vingboons.

The Bible Museum is packed with artifacts which attempt to give historical weight to Bible stories. Displays feature models of historical sites, and there are archaeological finds from Egypt and the Middle East. Highlights include a copy of the Book of Isaiah from the Dead Sea Scrolls, and the Delft Bible, dating from 1477. The museum also has a beautiful garden and two ceiling paintings by Jacob de Wit.

## Looier Kunst en Antiekcentrum **⑪**

Elandsgracht 109. **Map** 4 D1.
**[** 624 9038. **⤢** 7, 10, 13, 14, 17, 20. **◯** 11am–5pm Sat–Thu.
**⬤** public hols. **⌀** **♿**

A VAST NETWORK of ground-floor rooms in a block of houses has been turned into the Looier Antiques Centre. The market, named after its location near the Looiers-gracht (tanners' canal), boasts the largest collection of art and antiques in the Netherlands.

It has around 100 stalls selling everything from glassware to dolls. On Saturdays, anyone can rent a stall here and once a month the facility is rent-free. Lively bridge sessions, open to all, are always on the go.

**The Palladian façade of the 18th-century Felix Meritis Building**

## Felix Meritis Building **⑫**

Keizersgracht 324. **Map** 1 B5. **[** 623 1311. **w** www.felix.meritis.nl **⤢** 1 2, 5, 10, 13, 14, 17, 20. **Box office & enquiries ◯** 9am–7pm Mon–Fri, 5–8:30pm (or 9.15pm, depending on evening event) Sat & Sun. See **Entertainment** p246. **▨ ⌀ ♿**

T HIS NEO-CLASSICAL building is best viewed from the opposite side of the canal (see p96). Designed by Jacob Otten Husly, it opened in 1787 as a science and arts centre set up by the Felix Meritis society. The name means "happiness through merit". An association of wealthy citizens, the society was founded by watchmaker Willem Writs in 1777, at the time of the Dutch Enlightenment (see pp28–9).

Five reliefs on the façade proclaim the society's interest in natural science and art. The building was fitted out with an observatory, library,

laboratories and a small concert hall. Mozart, Edvard Grieg and Johannes Brahms are among the distinguished musicians who have given performances here.

In the 19th century, it became Amsterdam's main cultural centre, and its concert hall inspired the design of the Concertgebouw (see p128).

The Dutch Communist Party (CPN) occupied the premises from 1946, but cultural prominence was restored in the 1970s when the Shaffy Theatre Company used the building as a theatre and won acclaim for its avant-garde productions.

The building is now used by a reconstituted Felix Meritis Foundation, which specializes in progressive theatre.

## Houseboat Museum **⑬**

Prinsengracht, opposite no. 296.
**Map** 1 B5. **[** 427 0750. **@** info@
houseboatmuseum.nl **⤢** 1, 2, 5, 7, 10, 13, 14, 17. **◯** 11am–5pm Wed–Sun (Mar–Oct) 11am–5pm Fri–Sun (Nov–Feb). **▨ ◉**

M OORED ON the Princen-gracht canal on the edge of the Jordaan, the Hendrika Maria is a showcase of life aboard an Amsterdam house-boat. Built in 1914, it served as a barge and transported coal, sand and gravel until the 1960s when it was converted into a houseboat. Coffee is served in the spacious living room, formerly a cargo hold.

**Vintage robots on sale at the Looier Kunst en Antiekcentrum**

# EASTERN CANAL RING

STRETCHING SOUTH from Munttoren, part of a former city gate, this area lies wholly beyond the line of the medieval city wall. From the 1660s, the *Grachtengordel (see p43)* was extended further east towards the Amstel. One of Amsterdam's prettiest canals, Reguliers-gracht with its seven bridges, was cut at this time. Today, houses on the

**Sun motif on a café in Reguliersdwarsstraat**

major Canal Ring, such as the Van Loon, with its grand façade and fine interior, convey a sense of life in the Golden Age *(see pp24–7)*. Beyond is the 19th-century De Pijp, a working-class district built to relieve the overcrowded Jordaan. De Pijp is now a lively multicultural area, and home to the Albert Cuypmarkt, the city's biggest street market.

## SIGHTS AT A GLANCE

**Historic Buildings and Bridges**
Blauwbrug ❸
Magere Brug ❺
Amstelkerk ❻
Munttoren ⓫

**Cinemas**
Tuschinski
Theater ❿

**Squares and Markets**
Rembrandtplein ❶
Albert Cuypmarkt ❼
Bloemenmarkt ⓬

**Museums**
*Museum Willet-Holthuysen pp120–21* ❷
Six Collection ❹
Heineken Experience ❽
Museum van Loon ❾

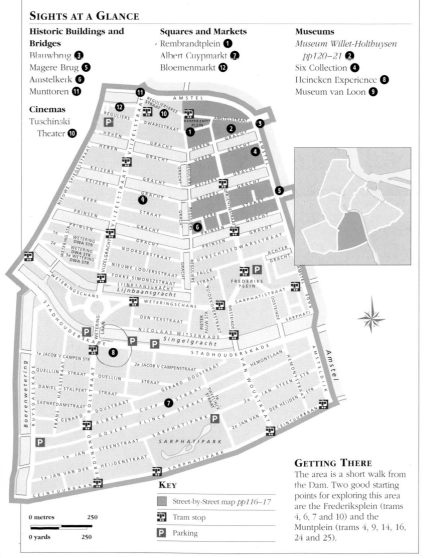

### KEY

| | |
|---|---|
| ▨ | Street-by-Street map *pp116–17* |
| 🚋 | Tram stop |
| 🅿 | Parking |

0 metres    250
0 yards     250

### GETTING THERE
The area is a short walk from the Dam. Two good starting points for exploring this area are the Frederiksplein (trams 4, 6, 7 and 10) and the Muntplein (trams 4, 9, 14, 16, 24 and 25).

◁ **Colourful display of flowers at the Albert Cuypmarkt, including roses, lilies and sunflowers**

# Street-by-Street: Amstelveld

THE EASTERN END of the *Grachtengordel* is quiet and largely residential, especially around the Amstelveld *(see p45)*, with its pretty wooden church and houseboats. A short walk will take you past shops and numerous cafés, particularly on the bustling Rembrandtplein. As you wander down the broad sweep of the Amstel river, Amsterdam suddenly loses its village atmosphere and begins to feel like a city.

★ **Rembrandtplein**
*Looking on to the former Botermarkt (butter market) and the cast-iron statue of Rembrandt, there are dozens of cafés dating from the 19th century, including the De Kroon at No. 17 (see p47)* ❶

**Café Schiller**
*(see p49)*

★ **Museum Willet-Holthuysen**
*This double canal house contains a number of period rooms, including the fine 19th-century-style garden room which looks out on to the restored 18th-century formal garden* ❷

**Amstelkerk**
*This wooden church was meant to be a temporary structure while money was raised to build a big new church on Rembrandtplein, but the grand scheme fell through. Today, the church houses offices and a restaurant (see p119)* ❻

## Blauwbrug

This cast-iron and stone bridge, inspired by the Alexander III bridge in Paris, is adorned with sculptures on nautical and marine themes **3**

**LOCATOR MAP**
See Street Finder maps 5 & 8

## Six Collection

Descendants of the original Six family still live in this splendid house, which is now a private museum **4**

0 metres          100
0 yards           100

**KEY**

‑ ‑ ‑     Suggested route

### STAR SIGHTS

★ **Rembrandtplein**

★ **Museum Willet-Holthuysen**

★ **Magere Brug**

**The Market Crier** statue commemorates Professor Kokadorus (1867–1934), one of Amsterdam's most famous street traders.

★ **Magere Brug**
The current wooden bridge is a 20th-century replica of the 17th-century original, but its mechanical drive was only installed in 1994 **5**

# Rembrandtplein ➊

**Map** 7 C5. 🚊 *4, 9, 14.*

FORMERLY CALLED the Botermarkt, after the butter market held here until the mid-19th century, this square acquired its present name when the statue of Rembrandt was erected in 1876.

Soon afterwards, Rembrandtplein developed into a centre for nightlife with the opening of various hotels and cafés. The Mast (renamed the Mille Colonnes Hotel) dates from 1889, and the Schiller Karena hotel *(see p221)* and the Café Schiller *(see p49)* both opened in 1892. De Kroon *(see p47)*, which epitomizes a typical grand café, dates from 1898. The popularity of Rembrandtplein has persevered, and the café terraces are packed during summer with people enjoying a pleasant drink and watching the world go by.

# Museum Willet-Holthuysen ➋

*See pp120–21.*

# Blauwbrug ➌

Amstel. **Map** 8 D5. 🚊 *9, 14.* Ⓜ *Waterlooplein.*

THE BLAUWBRUG (Blue Bridge) is thought to take its name from the colour of the wooden bridge that originally crossed this particular stretch of the Amstel in the 17th century. The present bridge is made of

**Two of the many outdoor cafés on Rembrandtplein**

stone. It was built in preparation for the World Exhibition, which attracted thousands of visitors to Amsterdam in 1883.

The Blauwbrug is decorated with sculptures of medieval boats, fish and the imperial crown of Amsterdam and is surmounted by ornate lamps. The design was inspired by the plans for the elaborate Alexander III bridge in Paris.

# Six Collection ➍

Amstel 218. **Map** 8 D5. 🚊 *4, 9, 14.* 🔴 *until further notice.*

THE SIX COLLECTION is made up of furniture, silver-ware, porcelain and fine paintings which belonged to Amsterdam burgomaster Jan Six (1618–1700). One of the richest men in the city, owning, it was said, "innumerable boxes of money", Six's collection is a treat for anyone interested

**Detail of the ornate stone carving on the Blauwbrug**

in the 17th century. Appointed burgomaster (mayor) of Amsterdam in 1691, Jan Six was also a friend and patron of Rembrandt *(see p62),* and several paintings by the artist are the treasures of the extensive art collection.

One, the *Portrait of Jan Six*, painted in 1654, is considered by many to be Rembrandt's finest portrait. It is believed that the painting was Rembrandt's way of paying back a 1,000-guilder loan he had received from Six. Another fabulous Rembrandt is the *Portrait of Anna Wijmer*, Six' mother. Jan Six' father-in-law was a model in Rembrandt's painting *The Anatomy Lesson of Dr Nicolaes Tulp*, now on show in the Mauritshuis *(see pp188–9).*

In addition to the Rembrandt paintings, the Six collection also includes works by other Dutch masters such as Frans Hals *(see pp178–9)*, Thomas de Keyser (1596–1667) and Albert Cuyp *(see p120)*. The seventeenth-century house was designed by Adriaan Dortsman and appears untouched by modernisation. Descendants of Jan Six, who now own the collection, are still in residence. A former arrangement with the Rijksmuseum no longer exists. Unfortunately, there are no plans to re-open the collection to the public.

## Magere Brug ❺

Amstel. **Map** 5 B3. 🚋 *4.*

O F AMSTERDAM'S 1,400 or so bridges, the Magere Brug (Skinny Bridge) is the city's best-known. The original drawbridge was built in about 1670. Tradition relates that it was named after two sisters called Mager, who lived on either side of the Amstel. However, it appears more likely that the bridge acquired the name from its narrow *(mager)* design.

The present drawbridge was put up in 1969 and, though wider than the original, it still conforms to the traditional double-leaf style. Constructed from African azobe wood, it was intended to last for 50

Magere Brug, a traditional double-leaf Dutch drawbridge

The Amstelkerk, built as a temporary church in the 17th century

years. About every 20 minutes, the bridge master has to let boats through the bridge. He then jumps on his bicycle and opens up the Amstelsluizen *(see p145)* and Hoge Sluis.

## Amstelkerk ❻

Amstelveld 10. **Map** 5 A3. 📞 *520 0060.* ⓦ *www.stadsherstel.nl* 🚋 *4.* ◻ *9am–5pm Mon–Fri.* ● *public hols.* ✝ *10:30am Sun.* 📷

D ESIGNED by Daniel Stalpaert in 1668, the wooden Amstelkerk was intended to be a temporary structure, while money was raised for a large new church on the Botermarkt (now Rembrandtplein). Sufficient funds for the grand scheme were never forthcoming however, so the

Amstelkerk was maintained. In 1825, the Protestant church authorities attempted to raise money to renovate the Amstelkerk's plain interior in a Neo-Gothic style. It was not until 1840, however, when Frederica Elisabeth Cramer donated 25,000 guilders to the project, that work began. The interior walls, pulpit, pews, and organ made by Jonathan Batz, all date from this period. The windows are older, dating from 1821.

In the late 1960s, the Amstelkerk underwent a substantial conversion, costing 4 million guilders. Glass-walled offices were installed inside the building. However, services are still held in the Amstelkerk and the nave, which was preserved in all its Neo-Gothic glory, now houses the modern Moko restaurant and café *(see p233).*

## HOW THE MAGERE BRUG WORKS

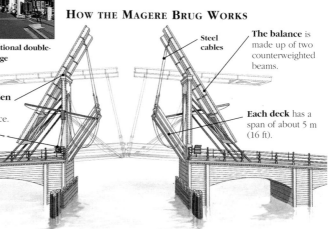

**Steel cables**

**The balance** is made up of two counterweighted beams.

**The arched wooden portal** provides a pivot for the balance.

**Mechanical chain-drive**

**Each deck** has a span of about 5 m (16 ft).

# Museum Willet-Holthuysen ❷

**Statue of Paris on stairway**

NAMED AFTER its last residents, the museum allows the visitor a glimpse into the lives of the merchant class who lived in luxury along the *Grachtengordel* (Canal Ring). The house was built in 1685 and became the property of coal magnate Pieter Holthuysen (1788–1858) in 1855. It passed to his daughter Sandrina and her art-connoisseur husband, Abraham Willet – both fervent collectors of paintings, glass, silver and ceramics. When Sandrina died childless in 1895, the house and its many treasures were left to the city. Some of the rooms remain unchanged, while others, such as the kitchen and Garden Room, have been restored in the style of the 18th century.

**The glass collection** includes several flute glasses engraved in the Netherlands in the 17th century.

**Portrait of Abraham Willet**
*Painted in 1877 by Abraham Mniszech, this full-length portrait shows the master of the house dressed in a 17th-century costume.*

| STAR FEATURES |
| --- |
| ★ **Blue Room** |
| ★ **Dining Room** |

Main room

Front room

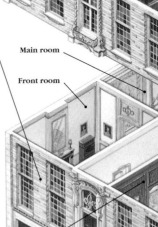

**★ Blue Room**
*Hung with heavy blue damask, the room boasts a chimney piece by Jacob de Wit (see p122), and was the exclusive preserve of the men of the house.*

Entrance

Ticket office

### Garden Room
*Now repainted in its original green, the Garden Room offers views over the intricate knot garden, laid out in 18th-century French style. It was used by the family to entertain guests to tea.*

### The Antiquities
**Room** was furnished in the last quarter of the 19th century in Dutch Renaissance style *(see p96)*, very popular at this time.

**Bedroom**

**VISITORS' CHECKLIST**

Herengracht 605. **Map** 8 D5. 523 1822. www.museum willetholthuysen.nl 4, 9, 14, 20. 10am–5pm Mon–Fri, 11am–5pm Sat & Sun. 1 Jan, 30 Apr, 25 Dec.

### Staircase
*The staircase was built in 1740 and has an elaborate gilded balustrade. The lower walls are painted to look like marble.*

**Hall**

### ★ Dining Room
*The wallpaper is a careful copy of the 18th-century silk original. The elaborate 275-piece Meissen dinner service provided up to 24 places.*

### The Blue
**Room** porcelain collection includes Chinese vases made during the Kangxi dynasty (1662–1722).

### Kitchen
*The 18th-century kitchen has been restored using items salvaged from similar houses, including the sink and pump.*

## Albert Cuypmarkt ❼

Albert Cuypstraat. **Map** 5 A5. ▦ *4, 16, 24, 25.* ◷ *9:30am–5pm Mon–Sat.*

THE MARKET running along Albert Cuypstraat began trading in 1904, shortly after the expansion of the city was completed. The wide street, once a canal, is named after the Dutch landscape painter Albert Cuyp (1620–91). It is located in the Pijp district, originally built for workers.

Described by the stallholders as "the best-known market in Europe", it attracts some 20,000 visitors on weekdays and often twice as many on Saturdays. The goods on sale at the 325 stalls range from fish, poultry, cheese, fruit and vegetables to clothes, and prices are among the cheapest in Amsterdam.

**Smoked fish in Albert Cuypmarkt**

## Heineken Experience ❽

Stadhouderskade 78. **Map** 4 F3. ☎ *523 9666.* ▦ *6, 7, 10, 16, 24, 25.* ◷ *10am–6pm Tue–Sun.* 🎫 📷

GERARD ADRIAAN HEINEKEN founded the Heineken company in 1864 when he bought the 16th-century Hooi-berg (haystack) brewery on the Nieuwezijds Voorburgwal. His readiness to adapt to new methods and bring in foreign brewers established him as a major force in Amsterdam's profitable beer industry.

In 1988, the company finally stopped producing beer in its massive brick brewery on Stadhouderskade, because it was unable to keep up with the demand. Production is now concentrated in two breweries, one in Zoeterwoude, near Den Haag, another in Den Bosch. Today, Heineken produces around half of the beer sold in Amsterdam, has production facilities in dozens of countries and exports all over the world.

The Stadhouderskade building now houses the Heineken Reception Centre, launched in 1991. Visitors can walk through the tiled brewhouse, with its enormous brewing coppers, and on through the renovated stables where the splendid dray horses are once more on show. Visitors to the museum can learn about the history of the company and of beer-making in general, a tradition which can be traced back to the Sumerians, who lived as long ago as 4000 BC. The offer of free beer makes a popular end to the tour, which is open to anyone over 18 years old.

**Formal rose garden at Museum van Loon**

## Museum van Loon ❾

Keizersgracht 672. **Map** 5 A3. ☎ *624 5255.* 🆆 *www.museumvanloon.nl* ▦ *16, 24, 25.* ◷ *11am–5pm Fri–Mon.* ⬤ *public hols.* 🎫 📷 🛒

VAN LOON was the name of one of Amsterdam's most prestigious families in the 17th century. They did not move into this house on the Keizersgracht, however, until 1884. Designed by Adriaan Dortsman, No. 672 is one of a pair of symmetrical houses built in 1672 for the Flemish merchant Jeremias van Raey. It was redecorated in 1752 when Dr Abraham van Hagen and his wife Catharina Elisabeth Trip moved in. Their surnames are incorporated in the copper staircase railing.

The house was opened as a museum in 1974, after 11 years of extensive restoration. It is now one of the most delightful canalside museums, managing to retain the original charming character of the house. It contains a collection of Van Loon family portraits, stretching back to the early 1600s. The period rooms are adorned with fine pieces of furniture, porcelain and sculpture. Some of the upstairs rooms contain sumptuous illusionistic wall paintings, which are known as *witjes* after their famous creator, Jacob de Wit (1695–1754). Outside, the formal rose garden contains a beautiful 18th-century coach house, which is now used as a private residence.

**Dray horse and beer wagon at the Heineken Brouwerij**

# Tuschinski Theater ⑩

Reguliersbreestraat 26–28. **Map** 7 C5.
📞 428 1060. 🚊 4, 9, 14.
**Box office** ⭕ noon–10pm. 📷
Jul–Aug: 10am Sun & Mon. 📷 📷

Abraham Tuschinski's cinema and variety theatre caused a sensation when it opened in 1921. Until then, Amsterdam's cinemas had been sombre places, but this was an exotic blend of Art Deco and Amsterdam School architecture *(see pp96–7)*. Its twin towers are 26 m (85 ft) in height. Built in a slum area known as the Duivelshoek (Devil's Corner), it was designed by Heyman Louis de Jong and decorated by Chris Bartels, Jaap Gidding and Pieter de Besten. In its heyday, Marlene Dietrich and Judy Garland performed here.

Now converted into a six-screen cinema, the building has been meticulously restored, both inside and out. The carpet in the entrance hall, replaced in 1984, is an exact copy of the original. Visitors may take a guided tour, but the best way to appreciate the opulence of the Tuschinski Theater is to

**Detail of Tuschinski Theater façade**

go and see a film. For just a few extra guilders, you can take a seat in one of the exotic boxes that make up the back row of the huge semi-circular, 1,472-seater main auditorium.

**View of the Munttoren at the base of Muntplein**

## Munttoren ⑪

Muntplein. **Map** 7 B5. 🚊 4, 9, 14, 16, 24, 25. **Munttoren** ⚫ to the public.
**Shop** ⭕ 10am–6pm Mon–Sat.

The polygonal base of the Munttoren (mint tower) formed part of the Reguliers-poort, a gate in Amsterdam's medieval city wall. The gate was destroyed by fire in 1618, but the base survived. In the following year, Hendrick de Keyser *(see p90)* added the clock tower, capped with a steeple and openwork orb. The carillon was designed by François Hemony *(see p68)* in 1699, and rings every 15 minutes. The tower acquired its name in 1673, during the French occupation of Amsterdam, when the city mint was temporarily housed here. An up-market gift shop is now found in the base of the tower.

## Bloemenmarkt ⑫

Singel. **Map** 7 B5. 🚊 1, 2, 4, 5, 9, 14, 16, 24, 25. ⭕ 9am–5pm Mon–Sat.

On the Singel, west of Muntplein, is the last of the city's floating markets. In the past, nurserymen sailed up the Amstel from their small-holdings and moored here to sell cut flowers and plants directly from their boats. Today, the stalls are still floating but are permanent. Despite the sellers' tendency to cater purely for tourists, the displays of fragrant seasonal flowers and bright spring bedding-plants are always beautiful to look at.

**Florist arranging his display at the Bloemenmarkt**

# MUSEUM QUARTER

UNTIL THE LATE 1800s, the Museum Quarter was little more than an area of farms and small-holdings. At this time, the city council designated it an area of art and culture and plans were conceived for constructing Amsterdam's great cultural monuments: the Rijksmuseum, the Stedelijk Museum and the Concertgebouw. The Van Gogh Museum followed in 1973, its striking extension

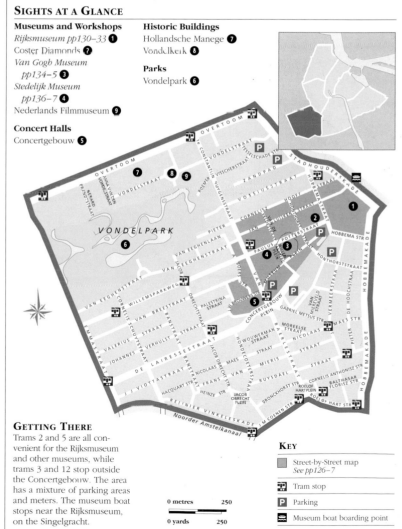

**"Russia" gablestone in Roemer Visscherstraat**

being added in 1999. The Museumplein has two memorials to the victims of World War II. The *plein* is still used as a site for political demonstrations. To the north and south are turn-of-the-century houses, where the streets are named after artists and intellectuals, such as the 17th-century poet Roemer Visscher. To the west, the Vondelpark offers a pleasant, fresh-air break from all the museums.

## SIGHTS AT A GLANCE

**Museums and Workshops**
*Rijksmuseum pp130–33* **1**
Coster Diamonds **2**
*Van Gogh Museum pp134–5* **3**
*Stedelijk Museum pp136–7* **4**
Nederlands Filmmuseum **9**

**Concert Halls**
Concertgebouw **5**

**Historic Buildings**
Hollandsche Manege **7**
Vondelkerk **8**

**Parks**
Vondelpark **6**

## GETTING THERE

Trams 2 and 5 are all convenient for the Rijksmuseum and other museums, while trams 3 and 12 stop outside the Concertgebouw. The area has a mixture of parking areas and meters. The museum boat stops near the Rijksmuseum, on the Singelgracht.

| 0 metres | 250 |
| 0 yards | 250 |

### KEY

| | Street-by-Street map *See pp126–7* |
| | Tram stop |
| P | Parking |
| | Museum boat boarding point |

◁ **Statue of the painter Pieter Aertsen (1509–75) on the façade of the Stedelijk Museum**

# Street-by-Street: Museum Quarter

THE GREEN EXPANSE of Museumplein was once bisected by a busy main road known locally as the "shortest motorway in Europe". But dramatic renovation between 1996 and 1999 has transformed it into a stately park, fringed by Amsterdam's major cultural centres. The district is one of the wealthiest in the city, with wide streets lined with grand houses.

**Statue on façade of Stedelijk**

After the heady delights of the museums, it is possible to window-shop at the up-market boutiques along the exclusive PC Hoofstraat and Van Baerlestraat, or watch the diamond polishers at work in Coster Diamonds.

★ **Van Gogh Museum**
*The new wing of the museum, an elegant oval shape, was designed by Kisho Kurokawa and opened in 1999. It is dedicated to temporary exhibitions of 19th-century art* ❸

**Van Baerlestraat** contains exclusive clothing shops *(see p238)*.

VAN DER VELDESTR

PAULUS POTTERSTRAAT

★ **Stedelijk Museum**
*Housing the civic collection of modern art, this museum also stages controversial contemporary art exhibitions. A sculpture garden is behind the building* ❹

VAN BAERLESTRAAT

**Concertgebouw**
*Designed by AL van Gendt, the building has a Classical façade and a concert hall with near-perfect acoustics* ❺

### Coster Diamonds

*Diamonds have been cut, polished and sold at Coster since 1840. The firm now occupies three splendid adjoining villas, built on Museumplein in 1896* ❷

**LOCATOR MAP**
*See Street Finder, map 4*

**Light lines**

HOBBEMASTRAAT

**Pond/ ice rink**

### ★ Rijksmuseum
*The heavily ornamented Neo-Gothic Rijksmuseum holds the magnificent Dutch national art collection of some 5,000 paintings, 30,000 pieces of applied art and 17,000 historical artifacts* ❶

**The Rijksmuseum**
is surrounded by gardens which contain statuary. This weathered bronze of Mercury, designed by Ferdinand Leenhoff (1841–1914), is found in the southeast garden.

MUSEUMPLEIN

**The Ravensbrück**
monument commemorates women victims of the Holocaust.

| 0 metres | 50 |
| 0 yards | 50 |

**KEY**

- - - Suggested route

### STAR SIGHTS

★ **Rijksmuseum**

★ **Van Gogh Museum**

★ **Stedelijk Museum**

## Rijksmuseum ❶

*See pp130–33.*

## Coster Diamonds ❷

Paulus Potterstraat 2–8.
**Map** 4 E3. 305 5555. *2, 5.*
9am–5pm daily.

ONE OF AMSTERDAM'S oldest
diamond factories, Coster
was founded in 1840. Twelve
years later, Queen Victoria's
consort, Prince Albert, honoured the company by giving
them the task of repolishing
the enormous *Koh-i-Noor*
(mountain of light) diamond.
This blue-white stone is one
of the treasures of the British
crown jewels and weighs in
at 108.8 carats. A replica of
the coronation crown, which
incorporates a copy of the
fabulous stone, is found in
Coster's spacious entrance hall.

More than 2,000 people visit
the factory each day to witness
the processes of grading, cutting and polishing the stones.
The goldsmiths and diamond-
cutters work together in the
factory to produce customized
items of jewellery, in a range
of styles, which are available
over the counter. For serious
diamond-buyers, such as the
jewellers who come to
Amsterdam from all over the
world, there is a series of
private sales rooms where
discretion is assured.

**A potential sale under discussion
at Coster Diamonds**

## Van Gogh Museum ❸

*See pp134–5.*

## Stedelijk Museum ❹

*See pp136–7.*

**Façade of the award-winning Concertgebouw (1881) by AL van Gendt**

## Concertgebouw ❺

Concertgebouwplein 2–6.
**Map** 4 D4. 671 8345. **W** www.
concertgebouw.nl *2, 3, 5, 12, 16.*
**Box office** 10am–7pm daily.
by arrangement.

FOLLOWING an open archi-
tectural competition held
in 1881, AL van Gendt (1835–
1901) was chosen to design a
vast new concert hall for
Amsterdam. The resulting
Neo-Renaissance building
boasts an elaborate pediment
and colonnaded façade, and
houses two concert halls.
Despite Van Gendt's lack of
musical knowledge, he managed to produce near-perfect
acoustics in the Grote Zaal
(main concert hall), which is
renowned the world over.

The inaugural concert at the
Concertgebouw was held on
11 April 1888, complete with
an orchestra of 120 musicians
and a choir of 600. A resident
orchestra was established at
the hall seven months later.

The building has been renovated several times over the
years, most recently in 1983,
when some serious subsi-
dence threatened the building's
entire foundation. To remedy
this, the whole superstructure
had to be lifted up off the
ground while the original supporting piles, which rested on
sand 13 m (43 ft) underground,
were removed and replaced
by concrete piles sunk into
the ground to a depth of 18 m
(59 ft). A glass extension and
new entrance were added by
Pi de Bruijn in 1988. The original entrance was relocated
round to the side of the
building. Though primarily

designed to hold concerts, the
Concertgebouw has become a
multi-functional building. It
has played host to business
meetings, exhibitions, conferences, political meetings and
occasional boxing matches.

**Bandstand in Vondelpark**

## Vondelpark ❻

Stadhouderskade. **Map** 4 E2. *1, 2,
3, 5, 6, 12.* **Park** 24hrs daily. **Open-
air theatre** Jun–last week Aug:
Wed–Sun.

IN 1864, a group consisting of
prominent Amsterdammers
formed a committee with the
aim of founding a public park,
and they raised enough money
to buy 8 hectares (20 acres) of
land. JD and LP Zocher, a
father-and-son team of landscape architects, were then
commissioned to design the
park in typical English landscape style. They used vistas,
pathways and ponds to create
the illusion of a large natural
area, which was opened to the
public on 15 June 1865, as the
Nieuwe Park. The park's
present name was adopted in
1867, when a statue of Dutch
poet Joost van den Vondel

(1586–1679) was erected in the grounds. The committee soon began to raise money to enlarge the park, and by June 1877 it had reached its current dimensions of 45 hectares (110 acres). The park now supports around 100 plant species and 127 types of tree. Squirrels, hedgehogs, ducks and garden birds mix with a huge colony of greedy, bright green parakeets, which gather in front of the pavilion every morning to be fed. Herds of cows, sheep, goats and even a lone llama graze in the pastures.

Vondelpark welcomes about 8 million visitors a year, and is popular with the locals for dog-walking, jogging, or just for the view. Free concerts are given at the *openluchttheater* (open-air theatre) or at the bandstand in the summer.

## Hollandsche Manege ❼

Vondelstraat 140. **Map** 3 C2. 🕿 *618 0942.* 🚋 *1, 6.* ⏰ *10am–midnight Tue–Fri, 10am–6pm Sat & Sun, 2pm–midnight Mon.* 📷 🔲

**Façade of the Hollandse Manege**

THE DUTCH RIDING SCHOOL was originally situated on the Leidsegracht *(see p111),* but in 1882 a new building was opened, designed by AL van Gendt and based on the Spanish Riding School in Vienna. The riding school was threatened with demolition in the 1980s, but was saved after a public outcry. Reopened in 1986 by Prince Bernhard, it has been restored to its former glory. The Neo-Classical indoor arena boasts gilded mirrors and moulded horses' heads on its elaborate plasterwork walls. Some of the wrought-iron stalls remain and sound is muffled by sawdust. At the top of the staircase, one door leads to a balcony overlooking the arena, another to the café.

## Vondelkerk ❽

Vondelstraat 120. **Map** 3 C2. 🚋 *1, 3, 6, 12.* 🚫 *to the public.*

THE VONDELKERK was the largest church designed by PJH Cuypers, architect of the Centraal Station *(see pp30–31).* Work began on the building in 1872, but funds ran out by the following year. Money gathered from public donations and lotteries allowed the building to be completed by 1880.

When fire broke out in November 1904, firefighters saved the nave of the church by forcing the burning tower to fall away into Vondelpark. A new tower was added later by the architect's son, JT Cuypers. The church was deconsecrated in 1979 and converted into offices in 1985.

## Nederlands Filmmuseum ❾

Vondelpark 3. **Map** 4 D2. 🕿 *589 1400.* 🌐 *www.filmmuseum.nl* 🚋 *1, 3, 6, 12.* **Library** ⏰ *10am–5pm Tue–Fri, 11am–5pm Sat.* ⬤ *public hols.* **Box Office** ⏰ *10am–10pm Mon–Fri, 6–10pm Sat, 2–10pm Sun.* **Screenings:** *from 7pm daily; plus 3pm Sun.* ♿ *for cinema.* 🚫 🔲 🍴

VONDELPARK'S pavilion was designed by the architects PJ Hamer (1812–87), and his son, W Hamer (1843–1913), and opened on 4 May 1881 as a café and restaurant. After World War II, it was restored and then reopened in 1947 as an international cultural centre. In 1991, the pavilion was renovated once more. The complete Art Deco interior of the Cinema Parisien, Amsterdam's first cinema, built in 1910, was moved into one of the rooms. It is now an important national film museum, showing more than 1,000 films a year. The museum owns a film poster collection, runs a public film library at Nos. 69–71 Vondelstraat and holds free outdoor screenings during summer.

**The terrace of Café Vertigo at the Filmmuseum**

# Rijksmuseum ❶

THE RIJKSMUSEUM, an Amsterdam landmark, possesses an unrivalled collection of Dutch art, begun in the early 19th century. The huge museum opened in 1885 to bitter criticism from Amsterdam's Protestant community for its Neo-Gothic style. The main building is undergoing extensive renovation between 2003 and 2008. However, all the highlights of the museum are on show in the Philips Wing during this period.

**Second floor**

**Winter Landscape with Skaters** *(1618)*
*Dumb painter Hendrick Avercamp specialized in intricate icy winter scenes.*

**The Gothic façade**
of Cuypers' building is red brick with elaborate decoration, including coloured tiles.

★ **The Kitchen Maid** *(1658)*
*The light falling through the window and the stillness of this scene are typical of Johannes Vermeer (see p194).*

**Stairw**

**Entrance**

## KEY TO FLOORPLAN

- ☐ Dutch history
- ☐ Dutch painting
- ☐ European painting
- ☐ Sculpture and decorative art
- ☐ Prints and drawings
- ☐ Asiatic art
- ☐ Temporary exhibitions
- ☐ Non-exhibition space

## STAR PAINTINGS

★ **The Night Watch by Rembrandt**

★ **St Elizabeth's Day Flood**

★ **The Kitchen Maid by Vermeer**

★ **St Elizabeth's Day Flood** *(1500)*
*An unknown artist painted this altar-piece, showing a disastrous flood in 1421. The dykes protecting Dordrecht were breached, and 22 villages were swept away by the flood water.*

**Entrance**

**Study collections**

**VISITORS' CHECKLIST**

Stadhouderskade 42. **Map** 4 E3.
674 7047. 2, 5, 6, 7,
10, 20. Stadhouderskade.
10am–5pm daily.
1 Jan.
www.rijksmuseum.nl

★ **The Night Watch** *(1642)*
*The showpiece of Dutch 17th-century art, this vast canvas was commissioned as a group portrait of an Amsterdam militia company.*

**Philips Wing**

**GALLERY GUIDE**
*There are entrances on either side of the street under the building – the left leads into the Dutch history section, the right to prints and drawings, sculpture and applied art, and then continues on up the stairs. On the first floor is a huge ante-chamber, with an information desk and shop. The entrance on the left starts with 16th- to 19th-century painting. The museum is undergoing renovation, but all the highlights are on show throughout the Philips Wing.*

**First floor**

**St Catherine** *(c.1465)*
*This sculpture by the Master of Koudewater shows the saint stamping on Emperor Maxentius, who allegedly killed her with his sword*

**Philips Wing**

**GENRE PAINTING**

For the contemporaries of Jan Steen (1625–79), this cosy everyday scene was full of symbols that are obscure to the modern viewer. The dog on the pillow may represent fidelity, and the red stockings the woman's sexuality; she is probably a prostitute. Such genre paintings were often raunchy, but nearly always had a moral twist *(see p189)* – domestic scenes by artists such as ter Borch and Honthorst were symbolic of brothels, while other works illustrated proverbs. Symbols like candles or skulls indicated mortality.

**Ground floor**

**Jan Steen's *Woman at her Toilet* was painted in about 1660**

# Exploring the Rijksmuseum

THE RIJKSMUSEUM is almost too vast to be seen in a single visit. It is famous for owning probably the best collection of Dutch art in the world, from early religious works to the masterpieces of the Golden Age. However, the applied art and sculpture sections, and the Asiatic artifacts, are equally wonderful, and the Dutch history section only slightly less rewarding. Those with just one chance to visit the museum should definitely start with the incomparable 17th-century paintings, taking in Frans Hals, Vermeer and scores of other Old Masters, to arrive finally at Rembrandt's *The Night Watch*.

**Feeding the Hungry from a series of seven panels by the Master of Alkmaar**

## DUTCH HISTORY

THE TURBULENT HISTORY of the Netherlands is encapsulated in this section. In the opening room is the medieval altar painting of *St Elizabeth's Day Flood (see p130)*. The central room has 17th-century models of ships, artifacts salvaged from shipwrecks and paintings of factories and townscapes from the days of the Dutch Empire. Later displays recall battles in naval history; exhibits from the 18th century deal with the impact of revolutionary France on Amsterdam, ending in 1815 after the Napoleonic Wars.

## EARLY PAINTING AND FOREIGN SCHOOLS

ALONGSIDE a small collection of Flemish and Italian art, including portraits by Piero di Cosimo (1462–1521), are the first specifically "Dutch" paintings. These works are mostly religious, such as *The Seven Works of Charity* (1504) by the Master of Alkmaar, Jan van Scorel's quasi-Mannerist *Mary Magdalene* (1528) and Lucas van Leyden's triptych, *Adoration of the Golden Calf* (1530). As the 16th century progressed, religious themes were superseded by pastoral subjects; by 1552, paintings like Pieter Aertsen's *The Egg Dance* were full of realism, by then the keystone of much Dutch art.

## 17TH-CENTURY PAINTING

BY THE ALTERATION in 1578 *(see pp22–3)*, Dutch art had moved away completely from religious to secular themes. Artists turned to realistic portraiture, landscapes, still lifes, seascapes, domestic interiors, including genre work *(see p131)*, and animal portraits.

Rembrandt *(see p62)* is the most famous of many artists who lived and worked around Amsterdam at this time. Examples of his work hanging in the Rijksmuseum include *Portrait of Titus in a Monk's Habit* (1660), *Self Portrait as the Apostle Paul* (1661), *The Jewish Bride (see p40)* and the incredible *Night Watch (see p131)*. Look out too for the work of his many pupils, who included Nicolaes Maes and Ferdinand Bol.

Don't miss Jan Vermeer's (1632–75) serenely light-filled interiors including *The Kitchen Maid, (see p130)*, and *The Woman Reading a Letter* (1662). Of several portraits by Frans Hals *(see pp1 /8–9)* the best known are *The Wedding Portrait* and *The Merry Drinker* (1630). *The Windmill at Wijk* by Jacob van Ruisdael (1628–82) is a great landscape by an artist at the very height of his power. Other artists whose works contribute to this unforgettable collection include Pieter Saenredam, Jan van de Capelle, Jan Steen *(see p131)* and Gerard ter Borch.

## 18TH- AND 19TH-CENTURY PAINTING

IN MANY WAYS, 18th-century Dutch painting merely continued the themes and quality of 17th-century work.

**The Wedding Portrait (c. 1622) by Frans Hals**

This is particularly true of portraiture and still lifes, with the evocative *Still Life with Flowers and Fruit* by Jan van Huysum (1682–1749) standing out. A trend developed later for elegant "conversation pieces" by artists such as Adriaan van der Werff (1659–1722) and Cornelis Troost (1696–1750). Most had satirical undertones, like *The Art Gallery of Jan Gildemeester Jansz* (1794) by Adriaan de Lelie (1755–1820), showing an 18th-century salon whose walls are crowded with 17th-century masterpieces.

## HAGUE SCHOOL AND THE IMPRESSIONISTS

THE SO-CALLED Hague School was made up of a group of Dutch artists who came together around 1870 in Den Haag. Their landscape work, which earned them the alternative title the "Grey" School for their overcast skies, captures the atmospheric quality of subdued Dutch sunlight. One of the prizes of the Rijksmuseum's 19th-century collection is *Morning Ride on the Beach* (1876) by Anton Mauve (1838–88), painted in soft pearly colours. Alongside hangs the beautiful polder landscape, *View near the Geestbrug* by Hendrik Weissenbruch (1824–1903). In contrast, the Dutch Impressionists, closely linked to the French Impressionists, preferred active subjects such as *The Bridge over the Singel at Paleisstraat, Amsterdam* (1890) by George Hendrik Breitner (1857–1923).

## SCULPTURE AND APPLIED ARTS

BEGINNING WITH religious medieval sculpture, this section moves on to the splendour of Renaissance furniture and decoration. Highlights that capture the wealth of the Golden Age include an exquisite collection of glassware, Delftware (*see p195*) and diamond-encrusted jewellery. A late 17th-century 12-leaf Chinese screen incorporates European figures on one side, a phoenix on the other; and two dolls'

*Still Life with Flowers and Fruit* (c. 1730) by artist Jan van Huysum (1682–1740), one of many still lifes exhibited in the Rijksmuseum

houses are modelled on contemporary town houses. Some outstanding 18th-century Meissen porcelain and Art Nouveau glass complete the collection.

## PRINTS AND DRAWINGS

THE RIJKSMUSEUM owns about a million prints and drawings. Although the emphasis is on Dutch works (most of Rembrandt's etchings as well as rare works by Hercules Seghers (c. 1589–1637) are here), there are prints by major European artists, including Dürer, Tiepolo, Goya, Watteau and Toulouse-Lautrec as well as a set of coloured Japanese woodcuts. Small exhibitions are held on the ground floor of the museum, but particular prints can be viewed with special permission from the Study Collection in the basement.

## ASIATIC ART

REWARDS OF the Dutch imperial trading past are on show in this department, which has a separate entrance at the rear of the museum. Some of the earliest artifacts are the most unusual: tiny bronze Tang dynasty figurines from 7th-century China and gritty, granite rock carvings from Java (c. 8th century). Later exhibits include a lovely – and extremely explicit – Hindu statue entitled *Heavenly Beauty*, luscious Chinese parchment paintings of tigers, inlaid Korean boxes and Vietnamese dishes painted with curly-tailed fish. This is a veritable hoard of delights and, above all, a monument to the sophistication and skill of craftsmen and artists in early Eastern cultures.

Late 7th-century Cambodian *Head of Buddha*

# Van Gogh Museum ❸

THE VAN GOGH MUSEUM is based on a design by De Stijl architect Gerrit Rietveld *(see p136)* and opened in 1973. A new, freestanding wing, designed by Kisho Kurokawa, was added in 1999. When Van Gogh died in 1890, he was on the verge of being acclaimed. His younger brother Theo, an art dealer, amassed a collection of 200 of his paintings and 500 drawings. These, combined with around 850 letters by Van Gogh to Theo, and selected works by his friends and contemporaries, form the core of the museum's outstanding collection.

**★ The Bedroom at Arles** *(1888)*
*One of Van Gogh's best-known works, this was painted to celebrate his achievement of domestic stability at the Yellow House in Arles. He was so delighted with the colourful painting that he did it twice.*

**★ Vase with Sunflowers**
*The vivid yellows and greens in this version of Van Gogh's Sunflowers (1889) have been enriched by broad streaks of bright mauve and red.*

**Third floor**

**Stairwell**

**Second floor (study collection)**

**First floor**

**19th-century art**

**Entrance**

**Ground floor**

**Shop**

## STAR PAINTINGS

- **★ Vase with Sunflowers**

- **★ The Bedroom at Arles**

- **★ Wheatfield and Crows**

## MUSEUM GUIDE

*Paintings from Van Gogh's Dutch period and from his time in Paris and Provence are on the first floor. The study collection, occasional exhibits of Van Gogh's drawings and other temporary exhibitions are on the top two floors. Works by other 19th-century artists are on the ground floor, along with the bookshop and café. The new wing houses temporary exhibitions.*

## AN ARTIST'S LIFE

Vincent van Gogh (1853–90), born in Zundert, began painting in 1880. He worked in the Netherlands for five years before moving to Paris, later settling at Arles in the south of France. After a fierce argument with Gauguin, he cut off part of his own ear and his mental instability forced him into an asylum in Saint-Rémy. He sought help in Auvers, where he shot himself, dying two days later.

**Van Gogh in 1871**

## VISITORS' CHECKLIST

Paulus Potterstraat 7. **Map** 4 E3.
[] 570 5200. [W] www.
vangoghmuseum.nl [] 2, 3, 5, 12,
16. [] 10am–5pm daily. [] 1
Jan. [] [] [] [] [] [] []

**Pietà (after Delacroix)** *(1889)*
*Van Gogh painted this work while in the asylum at Saint-Rémy. The figure of Christ is thought to be a self-portrait.*

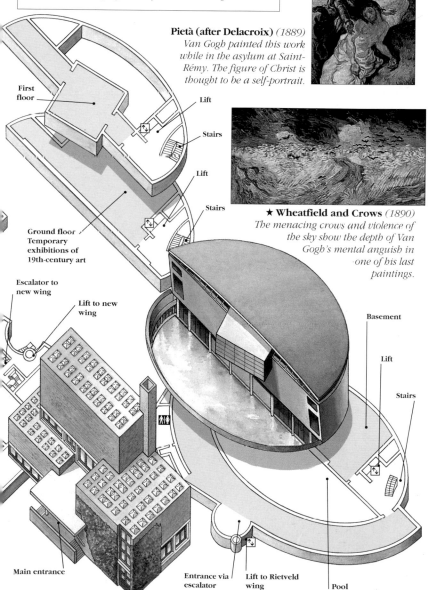

★ **Wheatfield and Crows** *(1890)*
*The menacing crows and violence of the sky show the depth of Van Gogh's mental anguish in one of his last paintings.*

**First floor**

Lift

Stairs

Lift

Stairs

**Ground floor**
Temporary exhibitions of 19th-century art

**Escalator to new wing**

**Lift to new wing**

**Basement**

Lift

Stairs

**Main entrance**

**Entrance via escalator**

**Lift to Rietveld wing**

**Pool**

# Stedelijk Museum ➍

THE STEDELIJK MUSEUM was built to house a personal collection bequeathed to the city in 1890 by art connoisseur Sophia de Bruyn. In 1938, the museum became the national museum of modern art, displaying works by artists such as Picasso, Chagall, Mondriaan and Cézanne. Exhibitions change constantly and recent acquisitions reflect developments after 1945, with works by Newman, Judd, Ryman and Sol Lewitt.

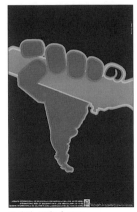

**Portrait of the Artist with Seven Fingers** *(1912)*
*Marc Chagall's self-portrait is heavily autobiographical; the seven fingers of the title allude to the seven days of Creation and the artist's Jewish origins. Paris and Rome, the cities Chagall lived in, are inscribed in Hebrew above his head.*

**Solidaridad con America Latina** *(1970)*
*The Stedelijk's collection of rare posters comprises some 17,000 works, including this graphic image by the Cuban human rights campaigner Asela Perez.*

## THE MUSEUM BUILDING

The Neo-Renaissance building was designed by AW Weissman (1858–1923) in 1895. The façade is adorned with turrets and gables and with niches containing statues of artists and architects. Inside, it is ultra-modern. The museum will be undergoing renovation between 2004 and 2006.

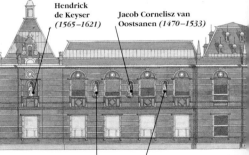

Hendrick de Keyser *(1565–1621)*

Jacob Cornelisz van Oostsanen *(1470–1533)*

Pieter Aertsen *(1509–75)*

Joost Jansz Bilhamer *(1541*

Gerrit Rietveld's *Red Blue Chair* (1918)

## DE STIJL MOVEMENT

The Dutch artistic movement known as De Stijl (The Style) produced startlingly simple designs which have become icons of 20th-century abstract art. These include Gerrit Rietveld's famous *Red Blue Chair* and Pieter Mondriaan's *Composition in Red, Black, Blue, Yellow and Grey* (1920). The movement was formed in 1917 by a group of artists who espoused clarity in their work, which embraced the mediums of painting, architecture, sculpture, poetry and furniture design. Many De Stijl artists, like Theo van Doesburg, split from the founding group in the 1920s, and their legacy can be seen in the work of the Bauhaus and Modernist schools which followed.

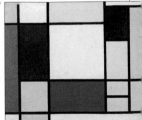

*Composition in Red, Black, Blue, Yellow and Grey* by Mondriaan

### Dancing Woman (1911)
*Ernst Ludwig Kirchner (1880–1938) was inspired by the primitive art of African and Asian cultures, and by the natural qualities of the materials he worked with.*

**Man and Animals** (1949)
*Karel Appel (born 1921) was a member of the short-lived, experimental Cobra movement. The human figure, dog fish and mythical creature are painted in the naïve style of a child.*

Elaborate bell tower

Thomas de Keyser (1596–1667)

Jan van der Heyden (1637–1712)

Jacob van Campen (1595–1657)

**Untitled** (1965)
*Jasper Johns (born 1930) believed viewers should draw their own conclusions from his work. This huge canvas, with its bold rainbow (red, blue and yellow) streaks and slabs), invites the viewer to think about the symbolism of colour.*

---

### STAR COLLECTIONS

★ **Works by Mondriaan**

★ **Cobra Collection**

★ **Works by Malevich**

---

### VISITORS' CHECKLIST

Paulus Potterstraat 13. **Map** 4 D3.
**☎** 573 2911 **W** www.stedelijk.nl
**🚊** 2, 3, 5, 12, 16. **◷** 11am–5pm daily. **●** 1 Jan. **🅿** **🚫**
**♿** **🚻** **📷** *The museum is currently being renovated.*

---

### PERMANENT ARTISTS

Works by inventive photographer Man Ray, Russian artist Kazimir Malevich and sculptor Jean Tinguely are usually on show in the museum.

**Man Ray** (1890–1977)
*elevated photography to an art form, and was a major influence on the Surrealists.*

**Kazimir Malevich** (1878–1935) founded Suprematism, an abstract movement which experimented with colour.

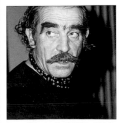

**Jean Tinguely** (1925–1991) created humorous, moving sculptures, welded together from junk and recycled metal.

# PLANTAGE

NOWN AS the "plantation", this area was once green parkland beyond the city wall, where 17th-century Amsterdammers spent their leisure time. From about 1848, it became one of Amsterdam's first suburbs. The tree-lined streets around Artis and Hortus Botanicus are still popular places to live. In the 19th century, many middle-class Jews prospered in the area, mainly in the

**Pillar decoration on Theater Carré**

diamond-cutting industry. They formed a large part of the Diamond Workers' Union, whose history is recorded at the Nationaal Vakbondsmuseum. From the Werf 't Kromhout, once a thriving shipyard, there is a fine view of De Gooyer Windmill, one of the few in Amsterdam to survive. The national maritime collection is kept at the Scheepvaart Museum, a former naval storehouse.

## SIGHTS AT A GLANCE

**Museums**
De Burcht
  (Vakbondsmuseum) **2**
Hollandse Schouwburg **3**
Geologisch Museum **5**
Museum 't Kromhout **11**
*Nederlands Scheepvaart-
  museum pp146–7* **12**
Verzetsmuseum **15**

**Historic Buildings
and Structures**
Entrepotdok **8**
Muiderpoort **9**
De Gooyer Windmill **10**
Amstelsluizen **14**

**Sights of Scientific Interest**
Artis **4**
Aquarium **7**
Planetarium **6**

**Botanical Gardens**
Hortus Botanicus Amsterdam **1**

**Theatres**
Koninklijk Theater Carré **13**

**GETTING THERE**
Trams 6, 9 and 14 pass Artis and Hortus Botanicus; buses 22 and 32 stop at the Scheepvaartmuseum. Weesperplein metro station is located in the southwest of Plantage. It can be intimidating at night, so use the nearby Waterlooplein station.

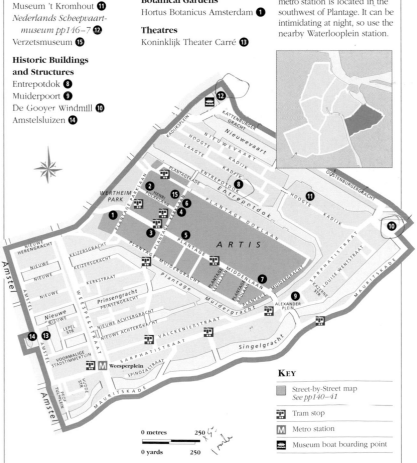

## KEY

| | |
|---|---|
| ▨ | Street-by-Street map *See pp140–41* |
| 🚋 | Tram stop |
| Ⓜ | Metro station |
| ⛴ | Museum boat boarding point |

0 metres 250

0 yards 250

◁ **Replica of the *Amsterdam*, an East Indiaman, moored alongside the Scheepvaart Museum**

# Street-by-Street: Plantage

**Elephant from Artis zoo**

WITH ITS WIDE, TREE-LINED streets and painted, sandstone buildings, the Plantage is a graceful and often over-looked part of the city. Though it seems like a quiet part of town, there is a lot to see and do. The area is dominated by the Artis complex. It has a diverse range of popular attractions which can get very busy on sunny days. The area has a strong Jewish tradition, and several monuments commemorate Jewish history in Amsterdam, including a basalt memorial in the Hollandse Schouwburg. The cafés of the Entrepotdok offer a pleasant setting for a relaxing coffee, within earshot of the zoo.

**De Burcht (Vakbondsmuseum)**
*Inspired by an Italian palazzo, its museum displays trade-union memorabilia* ❷

★ **Artis**
*More than 5,000 species, including a variety of reptiles, live in the zoo complex, which occupies a beautifully laid out garden site* ❹

**Moederhuis**, Aldo van Eyck's refuge for pregnant women, has a colourful, modern façade intended to draw people inside.

★ **Hortus Botanicus Amsterdam**
*The old glasshouses have been restored, and this new one put up to hold tropical and desert plants* ❶

### STAR SIGHTS

- ★ Artis
- ★ Hollandse Schouwburg
- ★ Hortus Botanicus Amsterdam

★ **Hollandse Schouwburg**
*Little remains of this former theatre, now a sombre monument to the deported Jews of World War II* ❸

### Entrepotdok
*This was the largest warehouse develop-ment in Europe dur-ing the 19th century. It has recently been redeveloped and transformed into an attractive quayside housing, office and leisure complex* **8**

**LOCATOR MAP**
*See Street Finder maps 5 & 6*

### Planetarium
*Part of the Artis complex, the domed Planetarium explores man's relationship with the stars. Stellar maps plot the night sky, while interactive displays show the positions of the planets. Model spacecraft are on display in the hall around the auditorium* **6**

### Geologisch Museum
*This updated exhibition covers planet earth, dinosaurs and fossils* **5**

**St Jacob's** incor-porates the stone portal from an old peoples' home formerly on this site.

```
0 metres        100
0 yards         100
```

**KEY**

– – –  Suggested route

### Aquarium
*The fine Neo-Classical building is home to thousands of aquatic species, ranging from tiny, fluorescent tropical fish to gigantic, European moray eels* **7**

**Tropical plants in the Hortus Botanicus**

# Hortus Botanicus Amsterdam ❶

Plantage Middenlaan 2. **Map** 6 D2.
🛈 625 8411. W www.hortus-
botanicus.nl 🚊 6, 9, 14.
Ⓜ Waterlooplein. ◯ 9am–5pm
Mon–Fri, 11am–5pm Sat, Sun &
public hols (Nov–Mar closes 4pm).
● 1 Jan, 25 Dec. 🎴 🔲 ♿
🗷 🔲 🚻

THIS NEAT botanical garden
began as a small apothe-
caries' herb garden in 1682,
and now contains one of the
world's largest botanical collections. Its range of flora expanded when tropical plants
were brought back by the
Dutch East India Company (see
pp26–7). In 1706, it became
the first place outside Arabia
to succeed in cultivating the
coffee plant (Coffea arabica).
    The glass-domed Palm
House, built in 1912,
contains a 400-year-old
cycad (palm fern). Art
shows with a botanical
theme are also held here.
    A modern glass and alu-
minium construction, designed
by Moshé Zwarts and Rein
Jansma, was opened in 1993
to make room for the tropical,
sub-tropical and desert plants.

# De Burcht (Vak-bondsmuseum) ❷

Henri Polaklaan 9. **Map** 5 C2.
🛈 624 1166. W www.deburcht-
vakbondsmuseum.nl 🚊 6, 9, 14.
◯ 11am–5pm Tue–Fri, 1–5pm Sun.
● public hols. 🎴 🔲 ♿ 🔲 🚻

THIS SMALL MUSEUM, housed
in the headquarters of the
General Dutch Diamond
Workers' Union (ANDB), outlines the history of the Dutch
trade union movement.
Founded in 1894, the ANDB

was the first, largest and
wealthiest union in the
Netherlands.
    The red-brick crenel-
lated building, known
locally as "the castle",
was designed by HP
Berlage (see p79) in
1900. It has a beautiful
interior, with murals by
the socialist artist Richard
Roland Holst of the
Amsterdam School (see p97),
and a spectacular arched
foyer. But the material on
show will be best enjoyed by
Dutch speakers.

# Hollandse Schouwburg ❸

Plantage Middenlaan 24. **Map** 5 C2.
🛈 626 9945. 🚊 6, 9, 14. ◯
11am–4pm. ● Yom Kippur. 🔲 ♿

FORMERLY A THEATRE, this is
now a memorial to the
104,000 Dutch Jewish victims
of World War II., More than
60,000 of them were detained
here before being deported to
concentration camps. After the

war, the building was abandoned until 1962 when a garden was laid out in the former
auditorium. A basalt column
with a base in the shape of the
Star of David was erected on
the site of the stage and behind
it is written: "To the memory
of those taken from here".
    The façade and foyer were
restored in 1993, and became
an education centre. On the
ground floor, a candle illuminates the names of the war
victims. Upstairs, exhibits
especially for children explain
the fate of the city's Jewish
community and the dark role
played by the theatre.

# Artis ❹

Plantage Kerklaan 40. **Map** 6 D2.
🛈 523 3400. W www.artis.nl
🚊 6, 9, 14. ◯ 9am– 5pm daily.
🎴 🔲 🍴 🔲 🗷 11am Sun.

ARTIS IS the oldest surviving
zoological complex in the
Netherlands. It was founded
in 1838 by Dr GF Westerman,
president of the Natura Artis

**Decorative tiles on the staircase of the Vakbondsmuseum**

Seals basking in their pool in Artis zoo complex

Magistra (Nature the Teacher of Art) association. Since its inception biologists have worked here and later the general public were allowed in to admire the collection of plants, trees and animals.

The complex has more than 5,000 animal species, as well as three greenhouses, the Planetarium, Geologisch Museum, Aquarium, Amfibarium and Zoölogisch Museum. Footpaths weave past mature trees, ponds, sculptures and animal enclosures.

While some of the spaces for the animals are cramped, the zoo's attractions include big cats, giraffes, polar bears, penguins, hippos and seals. It also contains a steamy reptile house, nocturnal house, aviary, ape house and flamingo lake. Children can clamber on model animals in the playground or pat the sheep and goats in the farmyard.

## Geologisch Museum ❺

Plantage Kerklaan 40. **Map** 6 D2.
[ 523 3400. 🚋 6, 9, 14.
⬤ 9am–5pm daily. 🅾 🐾 ✅

LOCATED AT the southwest corner of the Artis complex, the Geologisch Museum offers an entertaining introduction to planet earth. The admission charge is automatically covered by the entry ticket to Artis.

The first gallery on the ground floor is devoted to the evolution of life on earth. Displays trace the gigantic leap from single-cell life forms, via dinosaurs, to mammals. The second gallery on the ground floor deals imaginatively with the interacting elements of the earth and the forces which control it. The gallery's central attraction is the Earth Machine, which features rotating components to represent the biosphere (the area inhabited by living things), hydrosphere (water), atmosphere (air) and geosphere (the earth's solid crust). Upstairs, there is an extensive display of fossils, minerals and stones.

Ammonite fossil at the Geologisch Museum

## Planetarium ❻

Plantage Kerklaan 40. **Map** 6 D2.
[ 523 3452. 🚋 6, 9, 14.
⬤ Apr–Sep: 9am–5.30pm daily; Oct–Mar: 9am–4.30pm Mon–Sat, 9am–5pm Sun. 🅾 🐾 ✅

BUDDING astronomers should not miss the show at the Planetarium, which takes place on the hour every hour. In this large, domed building a powerful projector reproduces the night sky and shows how the planets constantly change positions in relation to the constellations. Adult and children's programmes are shown alternately and, although the commentary is in Dutch, there are summaries in English, French and German.

Around the edge of the Planetarium, stellar and planetary systems are mapped out using models, photographs, videos and push-button exhibits. There are also educational computer games and displays on exploration and astronomy.

## Aquarium ❼

Plantage Kerklaan 40. **Map** 6 D3.
[ 523 3400. 🚋 6, 9, 14.
**Aquarium** ⬤ 9am–5pm daily.
**Zoölogisch Museum** ⬤ 9am–5pm daily. 🅾 🐾 ✅

PERHAPS THE best feature of the Artis complex is its Aquarium, which opened in 1882 in a grand Neo-Classical building. Mainly housed on the first floor, there are now four separate aquatic systems: one freshwater and three saltwater. Together they hold almost a million litres (220,000 gallons) of water. These tanks, each kept at a different temperature, contain almost 500 species of fish and marine animals that can all be viewed at close quarters.
They range from simple invertebrates to piranhas, sharks and massive marine turtles. Look out for the vivid coral fish and charming sea horses housed at the far end of the gallery.

The Amfibarium is housed in the basement of the Aquarium building. This hall contains a substantial collection of frogs, toads and salamanders in all shapes, sizes and colours.

The building also houses the small Zoölogisch Museum, which is as old as the park itself. The museum has a more academic flavour, and its exhibition halls hold temporary shows on such themes as the history of the dodo or aspects of animal behaviour.

Tropical fish at the Aquarium, home to almost 500 marine species

# Entrepotdok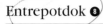

**Map** 6 D2. 6, 9, 14.

THE REDEVELOPMENT of the old VOC *(see pp26–7)* warehouses at Entrepotdok has revitalized this dockland area. It was once the greatest warehouse area in Europe during the mid-19th century, being a customs-free zone for goods in transit. The quayside buildings of Entrepotdok are now a lively complex of offices, homes and eating places. Some of the original façades of the warehouses have been preserved, unlike the interiors, which have been opened up to provide an attractive inner courtyard. Café tables are often set out alongside the canal. On the other side, brightly coloured houseboats are moored side by side, and herons doze at the water's edge.

## Muiderpoort 9

Alexanderplein. **Map** 6 E3. 7, 9, 10, 14. to the public.

FORMERLY A CITY GATE, the Muiderpoort was designed by Cornelis Rauws in about 1770. The central archway of this Classical structure is topped with a dome and clock tower. Napoleon entered the city through this gate in 1811 and, according to legend forced the citizens to feed and house his ragged troops.

**The grand dome and clock tower of the Muiderpoort**

## De Gooyer Windmill 10

Funenkade 5. **Map** 6 F2. 7, 10. to the public.

OF THE SIX remaining windmills within the city's boundaries, De Gooyer, also known as the Funenmolen, is the most central. Dominating the view down the Nieuwevaart, the mill was built around 1725, and was the first corn mill in the Netherlands to use streamlined sails.

It first stood to the west of its present site, but the Oranje Nassau barracks, built in 1814, acted as a windbreak, and the mill was then moved piece by piece to the Funenkade. The octagonal wooden structure was rebuilt on the stone foot of an earlier water-pumping mill, demolished in 1812.

By 1925, De Gooyer was in a very poor state of repair and was bought by the city council, which fully restored it. Since then, the lower part of the mill, with its neat thatched roof and tiny windows, has been a private home, though its massive sails still creak into action sometimes. Next to the mill is the IJ brewery *(see p48)*, one of two independent breweries in the city.

## Museum 't Kromhout 11

Hoogte Kadijk 147. **Map** 6 D1. 627 6777. W www.machine kamer.nl 6, 7, 9, 10, 14. 22, 32. Oosterdok or Kattenburgergracht. 10am–3pm Tue.

THE MUSEUM 'T KROMHOUT is one of the oldest working shipyards in Amsterdam, and is also a museum. Ships were built here as early as 1757. In the second half of the 19th century, production changed from sailing ships to steamships. As ocean-going ships got bigger, the yard, due to its small size, turned to building lighter craft for inland waterways. It is now used only for restoration and repair work.

**Spout-gable façades of former warehouses along Entrepotdok**

The 18th-century De Gooyer windmill, with its renovated balcony

The museum is largely dedicated to the history of marine engineering, concentrating on work carried out at the shipyard, with engines, maritime photographs and ephemera, and a well-equipped forge.

## Nederlands Scheepvaartmuseum ⑫

See pp146–7.

## Koninklijk Theater Carré ⑬

Amstel 115–125. **Map** 5 B3. 524 9494. www.theatercarre.nl 4, 6, 7, 9, 10, 14. Weesperplein.
**Box office** 9am–9pm daily. See **Entertainment** p246. 3pm Wed & Sat (phone in advance).

DURING the 19th century, the annual visit of the Carré Circus was a popular event. In 1868, Oscar Carré built wooden premises for the circus on the banks of the Amstel river. The city council considered the structure a fire hazard, so Carré persuaded them to accept a permanent building modelled on his other circus in Cologne. Built in 1887, the new structure included both a circus ring and a stage. The Classical façade is richly decorated with sculpted heads of dancers, jesters and clowns.

The Christmas circus is still one of the annual highlights at the theatre, but for much of the year the recently enlarged stage is taken over by concerts and big-show musicals.

Werf 't Kromhout Museum and working shipyard

## Amstelsluizen ⑭

**Map** 5 B3. 4, 6, 7, 9, 10, 14. Weesperplein.

THE AMSTELSLUIZEN, a row of sturdy wooden sluice gates spanning the Amstel river, form part of a complex system of sluices and pumping stations that ensure Amsterdam's canals do not stagnate. Four times a week in summer and twice a week in winter, the sluices are closed while fresh water from large lakes north of the city, is allowed to flow into Amsterdam's canals. Sluices to the west of the city are left open, allowing the old water to flow, or be pumped, into the sea.

The Amstelsluizen date from the 18th century, and were operated manually until 1994, when they were mechanized.

## Verzetsmuseum ⑮

Plantage Kerklaan 61. 620 2535. www.verzetsmuseum.org 6, 9, 14, 20. 10am–5pm Tue–Fri, noon–5pm Sat & Mon. 1 Jan, 30 Apr, 25 Dec.

Carving on façade of Koninklijk Theater Carré

PREVIOUSLY based in a former synagogue in Nieuw Zuid (New South), now moved to this site in the Plantage, the Resistance Museum holds a fascinating collection of memorabilia recording the activities of Dutch Resistance workers in World War II. It is run by former members of the Resistance and focuses on the courage of the 25,000 people actively involved in the movement. On display are false documents, weaponry, film clips, slide shows, photographs and equipment.

By 1945 there were 300,000 people in hiding in the Netherlands, including Jews and anti-Nazi Dutch. Subsequent events organized by the Resistance, like the February Strike against deportation of the Jews (see p33), are brought to life by exhibits showing where the refugees hid and how food was smuggled in. The museum complements the Anne Frankhuis (see p90) perfectly.

# Nederlands Scheepvaartmuseum ⑫

ONCE THE ARSENAL of the Dutch Navy, this vast Classical sandstone building was built by Daniel Stalpaert in 1656. It was constructed round a massive courtyard and supported by 18,000 piles driven into the bed of the Oosterdok. The Navy stayed in residence until 1973, when the building was converted into the Netherlands Maritime Museum, holding one of the world's largest maritime collections. Displays of boats, models and maps give a survey of Dutch naval history.

*Ornate 17th-century brass sextant*

**Ajax**
*This figurehead is from a ship built in 1832. It portrays Ajax, a hero of the Trojan War, who killed himself in despair when Achilles' armour was given to Odysseus.*

First floor

★ **The Orrery of Jan van den Dam** *(1750)*
*With a copper ball at its centre to represent the Sun, this is the oldest working orrery in the Netherlands.*

## MUSEUM GUIDE

*The museum is arranged chronologically. The first floor covers the early maritime history of the Netherlands. The second floor spans merchant shipping from the 19th century to date, including technical developments. A cinema is on the first floor, and a full-size model of the East Indiaman, Amsterdam, is docked at the quayside.*

### STAR EXHIBITS

★ **Royal Barge**

★ **The Amsterdam**

★ **The Orrery of Jan van den Dam**

Classical sandstone façade

**Map of the World**
*This map of Asia forms part of a series of five published in the Netherlands in 1780. Too inaccurate for navigation, they were used as wall decorations.*

Main entrance

**VISITORS' CHECKLIST**

Kattenburgerplein 1. **Map** 6 D1.
523 2222. W www.
scheepvaartmuseum.nl 22, 32.
Oosterdok, Kattenburger-
gracht. 10am–5pm Tue–Sun &
public hols; mid-Jun–mid-Sep also
10am–5pm, Mon. 1 Jan, 30
Apr, 25 Dec.

★ **The Amsterdam**
The Amsterdam is "crewed" by actors.
The captain of an East Indiaman
lived in considerable, if cramped,
luxury at the stern of the boat.

**KEY TO FLOORPLAN**

| | 17th-century collection |
| --- | --- |
| | 18th- and 19th-century collection |
| | 20th-century collection |
| | Water sports and yachting |
| | Temporary exhibitions |
| | Non-exhibition space |

**Full-size model
of a Dutch East
Indiaman**
(see pp26–7)

Second
floor

Steps down
to wooden
walkway

Ground
floor

Wooden
walkway

Library

**Artillery Courtyard**
The navy used to store its artillery in
the arsenal's internal courtyard.
Beneath it lie four massive vaults in
which fresh drinking water was kept.

★ **Royal Barge**
This gilded barge was
made in 1818 for King
William I. It is 17 m (54 ft) long
and was propelled by 20 oars-
men. It was last used in 1962,
during Queen Juliana's 25th wedding anniversary celebrations.

# FURTHER AFIELD

GREAT ARCHITECTURE and good town planning are not confined to central Amsterdam. Parts of the Nieuw Zuid (New South) bear testament to the imagination of the innovative Amsterdam School architects *(see p97)* under the auspices of the Municipal Councils. Many fine buildings can be found in De Dageraad Housing complex and the streets around the Olympic Quarter. If you are seeking old-world charm, the historic small town of Ouderkerk aan de Amstel, nestling on the southern fringes of the

**Sculpture on the fountain at Frankendael**

city, prides itself on being older than Amsterdam. There are also fine parks just a short tram ride from the city centre, which offer a whole host of leisure activities. Visitors can view the lakes, woods and parkland of the Amsterdamse Bos *(see pp32–3)* from the deck of an antique tram which tours the park from the Electrische Museumtramlijn. The more formal horticulture of the Amstelpark can be viewed aboard a miniature train. There is also a clutch of instructive museums to be found in the suburbs of Amsterdam.

## SIGHTS AT A GLANCE

**Historic Monuments, Buildings and Districts**
Frankendael ❶
De Dageraad Housing ❺
Ouderkerk aan de Amstel ❽
Olympic Quarter ❾

**Parks and Gardens**
Amstelpark ❼
Amsterdamse Bos ⓫

**Museums and Exhibition Halls**
*Tropenmuseum see pp152–3* ❷
Nemo ❸
Gemeentearchief Amsterdam ❹
Amsterdam RAI ❻
Electrische Museumtramlijn ❿
Nationaal Luchtvaartmuseum
  Aviodome ⓬

**KEY**

Central Amsterdam
Greater Amsterdam
✈ Airport
Major road
Minor road

0 kilometres     2
0 miles          2

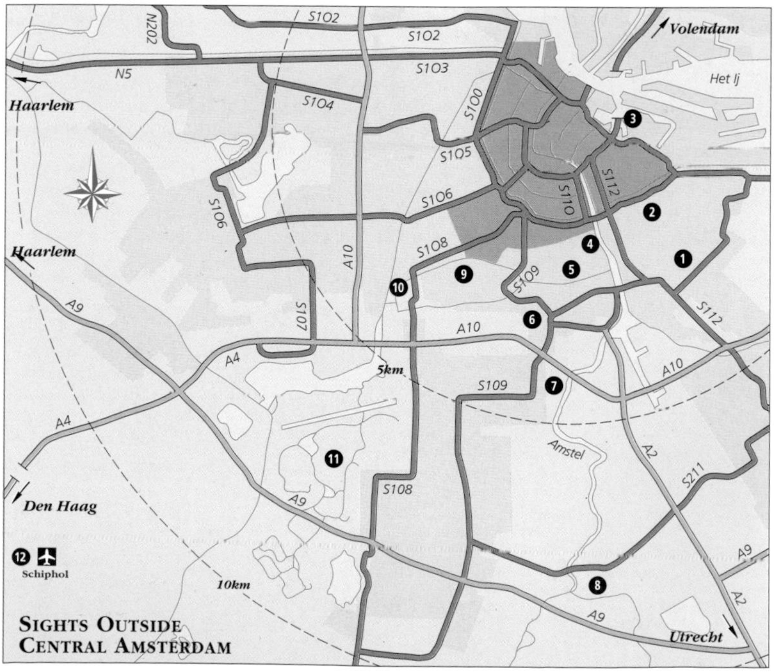

**SIGHTS OUTSIDE CENTRAL AMSTERDAM**

◁ **Moored sailing boat on the river at Ouderkerk aan de Amstel**

# Frankendael ❶

Middenweg 72. **Map** 6 F5. 🚊 9.
🚌 59, 120, 126, 136. **Gardens**
📞 568 7811. ⭘ dawn–dusk.

**D**URING THE early part of the
18th century, many of
Amsterdam's wealthier citizens
built country retreats south of
Plantage Middenlaan on reclaimed land called the Water-
graafsmeer. The elegant Louis
XIV-style Frankendael is the
last survivor. The house is
closed to the public and the
best views of the ornamented
façade are from Middenweg.
This is also the best place to
view the fountain made by
Ignatius van Logteren in 1714,
complete with reclining river
gods, in the front garden.

The rear gardens, however,
are open to the public, and
offer a peaceful, if unkempt,
refuge where overgrown
shrubs and ancient trees line
the footpaths. There are also
large nurseries into which
visitors are free to wander.

The late-19th-century façade of the Gemeentearchief Amsterdam

**Ignatius van Logteren's fountain
in the grounds of the Frankendael**

# Tropenmuseum ❷

See pp152–3.

# Nemo Science Center Amsterdam ❸

Oosterdok 2. **Map** 2 F4. 📞 531 32
33. 🌐 www.e-nemo.nl 🚌 22, 32.
⭘ 10am–5pm Tue–Fri (daily during
public hols). 🎦 🔊 📷 ♿ 🍴 🛍

**I**N JUNE 1997 Holland's
national science centre
moved to this dazzling
curved building which
protrudes 30 m (99 ft) over
water. Nemo presents
technological innovations in a
manner which allows visitors'
creativity full expression.
You can interact with virtual
reality, operate the latest
industrial equipment under
expert supervision and
harness science to produce
your own art. The Centre is
divided into five themed
zones (Interactivity, Technology, Energy, Science and
Humanity), each of which is
revamped every three years to

**Striking architecture of Nemo Science and Technology Centre**

keep pace with scientific evolution. Visitors – who in this setting might equally be termed explorers – can participate in games, experiments, demonstrations and workshops or take in lectures, films and even educational stage shows.

Sadly, the Centre is currently suffering financial problems and its future is uncertain.

## Gemeentearchief Amsterdam ❹

Amsteldijk 67. **Map** 5 B5.
572 0202. 3, 4.
10am–5pm Mon–Sat. public hols, Jul–Aug. Sat.

THIS ELABORATE 19th-century building, with its ornate Neo-Renaissance façade, used to be the town hall of Nieuwer Amstel, a small community partly annexed by Amsterdam in 1869. It has been home to the city's municipal archives since 1914 and major extensions have been added.

The oldest document in the archives is the Toll of Privilege of 1275, by which Floris V granted freedom from tolls "to the people living near the Dam in the river Amstel" (see p19). The city records include a register of baptisms, marriages and burials dating back to 1550, and a collection of drawings, books, newspapers and audiovisual material. Good exhibitions are often held here.

Interior of Amsterdam RAI with trade fair in progress

## De Dageraad Housing ❺

Pieter Lodewijk Takstraat. 4, 12, 25. to the public.

ONE OF THE best examples of Amsterdam School architecture (see p97), De Dageraad housing project was developed for poorer families following the revolutionary Housing Act of 1901 by which the city council was forced to condemn slums and rethink housing policy.

Socialist architect HP Berlage (see p79) drew up ingenious plans for the suburbs, aiming to integrate rich and poor by juxtaposing their housing. After Berlage's death, Piet Kramer and Michel de Klerk of the Amsterdam School adopted his ideas. Between 1918 and 1923, they designed this complex for a housing association known as De Dageraad (the Dawn).

Imposing corner block of De Dageraad public housing

They used a technique called "apron architecture" in which an underlayer of concrete allows for tucks, folds and rolls in the brick exterior, which was then subtly coloured and interspersed with decorative doors and windows. Each house mirrors the one opposite and there is a corner tower at the end of every block. The façades of the buildings were designed to give the impression of horizontal movement, an effect which is produced by the streamlined windows and the undulating roofs.

## Amsterdam RAI ❻

Europaplein. 549 1212.
www.rai.nl 4. RAI.
15, 66, 199. depending on exhibition. **Office & enquiries**: 8am–6pm Mon–Fri. with assistance.

AMSTERDAM RAI is one of the largest exhibition and conference centres in the country. It hosts more than a thousand events annually, from cabaret to horse shows and trade fairs.

The first Amsterdam trade fair was a bicycle exhibition held in 1893. Subsequent shows included cars and became an annual event known as the "RAI" (Rijwiel Automobiel Industrie). The present complex on Europaplein opened in 1961. It has undergone several extensions and now boasts 11 exhibition halls, 22 congress halls and seven restaurants.

# KIT Tropenmuseum ❷

BUILT TO HOUSE the Dutch Colonial Institute, this vast complex was finished in 1926 by architects MA and J Nieukerken. The exterior is decorated with symbols of imperialism, such as stone friezes of peasants planting rice. When the building's renovation was completed in 1978, the Royal Tropical Institute opened a museum, with a huge central hall and three levels of galleries. The institute's aims are to study and to help improve the lives of the indigenous populations of the tropics. The displays reflect this, focusing on development issues regarding daily life, education and colonization.

**Nomad's Felt Tent**
*Made of felt, with a homely interior, this is a recreated nomad's tent from Afghanistan.*

★ **Mask Collection**
*Feathered fertility masks from Zaire and this carved wooden mask from Central America are included in this collection.*

First floor

Great hall

★ **Bisj Poles**
*The roots of massive mangrove trees were used to make these exotic, painted ritual totem poles from New Guinea.*

**GALLERY GUIDE**
*Temporary exhibitions are held in the Great hall on the ground floor. On the upper floors, the permanent exhibitions combine static and interactive displays covering diverse topics. The shop on the ground floor has a range of gifts from developing countries, and in the basement are a restaurant, café and theatre. There is a visitors guide, '80 Minutes in Another World'.*

Main entrance

Basement

---

**STAR EXHIBITS**

★ **Bisj Poles**

★ **Diorama**

★ **Mask Collection**

Second floor

Park Hall

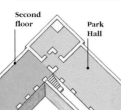

★ **Diorama** (1819)
*Gerrit Schouten used papier-mâché and painted wood to create this colourful scene of life in Surinam.*

**Javanese Stone Friezes**
*The stone friezes decorating the main stairs are copies from a Javanese monument from about AD 800. This section shows two Buddhas praying under ornate temple awnings.*

**Jeepney**
*Old army trucks left behind by the Americans after World War II are used as taxibuses or jeepneys in Manila. The one housed here is a typically colourful example.*

## KEY TO FLOORPLAN

- ☐ SE Asia & Textiles in Indonesia
- ☐ W Asia & N Africa
- ☐ Latin America & the Carribean
- ☐ Man & the Environment
- ☐ Music, Dance & Theatre
- ☐ Africa
- ☐ Dutch Colonialism
- ☐ Dutch New Guinea
- ☐ KIT Kindermuseum
- ☐ Temporary exhibition space
- ☐ Non-exhibition space

## KIT KINDERMUSEUM (CHILDREN'S MUSEUM)

Admission to the children's museum is by appointment only; adults are not admitted unless accompanied by a child. The museum is aimed at six- to 12-year-olds and takes a "hands-on" approach – visitors can examine and explore the exhibits. Guided tours (in Dutch) are available to help younger children gain the most from the collection, which is geared to bringing objects alive through their history and culture. Part of the exhibition is permanent, but much of the space is given over to temporary displays exploring specific topics.

**Tiger protector mask and model from Bali**

**Amstelpark's Rieker windmill**

# Amstelpark ❼

Europaboulevard. 🚊 4. Ⓜ 🚉 RAI.
🚌 66, 199. ◯ dawn–dusk.

SITUATED in the suburb of Buitenveldert, southwest of Amsterdam, this large park was created in 1972. Among its attractions are a rose garden, rhododendron walk and model garden with nursery.

The park offers good facilities for children, including a playground, pony rides, mini-golf and mini-football. The well-preserved Rieker windmill (1636) stands at the southern tip of the park, and art exhibitions are held in the Glazen Huis (Glass House) and the Papillon Gallery. From Easter to October, you can tour the park in a miniature train.

# Ouderkerk aan de Amstel ❽

Ⓜ 🚉 Bijlmer. 🚌 175 from Bijlmer station. **Wester Amstel Garden** ◯ dawn–dusk.

THIS PRETTY VILLAGE at the junction of the Amstel and the Bullewijk rivers has been a favourite with Amsterdammers since the Middle Ages. They had no church of their own until 1330 (see pp66–7), and worshippers had to travel to the 11th-century Ouderkerk that gave the village its name. The Old Church was destroyed in a tremendous storm in 1674, and a fine 18th-century church now stands on its site. Opposite is the Beth Haim Jewish cemetery, where more than 27,000 Jews from Amsterdam have been buried since 1615. The elders of the Jewish community bought this land to use as a burial ground because Jews were forbidden to bury their dead inside the city.

Today Ouderkerk aan de Amstel is popular with cyclists who come to enjoy the ambience of its waterfront cafés and restaurants. The skyline is dominated by the 50-m (160-ft) spire of the Urbanuskerk, a Catholic church designed by PJH Cuypers (see pp30–31) and consecrated in 1867.

A short walk upriver along Amsteldijk, there are two 18th-century country houses. While there is no access to the first, the restful wooded garden of the second house, Wester Amstel, is open to the public. The house, built in 1720, has a fine Louis XV-style gateway.

# Olympic Quarter ❾

🚊 6, 16, 24. 🚌 15, 23, 65, 142, 165, 170, 172.

DEVELOPMENT OF the western side of the Nieuw Zuid (New South) began during the run up to the Olympic Games, held here in 1928. Many of the streets and squares were given Grecian names, like Olympiaplein and Herculesstraat.

The Stadium was designed by J Wils and C van Eesteren. Its stark vertical lines and soaring torch tower recall the work of the American architect Frank Lloyd Wright. Once threatened with demolition, it has recently been renovated.

The sturdy bridge across the Noorder Amstel Kanaal at Olympiaplein is typical Amsterdam School design. It is the work of PL Kramer and the sculptor H Krop. Beyond the bridge, the Amsterdams Lyceum (a secondary school) shows the style at its best.

**The peaceful waterfront at Oudekerk aan de Amstel, south of Amsterdam**

**Pedalos on a lake in the Amsterdamse Bos**

## Electrische Museumtramlijn ⑩

Amstelveenseweg 264. *423 1100 or 673 7538* *6, 16, 24.* *15, 23, 170, 172.* *Easter–Oct: 11am–5pm Sun; Jun–Aug also Wed pm and on request.*

NOT A MUSEUM, as the name suggests, but a tram ride that operates from Haarlemmermeerstation and the southern tip of the Amsterdamse Bos. The tramcars, which date from 1910 to 1950, come from all over the Netherlands, Vienna, Prague and Berlin. The fleet is run by a group of enthusiasts along traditional lines and cars depart regularly from either terminus. A one-way journey takes about 20 minutes and provides a good view of the Olympic Stadium.

**Classic tram from the Museumtramlijn**

## Amsterdamse Bos ⑪

Amstelveenseweg. *Electrische Museumtramlijn (see entry 11).* *170, 172.* **Theatre** *643 3286 (after 6pm Jul & Aug).*

THIS WOODLAND PARK is the largest recreational area in Amsterdam. It was laid out in the 1930s, in a project to reduce unemployment in the city *(see p33)*. Extensive wooded areas, interspersed with grassy meadows, lakes, waterways and even a hill, were created on reclaimed land that lies 3 m (13 ft) below sea level. The park was enlarged periodically until 1967, when it reached its present size of more than 800 ha (2,000 acres).

Today, the marshy areas around Nieuwe Meer and the lakes at Amstelveense Poel and Kleine Poel are nature reserves. Other highlights include an animal enclosure with gigantic European bison, a goat farm, the Vogeleiland botanical gardens and the Bosmuseum, which has exhibits on the natural and social history of the park.

Among the facilities are an extensive network of planned walks, cycle paths and bridle ways, as well as water sports and an open-air theatre *(see p245)* during the summer.

## Nationaal Luchtvaartmuseum Aviodome ⑫

Constellationboulevard 1, Lelystad. *320 289 840.* *Lelystad, then* *145 to Harderwijk. Alight at Lelystad Airport/Aviodome stop.* *Apr–Oct: 10am–6pm daily; Nov–Mar: 10am–5pm daily.* *1 Jan, 25 Dec, 31 Dec.* www. aviodome.nl

THE DUTCH National Aviation Museum recently moved from Schiphol Airport to new premises at Lelystad Airport. This interactive aviation theme park has more than 30 aircraft, models and spacecraft tracing the history of aviation and space exploration.

Exhibits include the American Wright Flyer of 1903, and the Spider, brainchild of the Dutch engineer Anthony Fokker. His Triplane, flown by the famous Red Baron, was the best-known German aeroplane in World War I.

Visitors can see a genuine German "*Messerschmidt* hanger", a replica World War II British T-2 hangar, and also board a 1930's KLM Fokker air liner for a simulated flight from pre-war Schiphol Airport.

Visitors can see videos about flight, try their hand at the controls of coin-operated flight-simulators, make a virtual skydive and there are also occasional events enabling flights in helicopters or vintage aeroplanes.

**The Fokker Triplane from World War I, on view in the Aviodome**

# Two Guided Walks

MANY OF AMSTERDAM'S most important historical landmarks, and several fine examples of 16th- and 17th-century architecture, can be enjoyed on both of these walks. The first takes the visitor through the streets of the Jordaan, a peaceful quarter known for its narrow, pretty canals, houseboats and traditional architecture. The route winds through to the man-made Western Islands of Bickerseiland, Realeneiland and Prinseneiland, built in the 17th century to accommodate the expansion in Amsterdam's overseas trade. The area, with its rows of warehouses and

**Wall plaque at No. 6 Zandhoek**

wharves, is a reminder of the city's erstwhile supremacy at sea. The city's maritime heritage is also evident on the second walk, which starts off from the Schreierstoren, where women waved their husbands off to sea in the 17th century, and finishes at the Nederlands Scheepvaart Museum. On the way, the walk passes the original city boundaries, countless converted warehouses and along streets named after the spices brought in by the East India Company (VOC). On any weekday, there is also the opportunity to spend a few pleasurable hours browsing round the Waterlooplein flea market.

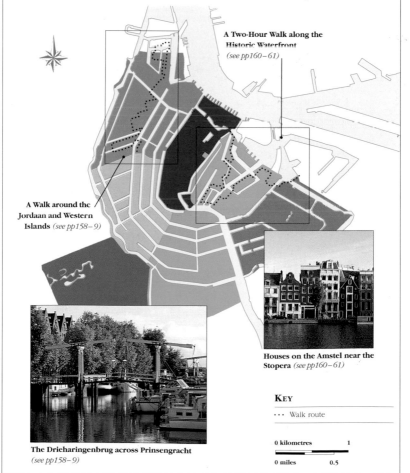

**A Two-Hour Walk along the Historic Waterfront** *(see pp160–61)*

**A Walk around the Jordaan and Western Islands** *(see pp158–9)*

**Houses on the Amstel near the Stopera** *(see pp160–61)*

**The Drieharingenbrug across Prinsengracht** *(see pp158–9)*

**KEY**

··· Walk route

0 kilometres     1

0 miles     0.5

◁ View from the tower of the Westerkerk across the Jordaan, with Prinsengracht in the foreground

# A Walk around the Jordaan and Western Islands

THE JORDAAN is a tranquil part of the city, crammed with canal houses, old and new galleries, restaurants, craft shops and pavement cafés. The walk route meanders through narrow streets and along enchanting canals. It starts from the Westerkerk and continues past Brouwersgracht, up to the IJ river and on to the Western Islands. These islands have now been adopted by the bohemian artistic community as a fashionable area to live and work.

Plaque on No. 8 Zandhoek, a former sailors' hostel

### Prinsengracht to Westerstraat

Outside Hendrick de Keyser's Westerkerk ① *(see p90)* turn left up Prinsengracht, past the Anne Frankhuis ② *(see p90)*, and cross over the canal. Turn left down the opposite side of Prinsengracht and walk along Bloemgracht – the prettiest canal in the Jordaan. Before crossing the second bridge, look out for the three identical canal houses called the Drie Hendricken (the three Henrys) ③ *(see p91)*. Continue up 3e Leliedwarsstraat, with its cafés and old shops in the first half of the street, turn right and walk past the St Andrieshofje ④, one of the numerous well-preserved almshouses in the city. It is worth pausing to take a look across Egelantiersgracht at No. 360, a rare example of an Art Nouveau canal house.

Follow the bank to the end, turn left on to Prinsengracht, passing the Café 't Smalle, and turn left into Egelantiersstraat. In 1e Egelantiersdwarsstraat can be found a group of 17th-century almshouses, known as

the Claes Claeszhofje ⑤ *(see p92)*. Follow this tiny street past several cafés as well as many unusual shops selling clothes, bric-a-brac, pottery and paintings, to Westerstraat.

**Simple wooden gable with hoisting hook on Westerstraat**

### Westerstraat to Bickerseiland

Cross the street – Westerstraat originally bordered a canal, now filled in – and turn right. The gabled houses are typical of the late-17th-century style of the Jordaan. Walk along for one block and take the first left into 1e Boomdwarsstraat, then right to the Noorderkerk ⑥ *(see p92)*. Each Monday morning, a lively flea market takes place in the Noordermarkt *(see p92)*. Continue on to the south side

of the Lindengracht. To the left, at Nos. 149–163, is the Suyckerhofje ⑦, a former refuge for abandoned women. Turn right and you will pass a wall plaque on No. 55 Lindengracht depicting fish swimming in trees and echoing an inverted view of houses reflected in the city's canals. The statue on Lindengracht is of the writer and educationalist, Theo Thijssen. Turn left down Brouwersgracht *(see p93)*, which is lined with colourful houseboats. Cross the first lift bridge and go into Binnen Oranjestraat, then under the railway bridge onto Bickerseiland, which is named after one of the city's most wealthy 17th-century families.

**Ornate step gables (1642) at Nos. 89 and 91 Bloemgracht**

### KEY

··· Walk route

0 metres 200
0 yards 200

A view of houseboats and gabled houses from Galgenstraat ⑨

## The Western Islands

The Western Islands are made up of Bickers-, Prinsen- and Realeneiland *(see p93)*. They were created in the early 17th century to cope with the city's need for warehouses as a result of Amsterdam's maritime trading success. Their quays were lined with ships, while sailors and dockworkers lived in nearby canal houses.

Cross the Hendrik Jonkerplein ⑧ and go on to Bickersgracht where the boatyards are still operational. The first bridge to the left leads on to Prinseneiland and then into Galgenstraat (gallows street) ⑨, so called because the view from here in the 17th century was of the gallows across the IJ.

Turning right, follow the bend and cross the wooden drawbridge on to Realeneiland. Turn right along Realengracht, take the first left, then right into Jan Mensplein and through to Taanstraat, first looking back along Vierwindenstraat where there stands a series of sombre old warehouses, once used for storing grain, hemp and flax. At the end, turn right down Zandhoek (sand corner) ⑩ *(see p93)*, with its rows of charming 17th-century houses. The name originates from the sand market which once took place here.

Follow Zandhoek and cross the wooden bridge (a 1983 replica of the original). Stay on the canal and follow the footpath that runs along Bickersgracht. Keep your eyes on the water and you might see a blue-grey heron looking for fish. Walk along Grote Bickersstraat and you will find yourself back where you started, at the bridge leading on to Prinseneiland. To leave the islands and return to the city centre, retrace your steps to Haarlemerdijk and turn left.

The tranquil, tree-lined Egelantiersgracht

### TIPS FOR WALKERS

**Starting point**: Outside the Westerkerk on the Prinsengracht.
**Length**: 4.5 km (2.8 miles).
**Duration**: One and a half hours.
**Getting there**: Buses 21, 142, 170, 171 and 172. Trams 13, 14, 17 and 20 from Centraal Station.
**Stopping-off points**: The Jordaan is packed with cafés and bars. On the Egelantiersgracht, 't Smalle is particularly atmospheric and there are bars in Noordermarkt, Haarlemmerdijk and Hendrik Jonkerplein. De Gouden Reaal in Zandhoek is ideal to rest in before the trip home.

# A Two-Hour Walk along the Historic Waterfront

**B**EGIN THE WALK at the Schreierstoren *(see p67)*, once a
defence tower in the medieval town wall. The route
follows the development of Amsterdam as a great trading
city, as wharves, warehouses and houses were built to
accommodate the boom in overseas trade and in population. The city's expansion was carefully planned; as
existing waterfronts became overcrowded, more islands
were created to the east, slowly reclaiming the surrounding marshy countryside. The walk takes in a number of
reminders of the Dutch East India Company (VOC) *(see
pp26–7)*, such as the streets named after spices, and ends
up at the imposing Nederlands Scheepvaart Museum.

16th-century stone tablet near the
main door, Schreierstoren ①

Gables and façades along the
right bank of Krommewaal

## Schreierstoren to
## St Antoniesbreestraat

From the Schreierstoren ①,
walk along Prins Hendrikkade,
turning at Krommewaal and
following the right bank, with
its series of rich façades and
gables, to Lastageweg ②.
Lastage is an area which was
developed for trade after the
fire of 1452 *(see p21)*. The expansion which followed in the
16th century *(see p23)* brought
Lastage within the city walls.
   Continue to Recht Boomssloot and turn right and keep
going until you reach Geldersekade, one of the town
boundaries in the 15th century.
Follow along Recht Boomssloot,
then along the side of Krom
Boomssloot, until you see the
Schottenburch warehouses ③
at Nos. 18–20. Built in 1636,
these are among the oldest in
the city and are now converted
into apartments. Next door is
an Armenian church, converted
from a warehouse in the mid-
18th century. Then follow
Snoekjesgracht, turning left
into St Antoniesbreestraat ④.

## St Antoniesbreestraat to
## Uilenburg Island

On St Antoniesbreestraat,
cross the road at Elias
Bouwman's Pintohuis ⑤
*(see p66)*, the only surviving
building from the original
street. Enter the Zuider-
kerk ⑥ yard opposite
through its skull-
adorned gateway.
The church was
built by Hendrick
de Keyser *(see p90)*
in 1603 and now
hosts a permanent
exhibition on vari-
ous aspects of
urban renewal.

*Schreierstoren*

*Montelbaanstoren*

*Waalseilandsgracht*

*Oudeschans*

*Uilenburgergracht*

*Stopera*

Lift bridge on Staalstraat,
crossing Groenburgwal

0 metres                    200

0 yards                     200

**KEY**

••• Walk route

Ⓜ Metro station

Cross the square and continue to Zandstraat. Continue on to Kloveniersburgwal and turn left along the canal on to Staalstraat, where another left turn takes you past the Saaihal ⑦ (the draper's hall), with its unusual trapezoid gable. The first bridge crosses the Groenburgwal, with splendid views of the Amstel to the right. The next bridge leads to the Stopera ⑧ (see p63), and Waterlooplein flea market ⑨ (see p63). Follow the market stalls and half way along turn left towards Jodenbreestraat,

**Wall plaque at Museum Het Rembrandthuis**

transformed since it was the heart of Jewish Amsterdam. To the left on Jodenbreestraat is the Museum Het Rembrandthuis ⑩ (see p62). Cross the road and continue on to Nieuwe Uilenburgerstraat and on to the island of Uilenburg, built in the late 16th century to take housing for the poor. On the right can be seen the vast Gassan Diamonds factory ⑪, with two synagogues in the yard, a reminder of the time when diamond polishing was one of the few trades open to Jews (see p64).

**Uilenburg to the Eastern Islands**

Turn left into Nieuwe Batavierstraat and then right at Oude Schans, a broad canal with former warehouses and quays full of

*Oosterdok*

*Oosterdok*

*Scheepvaart Museum* ⑭

eccentric-looking houseboats. On the opposite bank of the canal is the Montelbaanstoren ⑫ (see p66), an old defence tower. At the bend, cross over the Rapenburgwal

The 16th-century Montelbaanstoren, part of the city defences ⑫

bridge until you reach Peperstraat. Like other streets on these man made islands, Peperstraat was named after a commodity imported by the VOC (see pp26–7) in the 17th century. From here, turn right on to the main road of Prins Hendrikkade and then into Nieuwe Foeliestraat. Turn left onto Rapenburg, then left again onto Rapenburger Plein. Take the bridge across Nieuwe Herengracht to the gateway of the Entrepotdok ⑬ (see p144). Turn left into Kadijksplein, continue along Prins Hendrikkade and across the Nieuwevaart bridge from which you can see Daniel Stalpaert's Oosterkerk. Continue on to the Eastern Islands, built in 1658 to create more shipyards. The Nederlands Scheepvaart Museum ⑭ (see pp146–7) dominates the Oosterdok to the left. To return to the centre, follow Prins Hendrikkade westwards.

## TIPS FOR WALKERS

**Starting point**: The Schreierstoren on Prins Hendrikkade.
**Length**: 6 km (4 miles).
**Duration**: Two hours.
**Getting there**: Some buses go along Prins Hendrikkade, but it is easier to take a tram to Centraal Station (see p79) and walk along the IJ. To pick up the walk halfway, tram 9 goes to Waterlooplein.
**Stopping-off points**: There are cosy brown cafés (see pp 48 and 236) along the start of the walk and at the Stopera (see p63). There are also bars on Schippersgracht and within the Entrepotdok.

Antiques and bric-a-brac at Waterlooplein flea market ⑨

# Beyond Amsterdam

# BEYOND AMSTERDAM

AMSTERDAM IS AT THE HEART *of a region known as the Randstad, the economic powerhouse of the Netherlands. The city is a haven for tourists; within easy reach are the ancient towns of Leiden and Utrecht, as well as Den Haag and Haarlem with their exceptional galleries and museums. The Randstad extends south as far as Rotterdam, a thriving modern city full of avant-garde architecture.*

Much of the land comprising the Randstad has been reclaimed from the sea during the last 300 years, and the fertile soil is farmed intensively. Production is centred around early season greenhouse crops, like tomatoes and cucumbers and the incomparable Dutch bulbs. Spreading to the southwest in spring, dazzling colours carpet the fields, and the exquisite gardens at Keukenhof *(see p181)* are the showcase of the bulb industry.

Reclamation continues apace, and Flevoland, the Netherlands' newest province, consists entirely of polder. This flat marshy land, interspersed with drainage channels, has been created since 1950 by draining 1,800 sq km (695 sq miles) of the IJsselmeer. The flat terrain provides shelter for wild birds such as herons, swans and grebes, which nest along the reed-fringed canals. The area beyond Utrecht, to the east of Amsterdam, is much less populated than the Randstad, with vast tracts of unspoilt forest, moorland and peat bog, home to red deer and wild boar.

North of Amsterdam, the traditional fishing communities that depended on the Zuiderzee before it was closed off from the sea in 1932 *(see p170–71)*, have now turned to tourism for their income.

The coast round Zandvoort, lying to the west of Amsterdam, takes the full brunt of vicious North Sea storms in winter, but maritime vegetation and wild birds find shelter among the sandbanks of the exposed coastline.

**Lift bridge and canalside café at Enkhuizen – a popular haunt for visitors to the Zuiderzee Museum**

◁ **Traditional working smock mills** *(see p173)* **at Zaanse Schans**

# Exploring the Netherlands

AMSTERDAM IS AT THE CENTRE of a part of the Netherlands where there are many places of interest within easy reach. Haarlem is just 15 minutes away, and it takes less than half an hour to get to the cheese markets of Edam and Gouda. To the north, the Zuiderzee Museum recreates an old fishing community, and to the south lies historic Utrecht. The east offers the wilderness of the Nationaal Park de Hoge Veluwe, and the stately Paleis Het Loo, a hunting lodge and summer residence of the Dutch royal family since 1692.

Catamarans at Scheveningen

*Groningen, Leeuwarden*

Den Helder

HOORN ❸

ALKMAAR ❶

EDAM ❹

VOLENDAM ❼

ZAANSE SCHANS ❽

MARKEN ❻

MONNICKENDAM ❺

AMSTERDAM

*Noordzeekanaal*

*NOORDZEE*

HAARLEM ❾

*IJmee*

BULBFIELDS ❿

KEUKENHOF ⓭

LISSE ⓬

AALSMEER ⓫

LEIDEN ⓮

SCHEVENINGEN ⓰

DEN HAAG ⓯

UTRE

DELFT ⓱

GOUDA ⓲

*Oude Rijn*

*Hollandsche IJ*

ROTTERDAM ⓳

*Nieuwe Maas*

*Antwerpen*

*Breda*

*Nieuwe Waterweg*

*Calandkanaal*

## KEY

🞖 Motorway

🞖 Major road

🞖 River or canal

0 kilometres    10

0 miles            10

Suspension bridge crossing the Maas river at Rotterdam

**ZUIDERZEE MUSEUM** ②

MARKER MEER

N302

Groningen, Leeuwarden

N302

A6

N305

N302

N302

N303

A27

A28

N30

Lemmeer

A12

A1

A28

A12

A50

N30

N225

Amsterdam-Rijnkanaal

Neder-Rijn    Düsseldorf

**PALEIS HET LOO** ㉓

APELDOORN

Enschede

AMERSFOORT

**DE HOGE VELUWE** ㉑

**ARNHEM** ㉒

Traditional wooden fishing boats in the harbour at Hoorn

## GETTING AROUND

Amsterdam sits at the hub of the Dutch transport system, with fast road and rail links to towns and cities throughout the Netherlands. The A9 and A7 motorways connect the capital with Alkmaar and Hoorn in Noord Holland, and a network of motorways and first class roads cuts across the provinces to the south and east. It is not vital to have a car, as regular buses run to all major towns from Amsterdam, and the rail service, using modern double-decker trains, is even better. Cycling is the ideal way to take in the beauty of the spring bulbfields.

An elaborate gabled façade in Monnickendam

## SIGHTS AT A GLANCE

Children in national costume at the Zuiderzee Museum

Renaissance façade and bell tower of Alkmaar's Waaggebouw (1582)

# Alkmaar ❶

40 km (25 miles) NW of Amsterdam. 👥 94,000. 🚉 🛈 Waaggebouw, Waagplein 2–3. (072) 5114 284. 🗓 cheese market: mid Apr–mid Sep: 10am–12:30pm Fri; main market: Sat.

Alkmaar is an attractive old town with tree-lined canals and an historic centre, scene of an unsuccessful siege by the Spanish in 1573. It is one of the few Dutch towns to maintain its traditional cheese market, which is held every Friday morning in summer. Local producers lay out Gouda cheeses and some rounds of Edam in the Waagplein, and from here porters take them off on sledges for weighing. The porters, who sport colourful straw hats, belong to an ancient guild and indulge in

good-natured rivalry for the benefit of onlookers. The streets around the Waagplein are packed with stalls which sell everything from cheese to locally made pottery.

## 🏛 Waaggebouw

Waagplein 2. (072) 5114 284. **Hollands Kaasmuseum** 🗓 Apr–Oct: 10am–4pm Mon–Sat, 9am–4pm Fri. 🚫 ♿

The focal point of the cheese market is the imposing Waaggebouw (weigh house), which was altered in 1582 from a 14th-century chapel. It now contains the Hollandse Kaasmuseum, where local cheese-making techniques are revealed. Each day on the hour, mechanical knights, under the clock of the Waaggebouw, stage a jousting tournament while a clarion blower sounds his trumpet.

## 🛈 Grote Kerk

Kerkplein, Koorstraat. (072) 5140 707. 🗓 Jun–Aug: 10am–5pm Tue–Sun.

This imposing Gothic church contains the tomb of Floris V (see p19), whose body was exhumed and brought here when the building was completed in 1520. The 17th-century organ, built by Jacob van Campen (see p74) and painted by Cesar van Everdingen, dominates the Grote Kerk's nave.

# Zuiderzee Museum ❷

See pp170–71.

# Hoorn ❸

40 km (25 miles) N of Amsterdam. 👥 63,000. 🚉 🛈 Veemarkt 4. (0900 403 1055). 🗓 Wed (for tourists), Sat.

Hoorn was the capital of the ancient province of West Friesland and one of the great seafaring towns of the Golden Age (see pp24–7). The collection of ornate patrician houses in the streets around Rode Steen, Hoorn's main square, attest to the town's prosperous history. Several famous maritime heroes were born here, including Willem Schouten (1580–1625), who named the tip of South America Cape Horn after his birthplace, and Abel Tasman (see pp26–7). A statue in Rode Steen commemorates Jan Pietersz Coen (1587–1629), a famous explorer who went on to found Batavia, now known as Jakarta, the capital of Indonesia (see pp26–7).

**Painted unicorn, Westfries Museum**

## 🏛 Westfries Museum

Rode Steen 1. (0229) 280 020. 🖳 www.wfm.nl 🗓 11am–5pm Mon–Fri, 2–5pm Sat & Sun. ● 1 Jan, 30 Apr, 3rd Mon in Aug, 25 Dec. 🚫

The building that houses the Westfries Museum in Rode Steen was built in 1632 as a prison – the square takes its name, "red stone", from the blood spilt at executions there.

The three-tiered gable of this splendid building is decorated with heraldic figures carrying the coats of arms of the towns that made up the province of West Friesland. Inside, the museum is little changed since Aldous Huxley, the English writer, described it affectionately in 1925 as "filled with mixed rubbish". There is much to enjoy here, from the archaeological displays in the basement to the 17th-century period rooms filled with rich furniture and antique clocks.

Porters carrying cheese on sledges in Alkmaar's traditional market

**Wooden clogs outside a restored fisherman's cottage in Monnickendam**

# Edam ❹

22 km (14 miles) N of Amsterdam.
🏠 7,200. 🚊 🛈 *Damplein 1.
(0299) 315 125.* 🧀 *cheese market:
Jul–mid-Aug: 10:30am–12:30pm
Wed; general market: every Wed.*

THE NAME OF EDAM is known
throughout the world for
its ball-shaped cheeses which
are wrapped in wax – red for
export, and yellow for local
consumption. In the summer,
cheese lovers should head for
the *kaasmarkt* (cheese market),
held in the main square, which
is called Damplein. The *kaasmarkt's* single-gabled weigh
house dates from 1592 and
has a gaudy painted façade.
Nowadays, cheese-making is
an automated process and
some of the factories around
the outskirts of the town offer
guided tours for visitors.

Edam itself is exceptionally
pretty, full of narrow canals
bordered by elegant, gabled
Golden Age canal houses and
crossed by wooden lift bridges.
The imposing Grote Kerk is
noted both for its 16th-century
carillon, and its stained-glass
windows (1606–24), which
are among the most beautiful
in the Netherlands. The harbour to the east of the town
was built in the 17th century,
in the days when Edam was a
prominent whaling centre.

## 🏛 Edams Museum
Damplein 8. 📞 *(0299) 372 644.*
⭕ *Apr–Oct: Tue–Sat 10am–4.30pm,
Sun 1.30–4.30pm.* ⬤ *30 Apr.* 📷
This amazing Gothic building
(1530) is home to an eccentric
museum of local history. The
timbered interior and steep,

narrow stairs look like the
inside of a ship. According to
some, the house was built for
a retired sea captain who
could not bear sleeping on dry
land, so he created a cabin.
The unusual floating cellar,
has a floor which rises and
falls with fluctuations in the
water table. Just as strange are
the 17th-century portraits of
odd-looking locals, such as
Trijntje Kever, who was said
to be almost 2.8 m (9 ft) tall.

# Monnickendam ❺

16 km (10 miles) N of Amsterdam.
🏠 10,000. 🚊 🛈 *Nieuwpoortslaan
15, Edam. (0299) 651 998.* 🅰 *Sat.*

VISITORS FLOCK to this beautifully preserved port to
admire the gabled houses and
the renovated fishermen's
cottages in the narrow streets
around the harbour. Freshly
smoked local eel can be
bought here, and the fish
restaurants have become a
popular draw for tourists.

The **Museum de Speeltoren**
is dedicated to the history of
Monnickendam. It is housed in
the clock tower of the Stadhuis,
with its ornate 15th-century
carillon. When bells chime the
hour, the clockwork knights
in armour parade around the
exterior of the tower.

## 🏛 Museum de Speeltoren
Noordeinde 4. 📞 *(0299) 65 22 03.*
⭕ *mid-Apr–Whitsuntide, Sep–mid-
Oct: 11am–5pm Sat, 1–5pm Sun;
Whitsuntide–Aug: as above & 11am–
5pm Mon–Fri.* ⬤ *public hols.* 📷

**Lift bridge on one of the canals at Edam**

# Zuiderzee Museum ❷

ENKHUIZEN was one of several villages around the
edge of the Zuiderzee whose fishing-based economy
was devastated when access to the North Sea was
blocked by construction of the Afsluitdijk in 1932 *(see
p165)*. The village's fortunes were revived with the
opening of this museum complex. Seven centuries of
Zuiderzee history is depicted in the Binnenmuseum
(indoor museum). There is also a display of historic
boats. The Buitenmuseum (open air museum) consists
of rescued buildings, reconstructed to create a typical
Zuiderzee village, with demonstrations of local crafts.

**★ Houses from Urk**
*Buildings from the little island
of Urk have been rebuilt in the
open air museum. Daily life on
the island in 1905 is recreated
by actors in role play.*

**Smoke-houses from
Monnickendam**

**Entrance to
Buitenmuseum**

**Childrens's
Island**

**Reconstruction of
Marken harbour**

**★ Marine Hall**
*Housed in an old ware-
house of the Dutch East
India Company (see
pp26–7), the indoor
museum's Marine Hall
contains sailing and
fishing boats. A small
pleasure boat is rigged
up for children to play in.*

**Sail-maker's Shop**
*Until the early 20th cent-
ury, most Dutch ships
and fishing boats had
sails. The ancient craft
of sail-making is kept
alive in this workshop.*

**Barges** carry
visitors to the
open air
museum.

**Entrance to open
air museum**

**★ Lime Kilns**
*Bottle-shaped kilns were
used to burn shells dredged
from the sea bed. The
resulting quicklime was
used as an ingredient in
mortar for bricklaying.
These kilns are from
Akersloot in Noord Holland.*

### VISITORS' CHECKLIST

50 km (31 miles) NE of Amsterdam.
Wierdijk 12–22, Enkhuizen.
**C** (0228) 351111. **W** www.
zuiderzeemuseum.nl
**Indoor** ○ 10am–5pm daily.
● 1 Jan, 25 Dec. **Open Air**
○ Apr–Oct: 10am–5pm daily.
● Nov–Mar. ▣ Enkhuizen.
▭ leaves from behind train
station.

**★ Apothecaries' Gapers**
*The Apothecary has a wonderful Art Nouveau façade and,
inside, a display of "gapers": brightly painted heads placed
outside Dutch chemists' shops and
used as advertising signs.*

**Shed for
refitting
barges**

**Fish Smoking**
*Herrings, the main catch of the
former Zuiderzee, are preserved
by smoking them over
smouldering woodchips.
They are then ready
for visitors
to eat.*

**Houses brought
from the nearby
island of Urk**

**Houses in this area**
are from Zoutkamp, a
fishing village once on
the Zuiderzee.

**A working windmill**
shows how excess
water was cleared from
the dykes to create
polders *(see pp22–3).*

| 0 metres | 50 |
|---|---|
| 0 yards | 50 |

**The Church**
*The builders of this late-
19th-century church, from
the island of Wieringen,
disguised the organ in a
cupboard to avoid the tax
then levied on church organs.*

### STAR FEATURES

★ **Houses from Urk**

★ **Marine Hall**

★ **Apothecaries' Gapers**

## Marken ⑥

16 km (10 miles) NE of Amsterdam.
🏠 *2,000.* 🚌 🚲 ℹ️ *Damplein 1,*
*Edam. (0299) 315 125.*

UNTIL RECENTLY, Marken was an island fishing community that had changed very little over 200 years. However, the construction of a causeway link between the village and the mainland in 1957 brought an abrupt end to its isolation.

Though the appearance of the village may seem slightly artificial, it is extremely popular with tourists, who are drawn here by its old-world character. The local inhabitants still wear traditional dress and the gabled timber houses are painted in the rather sombre shades of black and green.

Marken's transition from fishing community to tourist centre is neatly symbolized by the local heritage centre, the **Marker Museum** – a cramped fisherman's house packed with brightly painted furniture.

### 🏛 Marker Museum

Kerkbuurt 44. 📞 *(0299) 601904.*
🕐 *Apr–Oct: daily.* 📷

**Yachts and pleasure boats in Volendam's marina**

## Volendam ⑦

18 km (11.5 miles) NE of Amsterdam.
🏠 *18,000.* 🚌 ℹ️ *Zeestraat 37.*
*(0299) 363747.* 🗓 *Sat.*

THE HARBOUR in Volendam is now overrun with tourists and souvenir shops, but the village is still worth exploring for the narrow canals and streets behind the main dykes, an area known as the Doolhof. The residents wear traditional costume: tight bodices, winged lace caps and striped aprons for the women; baggy trousers and jerseys for the men.

Artists flocked to Volendam in the late 19th century to paint views of this pretty town. Many stayed at the Spaander Hotel at No. 15 Haven, and the walls of the hotel's café are covered with paintings accepted by the owners in lieu of payment.

## Zaanse Schans ⑧

Schansend 1, Zaandam 13 km (8 miles)
N of Amsterdam. 🚉 *Koog-Zaandijk*
🏠 *50.* ℹ️ *Zaandam.* 📞 *(075) 6168*
*218.* 🕐 *8:30am–5pm daily (some*
*attractions closed during the week in*
*winter).* 📷 *for some buildings.*
🌐 *www.zaanseschans.nl*

PART OF THE TOWN of Zaandam, Zaanse Schans was created in 1960 as a monument to village life in the 17th century. Shops, cottages, windmills, houses and historic buildings from all over the Zaan region have been relocated here to create a museum village in which people can live and work.

The local community is dedicated to preserving the traditional Dutch way of life, and Zaanse Schans is run as a piece of living history. The inhabitants operate the carefully restored windmills themselves; these include a mustard mill, the last working oil mill still in existence, and mills that generate power. The energy they produce goes to sawing logs for building timber, and to grinding minerals to make pigments used in paint.

In summer, cruises can be taken in open-topped boats along the surrounding dykes.

**A typical 17th-century gabled timber house in Marken**

# Windmill Technology

WINDMILLS HAVE been a familiar feature of the Dutch landscape since the 13th century. They had many uses, including grinding corn, crushing seed to make oil and driving sawmills. However, as much of the Netherlands lies below sea level, their most vital function was to drain the land of lakes and marshes, and extend the shoreline to create fertile farmland called *polder*. Subsequently, the windmills have had to cope with the constant threat of flooding. To help prevent this, canals were dug to drain water from the soil; the mills then pumped excess water via a series of stepped canals until it drained into the main river system. Today, most land drainage is carried out by electric pumps driven by wind turbines. Of the thousands of windmills that once dotted the Dutch countryside, about 950 survive, many preserved in working order.

**Miller in cap and apron**

**Modern aerogenerators**, or wind turbines, are widely used in the Netherlands. They harness strong gusts of wind to create electricity without the pollution caused by burning fossil fuels such as gas or coal.

**Smock mills**, shaped like peasants' smocks, were drainage mills used, from the 17th century, in groups known as gangs. The Archimedes' screw rotated to force the water upwards.

Trelliswork and canvas sail

Drive shaft

Archimedes' screw

Upper channel

**The sails** of this traditional windmill transmit power via mechanical gears. A rotating cog operates an adjacent wheel to drive the water pump.

**Flour mills**, thatched with reeds and shaped like giant pepperpots, were vital to Dutch daily life. Sophisticated internal mechanisms were used to grind the wheat, barley and oats which formed the basis of the community's diet.

Furled sails at rest

The cap could be turned on its axis to face the wind.

Main axle

**Grain** was ground by two vast millstones.

**Canvas cloth** was stretched over the blades.

Wooden sail

**Chutes** carried the flour to be bagged.

# Street-by-Street: Haarlem 🟒

**Misericord in the Grote Kerk**

H AARLEM is the commercial capital of Noord Holland province and the eighth largest city in the Netherlands. It is the centre of the Dutch printing, pharmaceutical and bulb-growing industries, but there is little sign of this in the delightful pedestrianized streets of the historic heart of the city. Most of the sites of interest are within easy walking distance of the Grote Markt, a lively square packed with ancient buildings, cafés and restaurants. Old bookshops, antique dealers and traditional food shops are all to be discovered in nearby streets.

**Statue of Laurens Coster**
*According to local legend, Haarlem-born Laurens Jansz Coster (1370–1440) invented printing in 1423, 16 years before Gutenberg. The 19th-century statue in the Grote Markt celebrates the claim.*

**No. 39 Nieuwe Groenmarkt** is an exceptional cheese shop.

**The Hoofd-wacht** is a 17th-century, former guard house.

**Stadhuis**
*Lieven de Key's allegorical figure of* Justice *(1622) stands above the main entrance. She carries a sword and the scales of justice.*

**Vleeshal** *(1603)*
*The old meat market is part of the Frans Hals Museum (see pp178–9).*

**Grote Markt**
*The tree-lined market square is bordered with busy pavement restaurants and cafés. It has been the meeting point for the townspeople for centuries.*

**★ Grote Kerk**
*The huge church (see p176) is dominated by a decorative organ with soaring pipes (1735), which drew many famous composers to Haarlem.*

**VISITORS' CHECKLIST**

20 km (12.5 miles) W of Amsterdam. 153,000. Stationsplein. Stationsplein 1 (0900) 616 1600. Mon & Sat. Haarlem Jazz Festival: mid Aug; Bloemen Corso: end Apr.

**Shops and houses** cling to the walls of the Grote Kerk.

**★ Teylers Museum**
*Physical and astronomical instruments, like this brass electrostatic generator by Pieter van Marum (1784), form part of the collection in this museum of science, technology and art (see p177).*

JANSSTRAAT

BEGIJNESTRAAT

WIJDE APPELAARSTEEG

KLOKHUIS-PLEIN

NAUWE APPELAARSTEEG

BAKENESSERGRACHT

DONKERE SPAARNE

BINNEN SPAARNE

SPAARNE

**Gravestenenbrug**
*This lift bridge crosses the river Spaarne. Located on the south bank is the embarkation point for boat trips along the river and canals.*

**KEY**

– – –  Suggested route

0 metres    50
0 yards     50

**STAR SIGHTS**

★ Grote Kerk

★ Teylers Museum

# Exploring Haarlem

HAARLEM BECAME A CITY in 1245, and had grown into a thriving clothmaking centre by the 15th century. But in the Spanish siege of 1572–3 the city was sacked, and a series of fires wreaked further destruction in 1576. The town's fortunes changed in the 17th century, when industrial expansion ushered in a period of prosperity lasting throughout the Golden Age *(see pp24–7)*. The centre was largely rebuilt by Lieven de Key (1560–1627) and still retains much of its character. The Grote Kerk continues to overlook the city's *hofjes* (almshouses), and the brick-paved lanes around the Grote Markt are little changed.

*Grote Markt, Haarlem* (c.1668) by Berckheyde, showing the Grote Kerk

## 🏛 Frans Hals Museum
See pp178–9.

## ⛪ Grote Kerk
Oude Groenmarkt 23. 📞 (023) 5532 040. 🌐 www.bavo.nl 🕐 10am–4pm Mon–Sat. 📷 ♿

The enormous Gothic edifice of Sint Bavo's great church, often referred to simply as the Grote Kerk, was a favourite subject of the 17th-century Haarlem School artists Pieter Saenredam (1597–1665) and Gerrit Berckheyde (1639–98). Built between 1400 and 1550, the church and its ornate bell tower dominate the market square. Clinging on to the exterior of the south wall is a jumble of 17th-century shops and houses. The rents raised from these ramshackle, untidy buildings contributed to the maintenance of the church.

Today, the entrance to the Grote Kerk is through one of the surviving shops, a tiny antechamber that leads straight into the enormous nave. The church has a high, delicately patterned, vaulted cedarwood ceiling, white upper walls, and 28 supporting columns painted in greens, reds and golds. The intricate choir screen, like the magnificent brass lectern in the shape of a preening eagle, was made by master metal worker Jan Fyerens in about 1510. The choirstalls (1575) are painted with coats of arms, and the armrests and misericords are carved with caricatures of animals and human heads. Not far away is the simple stone slab covering the grave of Haarlem's most famous artist, Frans Hals.

The Grote Kerk boasts one of Europe's finest and most flamboyant organs, built in 1735 by Christiaan Müller. In 1738 Handel tried the organ and pronounced it excellent. It also found favour with the infant prodigy Mozart, who shouted for joy when he gave a recital on it in 1766. The organ is still often used for concerts, recordings and teaching.

## 🏛 Stadhuis
Grote Markt 2. 📞 (023) 5113 000. 🕐 by appt only or go to reception. ♿

Haarlem's Stadhuis (town hall) has grown rather haphazardly over the centuries and is an odd mixture of architectural styles dating from 1250. The oldest part of the building is the beamed medieval banqueting hall of the counts of Holland *(see p19)*, originally known as the Gravenzaal. Much of this was destroyed in two great fires in 1347 and 1351, but the 15th-century panel portraits of the counts of Holland can still be seen.

The wing of the town hall bordering the Grote Markt was designed by Lieven de Key in 1622. It is typical of Dutch Renaissance architecture, combining elaborate gables, ornate painted detail and Classical features, such as pediments over the windows. In a niche above the main entrance is a plump allegorical figure of Justice, bearing a sword in one hand and scales in the other as she smiles benignly upon the pavement cafés in the market below. To the left, in Koningstraat, an archway leads to the university buildings behind the Stadhuis, where there is a 13th-century cloister and library.

## 🏛 De Hallen (Vleeshal and Verweyhal)
Grote Markt 16. 📞 (023) 5115 775. 🕐 as Frans Hals Museum (p179). ⬤ 1 Jan, 25 Dec. 📷

De Hallen (the halls) is the collective name for two buildings in the Grote Markt which are part of the Frans Hals Museum *(see pp178–9)*. The more recent Verweyhal accommodates exhibitions of Dutch Expressionism, the Cobra School, Impressionism and contemporary works. It is named after the painter Kees Verwey, whose Impressionist still lifes are an important feature of the collection. The heavily ornamented Vleeshal (meat market) is situated just to the west of the church

**Detail on Vleeshal façade by Lieven de Key**

**The west gate of the Amsterdamse Poort (1355)**

and houses temporary exhibitions of modern art. It was built in 1602 by the city surveyor, Lieven de Key, and has a steep step gable which disguises the roof line. The extravagantly over-decorated miniature gables above each dormer window bristle with pinnacles. A giant painted ox's head on the building's façade signifies its original function.

### ⛩ Amsterdamse Poort

Nr Amsterdamsevaart. 🔴 to public.
The imposing medieval gateway that once helped protect Haarlem lies close to the west bank of the river Spaarne. The Amsterdamse Poort was one of a complex of 12 gates guarding strategic transport routes in and out of Haarlem. The gate was built in 1355,

though much of the elaborate brickwork and tiled gables date from the late 15th century.

The city defences were severely tested in 1573, when the Spanish, led by Frederick of Toledo, besieged Haarlem for seven months during the Dutch Revolt *(see pp22–3)*. The city fathers agreed to surrender the town on terms that included a general amnesty for all its citizens. The Spanish appeared to accept, but once the city gates were opened, they marched in and treacherously slaughtered nearly 2,000 people – almost the entire population of the city.

### 🏛 Teylers Museum

Spaarne 16. 🔲 *(023) 5319 010.*
🆅 www.teylersmuseum.nl
🅾 *Tue–Sun.* 🔴 *1 Jan, 25 Dec.* 🈺 ♿
This was first major public museum to be founded in the Netherlands. It was established in 1778 by the silk merchant Pieter Teyler van der Hulst to encourage the study of science and art. The museum's eccentric collection of fossils, drawings and scientific paraphernalia is displayed in Neo-Classical splendour in a series of 18th-century rooms. The two-storey Oval Hall was added in 1779, and contains bizarre glass cabinets full of minerals and cases of intimidating medical instruments. A significant collection of sketches by Dutch and Italian masters, including Rembrandt and Michelangelo, are shown a few at a time.

**Tiles in Haarlem Station**

### 🏛 St Elisabeth's Gasthuis Historisch Museum Kennemerland

Groot Heiligland 47. 🔲 *(023) 5422 427.* 🅾 *Tue–Sun.* 🔴 *1 Jan, 25 Dec.*
Haarlem is well known for its *hofjes* (almshouses) that were set up to minister to the poor and sick *(see p93)*. Almshouses began to appear in the 16th century, and were run by rich guild members, who took over the role traditionally filled by the monasteries until the Alteration of 1578 *(see pp22–3)*.

St Elisabeth's Gasthuis was built in 1610, around a pretty courtyard opposite what is now the Frans Hals Museum. A stone plaque carved above the main doorway in 1612 depicts an invalid being carried off to hospital. After extensive restoration this almshouse was opened in 1995 as Haarlem's principal historical museum.

### 🚉 Haarlem Station

Stationsplein. 🔲 *0900 92 92.*
The first railway line in the Netherlands opened in 1839 and ran between Haarlem and Amsterdam *(see pp30–31)*. The original station, built in 1842, was reworked in Art Nouveau style between 1905–8. It is a grandiose brick building with an arched façade and square towers. The green and beige interior is decorated with brightly coloured tiles depicting modes of transport. Other highlights are the timberwork of the offices and highly decorative wrought-iron staircases.

**17th- and 18th-century gabled houses along the river Spaarne in Haarlem**

# Frans Hals Museum

HAILED AS the first "modern" artist, Frans Hals (c.1582–1666) introduced a new realism into painting. While contemporary painters aimed for an exact likeness, Hals captured the character of his sitters through a more impressionistic technique. In his eighties, he still painted passionate portraits, such as *The Governesses of the Old Men's Home* (1664). The Old Men's Home, one of many in Haarlem, became the Frans Hals Museum in 1913. Besides his work, there is a selection of Dutch painting and applied art from the 16th and 17th centuries.

**Mother and Child**
*Following the Alteration (see pp22–3), artists like Pieter de Grebber (1600–53) often painted secular versions of religious themes. This painting (c.1630) of a woman suckling her baby recalls the Virgin Mary with Jesus.*

## STAR PAINTINGS

- ★ **Banquet of the Officers by Frans Hals**

- ★ **Still Life by Floris van Dijck**

- ★ **Mercury by Hendrick Goltzius**

## KEY TO FLOORPLAN

- ☐ Works by Frans Hals
- ☐ Renaissance Gallery
- ☐ Old Masters
- ☐ Applied art and design
- ☐ Temporary exhibitions
- ☐ Non-exhibition space

Chapel

Hals's Civic Guard portraits

18th-century doll's house

**★ Banquet of the Officers of the Civic Guard of St George** *(1616)*
*The characteristics of each of the 12 Civic Guards and the opulence of their banqueting hall are superbly portrayed in this formal group portrait by Frans Hals.*

**Delft Dish** *(1662)*
*This blue-and-white earthenware dish by M Eems shows the Grote Kerk and Grote Markt in Haarlem (see p176).*

**Doll's House** *(c. 1750)*
*This 11 room house, which belonged to Sara Rothé, is made to a scale of 1:10. Its representation is so realistic that it offers a good view into what it was like inside an 18th-century canal-side mansion (see pp28–9).*

**VISITORS' CHECKLIST**

Groot Heiligland 62, Haarlem.
📞 *(023) 511 5775.* W www.
franshalsmuseum.nl 🚉 *Haarlem.*
⏰ *11am–5pm Tue–Sat (last adm 4:30pm); noon–5pm Sun & public hols.* ● *1 Jan, 25 Dec.* 📷
📷 ♿ 🚻 🍴 🛗

★ **Mercury** *(1611)*
*Hendrick Goltzius (1558–1617) painted a lot of biblical and mythological scenes. This canvas was commissioned by a wealthy Haarlem burgomaster as one of a series of three.*

Small courtyard

**MUSEUM GUIDE**
*The entrance leads into a modern wing with a museum shop. The best route is anti-clockwise; displays of Frans Hals' work, other portraits, still life and many other paintings are usually reordered each year. Exhibits of modern art are held in De Hallen (Vleeshal and Verweyhal) which are in the Grote Markt (see p176).*

**An Allegory on Tulip Mania** *(c. 1640)*
*Jan Breughel II's painting ridicules the obsession with tulips that was gripping Holland at the time.*

Main entrance

★ **Still Life** *(1613)*
*Precise attention to detail and texture was the hallmark of Floris van Dijck (1575–1651). The damask tablecloth shown in the painting was a product of Haarlem's thriving linen industry.*

# A Tour of the Bulbfields ⑩

OCCUPYING A 30-KM (19-MILE) STRIP between Haarlem and Leiden, the Bloembollenstreek is the most important bulb-growing area in the Netherlands. From late January, the polders bloom with a succession of vividly coloured bulbs, beginning with early crocuses and building to a climax around mid-April when the tulips flower. These are followed by late-blooming flowers like lilies, which extend the season into late May. If you don't have a car, the VVV *(see p256)* has details on a variety of tours. Alternatively, you can hire a bicycle at Haarlem railway station and drop it off at Leiden station.

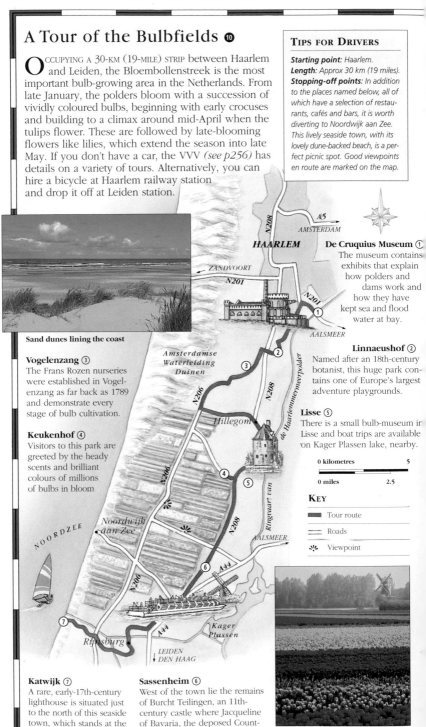

## TIPS FOR DRIVERS

**Starting point:** *Haarlem.*
**Length:** *Approx 30 km (19 miles).*
**Stopping-off points:** *In addition to the places named below, all of which have a selection of restaurants, cafés and bars, it is worth diverting to Noordwijk aan Zee. This lively seaside town, with its lovely dune-backed beach, is a perfect picnic spot. Good viewpoints en route are marked on the map.*

**Sand dunes lining the coast**

**De Cruquius Museum ①**
The museum contains exhibits that explain how polders and dams work and how they have kept sea and flood water at bay.

**Linnaeushof ②**
Named after an 18th-century botanist, this huge park contains one of Europe's largest adventure playgrounds.

**Lisse ⑤**
There is a small bulb-museum in Lisse and boat trips are available on Kager Plassen lake, nearby.

**Vogelenzang ③**
The Frans Rozen nurseries were established in Vogelenzang as far back as 1789 and demonstrate every stage of bulb cultivation.

**Keukenhof ④**
Visitors to this park are greeted by the heady scents and brilliant colours of millions of bulbs in bloom

| 0 kilometres | | 5 |
| 0 miles | | 2.5 |

### KEY

| | |
|---|---|
| ▬ | Tour route |
| ⋯ | Roads |
| ✲ | Viewpoint |

**Katwijk ⑦**
A rare, early-17th-century lighthouse is situated just to the north of this seaside town, which stands at the mouth of the Oude Rijn.

**Sassenheim ⑥**
West of the town lie the remains of Burcht Teilingen, an 11th-century castle where Jacqueline of Bavaria, the deposed Countess of Holland, died in 1436.

**A tulip field in the Bloembollenstreek**

## DUTCH BULBS

The most cultivated bulbs in the Netherlands include gladioli, lilies, daffodils, hyacinths, irises, crocuses and dahlias. Tulips, however, are still far and away the country's most cultivated flower. Originally from Turkey, the tulip was first grown in Dutch soil by Carolus Clusius in 1593.

**Aladdin tulips**

**China pink tulips**

**Tahiti daffodils**

**Minnow daffodils**

**Blue jacket hyacinths**

An array of bulbs in flower in the wooded Keukenhof park

## Aalsmeer ⑪

10 km (6 miles) south of Amsterdam. 🏠 22,000. 🚉 🛈 Driekolommen-plein 1. (0297) 325374. 🗓 Tue.

Aalsmeer is home to the largest flower auction in the world, the Bloemenveiling. Visitors can watch the colourful proceedings from a special viewing gallery, suspended above the frenetic activity on the trading floors. As the 3.5 billion cut flowers and 400 million pot plants sold here annually all have a short shelf-life, speed is of the essence. A clock above the auctioneer's head shows the prices falling as the hand sweeps round, from 100 to 1. When it reaches the price that bidders are willing to pay, the clock stops.

## Lisse ⑫

35 km (22 miles) west of Amsterdam. 🏠 26,000. 🚉 🛈 Grachtweg 53. (0252) 414262.

The best time to visit Lisse is at the end of April, when the town mounts a series of colourful flower parades.

The **Museum de Zwarte Tulp** (the Black Tulip Museum), has displays on the history and life cycle of bulbs.

Imported from Turkey in the early 17th century, by the mid-1630s "tulip mania" gripped the nation (see pp24–5). At the height of the boom rare bulbs were sold for their weight in gold. By February 1637 however, the market had collapsed leaving bankruptcy in its wake.

### 🏛 Museum de Zwarte Tulp

Grachtweg 2a. 📞 (0252) 417 900. 🗓 Tue–Sun. 🔴 1 Jan, 25 & 26 Dec. 🌐

## Keukenhof ⑬

Stationsweg, Lisse. 📞 (0252) 465555. 🗓 late-Mar–mid-May daily. 🌐

Set in 28 ha (70 acres) of wooded park on the outskirts of Lisse, Keukenhof is one of the most spectacular flower gardens in the world. It was set up in 1949 as a showcase for Dutch bulb growers and is now planted with some 7 million bulbs. It is at its most spectacular from late March to late May, when drifts of daffodils, hyacinths or tulips are in bloom. The array of flowers is complemented by the snowy blossom of Japanese cherry trees early in the season, and by showy splashes of azaleas and rhododendrons later in the year.

# Street-by-Street: Leiden ⑭

**L**EIDEN IS A PROSPEROUS university town, with its origins in Roman times. It grew due to its position on a branch of the Rijn (Rhine) and is still an important commercial crossroads. During term-time, the streets are crowded with students cycling between lectures or packing the cafés and bookshops. A number of exceptional museums document Leiden's turbulent history, including the Golden Age, when the town was a centre for world-wide trade *(see pp24–5)*. The wall plaque on the façade of Rembrandt's house in Weddesteeg marks his birthplace in June 1606 *(see p62)*.

**Statue of Justice on Stadhuis wall**

**★ Rijksmuseum van Oudheden**
*This squat statue of a kneeling treasury scribe is among the many Egyptian artifacts in the museum.*

**John Robinson** *(see p185)* lived in the Jan Pesijnshofje.

LANGEBRUG

PAPENGRACHT

SCHOOLSTEEG

GERECHT

HOUTSTRAAT

RAPENBURG

**★ Hortus Botanicus**
*The botanical gardens (see p184) are owned by Leiden University, and were laid out initially as a study aid for botany students in 1587.*

KLOKSTEEG

NONNENSTRAAT

**Oude Rijn**
*Many of the gabled houses along Leiden's canals have shops and cafés on the ground floor.*

**Neo-Classical houses on Rapenburg**

**University library**

**Het Gravensteen**
*The university's law faculty lies behind the Classical façade of this complex of buildings, which grew up between the 13th and 17th centuries.*

**Hoogstraat**
*Crossing the meeting point of the Rijn (Rhine) canals, Hoogstraat is popular for its floating cafés and restaurants.*

**Pieterskerkhof** is a cobbled lane with antiquarian bookshops.

**Korenbeursbrug**
*The stone bridge over the Nieuwe Rijn was roofed over in 1825 in Neo-Classical style to shelter corn merchants' stalls.*

**Stadhuis (1595) by Lieven de Key**

**★ Pieterskerk**
*This ethereal tombstone marks the oldest intact grave in the Netherlands – that of 15th-century merchant Floris van Boschuysen and his wife.*

**STAR SIGHTS**

★ **Rijksmuseum van Oudheden**

★ **Pieterskerk**

★ **Hortus Botanicus**

**KEY**

- - - Suggested route

0 metres 50
0 yards 50

# Exploring Leiden

L EIDEN IS FAMOUS for its university, the oldest and most prestigious in the Netherlands. It was founded in 1575 by William of Orange, a year after he relieved the town from a year-long siege by the Spanish *(see pp22–3)*. As a reward for their endurance, William offered the citizens of Leiden a choice of the building of a university or the abolition of tax. They chose wisely, and the city's reputation as a centre of intellectual and religious tolerance was firmly established. English Puritan dissidents, victims of persecution in their homeland, were able to settle here in the 17th century before undertaking their epic voyage to the New World.

**Arched gazebo within a walled garden in the Hortus Botanicus**

## 🏛 Stedelijk Museum De Lakenhal

Oude Singel 28–32. 📞 *(071) 5165 360*. 🌐 www.lakenhal.nl 🕐 *Tue–Sun.* ⬤ *1 Jan, 25 Dec.* 📷 ♿ 🛍 🎁

The Lakenhal (cloth hall) was the 17th-century headquarters of Leiden's cloth trade. Built in 1640 in Dutch Classical style by Arent van 's Gravesande, it houses the municipal museum, with temporary exhibitions of modern art and furniture from the 16th century onwards.

The pride of the collection is Lucas van Leyden's Renaissance triptych of *The Last Judgment* (1526–7), rescued from the Pieterskerk during the religious struggles of 1566 *(see pp22–3)*. A wing built in the 1920s offers a silver collection, furniture and exhibits covering the local weaving industry. Not to be missed is a big bronze *hutspot*, or

cauldron, allegedly left behind by the Spanish when William of Orange broke the siege in 1574. The cauldron contained a spicy stew which the starving people ate. This meal is now cooked every year on 3 October, to commemorate Dutch victory over the Spanish.

## 🌿 Hortus Botanicus der Rijksuniversiteit Leiden

Rapenburg 73. 📞 *(071) 5277 249*. 🌐 www.hortus.leidenuniv.nl 🕐 *daily in summer, Sun–Fri in winter.* ⬤ *3 Oct, 25 Dec–1 Jan.* 📷 ♿ *partial.*

Leiden's botanical garden was founded in 1587 as part of the university. The varied trees and shrubs include a 350-year-old laburnum planted shortly after the gardens were

set up. Carolus Clusius, who was responsible for introducing the tulip to the Netherlands in 1593 *(see pp24–5)*, became the first professor of botany at Leiden University. Today the Hortus Botanicus contains a modern reconstruction of his original walled garden, called the Clusiustuin. Other delights include hothouses full of exotic orchids, rose gardens and colourful beds of tulips planted around ponds.

## 🏛 Museum Boerhaave

Lange St Agnietenstraat 10. 📞 *(071) 5214 224*. 🌐 www.museumboer haave.nl 🕐 *Tue–Sun.* ⬤ *1 Jan, 3 Oct.* 📷

The Leiden physician, Herman Boerhaave (1668–1738), wrote the definitive 18th-century medical textbook, called *Institutiones Medicae*. The museum

**Lucas van Leyden's triptych of *The Last Judgment* in the Stedelijk Museum de Lakenhal**

named after him is devoted to the development of science in the Netherlands and contains reconstructions of an anatomy theatre and hospital wards. The displays are arranged chronologically and include pendulum clocks made by Christiaan Huygens (1629–95), the discoverer of Saturn's rings, and thermometers by Gabriel Fahrenheit (1686–1736). The collection of surgical instruments is not for the squeamish.

## 🏛 Rijksmuseum voor Volkenkunde

Steenstraat 1. (071) 5168 800.
www.rmv.nl ⃝ Tue–Sun.
1 Jan, 3 Oct, 25 Dec.

This outstanding ethnological museum, founded in 1837, houses collections from non-western cultures. Individual displays are linked together to create a worldwide cultural journey that shows both the differences and connections between cultures. Temporary exhibitions feature living conditions across the world, from the Arctic wastes to the hills of China, adding to this eclectic museum's wide appeal to people of all age groups.

**Heraldic lion at De Burcht**

## 🏛 Stedelijk Molenmuseum de Valk

2e Binnenvestgracht 1. (071) 5165 353. ⃝ Tue–Sun. 1 Jan, 3 Oct, 25 Dec.
This towering grain mill, built in 1743, is Leiden's last remaining mill. It is an imposing seven storeys high, and now restored to its original working state. A tour takes in the living quarters on the ground floor, the repair workshop and a retrospective exhibition on the history of Dutch windmills.

## 🏛 Pieterskerk

Pieterskerkhof 1a. (071) 5124 319.
⃝ daily (opening times vary; phone in advance). 3 Oct, 31 Dec.
The magnificent Gothic church was built in the 15th century in rose-pink brick, and stands in a leafy square surrounded by elegant houses. Now a

---

## THE PILGRIM FATHERS

The Netherlands was proudly Protestant by the 17th century, giving refuge to Puritans fleeing persecution in England. Preacher John Robinson (1575–1625) established a church in Leiden in 1609, inspiring his congregation with visions of a new Jerusalem in the New World. The Pilgrim Fathers set sail from Delfshaven in 1620 in the *Speedwell*, which proved unseaworthy. Putting in at Plymouth, England, they crossed the Atlantic in the *Mayflower* to found Plymouth, Massachusetts. Robinson was too ill to travel, dying in Leiden in 1625.

**The *Mayflower* crossing the Atlantic Ocean**

community centre, the church is worth visiting for its austere interior and its organ, built by the Hagenbeer brothers in 1642 and enclosed in gilded woodwork. The floor of the nave is covered with worn slabs marking the burial places of 17th-century intellectuals like Puritan leader John Robinson and Golden Age artist, Jan Steen *(see p133)*.

## ♣ De Burcht

Nieuwe Rijn. **Battlements**
⃝ daily.
De Burcht is an odd 12th-century fortress with crenellated battlements. It sits between two channels of the Rijn (Rhine) atop a grassy, man-made mound, thought to be of Saxon origin. The fortress is reached by a wrought-iron gate covered in heraldic symbols. The top of the citadel offers superb views over Leiden.

---

## 🏛 Rijksmuseum van Oudheden

Rapenburg 28. (071) 5163 163.
www.rmo.nl ⃝ Tue–Sun.
1 Jan, 3 Oct, 25 Dec.
The Dutch museum of antiquities, established in 1818, is Leiden's main attraction. The centrepiece of the collection is the Egyptian Temple of Taffeh, reassembled in the main exhibition hall in 1978. It dates from the 1st century AD, and was dedicated to Isis, Egyptian goddess of fertility, from the 4th century AD.

The museum's collection of Egyptian artifacts is very rich indeed, and occupies much of the first two floors. Alongside there are impressive displays of musical instuments, textiles and shoes, expressive Etruscan bronzework and fragments of Roman mosaic and frescoes.

The upper floor of the museum holds an exhibition of Dutch archaeology which begins in prehistoric times and runs to the Middle Ages.

**A lift bridge across the Oude Rijn in Leiden**

# Den Haag ⓯

**Statue in
Binnenhof
courtyard**

D EN HAAG ('s-Gravenhage or The Hague) is
the political capital of the Netherlands,
home to prestigious institutions such as the
Dutch Parliament and International Court of
Justice, located in the Vredespaleis (see p190).
When Den Haag became the seat of government in 1586, it was a small town built around
the castle of the counts of Holland. That same
castle, much rebuilt, now stands at the heart of
a city which is home to half a million people.
It is surrounded by public buildings, such as
the Mauritshuis (see pp188–9), and protected
to the north by the remains of a moat which
forms the Hofvijver (lake). To the west is the
seaside town of Scheveningen (see p191).

## 🏛 Mauritshuis
See pp188–9.

## 🏰 Ridderzaal
Binnenhof 8a. 📞 (070) 364 6144. 🕐
Mon–Sat (phone in advance). ● Sun &
public hols. 🈺 🚻
By the side of the Hofvijver is
the Binnenhof courtyard. In
the centre of this stands the
fairy-tale, double-turreted
Gothic Ridderzaal (Hall of the
Knights). This was the 13th-
century dining hall of Floris V,
Count of Holland (see p19).
Since 1904, the hall's function
has been primarily ceremonial;
it is used for the opening of
the Dutch Parliament by the
monarch, and for other state
occasions. It is open to visitors
when parliament is not sitting
in its new premises in the
complex. A tour takes in the
two former debating chambers
and an exhibition about demo-
cracy in the Netherlands.

## 🏛 Museum Bredius
Lange Vijverberg 14. 📞 (070) 362
0729. W www.museumbredius.nl 🕐
Tue–Sun. ● 1 Jan & 25 Dec. 🈺 🚻
Dr Abraham Bredius was an art
historian and collector as well
as director of the Mauritshuis
(see pp188–9) from 1895 to
1922. On his death in 1946, he
bequeathed his vast collection
of 17th-century art to the city
of Den Haag. This bequest is
displayed in a distinguished
18th-century merchant's house
on the north side of the Hofvijver, and features around 200
Golden Age paintings – famous
works by Dutch Masters such
as Rembrandt (see p66) and
Jan Steen (see p133), and
others by lesser-known artists.
   The building itself has undergone considerable renovation,
and now contains an equally
impressive collection of antique
furniture, delicate porcelain
and elaborate silverware.

## 🄰 Grote Kerk
Rond de Grote Kerk 10. 📞 (070) 302
8630. 🕐 during exhibitions only. ♿
In its present form, the Grote
Kerk dates mainly from 1539,
but has undergone major rebuilding between 1985 and
1987. Its most impressive feature is a stained-glass window
which depicts Charles V, the
Holy Roman Emperor (see
pp22–3), kneeling at the feet
of the Virgin Mary. The church
is at the centre of Den Haag's
pedestrianized shopping area,
which has many upmarket
galleries selling works of art.

**Coat of arms on façade of
Rijksmuseum Gevangenpoort**

## 🏛 Rijksmuseum
## Gevangenpoort
Buitenhof 33. 📞 (070) 346 0861.
W www.gevangenpoort.nl
🕐 Tue–Sun. ● 1 Jan, 25 Dec.
🈺 🚻 🔲 🚻
The Gevangenpoort (prison
gate) was originally the main
gateway to the 14th-century
castle of the counts of Holland.
Later, it was turned into a jail,
becoming infamous during a
period of violent social unrest
in the late 17th century when
burgomaster Cornelis de Witt
(see p25) was confined and
tortured here. Both he and his
brother Jan were subsequently
tried for heresy, and torn limb
from limb outside the prison
gate by a rioting mob.
   Appropriately, the building
is now a prison museum. On
display is a unique collection
of torture instruments, accompanied by a stereo soundtrack
of blood-curdling screams.

**The Hofvijver and parliament buildings in Den Haag**

**Paintings in Galerij Prins Willem V**

🏛 **Galerij Prins Willem V**
Buitenhof 35. 📞 (070) 302 3456.
🌐 www.mauritshuis.nl 🕐 Tue–Sun.
⚫ 1 Jan, 25 Dec. 🎫 📷
In his youth, Prince William V (see p28) was a collector of Golden Age paintings. His collection was opened to the public in 1774, inside this former inn, which the prince had converted for use as his *kabinet* – the 18th-century Dutch word for an art gallery. The Galerij is the oldest art gallery in the Netherlands. The contemporary fashion for covering every available inch of wall space with paintings has been retained, and so several pictures are hung too high and too close together. Not all are annotated, which may lead to some confusion for the viewer, but many of Prince William's original purchases are still to be seen. Old Master paintings by Rembrandt, Jan Steen and Paulus Potter (1625–54) are included in a collection that consists principally of typically Dutch Golden Age landscapes, genre works, "conversation pieces" and recreations of historical events (see p132).

🏛 **Haags Historisch Museum**
Korte Vijverberg 7. 📞 (070) 364 6940.
🌐 www.haagshistorischmuseum.nl
🕐 Tue–Sun. ⚫ 1 Jan, 25 Dec. 🎫
♿ ⛔
Den Haag's history museum is in the Sebastiaansdoelen, a Dutch Classical mansion built in 1636 and the former headquarters of the Civic Guard of St Sebastian. Exhibitions tell the story of Den Haag's growth since the Middle Ages. The displays change periodic-ally and are drawn from the city's collection of landscapes, portraits and genre paintings (see pp132–3) as well as 17th- and 18th-century furnishings. There is also a luxurious 19th-century dolls' house.

**VISITORS' CHECKLIST**

56 km (35 miles) SW of Amsterdam. 🚗 446,000.
🚆 Koningin Julianaplein 10; Stationsplein 25.
ℹ Koningin Julianaplein 30. 0900 340 3505.
🚤 Mon, Wed, Fri, Sat.
🎉 Vlaggetjesdag Scheveningen: last Sat in May or first Sat in Jun; North Sea Jazz Festival: mid-Jul.

**The 17th-century façade of the Haags Historisch Museum**

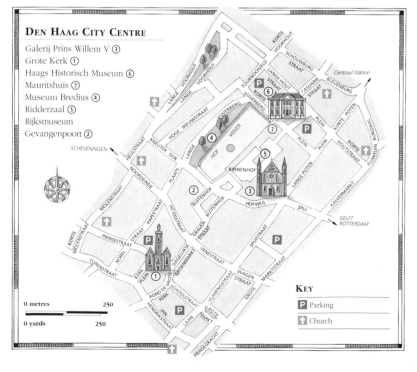

**DEN HAAG CITY CENTRE**

Galerij Prins Willem V ③
Grote Kerk ①
Haags Historisch Museum ⑥
Mauritshuis ⑦
Museum Bredius ④
Ridderzaal ⑤
Rijksmuseum
Gevangenpoort ②

**KEY**

🅿 Parking
⛪ Church

0 metres 250
0 yards 250

# The Mauritshuis

THE COUNT OF NASSAU, Johann Maurits, commissioned this graceful house after he retired as the governor of Brazil. It was completed in 1644 by Pieter Post in Dutch Classical style with influences from Italian Renaissance architecture, and enjoys wonderful views across the Hofvijver *(see p186)*. The mansion was bequeathed to the state after Maurits's death in 1679, and has been the home of the Royal Picture Gallery since 1821. The collection is small, but almost every painting is a superb work by one of the Old Masters. This, combined with the exquisite presentation in elegant period rooms, makes the Mauritshuis one of the finest galleries in the Netherlands.

★ **The Anatomy Lesson of Dr Nicolaes Tulp** *(1632)*
*Rembrandt's painting of surgeons examining a corpse reflects the burgeoning contemporary interest in anatomy and science.*

## GALLERY GUIDE

*The Mauritshuis, a small art gallery set on three floors, is packed with paintings. The displays are changed constantly in order to cover all aspects of the collection. Information sheets are available in English, listing the principal works. The arrangement of the paintings is delightfully jumbled, and many of the pictures are not labelled. If in doubt, ask for help from one of the well-informed gallery attendants. The permanent collection is subject to changes.*

**Portrait of Cornelis Schellinger** *(1584)*
*The verse on Pieter Pietersz's portrait refers to William of Orange's murder (see p195).*

Ground floor

Offices and administration

**Vase with Flowers** *(1618)*
*Ambrosius Bosschaert captured the beauty of early summer flowers, but the flies buzzing around them are there to remind us of our mortality.*

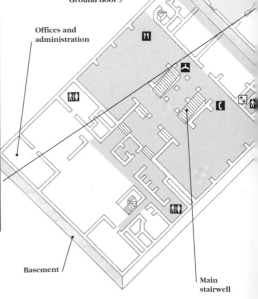

Basement

Main stairwell

**The Goldfinch** *(1654)*
*This tiny, delicate painting is by Carel Fabritius (1622–54), who was a pupil of Rembrandt.*

Main stairs (first floor)

First floor

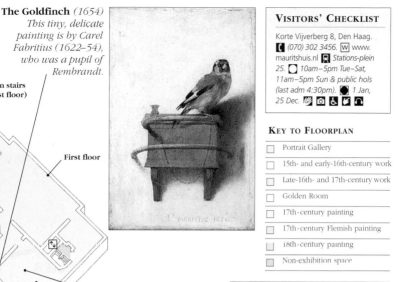

**KEY TO FLOORPLAN**

| | |
|---|---|
| ☐ | Portrait Gallery |
| ☐ | 15th- and early-16th-century work |
| ☐ | Late-16th- and 17th-century work |
| ☐ | Golden Room |
| ☐ | 17th-century painting |
| ☐ | 17th-century Flemish painting |
| ☐ | 18th-century painting |
| ☐ | Non-exhibition space |

**The Way You Hear It is the Way You Sing It** *(1665)*
*A serious moral is implicit in Jan Steen's allegorical genre painting (see p131) warning adults not to set a bad example to their offspring.*

★ **The Louse Hunt** *(1653)*
*Gerard ter Borch's painting is a scene of obsessive domesticity. It reflects the preoccupation of the 17th-century Dutch with order, cleanliness and social respectability.*

Main entrance

★ **Girl with a Turban** *(1660)*
*This haunting portrait was painted during the most successful middle period of Jan Vermeer's career. The model may have been his daughter, Maria.*

**STAR PAINTINGS**

★ **Girl with a Turban by Jan Vermeer**

★ **The Louse Hunt by Gerard ter Borch**

★ **The Anatomy Lesson of Dr Nicolaes Tulp by Rembrandt**

## ⚜ Vredespaleis

Carnegieplein 2. 📞 *(070) 302 4137.*
⊙ *Mon–Fri.* ⚿ *compulsory (phone in advance).* ● *public hols and when court is in session.* 📷

In 1899, Den Haag played host to the first international peace conference. This then led to the formation of the Permanent Court of Arbitration, which had the aim of maintaining world peace. To provide a suitably august home for the court, the Scottish-born philanthropist, Andrew Carnegie (1835–1918) donated £1 million towards the building of the mock-Gothic Vredespaleis (peace palace), which was designed by French architect Louis Cordonnier.

The enormous palace was completed in 1913, and many of the member nations of the Court of Arbitration contributed to the interior's rich decoration. Today the Vredespaleis is the seat of the United Nations' International Court of Justice, which was formed in 1946 as successor to the Permanent Court of Arbitration.

## 🏛 Haags Gemeentemuseum

Stadhouderslaan 41. 📞 *(070) 338 1111.* 🌐 *www.gemeentemuseum.nl*
⊙ *Tue–Sun.* ● *1 Jan, 25 Dec.* 📷 ♿ 🅿🛍📷

The Gemeentemuseum is one of the town's finest museums. The building was the last work of HP Berlage, the father of the architectural movement known as the Amsterdam School *(see p97)*. The museum was completed in 1935, a year after his death, and is built in sandy-coloured stone on two storeys round a central courtyard.

The exhibits are displayed in three sections. Highlights of the superb applied arts section include antique Delftware, Islamic and Oriental porcelain

Vredespaleis, home to the International Court of Justice

and the world's largest collection of paintings by Piet Mondriaan *(see p136)*. An annexe to the main building houses an exhibition of every-day costume worn in the 18th century onwards, including showcases on jewellery and fashion photography.

Probably the museum's main attraction is the collection of musical instruments which date from the 15th to 19th centuries. European instruments include harpsichords and pocket-size fiddles; more exotic is a Java-nese *gamelan*, which consists of gongs and drums.

## 🏛 Panorama Mesdag

Zeestraat 65. 📞 *(070) 310 6665.*
⊙ *daily.* ● *25 Dec.* 📷

This painted cyclorama is important both as a work of Dutch Impressionism and as a rare surviving example of 19th-century entertainment. The vast painting is 120 m (400 ft) around, and lines the inside wall of a circular, canopied pavilion. It shows the old fishing village of Scheveningen, 10 km (6 miles) north of Den Haag.

The astonishingly realistic effect of the painting is achieved through the brilliant use of perspective, enhanced by the natural daylight, which falls on to the canvas from above. Real sand and drift-wood piled at the foot of the painting add to the illusion. The canvas was painted in 1881 by members of the Dutch Impressionist School, led by HW Mesdag (1831–1915) and his wife, Sientje (1834–1909). George Hendrik Breitner (1857–1923) later added his personal touch by painting a group of cavalry officers charging along the beach on horseback.

Haags Gemeentemuseum (1935), designed by HP Berlage

### 🏛 Omniversum

President Kennedylaan 5. ☎ *(070) 354 5454.* ⬭ *daily.* 🖼 ♿ 🖵

The Omniversum is a cross between a planetarium and a space-age cinema, and is especially appealing to children. It has a high-tech sound system and a massive dome-shaped screen, on to which films and lasers are projected. These are combined to create stunning three-dimensional images of space exploration, volcanic eruptions and life beneath the ocean's surface.

### 🏛 Madurodam

George Maduroplein 1. ☎ *(070) 355 3900.* ⬭ *daily.* 🖼 ♿ 🍴 🚻

Madurodam is a model of a composite Dutch city, built to a scale of 1:25. It incorporates replicas of the Vredespaleis and Binnenhof in Den Haag, the canal houses of Amsterdam, Rotterdam's Europoort *(see p199)* and Schiphol Airport *(pp266–7)*, along with windmills, polders, bulbfields and a nudist beach. At night the streets and buildings are illuminated by 50,000 tiny lights.

The model city was opened by Queen Juliana in 1952. It was conceived by JML Maduro as a memorial to his son George, who died at Dachau concentration camp in 1945. All profits go to children's charities.

**Scale models in the miniature town of Madurodam**

## Scheveningen ⓰

45 km (28 miles) SW of Amsterdam. 🚶 *17,800.* 🚊 🛈 *Gevers Deijnootweg 1134 (0900 340 3505).* 🛍 *Thu.*

THE RESORT of Scheveningen is only a 15-minute tram-ride from the centre of Den Haag. Like many Dutch seaside towns, it had its heyday in the 19th century, and is now a mixture of faded gentility and seediness. Even so, it has retained its popularity as a holiday destination, mainly due to stretches of clean, sandy

beaches as well as a pier, built earlier this century, which is currently being restored. There is no shortage of places to eat, including some good seafood restaurants. The imposing French Empire-style Kurhaus, now a luxury hotel with its own casino, was built in 1885 when Scheveningen was still an important spa town.

Modern amenities include the **Sea Life Centre**, nearby, where visitors can walk in see-through tunnels for underwater views of stingrays, sharks and other forms of sea life. It is also a sanctuary for all kinds of wounded marine creatures.

The town has swallowed up the original fishing village of Scheveningen Haven, which has still managed to maintain some of its traditional fishing industry. The south side of the harbour is the departure point for tourists' fishing trips.

Close by is the small **Zee Museum** of marine biology. It is found in the former auction hall of the fish market and looks out across the marina. It houses exhibits of marine life from around the world

### 🐟 Sea Life Centre

Strandweg 13. ☎ *(070) 354 2100.* ⬭ *daily.* ● *25 Dec.* 🖼 ♿ 📷 🍴

### 🏛 Zee Museum

Dr Lelykàde 39. ☎ *(070) 350 2528.* ⬭ *daily.* ● *1 Jan, 25 Dec.* 🖼 ♿ 🚻

**Holiday-makers on Scheveningen's popular sandy beach**

# Street-by-Street: Delft 🔢

**19th-century Delft tile showing a church and barges**

THE ORIGINS OF DELFT date from 1075 and its prosperity was based on weaving and brewing. However, a massive explosion at the national arsenal destroyed much of the medieval town in October 1645. The centre was rebuilt in the late 17th century and the sleepy old town has changed little since then – gabled Gothic and Renaissance houses still line the tree-shaded canals. Activity centres on the market square, bordered by the landmarks of the Stadhuis and Nieuwe Kerk. Visitors can dip into the scores of shops selling antiques and expensive, hand-painted Delftware. Tours of local factories are available, and their shops are often reasonably priced.

**★ Stedelijk Museum Het Prinsenhof**
*Here you can see bullet holes where William of Orange was murdered in 1584*

**Volkenkundig Museum Nusantara**

**★ Oude Kerk**
*The 13th-century Oude Kerk contains tombs of eminent Delft citizens like Antonie van Leeuwenhoek, inventor of the microscope.*

**Oude Delft** is lined with Renaissance canal houses.

**Chapel of St Hippolytus**
*This simple, red-brick Gothic chapel (1396) was used as an ammunition store during the Alteration (see pp22–3).*

## STAR SIGHTS

★ Oude Kerk

★ Nieuwe Kerk

★ Stedelijk Museum Het Prinsenhof

**KEY**

- - - Suggested route

0 metres　　50
0 yards　　50

**View of Delft** *(c.1660)*
*Jan Vermeer's painting captures the town of Delft on a gloomy summer afternoon. The original spire of the Nieuwe Kerk is clearly visible in the distance.*

### Visitors' Checklist

50 km (31 miles) SW of Amsterdam. *95,000.* *Stationsplein.* *Markt 85. (0900) 335 3888.* *Thu, Sat.* *Jazz/Blues Festival: mid Aug; Delft Dag: last Sat in Aug.*

**Stadhuis** *(1618)*
*The Renaissance town hall was designed by Hendrick de Keyser and is adorned with stone lions' heads. It was built around a Gothic tower of the 13th-century.*

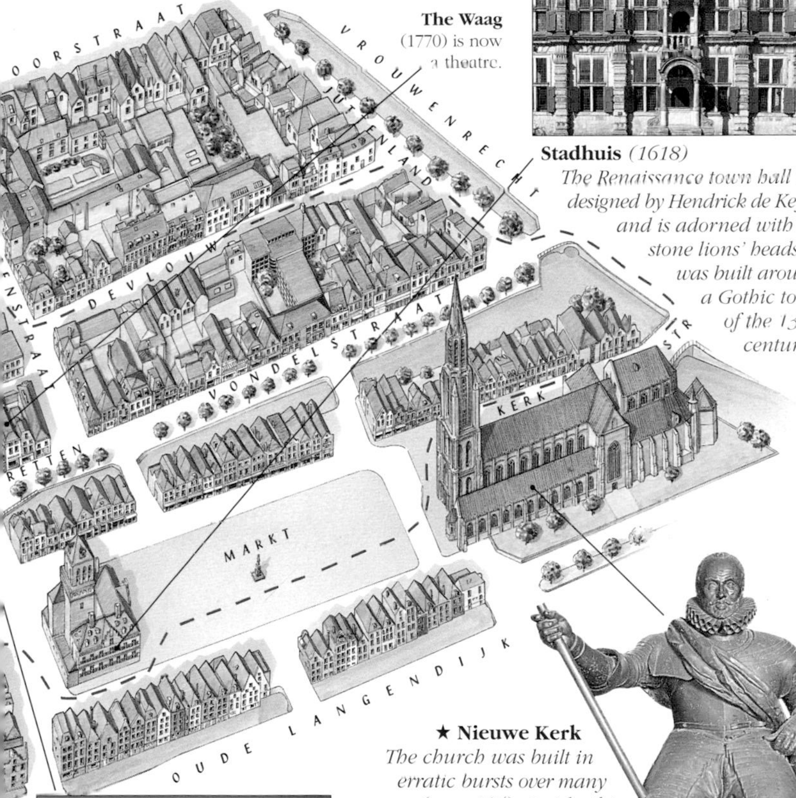


**The Waag** (1770) is now a theatre.

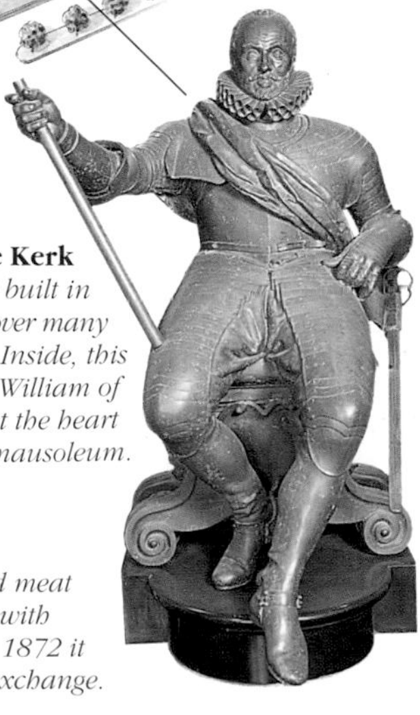

**★ Nieuwe Kerk**
*The church was built in erratic bursts over many years* (see p194)*. Inside, this statue of Prince William of Orange reclines at the heart of his elaborate mausoleum.*

**Vleeshal** *(1650)*
*The façade of the old meat market is decorated with animal heads. After 1872 it was used as a corn exchange.*

# Exploring Delft

THE CHARMING TOWN of Delft is known the world over for its blue-and-white pottery, but is equally famous as the resting place of William of Orange (1533–84), one of the most celebrated figures in Dutch history. He commanded the Dutch Revolt against Spanish rule from his headquarters in Delft, and his victory resulted in religious freedom and independence for the Dutch people (see pp22–3). Delft was also the birthplace of artist Jan Vermeer (1632–75), whose talent was so underrated during his lifetime that he died in extreme poverty.

**The imposing Renaissance pulpit (1548) of the Oude Kerk**

### Oude Kerk

Heilige Geestkerkhof. ( (015) 2123 015. ◯ Mon–Sat. ✎ ♿

Although a church has existed on this site since the 13th century, the original building been added to many times. The ornate, but leaning, clock tower was built in the 14th century, and the flamboyant Gothic north transept was added by Belgian architect Anthonis Keldermans in the early 16th century. The interior is dominated by the elaborately carved wooden pulpit with overhanging canopy. The floor is paved with 17th-century tomb slabs, many carved with skeletons and coats of arms. The simple stone tablet at the east end of the north aisle marks the burial place of Jan Vermeer. In the north transept lies Admiral Maarten Tromp (1598–1653), who routed the English fleet in 1652. Admiral Piet Heyn (1577–1629), who captured the Spanish silver fleet in 1628, is buried in the chancel.

### Nieuwe Kerk

Markt. ( (015) 2123 025. ◯ Mon–Sat. ✎

The Nieuwe Kerk was built between 1383 and 1510, but much of the original structure was restored following a fire in 1536 and an explosion at the national arsenal in 1645. Work on the church continued for many years, and it was not until 1872 that PJH Cuypers (see pp30–31) added the statuesque 100 m (320 ft) tower to the Gothic façade.

The burial vaults of the Dutch royal family are in the crypt of this empty, cavernous church, but the most prominent feature of the interior is the stately mausoleum of William of Orange. Set in the vast arched choir, the richly decorated tomb was designed by Hendrick de Keyser (see p90) in 1614 and is carved from black and white marble, with heavy gilded detailing. At its heart is a sculpture of William, resplendent in his battle dress, and at each corner stand bronze figures representing the Virtues. Close to William is the forlorn figure of his dog, who died days after him, and at the foot of the tomb is a trumpeting angel – symbol of Fame.

**The Nieuwe Kerk in Delft's market square**

## DELFTWARE

The blue-and-white tin-glazed pottery, known as Delftware, was developed from majolica and introduced to the Netherlands by immigrant Italian potters in the 16th century. Settling around Delft and Haarlem, the potters made wall tiles, adopting Dutch motifs such as animals and flowers as decoration. Over the next hundred years, trade with the east brought samples of delicate Chinese porcelain to the Netherlands, and the market for coarser Dutch majolica crashed. By 1650, local potters had adopted the Chinese model and designed fine plates, vases and bowls decorated with Dutch landscapes, and biblical and genre scenes. In 1652, De Porceleyne Fles was one of 32 thriving potteries in Delft. Today, it is one of two Delftware factories still in production, and is open for guided tours.

**Hand-painted 17th-century Delft tiles**

### 🏛 Koninklijk Nederlands Legermuseum

Korte Geer 1. 📞 (015) 2150 500. ◯ daily. ● 1 Jan, 25 Dec.
The Legermuseum (army museum) is housed in the Armamentarium, formerly the arsenal of the old provinces of West Friesland and Holland. The bluff, square armoury was built in 1692 and is still full of weaponry, now displayed with military uniforms, battle models and armoured vehicles. These exhibits trace developments in Dutch military history since the Middle Ages up to the present peace-keeping role of the Netherlands in the service of the United Nations.

**Coat of arms on façade of the Legermuseum**

### 🏛 Stedelijk Museum Het Prinsenhof

St Agathaplein 1. 📞 (015) 2602 358. ◯ Tue–Sun. ● 1 Jan, 25 Dec. 🖼
This tranquil Gothic building, formerly a convent, now houses Delft's historical museum, but is better known as the place where William of Orange was assassinated. He requisitioned the convent in 1572 for use as his headquarters during the Dutch Revolt. In 1584, by order of Philip II of Spain (see pp22–3), William was shot by Balthasar Geraerts, a fanatical Catholic. The bullet holes in the main staircase wall can still be seen today.

The crooked tiled floors and leaded windows of the convent provide the perfect backdrop for a rare collection of antique Delftware. This is displayed alongside tapestries, silverware, medieval sculpture and a series of portraits of the Dutch royal family, from William of Orange to today.

### 🏛 Volkenkundig Museum Nusantara

St Agathaplein 4. 📞 (015) 2602 358. ◯ Tue–Sun. ● 1 Jan, 25 Dec. 🖼
When William of Orange took over the Prinsenhof in 1572, the nuns moved into one of its wings across the square. This is now the home of the Nusantara ethnological museum. It is small, but has a wonderful collection of masks, carvings, textiles, jewellery and musical instruments brought back from Indonesia by traders working for the Dutch East India Company (see pp26–7). The museum shop sells unusual, but rather expensive, modern Indonesian crafts.

### 🏛 Museum Lambert van Meerten

Oude Delft 199. 📞 (015) 2602 358. ◯ Tue–Sun. ● 1 Jan, 25 Dec. 🖼
This small museum is located in an elegantly furnished 19th-century mansion, with paintings and architectural details recently salvaged from local 17th- and 18th-century buildings. Its main attraction is the antique hand-painted Delftware tiles and tile pictures from across the world.

**Fine gabled façades along Binnenwaterslot in the centre of Delft**

# St Janskerk, Gouda

THE ORIGINAL Catholic church of 1485 was rebuilt in Gothic style after it was razed by fire in 1552. Between 1555 and 1571, a series of remarkable stained-glass windows were donated to the church by wealthy Catholic benefactors such as Philip II of Spain. After the Alteration *(see pp22–3)* the church became Protestant, but even the iconoclasts could not bring themselves to destroy the windows – in fact Protestant patrons, such as the aldermen of Rotterdam, continued to donate windows until 1603. Depicting contemporary figures and events, the stained glass is rich in political symbolism, using biblical stories to make coded reference to the conflict between Catholic and Protestant, and Dutch and Spanish that led to the Dutch Revolt in 1572.

Donor's coat of arms (1601)

**The Nave**
At 123 m (403 ft), the nave is the longest in the Netherlands. Memorial slabs cover the floor.

**The Adulterous Woman** *(1601)*
*Dressed as a Franciscan monk, Jesus begs the people in the temple to forgive the adulterous wife, who is heavily guarded by Spanish soldiers.*

**Baptism of Christ**

North aisle

Visitors' entrance

Purification of the Temple

South aisle

**Judith Slays Holofernes**
*This detail is taken from a window which portrays the biblical story of the slaying of Holofernes by Judith. The glazier, Dirck Crabeth, shows John the Baptist holding a lamb. Next to him is the kneeling figure of Jean de Ligne, Count of Aremberg, who commissioned the window.*

**The Relief of Leiden** *(1603)*
*William of Orange is pictured here directing Leiden's heroic resistance to the Spanish siege of 1574 (see p184).*

View over Gouda with St Janskerk in the background

**Purification of the Temple**
*The window was donated by
William of Orange (see p22)
in 1567. The detail shows
dismayed traders watching
Jesus drive the moneylenders
from the temple. It represents
the Dutch desire to expel the
Spanish from their country.*

# Gouda ⑱

50 km (33 miles) S of Amsterdam.
🏠 71,000. 🚉 ℹ️ Markt 27. (0900)
468 3288. 🧀 cheese market.
mid Jun–Aug: 10am–12.30pm Thu;
general market: Thu & Sat; antiques:
Apr–Oct, Wed.

G OUDA received its charter
from Count Floris V *(see
p19)* in 1272. Situated at the
confluence of two rivers, the
town became the centre of a
successful brewing industry in
the 15th century. The growth
of the cheese trade during the
17th century brought more
prosperity. Today, the name
of Gouda is synonymous with
its famous full-bodied cheese.
There is a cheese market in
summer, and the twice-weekly
general market offers local
cheeses and crafts. There is
also a candlelit Christmas
market. All these markets take
place in the huge square
around the Stadhuis which,
dating from 1450, is one of the
oldest town halls in the Netherlands. The building bristles
with pinnacles and miniature
spires in Flemish Gothic style.
The elaborate façade includes
statues of Gouda's former
rulers. However, the principal
attraction of the town are the
superb stained-glass windows
found in St Janskerk.

### 🏛 Stedelijk Museum Het
### Catharina Gasthuis
Oosthaven 9. 📞 (0182) 588 440. 🕐
daily. ● 1 Jan, 25 Dec. 📷
An arched gatehouse (1609)
leads into the leafy courtyard
of this delightful museum. The
Catharina Gasthuis was built in

the 14th century as a hospice
for travellers, later becoming
an almshouse for the elderly.
Converted into a museum in
1910, it has a series of Civic
Guard portraits and landscapes
by Dutch Impressionists. The
more eccentric elements of
the collection include rather
gruesome surgical instruments
and a torture chamber.

### 🏛 Stedelijk Museum De
### Moriaan / The Blackamoor
Westhaven 29. 📞 (0182) 588 444.
🕐 daily. ● 1 Jan, 25 Dec. 📷
This little tobacco museum
was once a sugar refinery
and later a coffee and tobacco
shop. Behind the 1617 façade
it is packed with tobacco jars
and traditional clay pipes with
long stems and tiny bowls.

**Gatehouse of the Stedelijk
Museum Het Catharina Gasthuis**

**Baptism of Christ** *(1555)
John the Baptist is shown
baptizing Christ in the river
Jordan. The window was don-
ated by the Bishop of Utrecht.*

# Rotterdam ⑲

**R**OTTERDAM OCCUPIES a strategic position where the Rijn (Rhine), Europe's most important river, meets the North Sea. Barges from Rotterdam transport goods deep into the continent, and ocean-going ships carry European exports around the world. This made Rotterdam a prime target for aerial bombardment during World War II, and the city's ancient heart was destroyed. Much of the city has been rebuilt in experimental styles, resulting in some of Europe's most original and innovative architecture. The Europoort is now the world's largest container port, stretching for 37 km (23 miles) along the river banks.

Cabin on the warship *De Buffel*

🏛 **Maritiem Museum Rotterdam**
Leuvehaven 1. ☎ *(010) 413 2680.*
Ⓦ www.martiemmuseum.nl
◯ Tue–Sun & public hols; Jul & Aug: also Mon. ● 1 Jan, 30 Apr, 25 Dec.
Prince Hendrik, brother of King William III *(see pp30–31),* founded this museum in 1873. Its main highlight is an iron-clad warship called *De Buffel,* built in 1868. It boasts an opulent officers' quarters, which have the atmosphere of a gentleman's club. Other exhibits include a small fleet of barges and steamships.

🏛 **Historisch Museum Rotterdam**
Korte Hoogstraat 31. ☎ *(010) 217 6767.* Ⓦ www.hmr.rotterdam.nl
◯ Tue–Sun & public hols. ● 1 Jan, 30 Apr, 25 Dec.
Rotterdam's historical museum is in the Schielandshuis, a gracious town house built in 1665 by Jacob Lois. The museum charts the development of the city, and the urbane lifestyles of its people, through displays of paintings, silverware and furniture in elegant rooms.

Oudehaven, with the futuristic Kijk-Kubus houses in the background

## Exploring Rotterdam

Much of Oudehaven, the old harbour area of Rotterdam, was destroyed in bombing raids during World War II. It has largely been rebuilt in daring and avant-garde styles. The pyramid-shaped **Gemeente-bibliotheek** (public library) is similar to the Pompidou Centre in Paris: its yellow ventilation ducts and service piping are on the exterior of the building.

Piet Blom's **Kijk-Kubus** (cube houses) of 1982 are extraordinary apartments, set on concrete stilts and tilted at a crazy angle. Residents have specially designed furniture to fit the sloping rooms. Pavement cafés have sprung up along the harbour quayside, and apartment blocks with

undercover shopping arcades have now replaced the old wooden warehouses.

In the Golden Age, maritime trade brought wealth to Dutch towns with access to the sea. Delft *(see pp192–5)* lacked a harbour, so its citizens built a 12-km (7.5-mile) canal from the town to the Nieuwe Maas river, and constructed **Delfs-haven** – a purpose-built village complete with harbour. This has long been swallowed up by Rotterdam, but remains a pretty corner of the city, with 18th-century warehouses converted into apartments, galleries, restaurants and cafés.

🏛 **Museum Boijmans-van Beuningen**
See pp200–201.

Peaceful canal houses in a quiet corner of Delfshaven

## 🏛 Historisch Museum de Dubbelde Palmboom

Voorhaven 12. **[** *(010) 476 1533.*
**W** *www.hmr.rotterdam.nl* **○** *Tue–Sun and public hols.* **●** *1 Jan, 30 Apr, 25 Dec.* 📷 ♿ 🍴 📷

The museum "of the double palm tree" is in a twin-gabled, wooden warehouse dating to 1825. Its five storeys are open-plan with vast, beamed rooms. These display arts and crafts, photographs and scale models depicting life at the mouth of the Nieuwe Maas river, from the earliest Iron Age fishing settlements to the booming industrial port of present day.

## 🏛 Wereldmuseum Rotterdam

Willemskade 25. **[** *(010) 270 7172.*
**W** *www.wereldmuseum.rotterdam.nl* **○** *10am–5pm Tue–Sun & public hols.* 📷 ♿ 🍴 📷

During the 17th century, the city fathers amassed a superb ethnological collection. It is now in a museum, built in 1851, which uses audiovisual displays of theatre, film, dance and music. Permanent collections include Indonesian musical instruments, ancient folk art, masks and carvings.

Euromast against the skyline

## 📯 Euromast

Parkhaven 20. **[** *(010) 436 4811.*
**○** *daily.* 📷 ♿ 🍴 📷

Visitors ride a high-speed lift up the first 100 m (328 ft) of the Euromast to enjoy sweeping views of Rotterdam. This lower section, built in 1960, has a viewing platform with a restaurant and exhibition area. In 1970 the Space Tower added another 85 m (272 ft) in height

**VISITORS' CHECKLIST**

65 km (40 miles) SW of Amsterdam. 🏠 602,000. 🚉 *Stationsplein.* ✈ *6 km (4 miles) NW.* 🛈 *Coolsingel 67. 0900 403 4065.*
**W** *www.rotterdam.nl* 🚢 *Tue, Fri, Sat.* 🎦 *Rotterdam Film Festival: end Jan–begin Feb; Heineken Dance Parade: second Sat in Aug.*

to make this the tallest construction in the Netherlands. A covered "space cabin" attached to the outside of the tower ascends 58 m (190 ft) up from the viewing platform.

## Europoort

Leuvehoofd 5. **[** *(010) 413 5400.*
**Europoort** **○** *daily.* 🚢 *See Getting to Amsterdam By Ferry p268.* **Boat tours** **○** *daily.* 📷

The wharves and quays of the city's highly automated port service about 32,000 container ships a year. A boat tour is an ideal way of seeing the port, built between 1958 and 1975. Cyclists and motorists follow the 48-km (30-mile) Haven Route (harbour route) along the Nieuwe Maas, passing oil terminals, docks and tankers.

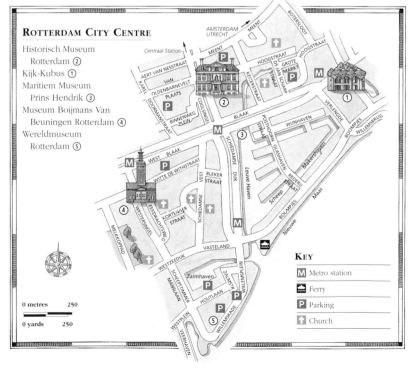

### ROTTERDAM CITY CENTRE

Historisch Museum Rotterdam ②
Kijk-Kubus ①
Maritiem Museum Prins Hendrik ③
Museum Boijmans Van Beuningen Rotterdam ④
Wereldmuseum Rotterdam ⑤

**KEY**

M Metro station
🚢 Ferry
P Parking
✝ Church

0 metres 250
0 yards 250

# Museum Boijmans Van Beuningen Rotterdam

THE MUSEUM IS NAMED after two art connoisseurs, FJO Boijmans, who bequeathed his paintings to Rotterdam in 1847, and DG van Beuningen, who donated works between 1916 and 1954. The resulting collection is one of the Netherlands' finest. First displayed in the nearby Schielandshuis, the collection was moved to the present gallery in 1935. Known mainly for its supreme series of Old Master paintings, the collection also covers the whole spectrum of Dutch art, from the medieval works of Jan van Eyck to rare glassware and recent installations using laser technology.

**The Pedlar** *(c.1502)*
*Jheronimus Bosch's, painting shows mankind, travelling through life with sin trying to trap him at every turn.*

**Three Marys at the Open Sepulchre** *(1430)*
*Brothers Jan and Hubert van Eyck collaborated on this colourful work, which shows the three Marys at the tomb of the resurrected Christ.*

Main stairwell

First floor

**La Méditerranée** *(1905)*
*Aristide Maillol's bronze was presented to the museum in 1961. He often used the female nude as a medium to express his philosophy of form.*

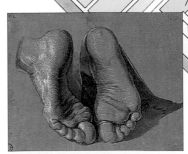

---

**STAR EXHIBITS**

---

★ **The Tower of Babel**
   by Pieter Bruegel

---

★ **Study of Two Feet**
   by Albrecht Dürer

---

★ **Titus at his Desk**
   by Rembrandt

---

★ **Study of Two Feet** *(1507)*
*Albrecht Dürer's study in grey and white ink is one of a series of preliminary sketches on the subject of the Assumption made for the Heller Altar in Frankfurt.*

**★ The Tower of Babel** (c.1553)
Pieter Bruegel took his theme from the
Old Testament, and showed the
elaborate ten-storey edifice teeming
with frenetic activity.

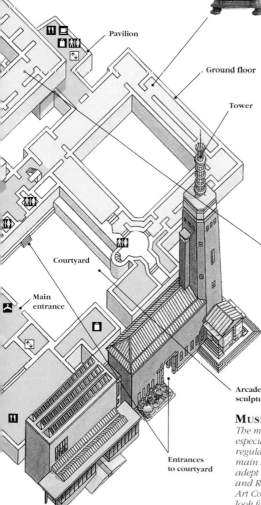

**VISITORS' CHECKLIST**

Museumpark 18–20, Rotterdam.
(010) 441 9400. W www.
boijmans.rotterdam.nl Centraal
Station. 10am–5pm Tue–Sat,
11am–5pm Sun & public hols.
1 Jan, 30 Apr, 25 Dec.

**Standing Clock** (1750)
Lourens Eichelar designed this
clock, which stands 215 cm (7 ft)
high. It is made of walnut root
wood and adorned with gilded
cherubs blowing long horns.

### KEY TO FLOORPLAN

| | |
|---|---|
| ☐ | Ancient Art |
| ☐ | Art: 1750-1930 |
| ☐ | Decorative Arts & Design |
| ☐ | 20th Century Art |
| ☐ | Graphic Cabinet |
| ☐ | Temporary Exhibition space |
| ☐ | Non-exhibition space |

**Pavilion**

**Ground floor**

**Tower**

**Courtyard**

**Main
entrance**

**Arcade with
sculptures**

**Entrances
to courtyard**

**★ Titus at his Desk** (1655)
Rembrandt portrayed his sickly
son in introspective mood,
bathed in a tender light which
heightens the ghostly pallor of his
brooding features.

### MUSEUM GUIDE
The museum is vast and can be confusing,
especially since the displays change
regularly. Signposting to the museum's four
main sections is clear and attendants are
adept at directing visitors. For Brueghel
and Rembrandt follow signs to the Ancient
Art Collection, and for Dali and Magritte
look for the 20th Century Art section.

# Utrecht ⑳

UTRECHT WAS FOUNDED by the Romans in AD 47 to protect an important river crossing on the Rijn (Rhine). The town was among the first in the Netherlands to embrace Christianity. In 700, St Willibrord (658–739), a missionary from northern England, established a bishopric here, known as Het Sticht. Utrecht grew in importance as a religious centre throughout the Middle Ages, extending its control over much of the Netherlands until 1527, when Bishop Hendrik of Bavaria was obliged to sell all his temporal powers to Charles V (see pp22–3). The city centre still retains many of its medieval churches and monasteries, but these now stand alongside modern blocks and a vast undercover shopping complex. The Oudegracht (old canal) threads its way through the city, flowing 5 m (16.5 ft) below ground level to prevent flooding. Today, it is lined with broad quays, cellar bars and cafés.

has a superb railway museum. The Spoorwegmuseum is in the former 19th-century Maliebaan station. Inside the old building, there are specialist technical displays, engines and modern rail accessories.

Outside, children can explore steam engines, carriages, trams and signal boxes. A highlight for many visitors of all ages is the simulated ride in the cab of a high-tech express train.

Organ in the Speelklok museum

### 🚩 Domtoren
Via 'Rondom', Domplein 9. 📞 (030) 233 3036. 🕐 10am–4pm Mon–Sat, noon–4pm Sun. ⬤ 1 Jan, 25 Dec. 🖼

The Gothic Domtoren

The soaring Domtoren is a Gothic masterpiece and one of the tallest towers in the Netherlands at 112 m (367 ft) high. It was completed in 1382, on the site of the small, 8th-century church of St Willibrord. The tower, which has always stood apart from the Domkerk, miraculously survived a massive hurricane in 1674 that destroyed the nave of the cathedral. The Domtoren continues to dominate Utrecht, and the viewing gallery in its spire still affords the best views across the city.

### ⛪ Domkerk
Achter den Dom 1.
🕐 daily; 🛠

Construction of Utrecht's cathedral began in 1254. Today, only the north and south transepts, two chapels and the choir remain, along with the 15th-century cloisters and a chapter house (1495), which is now part of the university. It was here that the Union of Utrecht (see p23) was signed in 1579 by John, Count of Nassau, brother of William of Orange. Outside the church stands a giant boulder, dated 980 and covered with runic symbols. It was presented to Utrect by the Danish people in 1936, to commemorate Denmark's early conversion to Christianity by missionaries from Utrecht.

### 🏛 Nederlands Spoorwegmuseum
Maliebaanstation. 📞 (030) 2306 206.
🖥 www.spoorwegmuseum.nl 🕐 Tue–Sun. ⬤ public hols. 🖼 🛠 🚻 🛠
The headquarters of the Dutch railways are based in Utrecht, so it is fitting that the town

### 🏛 Nationaal Museum van Speelklok tot Pierement
Buurkerkhof 10. 📞 (030) 2312 789.
🖥 www.museumspeelklok.nl
🕐 Tue–Sun. ⬤ 1 Jan, 30 Apr, 25 Dec.
🛠 🖼 🛠 🛠 🛠
This magical place – literally "from musical clock to street organ" – is located in the 13th-century Buurkerk, Utrecht's oldest church. It has a collection of mechanical musical instruments from the 18th century to the present day. Fairground organs compete with clocks, carillons, pianolas and automated birds. These instruments are demonstrated on guided tours, during which visitors are encouraged to sing and dance along.

### 🏛 Centraal Museum
Agnietenstraat 1. 📞 (030) 2362 362.
🖥 www.centraalmuseum.nl 🕐 Tue–Sun. ⬤ 1 Jan, 30 Apr, 25 Dec. 🖼 🛠 🛠 🛠
Housed in an old convent, Centraal Museum is only a ten-minute walk from the city centre. At the heart of the collection is a series of portraits by artist

Steam engine and guard's box, Nederlands Spoorwegmuseum

Gerrit Rietveld's Schröderhuis (1924), part of the Centraal Museum

Jan van Scorel (1495–1562). On visiting Rome, van Scorel absorbed ideas from Italian Renaissance painting and he became the first Dutch artist to paint group portraits. These established the tradition leading to the superb 16th-century Civic Guard portraits *(see p81)*.

Another of the museum's highlights is Gerrit Rietveld's Schröderhuis. Designed in 1924 and regarded as the apogee of De Stijl architecture *(see p136)*, it is open to the public at Prins Hendriklaan 50.

There is also a display of Dutch interior design from the Middle Ages to the 18th century.

### 🏠 Pieterskerk
Pieterskerkhof. 🕐 *sporadically.*
Built of tufa (limestone) with red sandstone columns, the church was completed in 1048. It is a rare Dutch example of German Romanesque architecture, and set in a crescent of elegant Golden Age houses.

### 🏛 Museum Catharijneconvent
Lange Nieuwstraat 38. ☎ (030) 2313 835. 🌐 www.catharijneconvent.nl
🕐 Tue – Sun. ⬤ 1 Jan & 30 Apr. 🚫
♿ 🛍 📷
The beautiful former convent of St Catherine (1562) is now home to this

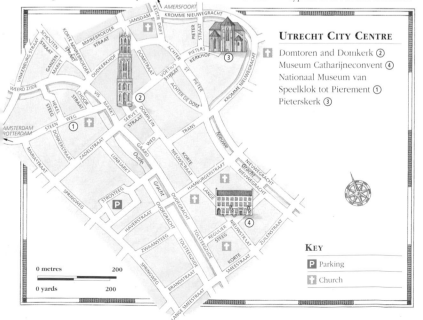

Sculpture in Catharijneconvent

fascinating museum. It deals with the troubled history of religion in the Netherlands and owns an award-winning collection of medieval art. Wooden and stone sculptures, gold and silver work, manuscripts, paintings and jewel-encrusted miniatures are displayed in rooms round the cloister. On the upper floors is a series of model church interiors, highlighting the great variety of Dutch religious philosophies through the ages. They range from the lavish statues, paintings and altar in a Catholic church to the plain interiors typical of Protestant churches.

## UTRECHT CITY CENTRE

Domtoren and Domkerk ②
Museum Catharijneconvent ④
Nationaal Museum van
Speelklok tot Pierement ①
Pieterskerk ③

### KEY

🅿 Parking

✝ Church

0 metres  200
0 yards  200

# Het Nationale Park De Hoge Veluwe ㉑

**M**ADE UP OF MORE THAN 5,500 ha (13,750 acres) of woodland, fen, heath and sand drifts, the Netherlands' largest nature reserve is home to thousands of rare plants, wild animals and birds. In order to preserve the natural habitat, cars are banned from large sections of the reserve. Also located in the park are the Museum Kröller-Müller, with 278 paintings by Van Gogh, and an outdoor sculpture garden, the Beeldentuin. Beneath the Visitors' Centre is the Museonder, with audiovisual displays about the earth's sub-surface, including an earthquake simulator.

**Jachthuis St Hubertus**
*This hunting lodge was built in 1920 by HP Berlage (see p79) for the park's wealthy patrons, the Kröller-Müllers.*

**★ Museum Kröller-Müller**
*Besides Van Gogh's Café Terrace at Night (1881), the museum has a collection of early Flemish masters and works by modern artists.*

**★ Beeldentuin**
*Jean Dubuffet's Jardin d'Emaille, shown here, is one of the striking modern sculpures on display in this 11-ha (27-acre) sculpture park. The Beeldentuin also provides an elemental setting for works by Auguste Rodin, Alberto Giacometti and Barbara Hepworth.*

**Nieuwe Plijmen game observation post**

OTTERLOSE ZAND

De Wetweg

**Otterlo entrance**

Houtkampweg

Moufflon

Kronkelweg

**Visitors' Centre and Museonder**

FRAN BER

PLIJMEN

Roe Deer

Wildbaanweg

OUD-REEMSTER ZAND

Wild Boar

**Bosje van Staf game observation post**

Reemsterweg

OUD-REEMSTE VELD

## Picnicking
*Tables are provided near the Visitors' Centre. Picnicking is allowed everywhere except in areas set aside for the animals.*

OUD-REEMST

Roe Deer

**Free White Bicycles**
*At the Visitors' Centre bikes are available for exploring the park.*

Camp site

Hoenderloo entrance

Roe Deer

*Houtkampweg*

De Klep game hide

P

Red Deer

**DEELENSE WAS**

ELENSE VELD

Schaarsbergen entrance

RBERG

**Game Hides and Observation Points**
*Special viewing areas (see map) allow the wildlife, like red deer, moufflon sheep and wild boar, to remain undisturbed.*

## VISITORS' CHECKLIST

80 km (50 miles) SE of Amsterdam.
Arnhem. **Entrances** at Otterlo, Schaarsbergen, Hoenderloo.
**Nationale Park Visitors' Centre**
Houtkampweg, Otterlo.
(0900) 464 3835.
Apr–Aug: 8am–dusk;
Sep–Mar: 9am–dusk.
www.hogeveluwe.nl
**Museum Kröller-Müller**
Houtkampweg 6, Otterlo.
(0318) 591 041.
www.kmm.nl 10am–5pm
Tue–Sun & public hols. 1 Jan.

**Park regulations**: Do not camp, or disturb the animals. Vehicles must not leave the road. Do not light fires outside designated areas. Keep dogs on a leash.

## KEY

— Main road
••• Walk route
Cycle path
Forest
Heath
Sand drifts
No access

0 kilometres      2

0 miles      1

## STAR SIGHTS

★ **Museum Kröller-Müller**

★ **Beeldentuin**

# Arnhem ㉒

80 km (50 miles) SE of Amsterdam.
136,000. Stationsplein 45.
0900 202 4075. Sat.

CAPITAL OF Gelderland province, Arnhem was all but destroyed between 17 and 27 September 1944, in one of the most famous battles of World War II. The city has since been largely rebuilt, but still retains a number of reminders of the conflict, such as the John Frost Bridge, scene of some of the heaviest fighting. The bridge is named after the commanding officer of the 2nd Parachute Battalion, which fought to hold the bridgehead for four days.

## Airborne Museum
Utrechtseweg 232, Oosterbeek.
(0263) 337 710.
www.airbornemuseum.com
daily. 1 Jan, 25 Dec.
The museum traces the course of the struggle to take Arnhem, using models, slides, and taped commentaries. The collection is in a villa near Oosterbeek, used by the Commander of the 1st British Airborne Division, General Urquhart. The war cemetery nearby is a reminder of all those who died.

**John Frost Bridge, Arnhem**

## Nederlands Openluchtmuseum
Schelmseweg 89. (0263) 576 100.
www.openluchtmuseum.nl
Apr–Oct: daily.
Situated in a 44-ha (110-acre) wooded park, the Nederlands Openluchtmuseum recreates the traditional architecture and folklore of the Netherlands from 1800 to 1950. Founded in 1912, about 100 farmhouses, barns, windmills and workshops have since been erected here, many of them furnished in period style. The museum staff dress up in traditional costume and demonstrate the old rural way of life, handicrafts and industry.

# Paleis Het Loo ❷

STADHOLDER WILLIAM III *(see p28)* built Het Loo in 1686 as a royal hunting lodge. Generations of the House of Orange used the lodge as a summer palace. Because of its magnificence, it was regarded as the "Versailles of the Netherlands". The main architect was Jacob Roman (1640–1716); the interior decoration and layout of the gardens were the responsibility of Daniel Marot (1661–1752). The building's Classical façade belies the opulence of its lavish interior; after extensive restoration work was completed on both in 1984, the palace was opened as a museum.

**Coat of arms** (1690) of William and Mary, future king and queen of England.

★ **Royal Bedroom of Stadholder William III** *(1713)*
*Recently refurbished, the wall coverings and draperies in this luxurious bedroom are of rich orange damask and purple silk.*

**King William III's bedroom**

**King's Garden**

**Stadholder William III's Closet** *(1690)*
*The walls of William's private study are covered in embossed scarlet damask. His favourite paintings and Delftware pieces are exhibited here.*

**Classic Cars**
*This 1925 Bentley, nicknamed Minerva, was owned by Prince Hendrik, husband of Queen Wilhelmina. It is one of the royal family's many vintage cars, which are on display in the stable block (1910).*

| STAR FEATURES |
| --- |
| ★ **Old Dining Room** |
| ★ **Royal Bedroom** |
| ★ **Formal Gardens** |

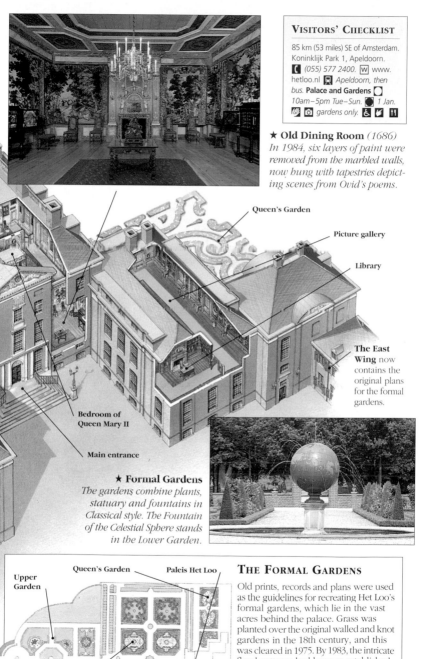

★ **Old Dining Room** (1686)
*In 1984, six layers of paint were removed from the marbled walls, now hung with tapestries depicting scenes from Ovid's poems.*

**Queen's Garden**

**Picture gallery**

**Library**

**The East Wing** now contains the original plans for the formal gardens.

**Bedroom of Queen Mary II**

**Main entrance**

★ **Formal Gardens**
*The gardens combine plants, statuary and fountains in Classical style. The Fountain of the Celestial Sphere stands in the Lower Garden.*

**Upper Garden**

**Queen's Garden**

**Paleis Het Loo**

**Lower Garden**

**King's Garden**

## THE FORMAL GARDENS

Old prints, records and plans were used as the guidelines for recreating Het Loo's formal gardens, which lie in the vast acres behind the palace. Grass was planted over the original walled and knot gardens in the 18th century, and this was cleared in 1975. By 1983, the intricate floral patterns had been re-established, replanting had begun, the Classical fountains were renovated and the water supply fully restored. The garden reflects the late 17th-century belief that art and nature should operate in harmony.

**Layout of the formal section of the gardens**

# TRAVELLERS' NEEDS

# WHERE TO STAY

A MSTERDAM PROVIDES top-quality, city-centre accommodation to suit everyone's budget. It ranges from a clutch of luxurious five-star hotels that should impress the most hedonistic traveller to the many cheap hostels for those on a budget. In between there are scores of B&Bs, many occupying pretty gabled houses, often with a canal view. We have inspected dozens of hotels in all price ranges, selecting those which are particularly friendly, comfortable, interesting or good value. They are described in the listings on pages 218–23. The *Choosing a Hotel* chart on pages 216–17 will help you to narrow down the available choice.

**The Van Ostade Bicycle Hotel in southern Amsterdam** *(see p223)*

## CHOOSING A HOTEL

M OST OF Amsterdam's tourist hotels lie in three areas: the historic centre, along the *Grachtengordel* (Canal Ring) and in the Museum Quarter. As central Amsterdam is compact, wherever you stay, you are still within walking distance of most of the city's major attractions. Most business-oriented hotels on the other hand are located in the Nieuw Zuid (New South), which is a little more remote.

Accommodation in Amsterdam's historic centre can often be disappointing. It mainly consists of chain hotels, seedy rooms above cafés and unenticing low-budget hotels around Centraal Station and the Red Light District. Fortunately, there are a handful of notable exceptions.

You will find the city's most charismatic hotels along the Canal Ring, the majority of which boast beautiful gabled façades and old-fashioned beamed interiors. Despite their charm, you may have to sacrifice some creature comforts, as the rooms can be small,

the facilities limited and the stairs treacherously steep.

The quiet 19th-century terraced streets between Leidseplein and Vondelpark house many modest but comfortable establishments which, although not as characterful as the canalside hotels, are situated close to the main museums and galleries. The Amsterdam Tourist Board *(see p256)* publishes a useful brochure which details the facilities, price and location of virtually all the 300 or so hotels in Amsterdam, with photographs and descriptions. It is on sale from the information desk at Schiphol Airport and Tourist Board offices in the city. It is also available by post from the Tourist Board and the **NBT** (Netherlands Board of Tourism) in your home country.

**Arena Hotel** *(see p223)*

## ROOM RATES

R OOM RATES usually include tax and a basic breakfast, except at large, expensive hotels where breakfast is almost invariably extra. For those on a tight budget many B&Bs and small private hotels have rooms without *en suite* facilities at rock-bottom prices. However, canalside accommodation can be expensive and some of these hotels charge a little extra for a room with a canal view.

Hostels are the cheapest option for single travellers as reductions on the double-room rate at hotels is small, typically around 20 per cent. Families and groups of friends, however, can make large savings by staying in family rooms, common in all types of hotel.

**De l'Europe, overlooking Muntplein** *(see p219)*

**An airy breakfast room in an Amsterdam hotel**

## SPECIAL OFFERS

MOST PRIVATE hotels drop their rates by a quarter or a third from the beginning of November to the end of March (except over Christmas and the New Year). Some even throw in a complimentary boat trip and free museum admissions. These hotels, which include a couple of dozen choices in all price categories, are featured in the *Winter the Amsterdam Way* brochure which is available by post from the Amsterdam Tourist Board or your local NBT office.

Amsterdam has a surfeit of chain hotels. Large operators such as **Best Western** and **Holiday Inn** frequently offer special discounts to attract guests, and their weekend rates are substantially cheaper than weekday rates off season.

## BOOKING AND PAYING

APRIL TO MAY (the tulip season) and July to August are the busiest times of year for tourists. During these periods, book at least a few weeks in advance, especially at weekends when reasonably priced accommodation can dry up completely. For popular hotels along the canals, book well in advance all year round.

As all Amsterdam hoteliers speak English, it is easy to make reservations direct with the hotel. While most take credit card reservations, some small places will ask for a deposit in the form of a cheque or postal order, usually for the full amount of the first night's stay. The **Netherlands Reservation Centre** makes hotel bookings free of charge if you are already in the Netherlands. It will charge a substantial fee should you reserve before you arrive in the country. If you arrive by plane without accommodation, the KLM desk at Schiphol Airport makes hotel reservations without charge. **Amsterdam Tourist Board offices** require a small fee for same-day bookings.

## HOTEL GRADINGS

THE NUMBER OF STARS (from one to five) meted out by the Benelux Hotel Classification system only indicates a hotel's level of facilities. Stars have no bearing on its appeal or location. Many of the city's small hotels are given a low star rating, despite their charm, due to a lack of facilities.

**The elegant foyer of the Amstel Inter-Continental *(see p223)***

**Dining room of the Canal House in the Western Canal Ring** *(see p220)*

## What to Expect

WHILE SOME stylish B&Bs boast an elegant lounge, only top-of-the-range hotels normally have a restaurant. The vast majority of hotels just offer bed and breakfast, and public areas are limited to a breakfast room and possibly a bar. A Dutch breakfast can include cold meats, cheeses and boiled eggs, but do not expect more than rolls, jams and a hot drink at a no-frills B&B.

It is important to get a detailed description of your room when you book, as many canalside hotels have a number of cramped rooms. In cheap B&Bs furnishings can be spartan, but all rooms usually include a TV. If there is a telephone, expect to pay double or treble the normal rate for any call you make.

**Wall plaque on the façade of the Radisson SAS** *(see p218)*

## Travelling with Children

WHILE A FEW, small upmarket hotels do not welcome children, many big chain hotels offer free accommodation to children under 12 when they share their parents'

room. Others offer a half-price rate or even free accommodation for children up to 18, so it is worth phoning around. Babies stay for free almost everywhere. Some places charge for the use of a cot.

The *Choosing a Hotel* chart on pages 216–17 shows which of our recommended hotels have special deals for children.

## Gay Hotels

A GAY COUPLE is unlikely to produce a raised eyebrow in most hotels in this tolerant city. Exclusively gay hotels, like the stylish and very popular **Aero Hotel**, have the advantage of providing a wealth of information on gay hangouts and events. Some hotels, although not exclusively gay, extend a particularly warm welcome to gay guests. Of these, the **Quentin** is now very popular with women, and the Waterfront *(see p220)* attracts a mainly male clientele.

English-language publications like *Men to Men* and *Best Guide to Holland* offer comprehensive listings. They can be found in bookshops such as **Intermale**.

## Disabled Travellers

THE INFORMATION about wheelchair access in our hotel listings relies on the hotels' own assessment of their suitability. The Amsterdam Tourist Board's hotel brochure indicates which four- and five-star hotels have wheelchair access. To avoid disappointment be sure to make your needs absolutely clear when you make a hotel reservation. Remember, the stairs in most of the old canalside hotels can be steep, and few have lifts. The website www.ttfa.nl also offers useful information.

## Hostels

HOSTELS are very much part of the mainstream tourist culture in Amsterdam. Their convivial cafés are a good place for meeting fellow travellers and finding out about popular nightspots. The Amsterdam Tourist Board hotel brochure lists a broad selection of hostels, and the best four are reviewed in this guide on pages 218–23.

Most of Amsterdam's hostels are independent, except two run by **Stayokay**, which offer discounts to members of the International Youth Hostel Federation (IYHF). Dormitory beds make up the bulk of accommodation in all hostels Many hostels impose a curfew at night and close for a couple of hours during the day.

## CAMPING

AMSTERDAM'S TOURIST BOARD hotel brochure details five campsites close to the city centre. Most open in spring and close at the end of October, but some, including **Zeeburg**, stay open all year. **Vliegenbos** and Zeeburg are closest, both about 5 km (3 miles) from the centre. They are open to everyone, but classified as youth sites. Families would do better to head for a quieter site, such as **Amsterdamse Bos**.

Local Tourist Board offices can provide information on campsites elsewhere in the Netherlands, and the NBT in your home country has brochures covering the whole country. The Netherlands Reservation Centre can make camping bookings.

## SELF-CATERING

APARTMENTS for short-term lets are limited, so canal-side self-catering accommo-dation tends to be expensive. Letting agencies are listed in the Amsterdam Tourist Board hotel brochure; others can be found in the Visitors' Guide section of the Yellow Pages (*Gouden Gids*) (see p256).

Agencies usually insist on a minimum stay of one week. Of the hotels recommended in this guide, the Amsterdam Renaissance (see p219), Waterfront (see p220) and Acacia (see p220) all offer self-catering facilities.

## STAYING IN PRIVATE HOMES

A BOOKLET ENTITLED **Bed & Breakfast Holland** offers a helping hand in finding Dutch homes that take in guests. Around 50 of these are in Amsterdam. Most homes have no more than two bedrooms and require guests to stay for at least two nights. Some offer evening meals. Prices are charged per person and are competitive with cheap B&Bs.

## BEYOND AMSTERDAM

THE NBT publishes a thick brochure covering more than 450 hotels throughout the Netherlands. Although this Eyewitness Travel Guide does not cover any hotels outside Amsterdam, the information provided here on booking and paying, hotel gradings, hostels, camping and staying in priv-ate homes is applicable.

The bar of Arena Hotel *(see p223)*, a hostel near Oosterpark

---

# Amsterdam's Best: Hotels

THE HOTELS RECOMMENDED on these two pages possess an individual charm and character not found in most of their chain-hotel counterparts. All of these recommendations have a typically Dutch atmosphere, ranging from the simple and homely to the ornate, and some have an historical interest. Many of these hotels are impeccably restored 17th-century canal houses offering both canal and garden views, in addition to steep and narrow staircases. So whether you are after a reasonably priced B&B or looking for luxury, there is a huge choice available in Amsterdam.

**Canal House**
*This atmospheric B&B has been restored to create an ambience of past grandeur* (See p220.)

*Western Canal Ring*

**Pulitzer**
*This surprising, labyrinthine hotel was created by joining together 24 old canal houses and their gardens.* (See p221.)

**HOTEL DE FILOSOOF**

**De Filosoof**
*Perhaps the city's most unusual hotel, "The Philosopher" has rooms named after the world's greatest thinkers, with thematic decor.* (See p222.)

*Central Canal Ring*

*Museum Quarter*

**Ambassade**
*This classy B&B is an ideal choice for those who want to stay in a characterful, gabled canal house without forgoing comfort.* (See p220.)

### Grand Hotel Krasnapolsky
*This 130-year-old institution has a good choice of restaurants, including the impressive Winter Garden shown left.* (See p219.)

### Grand Sofitel Demeure
*The newest of Amsterdam's set of luxury hotels has the air of an opulent country house.* (See p218.)

### Seven Bridges
*On a pretty canal, this refined B&B is filled with antiques and Persian rugs.* (See p221.)

| 0 metres | 500 |
| --- | --- |
| 0 yards | 500 |

### Prinsenhof
*The dedicated owners of this charmingly decor- ated, simple canal-house B&B provide delightful accommodation at a very reasonable price.* (See p221.)

### Amstel Inter-Continental
*Situated by the side of the Amstel, the city's number one hotel is serene, breath- takingly beautiful and utterly luxurious.* (See p223.)

# Choosing a Hotel

THE HOTELS and hostels on the following pages have all been inspected and assessed specifically for this guide. This chart shows some of the factors that may affect your choice. For more information on each entry see pages 218–23. They are listed by area and appear alphabetically within their price categories.

| | | NUMBER OF ROOMS | LARGE ROOMS | BUSINESS FACILITIES | UNDER 12s FREE IN ROOM | CLOSE TO SHOPS AND RESTAURANTS | QUIET LOCATION | CANAL VIEWS |
|---|---|---|---|---|---|---|---|---|
| **OUDE ZIJDE** *(see p218)* | | | | | | | | |
| Amstel Botel | €€ | 176 | | | | | | ▪ |
| NH Doelen | €€€ | 85 | | | | ▪ | | ▪ |
| Radisson SAS | €€€€ | 242 | | ▪ | | ▪ | | |
| The Grand Sofitel Demeure | €€€€€ | 182 | ● | ▪ | | ▪ | ● | ▪ |
| **NIEUWE ZIJDE** *(see pp218–19)* | | | | | | | | |
| Avenue | €€ | 80 | | | | ▪ | | |
| Rho | €€ | 160 | | | | ▪ | ● | |
| Singel | €€ | 32 | | | | ▪ | ● | ▪ |
| Tulip Inn Dam Square | €€ | 38 | | | ● | ▪ | | |
| Amsterdam | €€€ | 79 | | ▪ | | ▪ | | |
| Estheréa | €€€ | 75 | | | ● | ▪ | ● | ▪ |
| Die Port van Cleve | €€€€ | 120 | | | ● | ▪ | | |
| NH Hotel Krasnapolsky | €€€€ | 469 | ● | ▪ | | ▪ | | |
| Renaissance Amsterdam | €€€€ | 405 | | ▪ | ● | ▪ | | |
| Sofitel | €€€€ | 148 | | ▪ | | ▪ | | |
| Crowne Plaza Amsterdam City Centre | €€€€€ | 270 | | ▪ | ● | ▪ | | |
| De l'Europe | €€€€€ | 100 | ● | ▪ | | ▪ | | ▪ |
| NH Barbizon Palace | €€€€€ | 275 | | ▪ | ● | ▪ | | |
| Swissôtel Amsterdam | €€€€€ | 106 | | ▪ | ● | ▪ | | |
| Victoria Hotel Amsterdam | €€€€€ | 305 | | ▪ | ● | ▪ | | |
| **WESTERN CANAL RING** *(see p220)* | | | | | | | | |
| Acacia | € | 21 | | | | ▪ | | ▪ |
| The Shelter Jordan | € | 106 | | | | ▪ | ● | |
| Van Onna | € | 39 | | | | ▪ | ● | ▪ |
| Canal House | €€ | 26 | ● | | | ▪ | ● | ▪ |
| Toren | €€ | 43 | | | | ▪ | ● | ▪ |
| **CENTRAL CANAL RING** *(see pp220–21)* | | | | | | | | |
| Hans Brinker | € | 31 | | | | ▪ | | |
| Agora | €€ | 16 | | | | ▪ | | ▪ |
| Amsterdam Wiechmann | €€ | 40 | | | | ▪ | | ▪ |
| Hotel Maas | €€ | 28 | | ▪ | | ▪ | ● | ▪ |
| Ambassade | €€€ | 59 | ● | | | ▪ | ● | ▪ |
| Dikker & Thijs Fenice Hotel | €€€ | 42 | | ▪ | ● | ▪ | | ▪ |
| American | €€€€ | 174 | | ▪ | ● | ▪ | | ▪ |
| Pulitzer | €€€€€ | 230 | ● | ▪ | ● | ▪ | ● | ▪ |
| **EASTERN CANAL RING** *(see p221)* | | | | | | | | |
| Asterisk | € | 40 | | | | ▪ | ● | |
| De Admiraal | € | 9 | ● | | | ▪ | | ▪ |
| Prinsenhof | € | 11 | | | | ▪ | | ▪ |
| De Munck | €€ | 14 | | | | ▪ | ● | |
| Seven Bridges | €€ | 8 | ● | | | ▪ | ● | ▪ |
| NH Schiller | €€€€ | 95 | | | | ▪ | | |

**Price categories** for a standard double room per night, including breakfast, tax and service:
€ under €100
€€ €100–€200
€€€ €200–€300
€€€€ €300–€350
€€€€€ over €350

**LARGE ROOMS**
A significant proportion of standard rooms are larger than average.

**NUMBER OF ROOMS**
This chart only indicates the number of rooms for hotels, not hostels. The number of beds at each hostel is given in the listings (see pp218–23).

**BUSINESS FACILITIES**
Includes message-taking service, fax service, desk and telephone in every bedroom, and meeting rooms. Conference facilities are not necessarily available.

| | Number of Rooms | Large Rooms | Business Facilities | Under 12s Free in Room | Close to Shops and Restaurants | Quiet Location | Canal Views |
|---|---|---|---|---|---|---|---|
| **MUSEUM QUARTER** (see pp221–2) | | | | | | | |
| Stayokay Hostel Amsterdam Vondelpark € | | | | | | | |
| Wijnnobel € | 11 | ● | | | ■ | ● | |
| Acro €€ | 51 | | | | ■ | | |
| AMS Hotel Atlas €€ | 23 | | ■ | | ■ | | |
| De Filosoof €€ | 38 | | | | | ● | |
| Owl €€ | 34 | | | | ■ | | |
| Sander €€ | 20 | ● | | | ■ | | |
| Bilderberg Jan Luyken €€€ | 62 | | ■ | | ■ | | |
| Amsterdam Marriott €€€€€ | 392 | | ■ | | ■ | | |
| | | | | | | | |
| **PLANTAGE** (see pp222–3) | | | | | | | |
| Adolesce € | 10 | | ■ | | ■ | ● | ■ |
| The Bridge € | 36 | ● | | | | | ■ |
| Fantasia € | 19 | | | | | ● | ■ |
| Kitty Muijzers € | 10 | ● | | | | | |
| Amstel Inter Continental €€€€€ | 79 | ● | ■ | | | ● | ■ |
| | | | | | | | |
| **FURTHER AFIELD** (see p223) | | | | | | | |
| Van Ostade Bicycle Hotel € | 16 | | | | ■ | ● | |
| Arena Hotel €€ | 121 | | | | | | |
| Villa Borgmann €€ | 15 | ● | | | | ● | ■ |
| AMS Hotel Toro €€€ | 22 | ● | | | | ● | ■ |
| Amsterdam Hilton €€€€€ | 271 | | ■ | ● | | ● | ■ |
| Okura €€€€€ | 370 | ● | ■ | ● | | ● | ■ |

## OUDE ZIJDE

### Amstel Botel

Oosterdokskade 2–4, 1011 AE.
**Map** 8 E1. 📞 626 4247. 🇼
www.amstelbotel.com 📠 639 1952.
**Rooms:** 176. 🛏 1 🏋 📺 🔧 🍴
🅰 AE, DC, MC, V, JCB. €€

The Amstel Botel, a big, modern
boat moored close to Centraal
Station, is the only remaining
floating hotel in the city. More
romantic in aspect than reality, the
accommodation aboard is neat,
but uninspiring and cramped.
Although no more spacious, the
berths facing the water provide a
wonderful view of Amsterdam
across the Oosterdok.

### NH Doelen

Nieuwe Doelenstraat 24, 1012 CP.
**Map** 7 C4. 📞 554 0600.
📠 622 1084. 🇼 www.nh-
hotels.com **Rooms:** 85. 🛏 1 🏋
📺 🔧 🍴 🍴 🅰 AE, DC, MC,
V, JCB. €€€

A reproduction of Rembrandt's
*The Night Watch (see p131)* hangs
in this imposing Neo-Classical
building, a reminder that the
original hung here from 1642 to
1715. Stuccoed walls, marble steps
and copper candelabras reveal the
hotel's pedigree. Although it has
seen better days, it is one of the
few reasonably priced hotels in
central Amsterdam to retain its
interior character. Book one of the
charming bedrooms overlooking
the Amstel (for no extra cost), or
spoil yourself in one of the corner
suites, which have the best views;
some even have their own balcony.

### Radisson SAS

Rusland 17, 1012 CK. **Map** 7 C4.
📞 623 1231. 📠 520 8200.
🇼 www.radissonsas.com
**Rooms:** 242. 🛏 1 📺 📺 🍴
🍴 🅰 AE, DC, MC, V, JCB. €€€

Taking up most of the street, the
well-run Radisson SAS, which
opened in 1990, is set around a
dramatic state-of-the-art atrium.
Despite a modern appearance, the
hotel was developed on the site of
several old buildings. These
include an 18th-century vicarage,
features of which have been transformed into a candle-lit bar. The
bedrooms are imaginatively
themed in Scandinavian, Oriental,
Art Deco or Dutch styles. The
hotel also has its own private
health centre and conference
facilities in a building across the
road. Both amenities are linked to
the hotel by a connecting tunnel.

### The Grand Sofitel Demeure

Oudezijds Voorburgwal 197, 1012 EX.
**Map** 7 C3. 📞 555 3111. 📠 555
3222. 🇼 www.thegrand.nl **Rooms:**
182. 🛏 1 🏋 📺 🔧 🍴 🍴
🍴 🏋 🍴 🅿 🍴 🍴 🍴
🅰 AE, DC, MC, V, JCB. €€€€€

The Grand Amsterdam, opened in
1992, is situated on a peaceful canal
just south of the Red Light District.
The city's newest luxury hotel, it
occupies one of the most historic
locations in the city. The site, first
developed as a convent at the
beginning of the 15th century,
became a royal guest house in the
16th century. The present building,
constructed in 1661, was built for
the Admiralty and was later used
as the city hall. The magnificent
premises are set around their own
courtyard and a lovely enclosed
garden. Highlights inside include
luxurious bedrooms in English
country-house style and the striking
Art Deco Café Roux, serving
affordable high-quality food.

## NIEUWE ZIJDE

### Avenue

Nieuwezijds Voorburgwal 27, 1012 RD.
**Map** 7 C1. 📞 530 9530. 📠 530
9599. 🇼 www.avenue-hotel.nl
**Rooms:** 80. 🛏 1 📺 🔧 🍴
🍴 🍴 🅰 AE, DC, MC, V, JCB. €€

The six-storey black-brick Avenue
used to be a warehouse belonging
to the United East India Company.
Although traffic disturbs the front-
facing bedrooms of this modest
city-centre hotel, rooms at the
back are quieter. All the rooms are
attractive with wicker furniture.
Those on the upper floors at the
back have interesting roof-top
views. Downstairs, the little
breakfast room and bar are
functional rather than inviting.

### Rho

Nes 5–23, 1012 KC. **Map** 7 B3.
📞 620 7371. 📠 620 7826. 🇼
www.rhohotel.com **Rooms:** 160. 🛏
1 📺 📺 🍴 🍴 🔧 🍴 🅿 🍴
🅰 AE, MC, V. €€

The Rho is tucked away down the
Nes *(see p74)*, a narrow backstreet
running south from Dam square. It
enjoys both peace and quiet and a
central location. The hotel's vaulted
lobby, with hints of Art Nouveau
style, is an original feature of the
building, which was constructed in
1908 as a theatre. Bedrooms are
practical and modern without the
character of the period rooms on
the ground floor. The facilities on
offer makes this hotel good value.

### Singel

Singel 13–17, 1012 VC. **Map** 7 B1.
📞 626 3108. 📠 620 3777.
🇼 lempereur-hotels.nl **Rooms:** 32.
🛏 1 🏋 📺 🍴 🍴 🍴
🅰 AE, DC, MC, V, JCB. €€

This little hotel occupies three
17th-century canalside houses. It
is located on a pretty northern
stretch of the Singel overlooking
the Poezenboot (a barge inhabited
by scores of stray cats). Buffet
breakfasts are served in a lime-
green room on the ground floor.
The bedrooms are small but
characterfully shaped and brightly
decorated. All the rooms have
showers, except the family rooms
which have a bath.

### Tulip Inn Dam Square

Gravenstraat 12–16, 1012 NM.
**Map** 7 B2. 📞 623 3716. 📠 638
1156. 🇼 www.tulipinndamsquare.
com **Rooms:** 38. 🛏 🏋 📺 🔧 🍴
🍴 🍴 🅰 AE, DC, MC, V, JCB. €€

De Drie Fleschjes, an ancient
*proeflokaal (see p48)*, leans
against the handsome Tulip Inn,
which was built in 1880 as a
distillery. The hotel overlooks
perhaps the most atmospheric
cobbled square in the city.
Inside, the large open-plan
lobby-cum-breakfast area and
bar is functional and disappoint-
ingly modern. The best of the
modern-styled bedrooms have
been smartly decorated and
contain interesting angular
black and brown furniture.

### Amsterdam

Damrak 93–94, 1012 LP. **Map** 7 B2.
📞 555 0666. 📠 620 4716.
🇼 www.hotelamsterdam.nl
**Rooms:** 79. 🛏 1 🏋 📺 🍴 🍴
🍴 🍴 🍴 🍴 🅰 AE, DC,
MC, V, JCB. €€€

The best part of the hotel is at
street level, where you can sit
all hours of the day on the
covered terrace, drinking beer
and watching the world go by.
Behind this a restaurant serves
a good buffet breakfast and
specializes in traditional Dutch
cuisine. The bedrooms are well
equipped but plain; ask for one
at the back to avoid street noise.

### Estheréa

Singel 305, 1012 WJ. **Map** 7 A3.
📞 624 5146. 📠 623 9001.
🇼 www. estherea.nl **Rooms:** 75.
🛏 1 🏋 📺 🍴 🍴 🍴 🍴
🅰 AE, DC, MC, V, JCB. €€€

The Estheréa occupies four handsome 17th-century red-brick houses
on an elegant part of the Singel. It

is within easy walking distance of Dam square and Spui. This long-established hotel is popular with groups. More than half the bedrooms have a canal view, but rooms at the rear are bigger.

## Die Port van Cleve

Nieuwezijds Voorburgwal 176–180, 1012 SJ. **Map** 7 B3. **C** 624 4860. **FAX** 622 0240. **W** www.dieportvan cleve.com **Rooms**: 120.

AE, DC, MC, V, JCB. €€€€

The hotel boasts two atmospheric restaurants specializing in Dutch cuisine. Murals of old Amsterdam decorate De Poort restaurant, famous for its steaks, while the more formal De Blauwe Parade restaurant contains a beautiful Delft tile frieze. The hotel stands between two busy streets, near the up-market Magna Plaza shopping centre (see Postkantoor, p78), so bedrooms can be noisy. The bedrooms have recently undergone renovation and are less spartan than previously.

## NH Grand Hotel Krasnapolsky

Dam 9, 1012 JS. **Map** 7 C2. **C** 554 9111. **FAX** 622 8607. **W** www.nh-hotels.nl **Rooms**: 469.

AE, DC, MC, V, JCB. €€€€

This landmark hotel began life as a mere coffee house in 1866. It has since had guests as diverse as James Joyce and the Rolling Stones. There is a good choice of restaurants, with buffets in the Winter Garden, a Belle Epoque French brasserie and a stylish Japanese restaurant. Afternoon teas are served in the elegant lounge. Its conference and business facilities are good and the bedrooms are comfortable, but due to its location few are peaceful.

## Renaissance Amsterdam

Kattengat 1, 1012 SZ. **Map** 7 C1. **C** 621 2223. **FAX** 627 5245. **W** www.renaissancehotels.com/amsrd **Rooms**: 405.

AF, DC, M, V, JCB. €€€€

If you want the full range of facilities at a modest room rate, the spacious Amsterdam Renaissance is the best choice. There is a disco, extensive health facilities and a traditional brown café (see p48), along with other restaurants and bars. The hotel also rents out 43 self-catering apartments in old town houses it owns nearby. The

hotel also has a business and conference centre, which is located across the road in the Lutherse Kerk (see p78).

## Sofitel

Nieuwezijds Voorburgwal 67, 1012 RE. **Map** 7 B1. **C** 627 5900. **FAX** 623 8932. **W** www.sofitel.nl **Rooms**: 148.

AE, DC, MC, V, JCB. €€€€

This is a good-quality chain hotel, but somewhat noisy due to its location on a busy street. Like many hotels in the centre, its old gabled buildings now contain modern accommodation. However, the standard look is relieved by the beams in the hotel's dozen or so vaulted bedrooms on the top floor. Its striking bar has red velvet seating, panelled walls and windows to replicate a carriage from the Orient Express.

## Crowne Plaza Amsterdam City Centre

Nieuwezijds Voorburgwal 5, 1012 RC. **Map** 7 C1. **C** 620 0500. **FAX** 620 1173. **W** www.amsterdam-citycentre. crowneplaza.com **Rooms**: 270.

AE, DC, MC, V, JCB. €€€€€

The Crowne Plaza is a cut above the average Holiday Inn, with good business facilities, perky staff and a swimming pool. The hotel's original garden has been covered to make a courtyard café and a variety of Dutch delicacies can be enjoyed nearby at the Dorrius, a 100-year-old restaurant (see p231). The standard bedrooms are small, but pay a little more and you'll be rewarded with plenty of extra space.

## De l'Europe

Nieuwe Doelenstraat 2–8, 1012 CP. **Map** 7 C4. **C** 531 1777. **FAX** 531 1778. **W** www.leurope.nl **Rooms**: 100.

AE, DC, MC, V, JCB. €€€€€

The monolithic De l'Europe, dating from 1896, stands opposite the Muntplein, a confluence of waterways and streets carrying every kind of traffic. The location may be noisy, but if you have a weakness for chandeliers, plush drapes, classical music or bedrooms with fleur-de-lys wallpaper, a chaise longue and a tip-top marble bathroom, this is the place to stay. Added incentives include a serious French restaurant and an amazing swimming pool, which is

surrounded by statues and pillars. Many of the rooms have balconies that face directly on to the Amstel, as does the hotel's memorably picturesque waterside terrace.

## NH Barbizon Palace

Prins Hendrikkade 59–72, 1012 AD. **Map** 8 D1. **C** 556 4564. **FAX** 624 3353. **W** www.nh-hotels.com **Rooms**: 275.

AE, DC, MC, V, JCB. €€€€€

A predominantly modern exterior conceals 19 houses dating from the 17th century. Consequently, many of the bedrooms have attractive beamed ceilings. All have first-rate facilities. The chessboard floor and creamy pillars of the lobby, the sprinkling of antiques in the smart Vermeer restaurant (see p231) and the tiny panelled bar lend character to the hotel's public areas. Business and conference facilities are available in St Olofskapel.

## Swissôtel Amsterdam

Damrak 96–98, 1012 LP. **Map** 7 C2. **C** 522 3000. **FAX** 522 3223. **W** www.swissotel.com **Rooms**: 106.

AE, DC, MC, V, JCB. €€€€€

This smart establishment on the corner of Dam square should appeal to business people who are looking for something more intimate than a vast chain hotel. Breakfast, lunch and dinner are served in an attractive marbled, yet informal, French brasserie. Marble also features in the bathrooms of the hotel's stylish, modern and well-equipped bedrooms. Rooms facing the square are more expensive, but it is wiser to ask for a quieter room at the rear.

## Victoria Hotel Amsterdam

Damrak 1–5, 1012 LG. **Map** 7 C1. **C** 524 0620. **FAX** 627 4259. **W** www.parkplazaeurope.com **Rooms**: 305.

AE, DC, MC, V, JCB. €€€€€

Despite the trams, trains and canal cruises, which all depart from close to the front doors, the Park Plaza offers a world removed from the bustle of nearby Centraal Station and the neon of the Damrak. Within the grand Neo-Classical building, leather Chesterfields and oil paintings grace the bar, while pine and pot plants deck out the restaurant. The bedrooms are fresh, colourful and double-glazed, and the health centre boasts a pool.

## WESTERN CANAL RING

## Acacia

Lindengracht 251, 1015 KH. **Map** 1 B3. 🄲 *622 1460.* 🄵🄰🄷 *638 0748.* 🅆 www.acaciahotel.nl **Rooms**: *21.* 🛏 1 🎚 📺 🐾 ▶ 🅿 🕭 *MC, V.* €
Inside the wedge-shaped, end-of-terrace Acacia, guests must climb steep stairs to reach simple rooms with a little shower room and not much else. However, the breakfast room is charming, as are the young owners, the van Vliets. They also rent out a houseboat, which sleeps four and has a kitchenette, on an adjacent canal in this peaceful part of the Jordaan.

## The Shelter Jordan

Bloemstraat 179, 1016 LA. **Map** 1 A4. *Hostel.* 🄲 *624 4717.* 🄵🄰🄷 *627 6137.* 🅆 www.shelter.nl **Beds**: *106.* 📳 🎚 €
This spotlessly clean Christian hostel is not designed for late-night revellers. There is a midnight curfew (2am at weekends) and no drink is allowed on the premises. Optional Christian activities are laid on.

## Van Onna

Bloemgracht 102/104/108, 1015 TN. **Map** 1 A4. 🄲 *626 5801.* 🅆 www. netcentrum.com/onna **Rooms**: *41.* 🛏 1 🎚 €
Charismatic Loek van Onna's B&B is made up of three canalside houses. He is justifiably proud of the recent modernization of the middle house, which contains an attractive staircase and breakfast room, and neat, modern rooms with *en suite* bathrooms. The untouched old buildings on either side offer much more basic accommodation with shared bathrooms.

## Canal House

Keizersgracht 148, 1015 CX. **Map** 7 A1. 🄲 *622 5182.* 🄵🄰🄷 *624 1317.* 🅆 www.canalhouse.nl **Rooms**: *26.* 🛏 1 🐾 🕭 *AE, DC, MC, V.* €€
This small-scale hotel occupies two old houses. Downstairs, there is an atmospheric bar hung with gilt mirrors and an ornate breakfast room-cum-lounge, with a grand piano under a chandelier and stuccoed ceiling. Antique furnishings also adorn a selection of the individually decorated bedrooms. Those at the front of the hotel have good views of the canal, while some of the back rooms overlook a small garden. To preserve the ambience, there·. is not a TV in sight, and children are not welcomed.

## Toren

Keizersgracht 164, 1015 CZ. **Map** 7 A1. 🄲 *622 6033.* 🄵🄰🄷 *626 9705.* 🅆 www. toren.nl **Rooms**: *43.* 🛏 1 🎚 📺 🅦 🐾 📳 🔆 🕭 *AE, DC, MC, V.* €€
The two old houses of the Toren on this ultra-civilized stretch of canal are overshadowed by the allure of the nearby Canal House. Bedrooms typically have dated furniture, but for a few extra euros you can have a canal view and a fair amount of space. Be careful to avoid the rooms in the middle of the hotel, which don't even have windows. However, the breakfast rooms and hotel bar display more character with their small chandeliers and panelled walls. The staff at Toren are helpful and keen to please.

## CENTRAL CANAL RING

## Hans Brinker

Kerkstraat 136–138, 1017 GR. **Map** 7 A5. *Hostel.* 🄲 *622 0687.* 🄵🄰🄷 *638 2060.* 🅆 www.brinker.nl/xxxclusive **Rooms**: *31.* **Beds**: *536.* 1 🎚 🕭 🐾 🔆 📳 🕭 *AE, DC, MC, V.* €
Conveniently close to the nightlife around Leidseplein, this hostel has small dormitories and its own disco. Despite being a bit pricey, it is very popular with backpackers. There is no curfew policy and the lively bar is open until 2am.

## Agora

Singel 462, 1017 AW. **Map** 7 B5. 🄲 *627 2200.* 🄵🄰🄷 *627 2202.* 🅆 www.hotelagora.nl **Rooms**: *16.* 🎚 *13.* 1 🎚 📺 🔆 🐾 🕭 *AE, DC, MC, V.* €€
This modern canalside terraced house has a classic city location overlooking the Singel, near the Bloemenmarkt *(see p123).* Friendly owners preside over a warren of simple rooms, which boast the odd antique desk or armchair. Those overlooking the canal can sometimes be noisy. The open-plan lounge and breakfast area are both smartly decorated.

## Amsterdam Wiechmann

Prinsengracht 328–332, 1016 HX. **Map** 1 B5. 🄲 *626 3321.* 🅆 www. wiechmann.nl 🄵🄰🄷 *626 8962.* **Rooms**: *40.* 🛏 1 📺 🎚 🔆 €€
The charming Mr Boddy from Oklahoma has been taking in guests at this B&B for some 40 years. His hotel is made up of three canal houses. The corner house, now an attractive blue-tiled breakfast room, was built as a café in 1912. The rest of the hotel

seems much older. Persian rugs on polished dark wood floors, beams, antiques and even a suit of armour characterize the elegant reception and lounge bar. Some antique furniture also graces the fetching, unfussy bedrooms, most of which have a canal view.

## Hotel Maas

Leidsekade 91, 1017 PN. **Map** 4 D1. 🄲 *623 3868.* 🄵🄰🄷 *622 2613.* 🅆 www.hemhotels.nl **Rooms**: *28.* 📳 🛏 1 🎚 📺 🐾 🔆 🅈 🕭 *AE, DC, M, V.* €€

This 19th-century canal house hotel is situated on a quiet stretch of the Singel. Just round the corner, however, you'll find the vibrant nightlife of the Leidseplein and De Melkweg, the city's most famous venue for entertainment and culture of all sorts. The bedrooms are comfortable with coffee makers and mini bars. Some boast jacuzzis and waterbeds and many have lovely views over the canal. Children are welcome, with cots and babysitting available.

## Ambassade

Herengracht 335–341, 1016 AZ. **Map** 7 A4. 🄲 *555 0222.* 🄵🄰🄷 *555 0277.* 🅆 www.ambassade-hotel.nl **Rooms**: *59.* 🛏 1 🎚 📶 📺 🐾 🔆 🛏 🕭 *AE, DC, MC, V.* €€€
This is Amsterdam's most luxurious canalside B&B. Favoured by illustrious writers such as Umberto Eco, the hotel is stylish, comfortable and professionally run. It comprises eight beautiful patrician 17th-century houses. The lounges have chandeliers, rugs on parquet floors and ornate French antiques. The most memorable bedrooms, located at the top of the houses, have beamed, vaulted ceilings and miniature windows. The rooms on lower floors are often spacious and have as many as four canalside windows. The 24-hour room service provides simple meals and drinks.

## Dikker & Thijs Fenice Hotel

Prinsengracht 444, 1017 KE. **Map** 4 E1. 🄲 *620 1212.* 🄵🄰🄷 *625 8986.* 🅆 www.dtfh.nl **Rooms**: *42.* 🛏 🎚 1 📺 🅈 🐾 🅈 📳 🕭 *AE, DC, MC, V, JCB.* €€€
Located near Leidseplein, the privately owned and recently refurbished Dikker & Thijs offers a change of tempo from the city's traditional canalside residences. Three floors of stylized rooms are predominantly decorated in blacks, pinks and greys, reflecting the hotel's austere, angular Art Deco exterior. Bedrooms looking onto Prinsengracht are the quietest.

## American Hotel

Leidsekade 97, 1017 PN. **Map** 4 E2.
▮ *556 3000*. ▮**FAX** *556 3001*. ▮**w** www.
amsterdam-american.crowneplaza.com
***Rooms****: 174.* ▮ ▮ ▮ ▮ ▮ ▮
▮ ▮ ▮ ▮ ▮ ▮ ▮ ▮ ▮
*AE, DC, MC, V, JCB.* €€€€€

The spectacular American Hotel
dates from the turn of the century
and is one of Amsterdam's most
distinctive landmarks (*see p110*).
The impressive façade and turreted
clock tower bristle with Art Nouveau flourishes. Over the years,
bedrooms have lost their authentic
period details but, thanks to the
installation of double glazing, noise
has been reduced. Fortunately, the
famous Café Américain (*see p46*),
constantly packed with locals and
tourists, has remained largely
unchanged, down to library-style
desks on which newspapers are
read. The hotel's terrace fills a
corner of the city's busiest entertainment spot, Leidseplein.

## Pulitzer

Prinsengracht 315–331, 1016 GZ.
**Map** 1 B5. ▮ *523 5235*. ▮**FAX** *627
6753*. ▮**w** www.pulitzer.nl
***Rooms****: 230.* ▮ ▮ ▮ ▮ ▮ ▮
▮ ▮ ▮ ▮ ▮ ▮ *AE, DC,
MC, V, JCB.* €€€€€

The luxury Pulitzer is probably the
city's most imaginative canal house
conversion. No fewer than 24
houses along Prinsengracht and
Keizersgracht offer bedrooms that
cleverly combine 17th- and 18th-
century architecture with stylish
modern furnishings and art. The
complex is set around a lovely
courtyard garden, where you can
wine and dine in summer. Other
highlights include the hotel's tiled
brasserie, an Art Nouveau garden
room and a snug bar. In the
summer, champagne cruises leave
from the hotel's own landing stage.

## EASTERN CANAL RING

## Asterisk

Den Texstraat 14–16, 1017 ZA.
**Map** 5 A4. ▮ *626 2396*. ▮**w** www.
asteriskhotel.nl ▮**FAX** *638 2790*. ***Rooms*:**
*40.* ▮ *25.* ▮ ▮ ▮ ▮ ▮ ▮ ▮
*MC, V.* €

As the Asterisk is a little way from
the centre of town, on a residential
backstreet near the Heineken
Brouwerij (*see p122*), its rates are
good value. Bedrooms within the
handsome, four-storey, 19th-cent-
ury house are a decent size and are
furnished with good-quality modern units, Impressionist prints and
aerial photographs of the city. In
the breakfast room, mirrors and

stuccowork offer a touch of style.
Breakfast is inclusive with cash payment, but extra for credit cards.

## De Admiraal

Herengracht 563, 1017 CD. **Map** 7
C5. ▮ *626 2150*. ▮**FAX** *623 4625*.
***Rooms****: 9.* ▮ *6.* ▮ ▮ ▮
▮ *AE, DC, MC, V.* €

This engagingly laid-back B&B
stands next to a saucy-looking
cabaret off Rembrandtplein and
should be avoided by early-to-
bedders. Breakfast, served in an
amazingly cluttered room full of
plants, carriage clocks and paintings, is extra as guests often
spend the morning in bed. Many
of the atmospheric, beamed bedrooms are massive, particularly
the family rooms. No. 12 also
has a balcony. There is a five
per cent surcharge for credit-
card payments.

## Prinsenhof

Prinsengracht 810, 1017 JL. **Map** 5 A3.
▮ *623 1772*. ▮**FAX** *638 3368*.
▮**w** www.hotelprinsenhof.com ***Rooms*:**
*11.* ▮ *3.* ▮ ▮ ▮ *AE, MC, V.* €

The Prinsenhof is one of the
best-kept and prettiest of the
city's simple canalside B&Bs.
With its attractive breakfast room
and tastefully decorated
bedrooms, the hotel is a good
choice if you don't mind sharing
a bathroom and can cope with
very steep stairs. The first flight
of stairs leads straight from the
front door, which is operated by
a pulley system at reception on
the first floor. The many bistros
along Utrechtsestraat are a short
walk away. Credit card payments
incur a five per cent surcharge.

## De Munck

Achtergracht 3, 1017 WL. **Map** 5 B3.
▮ *623 6283*. ▮**FAX** *620 6647*. ▮**w** www.
hoteldemunck.com ***Rooms****: 14.*
▮ *12.* ▮ ▮ ▮ ▮ €€

The two old gabled buildings of
the De Munck rest peacefully on
the corner of a leafy little square
and cul-de-sac canal. The owner
loves 50s and 60s pop music, so
pride of place in the lovely basement breakfast room goes to a
gold-plated Elvis record and a juke-
box. Credit cards can be used to
make a reservation but once there
you have to pay in cash.

## Seven Bridges

Reguliersgracht 31, 1017 LK. **Map** 5 A3.
▮ *623 1329*. ***Rooms****: 8.* ▮ ▮ ▮
*AE, MC, V.* €€

Sitting inconspicuously on arguably
Amsterdam's prettiest little canal,
the Seven Bridges has evolved over
the last 20 years into one of the

city's most stylish B&Bs. Although
it has no public rooms, steep stairs
and a less-than-eager attitude towards children, you may need to
book at least a month in advance
to stay in one of its beautiful bedrooms. Stripped floorboards,
Persian rugs and antique cabinets
distinguish both the grand and
small rooms. Breakfast is served in
your room on fine English china.

## NH Schiller

Rembrandtplein 26–36, 1017 CV.
**Map** 7 C5. ▮ *554 0700*. ▮**FAX** *624
0098*. ▮**w** www.nh-hotels.com
***Rooms****: 95.* ▮ ▮ ▮ ▮ ▮ ▮
▮ ▮ ▮ ▮ ▮ *AE, DC, MC, V, JCB.*
€€€€

The most distinctive feature of the
old-fashioned Schiller is the vast
collection of paintings which hangs
throughout the hotel's public areas,
all the work of the original owner
Fritz Schiller. The late 19th-century
building has its own café terrace
on lively Rembrandtplein. Behind
the café lies a big airy dining
room with attractive stained-glass
sun-lights, oak beams and
panelling. For peace and quiet,
request a bedroom at the back of
the hotel. All the rooms tend to be
a little shabby in places.

## MUSEUM QUARTER

## Stayokay Hostel
## Amsterdam Vondelpark

Zandpad 5, 1054 GA. **Map** 4 D2.
*Hostel.* ▮ *589 8996*. ▮**FAX** *589 8955*.
▮**w** www.stayokay.com ***Beds****: 475.*
▮ ▮ ▮ ▮ ▮ €

Pleasantly situated in a chalet
on the eastern edge of Vondelpark
is one of the two hostels in
Amsterdam belonging to the
Dutch Youth Hostels Association
(NJHC). Recently renovated, it
offers dormitory accommodation
as well as single and double
rooms, with a discount if you join
the International Youth Hostel
Federation on arrival.

## Wijnnobel

Vossiusstraat 9, 1071 AB. **Map** 4 E2. ▮
*662 2298*. ***Rooms****: 11.* ▮ ▮ ▮ €

The utterly basic Wynnobel, on a
quiet street off Vondelpark, is
geared towards a bohemian clientele and offers good value. Steep
stairs lead to simple but striking
rooms, typically with lino flooring,
a marble fireplace and old
wooden furniture. As none of the
rooms has its own bathroom, they
are often spacious. A modest
breakfast is served in the rooms
and each floor shares an old-
fashioned bathroom.

For key to symbols *see p211*

## Acro

Jan Luijkenstraat 44, 1071 CR.
**Map** 4 E3. **(** 662 0526. **FAX** 675
0811. **W** www.acro-hotel.nl
**Rooms**: 51. 🛏 🔟 💤 TV ⬆ ▸
🅿 AE, DC, MC, V, JCB. €€

What the Acro lacks in old-world
charm it makes up for in smart
modernity, value for money and
proximity to the up-market shops
along PC Hooftstraat *(see p242)*.
The hotel has a dapper little bar
off the foyer and a cafeteria-style
breakfast room in the basement.
Upstairs, the small bedrooms are
bright, well kept and each has an
*en suite* shower room. The hotel
is popular with tour groups.

## AMS Hotel Atlas

Van Eeghenstraat 64, 1071 GK.
**Map** 3 C3. **(** 676 6336. **FAX** 671
7633. **W** www.ams.nl **Rooms**: 23.
🛏 🔟 💤 24 TV ⬆ ▸ 🍽 💤
🅿 AE DC, MC, V, JCB. €€

Atlas is one of the city's unheralded
architectural delights. This large,
detached Art Nouveau house on
the southern edge of Vondelpark
has floral indulgences on the façade
and Gaudiesque embellishments
over the windows. The interior is
plainer, but all the bedrooms are
smart and have good modern bathrooms. A modest menu of home-
made Dutch food is available in
the dining room and through room
service. The staff are experienced
and very welcoming.

## De Filosoof

Anna van den Vondelstraat 6,
1054 GZ. **Map** 3 C2. **(** 683 3013.
**FAX** 685 3750. **W** www.hotelfilosoof.nl
**Rooms**: 38. 🛏 🔟 💤 TV 🍽 🅿
AE, MC, V. €€

If the stimulants found in
Amsterdam's coffee shops *(see
p49)* don't deliver the meaning
of life to you, search out the
modest Hotel de Filosoof on the
northern side of Vondelpark. Run
by vivacious professional philosopher Ida Jongsma, regular
highbrow dinners and meetings
are held here and many of the
hotel's resident guests are
intellectuals. However, this is no
stuffy academic retreat. Murals of
Plato and Aristotle greet you at the
door and most bedrooms have
exuberant philosophical or cultural themes. For example, the
Plato room is dramatically decorated in black and white with
*trompe l'oeil* paintings mounted on
pedestals. Classical jazz is played
in the velvet-draped breakfast
room, which is lined with a library
of thought-provoking works, and
also in the eye-catching black and
white marbled bar.

## Owl

Roemer Visscherstraat 1, 1054 EV.
**Map** 4 D2. **(** 618 9484. **FAX** 618
9441. **W** www.owl-hotel.nl
**Rooms**: 34. 🛏 🔟 💤 TV 🗡
💤 🍽 🅿 AE, DC, MC, V, JCB.
€€

A stuffed owl in an alcove on the
exterior wall provides the name
for arguably the best of the many
hotels situated on this convenient,
quiet street between Leidseplein
and Vondelpark. A smart bar and
breakfast room downstairs lead
through to a neat and pretty
garden. Fresh flowers enliven
the rather plain, pine-furnished
bedrooms that show signs of
wear and tear in places. The
Kos-Brals family have been
providing a warm welcome
for many years.

## Sander

Jacob Obrechtstraat 69, 1071 KJ.
**Map** 4 D4. **(** 662 7574.
**FAX** 679 6067. **W** www.hotel-
sander.nl **Rooms**: 20. 🛏 🔟 💤
TV 🍽 💤 🅿 AE, DC, MC, V, JCB.
€€

This small, well-kept hotel
stands in a long terrace in the
Oud Zuid (Old South), not far
from the city's main museums.
It has an appealing bar and
breakfast room opening onto a
pretty little garden to the rear.
The bedrooms, although somewhat plain, are comfortable. The
more spacious ones even have
bays with seating areas.

## Bilderberg Jan Luyken

Jan Luijkenstraat 58, 1071 CS.
**Map** 4 E3. **(** 573 0730. **FAX** 676
3841. **W** www.janluyken.nl
**Rooms**: 62. 🛏 🔟 💤 TV 🍽 ▸
🔟 🗡 🍽 💤 🅿 AF, DC, MC,
V. €€€

The Bilderberg Jan Luyken is
located in three elegant 19th-
century houses, just a stone's
throw from the main museums
and best shops. This well-kept
hotel goes out of its way to woo
a wide range of guests. Along
with excellent business facilities,
it offers room service most hours
of the day, as well as snacks in
the cosy bar and on the garden
patio. It also provides an elaborate
buffet breakfast in the basement,
which is enlivened with attractive
stained-glass windows. Free
afternoon tea is served in the
smart peach-coloured lounge.
The comfortable, well-equipped
bedrooms are priced according
to their size. There are large
family rooms that also come
with a sofa bed.

## Amsterdam Marriott

Stadhouderskade 12, 1054 ES. **Map** 4
D2. **(** 607 5555. **FAX** 607 5511.
**W** www.marriott.com **Rooms**: 392.
🛏 🔟 💤 TV 💤 🍽 🗡 🍽 ▸
🏃 ♿ 💤 🅿 🍽 🍽 🍽 🅿 AE, DC,
MC, V, JCB. €€€€€

The multi-storeyed Marriott is by
no means a showpiece for this
American chain, yet it provides all
the facilities you would expect
from a large cosmopolitan hotel.
Business facilities include spacious
conference rooms, express check-
out and an executive floor. The
hotel also contains a number of
shops, as well as an attractive grill
and seafood restaurant. Front bedrooms face Leidseplein across a
busy main road and are noisy.
The rooms at the back are quieter
with views over Vondelpark. There
are bargain rates for bookings made
at least three weeks in advance.

## PLANTAGE

## Adolesce

Nieuwe Keizersgracht 26, 1018 DS.
**Map** 8 F5. **(** 626 3959. **FAX** 627
4249. **Rooms**: 10. ♿ (one room)
🛏 8 🔟 💤 🍽 MC, V. €

A cheerful canal-house hotel in a
quiet but central location on the
Keizersgracht, close to the eastern
bank of the Amstel. The bar is
cosy and the conservatory and
patio garden are great in summer.
The hotel serves no breakfast.

## The Bridge

Amstel 107–111, 1018 EM. **Map** 5
B3. **(** 623 7068. **FAX** 624 1565.
**W** www.thebridgehotel.demon.nl
**Rooms**: 36. 🛏 🔟 💤 TV 🍽 AE,
DC, MC, V. €

From the Bridge, it is less than a
ten-minute stroll along a lovely
stretch of the Amstel to the hub-
bub of Rembrandtplein. Unlike
many canalside hotels in the
centre of town, the three adjoining
brick houses are refreshingly
spacious. The roomy bedrooms
are furnished in pine with varying
degrees of modernity, and the
smart breakfast room is done out
in rattan style.

## Fantasia

Nieuwe Keizersgracht 16, 1018 DR.
**Map** 5 B3. **(** 623 8259. **FAX** 622
3913. **W** www.fantasia-hotel.com
**Rooms**: 19. 🛏 🔟 💤 🍽 AE, MC,
V. €

This canalside house, dating from
1773, faces the Amstelhof, a stately
retirement home, rather than the

usual gabled terraces. Here on the quiet eastern side of the Amstel, the pace of life is slower than on the more fashionable west side. Despite being within easy walking distance of the city centre, prices for the old-fashioned, simple bedrooms are very reasonable. The atmosphere is altogether homely, especially in the panelled breakfast room, where the resident cat is often to be found snoozing.

## Kitty Muijzers

Plantage Middenlaan 40, 1018 DG.
**Map** 6 D2. 622 6819.
***Rooms***: 10. 1 ⊞ €

Few traces of the 1990s appear in elderly Kitty Muijzer's somewhat bizarre pension. Situated opposite the zoo, the hotel is a 15-minute walk or a short tram ride from the centre of Amsterdam. Religious and Classical statues and a profusion of greenery decorate the turn-of-the-century house, which is flooded in a yellowy light from the glass-roofed stairwell. Unequivocally old-fashioned bedrooms, some with decades-old TVs and fridges, are big and comfortably furnished; none has a private bathroom, and basins are often hidden away in cupboards. Children under 12 years old are not welcome.

## Amstel
## Inter Continental

Prof. Tulpplein 1, 1018 GX. **Map** 5 B4.
622 6060. **FAX** 622 5808.
W www.amsterdam.intercontinenti.com
***Rooms***: 79. ⌂ 1 ⊞ 24 TV Y
⊠ ▤ ▮ ⬚ ▣ ◨ ⬆ P Y
▮▮ ⬚ *AE, DC, MC, V, JCB*
€€€€€

This is undisputably the city's top hotel. Opened in 1867 and painstakingly renovated in 1992 at a cost of some 70 million guilders, its grandeur is almost overwhelming. The breathtaking hallway is graced with two tiers of pillars and arches and a gilded ceiling. The Amstel's first-class restaurant, La Rive *(see p235)*, the conservatory sitting room and the elegant swimming pool all open on to a terrace beside the Amstel river. Beautiful fabrics, furniture and paintings adorn the stunning bedrooms. Each room also comes with its own superb bathroom, a drinks cabinet with cut-glass decanters and a personal fax machine. Additional treats include a Turkish bath, Rolls Royces and a motor yacht available for use by guests, and a limousine service to Schiphol Airport. For a five-star hotel the Amstel is comparatively small, so you often need to book well in advance to secure a room.

While the hotel is a 15-minute walk from the city centre, this doesn't dissuade guests from staying here, as the cost of a few taxis pales into insignificance beside the final hotel bill.

## FURTHER AFIELD

## Van Ostade
## Bicycle Hotel

Van Ostadestraat 123, 1072 SV.
**Map** 4 F5. 679 3452. **FAX** 671 5213. W www.bicyclehotel.com
***Rooms***: 16. ⌂ 1 ▣ P €

Two bicycles hang 6 m (20 ft) up on the wall of this most friendly of B&Bs in the untouristy De Pijp district, south of Sarphatipark. A youthful clientele is attracted by the cheapness of the spartan but decent bedrooms, the laid-back atmosphere in the pretty breakfast room and the convenience of being able to rent bikes on the spot. The helpful owners provide city maps and plenty of advice on alternative routes for guests who want to explore the city by bike.

## Arena Hotel

's-Gravesandestraat 51, 1092 AA.
**Map** 6 D4. 850 2400. **FAX** 850 2425. W www.hotelarena.nl
***Rooms***: 121. 1 ⊞ ▣ ◨ ⬚ P ⬆
Y ▮▮ ⬚ *AE, MC, V.* €€

A radical restoration has transformed this former hostel into a comfortable and spacious hotel. Located near the peaceful Oosterpark, the Arena also functions as an international centre for youth culture and tourism. Although it is quite a long way from the centre of town, the hostel has a lively bar, which is open until 2am at weekends, and organizes in-house youth-oriented events, club nights, gigs and exhibitions in the summer. Arena is also the third-largest pop music venue in Amsterdam. There is no curfew policy and bicycles are available for rent.

## Villa Borgmann

Koningslaan 48, 1075 AE.
**Map** 3 B4. 673 5252. **FAX** 676 2580. W www.bookings.nl ***Rooms***: 15. ⌂ 1 ⊞ TV ⬚ ◨ ⬆ ⬚
⬚ *AE, DC, MC, V, JCB.* €€

No match for the stylishness of the nearby Toro, this big, airy house built in 1905 nonetheless shares the same enviable peaceful location overlooking the canal on the southern side of Vondelpark. Wicker furniture and floral bed linen dominate the extremely pleasant bedrooms, some of which are very large.

## AMS Hotel Toro

Koningslaan 64, 1075 AG. **Map** 3 A4. 673 7223. **FAX** 675 0031.
W www.ams.nl ***Rooms***: 22. ⌂ 1
TV Y ⬚ *AE, DC, MC, V.* €€€

The Toro is situated in a smart residential district on the southwest corner of Vondelpark. This very peaceful spot is some way from the city centre – a 15-minute stroll through the park or a short tram ride. Consequently, its rates are an absolute bargain. Tasteful antiques, oil paintings, stained glass, chandeliers and a carved wooden staircase give the mansion the air of a small country house. Some of the Toro's very comfortable bedrooms overlook the park's canal and come with a balcony. The same view can also be admired through the French windows of the delightfully airy breakfast room.

## Amsterdam Hilton

Apollolaan 138, 1077 BG. **Map** 3 C5.
710 6000. **FAX** 710 6080.
W www.amsterdam.hilton.com
***Rooms***: 271. ⌂ 1 ▣ 24 TV Y
⊠ ▤ ▮ ◨ ⬚ ◨ ▣ P Y
▮▮ ⬚ *AE, DC, MC, V, JCB.*
€€€€€

As this Hilton is a monument to ugly, high-rise architecture, only the bedrooms on the two executive floors are recommended. Although no-one chooses to stay in the Nieuw Zuid (New South) district unless they have business in the area, John Lennon and Yoko Ono staged their famous "bed in" here in 1969. For a great deal of money, Beatles fans can stay in what was their suite with quotes, photographs and prints of the lovers on the walls. The room also houses a small library of Lennon books and CDs and, of course, a guitar.

## Okura

Ferdinand Bolstraat 333, 1072 LH.
**Map** 4 F5. 678 7111. **FAX** 671 2344. W www.okura.nl
***Rooms***: 370. ⌂ 1 ▣ 24 TV Y
⊠ ▤ ▮ ◨ ⬚ Cots. ⬚ ⬆ P
Y ▮▮ ⬚ *AE, DC, MC, V, JCB.*
€€€€€

The luxurious Okura is one of the leading five star hotels in the Netherlands. A five-minute walk from the RAI Congresgebouw *(see p151)*, the hotel is wholeheartedly geared to business travellers. There are ten banqueting rooms which can also be used for conferences. It has two Japanese restaurants and a French restaurant, perched on the 23rd floor. Most room rates are halved at weekends.

# RESTAURANTS, CAFÉS AND BARS

LTHOUGH the Netherlands does not enjoy the gastronomic reputation of France or Italy, the chances of finding good food at a reasonable price in Amsterdam are high. Many cafés and bars serve tempting snacks, and some, known as *eetcafés*, provide a full three-course menu *(see pp236–7)*. In addition to the city's selection of Dutch restaurants, where portions are invariably generous, there are also hundreds of other places to try, offering a range of culinary delights from around the world. The following pages will help you locate the best quality food and most exciting cuisine in all price categories. *Choosing a Restaurant* on pages 228–9 gives summaries of the key features of restaurants included in this guide. A detailed review on each of the selected restaurants is provided on pages 230–35.

**A typically cosy, atmospheric restaurant, Amsterdam**

## WHERE TO EAT

AMSTERDAM IS A small city, and most of the restaurants listed in this guide are fairly central and easy to find. The highest concentrations of restaurants are to be found along Van Baerlestraat in the Museum Quarter, in the Red Light District and along Spuistraat in the Nieuwe Zijde, on Reguliersdwarsstraat in the Eastern Canal Ring and in the Jordaan. Cheap meals can also be enjoyed in any of the city's *eetcafés*.

## WHAT TO EAT

IN THE PAST, Dutch home cooking and snacks were traditionally offered in *eetcafés*, and Indonesian-based cuisine was the main cheap alternative. French food was served in more expensive restaurants. Today, there is a much greater choice of international cuisine available and many of the city's restaurants combine French cooking techniques with seasonal Dutch ingredients.

Since much of Indonesia was once a Dutch colony, Amsterdam is one of the best places in Europe to sample its diverse flavours. Much of the cooking may lean too heavily towards the Chinese style for purists, but it is possible to sample genuine Indonesian recipes. Japanese and Thai food is also popular and affordable. Italian cooking is another favourite and the standard is improving. Indian, Mexican and African food can also be found, but the quality is variable.

On the whole, vegetarians are well catered for here. The chart on pages 228–9 shows which restaurants have a good selection of vegetarian dishes.

## WHAT TO DRINK

BEER IS THE DRINK of preference in most Dutch cafés and bars, and all have a wide selection of local and imported brews *(see p48–9)*. Wine is widely available and nearly all restaurants in Amsterdam offer a good choice, with emphasis on French wines. Most Spanish and Italian restaurants also have an interesting range of their own local wines. A special symbol is awarded to

**Amsterdam's famous floating Chinese restaurant, the Sea Palace** *(see p230)*

those restaurants listed in this guide that offer an exceptionally good choice of wines.

Restaurants specializing in traditional cuisine tend to have the best selection of *jenevers* (Dutch gin) *(see p48–9)*.

## How Much to Pay

DUTCH PEOPLE like to know exactly how much they are going to pay for a meal, so almost all restaurants display a menu in the window. This gives the prices, which include VAT (BTW) and service. Prices vary markedly in the city and a meal at a luxurious restaurant can cost more than €80 per head. However, if you are on a budget, Amsterdam has a wide choice of places serving meals at under €45 per head. The cost of drinks is invariably extra and the mark-up levied by a restaurant, especially on cheap wine, can be high.

**Enjoying attentive service – a feature of eating out in Amsterdam**

## Opening Times

SINCE THE DUTCH don't view lunch as the main meal of the day, few restaurants are open during the day. However, many designer bars and brown cafés *(see pp236–7)* serve lunch from around noon to 2pm. In most restaurants, dinner is served from 6pm onwards, and last orders are often taken as early as 10pm. Nowadays, however, some kitchens are deciding to stay open longer. Some restaurants, particularly those in the central areas, now take orders until 11pm, and a few remain open considerably later. Traditionally, many do not open at all on a Monday,

**Outdoor café life near the Waag in Nieuwmarkt**

although this is also changing. For details of café and bar opening times, see *Light Meals and Snacks* on pages 236–7.

## Making a Reservation

WHEN VISITING one of the city's more celebrated restaurants, it is always wise to book in advance. The listings on pages 228–35 indicate where booking is advisable.

Popular brown cafés and designer bars can also become crowded in the evening, but few of them take reservations.

## Reading the Menu

THE MENUS at many tourist restaurants are written in Dutch, French and English. However, as most waiters and waitresses in the city speak good English, and often another European language, it is rarely a problem ordering a meal anywhere in Amsterdam. For more details on what to order, see pages 226–7.

## Etiquette

MOST RESTAURANTS in Amsterdam are relaxed, so smart casual or semi-formal dress is suitable almost everywhere. Although there is nothing to stop you dressing up for special occasions, nowhere insists on a tie. For details of eating out with children, see page 253.

## Smoking

GENERALLY, there are no areas set aside for non-smokers in Amsterdam's restaurants, brown cafés or designer bars.

## Disabilities

DISABLED VISITORS will be able to get into the majority of ground-floor restaurants in the city. However, toilets can be difficult to get to as access to them is often via steep stairs.

## Tipping

A SERVICE CHARGE of 15 per cent is automatically included on bills in restaurants, cafés and bars. Most Amsterdammers, however, round up a small bill to the largest whole euro and larger ones to the nearest €5. The tip is left as change rather than included on a credit-card payslip.

### Using the Listings

Key to symbols in the listings on pp228–9.

|☜| fixed-price menu
V vegetarian dishes
♿ wheelchair access
▦ outdoor eating
♟ good wine list
♫ live music
★ highly recommended
🖰 credit cards accepted:
*AE* American Express
*DC* Diners Club
*MC* Master Card/Access
*V* Visa
*JCB* Japanese Credit Bureau

**Price categories** for a three-course meal for one, including cover charge, tax and service, but without wine or other drinks:
€ up to €25
€€ €26–€30
€€€ €31–€45
€€€€ over €45

# What to Eat in Amsterdam

*Patates frites* (French fries) and mayonnaise

TRADITIONAL DUTCH food is hearty and wholesome, prepared with simple ingredients. Bread, cold meat and cheese are often eaten for breakfast and lunch, with meat or fish in the evening. Snacks such as French fries are sold from street stalls *(see p236)* and there are many bakeries selling tempting cakes. Ethnic dishes are also popular, and the city enjoys some of the best Indonesian cuisine in Europe.

**Typical Dutch Breakfast**
*Breakfast usually consists of bread and butter with a slice of ham or cheese.*

**Bitterballen en Frikadellen**
*Deep-fried meat balls and spicy, sausage-shaped rissoles are served with mustard.*

**Uitsmijter**
*This filling snack consists of a slice of bread with cheese or ham, topped with a fried egg.*

**Crispbread with Hagelslag**
*Strands of chocolate (hagelslag) are sprinkled on bread.*

**Fresh Raw Herring**
*Raw herring is marinated and eaten as an entrée or snack with onion or gherkins.*

**Coffee and Speculaas**
*Spicy biscuits called speculaas are ideal with coffee, usually served strong and black.*

**Young Gouda**      **Nettle Gouda**

**Edam cheese**    **Rye bread**

**Bread and Cheeses**
*The most popular cheeses are Edam and Gouda, sometimes flavoured with herbs or seeds. Cheese is often eaten with rye, wholemeal or white bread.*

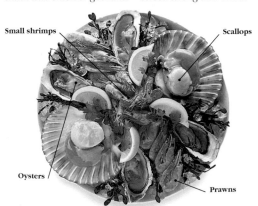

**Small shrimps**        **Scallops**

**Oysters**        **Prawns**

**Fruits de Mer**
*Fresh seafood such as oysters, prawns, shrimps and scallops are served on a bed of ice and seaweed.*

**Plaice with Vegetables**
*Grilled fish is often eaten as a main dish, served with butter, boiled potatoes and carrots.*

**Stamppot**
*This is a typical Dutch stew of puréed potatoes, vegetables and smoked sausage.*

**White Asparagus and Ham**
*Thick slices of boiled Dutch ham are served with white asparagus and melted butter.*

**Erwtensoep**
*A wholesome, thick pea soup, it is served with boiled, smoked sausage and bacon.*

**Large Pancake with Stroop**
Pannekoeken, *or pancakes, are a popular dessert, covered with a thick syrup or stroop.*

**Limburgse Vlaai**
*Served hot or cold, Limburg pie is made with bread dough and filled with fruit.*

**Strawberries and Yoghurt**
*Yoghurt is delicious as a light dessert, sprinkled with sugar and served with fresh fruit.*

## INDONESIAN CUISINE

Indonesian food, introduced from the former Dutch colony, is usually eaten in the form of a *rijsttafel* (rice table). It consists of a large, shared bowl of noodles or rice, with up to 25 smaller dishes of meat, fish and vegetables, with various sauces.

Stir-fried egg noodles

**Bami goreng (fried noodles, chicken, shrimps, garlic, chilli and vegetables)**

**Babi asam pedas (spicy pork)**

**Udang bakar (grilled tiger prawns)**

**Satay daging (marinated beef)**

**Satay ayam (chicken in peanut sauce)**

**Ayam panike (chicken in aromatic sauce)**

Spicy peanut sauce

Sambal (red chilli sauce)

Dark soy sauce with chillies

**Gado gado (vegetable salad with peanut sauce)**

**Nasi goreng (fried rice with beef or pork, mushrooms, soy sauce and shrimp paste)**

# Choosing a Restaurant

THE RESTAURANTS in this guide have been selected across a wide range of price categories for their good value, exceptional food and interesting locations. The chart below lists restaurants in Amsterdam by area; entries are alphabetical within each price category. Information on cafés and bars can be found on pages 236–7.

| | CREDIT CARDS | GOOD WINE LIST | GARDEN OR TERRACE | ATTRACTIVE SETTING |
|---|---|---|---|---|

## OUDE ZIJDE

**ORIENTAL CITY,** Oudezijds Voorburgwal 177-179. **Map** 7 C3. **€** 626 8352.
Very popular with the local Chinese, this is a large bustling restaurant with an extensive menu. Best time to go is Sunday lunchtime when families congregate for *dim sum* accompanied by Chinese tea. Same owner has Golden Chopsticks next door; a brightly lit canteen serving faster food. Try the roast duck, *won ton* soup or *bami* (noodle dishes). 🍴
€ | AE DC MC V

**HEMELSE MODDER,** Oude Waal 9. **Map** 8 E3. **€** 624 3203.
Located on a quiet canal-side with a smart looking interior offering international food with a strong French influence. Attractive restaurant originally set up by squatters who cooked at weekends as a hobby; times have changed over many years. The menu includes both fish and meat. A very Amsterdam place. ◐ *lunch; Mon.* 🍴 ♿
€€ | AE DC MC V | | ■ | ●

**KRUA THAI,** Staalstraat 22. **Map** 7 C4. **€** 620 0623.
Thai hospitality and enthusiasm add to this casual restaurant's fragrant specialities. Easiest way is to take one of the set menus. For a memorable meal ask the waiter to help select an interesting combination from the extensive selection of soups, curries and salads. Green curry is a favourite. ◐ *lunch; Mon* 🍴
€€ | MC V | ●

**SEA PALACE,** Oosterdokskade 8. **Map** 8 E1. **€** 626 4777.
If you cannot reach the floating emporiums in Hong Kong, then this is the next best thing, a Chinese restaurant offering a wonderful view of Amsterdam. The huge menu offers Cantonese staples such as *won ton* soup and more unusual dishes from Peking and Sichuan.
€€ | AE DC MC V JCB | | | ●

**BLAUW AAN DE WAL,** O.Z. Achterburgwal 99. **Map** 5 A1. **€** 330 2257.
Search for the doorway leading to a tiny alley, and you will be rewarded by one of the best restaurants in town. Choose from concise menu; scallops, *langoustine* with lemon marmalade or poached beef with truffle and bacon. Attractive interior includes a no-smoking section. ◐ *lunch; Sun.* 🍴 ♿ 🚭
€€€ | AE MC V | ● | ■

**CAFÉ ROUX/GRAND AMSTERDAM,** Oudezijds Voorburgwal 197. **Map** 7 C3. **€** 555 3560.
A unique opportunity to experience dishes made famous by Albert Roux at a very reasonable price, especially the fixed-price menu. Wonderful mix of French and British dishes with quality local products. Wine selection is excellent. The courtyard in summer is an oasis. 🍴
€€€ | AE DC MC V JCB | ● | ■

**IN DE WAAG,** Nieuwmarkt 4. **Map** 8 D3. **€** 422 7772.
Modern, bustling restaurant in the five hundred year old city gate and weigh-house where Rembrandt painted *The Anatomy Lesson*. Medieval atmosphere is enhanced by long tables and 300 candles; modern times with the internet bar. Eclectic menu ranges from Moroccan stew with mackerel to steaks. Great terrace in summer. 🍴
€€€€€ | AE DC MC V | | ■ | ●

## NIEUWE ZIJDE

**EERSTE KLAS,** Platform 2B, Centraal Station. **Map** 2 E3. **€** 625 0131.
The former first class waiting room on platform 2B at the Centraal Station wonderfully restored to its former glory is worth a visit for the interior alone. The restaurant/grand café serves everything from Dutch shrimp *croquettes* to classic sole Picasso and ending with *parfait* of honey with fresh fruit. 🍴 ♿
€€ | AE DC MC V | | | ●

**KANTJIL & DE TIJGER,** Spuistraat 291-293. **Map** 7 A3. **€** 620 0994.
The modern interior disguises the fact that this is one of the few restaurants serving really authentic Indonesian food. Menu features classic *nasi goring* along with lesser known regional dishes like *sate ikan* (fish sate) and *pepesan oedang* (steamed shrimp in banana leaf). *Rijsttafel* (*see p227*) offers a complete selection. ◐ *lunch.*
€€ | AE DC MC V | | ■

<table>
<tr><td colspan="2">

**Price categories** are for a three-course meal for one, excluding drinks, plus all unavoidable extra charges such as cover, service and tax:

€ up to €25
€€ €26–€30
€€€ €31–€45
€€€€ over €45

</td><td>

**CREDIT CARDS**
Indicates which major credit cards are accepted in those restaurants where the credit card symbol is shown..

**GOOD WINE LIST**
Denotes a wide selection of good wines.

**GARDEN OR TERRACE**
Weather permitting, meals can be served outside.

**ATTRACTIVE SETTING**
Restaurant with a striking interior design, or with a good view or pleasant setting such as an attractive canalside.

</td></tr>
</table>

| | CREDIT CARDS | GOOD WINE LIST | GARDEN OR TERRACE | ATTRACTIVE SETTING |
|---|---|---|---|---|
| **LUCIUS**, Spuistraat 247. **Map** 7 B3. **(** *624 1831*. €€<br>There are very few specialist sea-food restaurants in Amsterdam despite the fantastic range of fresh produce available. Lucius offers a full selection of Dutch flat fish, oysters and mussels. There are also more exotic fish such as swordfish and gold bream. Meat dishes are available, just in case.<br>● *lunch.* ¶●¶ & | AE DC MC V JCB | ● | ■ | |
| **D'ANTICA**, Reguliersdwarsstraat 80-82. **Map** 7 C5. **(** *623 3862*. €€€<br>Very Italian, family-run restaurant, bustling with extrovert service and producing authentic dishes prepared with good quality ingredients. Try the *salmone allo zafferano* (salmon with saffron) or *scaloppini marsala* (veal with marsala). Good Italian wines. Interior has a combination of *trattoria* and *ristorante*. ● *Sun lunch.* ¶●¶ | AE MC V | ● | | |
| **CENTRA**, Lange Niezel 29. **Map** 8 D2. **(** *622 3050*. €€€<br>Some places survive changes in fashion and public taste and this Spanish restaurant in the heart of the Red Light area is a good example. Spartan interior and a no-nonsense approach towards the repertoire of classic dishes such as *paella* and *tortilla* washed down with a good selection of Spanish wines. | | | | |
| **DE COMPAGNON**, Guldehandsteeg 17 (near Warmoesstraat).<br>**Map** 8 D1. **(** *620 4225*. €€€<br>Insiders gem tucked away in a small alley. A tiny restaurant in an old building with friendly service, offering gastronomic cuisine ranging from salmon lasagna with caviar and saffron mayonnaise to a classic-style *entrecôte* of Limousin beef. The quality of the products is shown by the sole with tomato and olive oil. Exceptional wine list. ● *Sat lunch, Sun.* ¶●¶ | AE DC MC V JCB | ● | ■ | |
| **DORRIUS**, Nieuwezijds Voorburgwal 5. **Map** 7 C1. **(** *420 2224*. €€€<br>First opened at the end of the 19th century, closed for many years and then revived with the re-discoverd original 1890 interior in a new location. One of the few places serving original Dutch food and drinks. Try the typical *erwtensoep* (thick pea soup) or for dessert, *hangop* (yoghurt, cinnamon, sugar and cream). ● *lunch.* & | AE DC MC V JCB | | | ● |
| **DE SILVEREN SPIEGEL**, Kattengat 4. **Map** 7 C1. **(** *624 6589*. €€€<br>There has been a restaurant on this site for the last 200 years and the building dates from 1614. The small and carefully tended dining-room retains the intimate historic atmosphere. Fresh, seasonal food includes *Texel* lamb with almonds and black pepper and ginger crème brûlée.<br>● *lunch; Sun.* ¶●¶ & | AE MC V | ■ | | ● |
| **TREASURE**, Nieuwezijds Voorburgwal 115. **Map** 7 B2. **(** *626 0915*. €€€<br>Most Chinese food in Amsterdam is a strange mixture of Indonesian inspired dishes cooked with fruit. Treasure is one of the few places where you can eat authentic specialities from Canton, Peking, Shanghai and Sichuan. The food is prepared with attention to detail and presentation. The *dim sum* bar offers enticing snacks. & | AE MC V JCB | | | |
| **VASSO**, Rozenboomsteeg 10-14. **Map** 7 B4. **(** *626 0158*. €€€<br>Quality products are the hallmark of the best Italian cooking. This attractive rustic restaurant with colour-washed walls and a wooden floor is the place to sample the ever changing menu of creatively produced regional and seasonal dishes. Excellent wine list. More than a pizza or a pasta. Book early. ● *lunch.* ¶●¶ | AE MC V | ● | ■ | ● |
| **D'VIJFF VLIEGEN**, Spuistraat 294-302. **Map** 7 A3. **(** *530 4060*. €€€<br>The "Five Flies" is a 350 year old restaurant with authentic period dining-rooms. Brass nameplates on the chairs display the names of famous guests, including Elvis Presley. The food is attempting to combine Dutch food with a modern cuisine. 50 Dutch gins are on offer. A touristic attraction.<br>● *lunch.* ¶●¶ | AE DC MC V JCB | ● | | ● |

For key to symbols *see p225*

<table>
<tr><td colspan="2">

**Price categories** are for a three-course meal for one, excluding drinks, plus all unavoidable extra charges such as cover, service and tax:

€ up to €25
€€ €26–€30
€€€ €31–€45
€€€€ over €45

</td><td>

**CREDIT CARDS**
Indicates which major credit cards are accepted in those restaurants where the credit card symbol is shown.
**GOOD WINE LIST**
Denotes a wide selection of good wines.
**GARDEN OR TERRACE**
Weather permitting, meals can be served outside.
**ATTRACTIVE SETTING**
Restaurant with a striking interior design, or with a good view or pleasant setting such as an attractive canalside.

</td></tr>
</table>

| | CREDIT CARDS | GOOD WINE LIST | GARDEN OR TERRACE | ATTRACTIVE SETTING |
|---|---|---|---|---|
| **SUPPER CLUB**, Jonge Roelensteeg 21. Map 1 C5. 344 6400. €€€€<br>Total hedonistic experience in a modern, lounging restaurant for the brave and trendy. Eat at 8pm while relaxing on a cushioned bed; listen to the DJ; get rid of stress with a *shiatsu* massage; marvel at the entertainment. Total experience for all the senses. A restaurant with attitude. Wear clean socks! *lunch.* | AE DC MC V | | | ● |
| **VERMEER/BARBIZON PALACE HOTEL**, Prins Hendrikkade 59-72. €€€€<br>Map 8 D1. 556 4885.<br>One of the finest star restaurants. The imaginative French-based cuisine of Pascal Jalhaij uniquely matches flavours and ingredients. Take the wine arrangement to fully appreciate the combination of contemporary dishes with classic wines. Scallops with fennel and a caper and duck *foie gras* alongside a *Condrieu* will impress. A real favourite. *Sat lunch; Sun.* | AE DC MC V JCB | ● | | |
| **WESTERN CANAL RING** | | | | |
| **BANANA RAMA**, Westerstraat 91. Map 1 B3. 638 1039. €<br>Combinations of flavours and taste are the key to Philippine food; influences from Malaysia, China and Spain are found in the creative cooking of Tani Morabe. Taro leaves with shrimps and coconut milk are wonderful. A menu with a wine arrangement is great value for money. *lunch.* | | | ■ | ● |
| **BURGER'S PATIO**, 2e Tuindwarsstraat 12 (near Westerstraat). €<br>Map 1 B3. 623 6854.<br>Good café restaurant that stands up to more the expensive competition. Fresh ingredients and organic meat and poultry are used in the Mediterranean-inspired dishes. Chips with mayonnaise provide a local touch. 1950's style interior with kitsch lighting sets the scene for a relaxed dinner with friendly service. *lunch.* | AE DC MC V | | ■ | |
| **CLAES CLAESZ**, Egelantiersstraat 24-26. Map 1 B4. 625 5306. €<br>This Dutch restaurant is situated in a former almshouse built in 1616, and has amusing touches such as the ice buckets made from tiny garden pails, and plates decorated with the Dutch children's alphabet. Portions are generous and seasonal dishes include asparagus and game. Live music at weekends and a relaxed Jordaan ambiance. *lunch; Mon.* Fri-Sun | MC V | | | |
| **BORDEWIJK**, Noordermarkt 7. Map 1 C3. 624 3899. €€<br>With a striking 1950's-cum-1980's interior this is one of the busiest and most highly regarded restaurants amongst locals. Well informed staff can help you select an ideal combination of creative food and interesting wine. A good example would be red mullet with wild spinach complemented by a Sancerre rosé. Book early. *lunch; Mon.* | AE DC MC V | ● | ■ | ● |
| **CHEZ GEORGES**, Herenstraat 3. Map 7 A1. 626 3332. €€<br>Despite the modest façade, this is a very busy place. Chef Georges François and his family are all involved in providing a friendly atmosphere where you can enjoy top quality dishes ranging from goose liver salad to a *bavarois* of coffee and rum. Reservations can take weeks. *lunch; Wed; Sun.* | AE DC MC V | ● | | |
| **GOUDEN REAEL**, Zandhoek 14. Map 1 C1. 623 3883. €€<br>The quiet location overlooking a canal and boats is not the only attraction in this French regional restaurant; there are also culinary delights from all over France. Wine by the glass combines with the variety of dishes; this is definitely worth a visit for a very enjoyable meal. | AE DC MC V | ● | ■ | ● |
| **PREGO**, Herenstraat 25. Map 7 A1. 638 0148. €€<br>Very popular with locals; tasty combination of Dutch and French Mediterranean food served in an austere, good-looking restaurant. Menu changes frequently and includes both good meat and fish dishes. Extensive wine list with some excellent Italian choices. Friendly, helpful staff. Book in advance. *lunch.* | AE MC V | ● | | |

**D'THEEBOOM**, Singel 210. **Map** 7 A3. [ 623 8420.
French chef Georges Thubert is a consummate professional with a talent
for enticing, well-priced food and wine in his attractive restaurant
overlooking a canal. A typical meal could include *velouté* of celeriac, rib-
eye steak with a black pepper sauce and a dessert of pears marinated in
*pinot noir* with yoghurt ice-cream. ● *Sat lunch & Sun.*

€€  AE DC MC V JCB

---

**TOSCANINI**, Lindengracht 75. **Map** 1 C3. [ 623 2813.
The spaciousness of this busy Italian restaurant is unusual in Amsterdam.
You can watch your authentic meal being prepared in the open kitchen.
Good selection of classic dishes. Service can be slow but this remains one
of the most popular restaurants with a good reputation for the quality of
the food. ● *lunch; Sun.* &

€€  AE DC MC V

---

**DE GROENE LANTEERNE**, Haarlemmerstraat 43. **Map** 2 D3. [ 624 1952.
French food served in an Old-Dutch restaurant, typically narrow and vertical.
The owner and his wife cook themselves. Wide choice of excellent wines at
all prices reflects the owners previous occupation as a *sommelier* and wine
merchant. French-based food is interesting. ● *lunch; Sun.* ¶●¶

€€€  AE DC MC V

---

**HEERLIJK**, Palmgracht 39. **Map** 1 B2. [ 421 5528.
Very friendly welcome in a small, personal restaurant with a compact,
modern interior off the tourist route in the Jordaan. Pleasing food
influenced by Europe and Asia. *Ravioli* with duck *ragout* and
forest mushroom sauce is very tasty. Concise, interesting wine list.
Very Amsterdam. ● *lunch; Mon & Tues.*

€€€  AE MC V

---

**LOF**, Haarlemmerstraat 62. **Map** 2 D3. [ 620 2997.
One of Amsterdam's very best restaurants, Lof has a new menu every day,
depending on what the market has to offer. Chef Sander Louwerens
maintains the highest standards, enuring a constant flow of Amsterdam's
"in" crowd. The restaurant gets very busy at weekends, so it is advisable to
book in advance. ● *Mon.* ¶●¶

€€€

---

**SUMMUM**, Binnen Dommersstraat 13. **Map** 1 C2. [ 770 0407.
A favourite with many people for the interesting food that uses Dutch,
Spanish and Italian ingredients, with good wine and a relaxed atmosphere.
Roasted artichoke with rocket and romanesco sauce, or duck with chestnut,
sage, celery and parmesan, show the creative side of the menu. A little
difficult to find but worth the effort. ● *lunch; Mon.* &

€€€  AE DC MC V

---

**CHRISTOPHE**, Leliegracht 46. **Map** 7 A2. [ 625 0807.
The south west of France influences star chef, Jean-Christophe Royer.
He concentrates on high quality, full flavoured dishes enhanced by an
attractive restaurant. Favourites are pigeon roasted in a salt crust and *crème
brûlée* with honey and saffron. Special wines from Madiran, Limoux and
Jurançon. ● *lunch; Mon; Sun.* ¶●¶

€€€€  AE DC MC V

---

## CENTRAL CANAL RING

**MAYUR**, Korte Leidsedwarsstraat 203. **Map** 4 E2. [ 623 2142.
Authentic tandoori dishes cooked in a clay oven are the speciality of this
spacious restaurant near Leidseplein. Many Dutch people have not
acquired the taste for Indian food so there are a lot of tourists; do not let
this put you off. A welcoming, friendly atmosphere. ● *lunch.* ¶●¶ &

€  AE DC MC V JCB

---

**SWAAGAT**, Lange Leidsedwarsstraat 76. **Map** 4 E2. [ 638 4702.
Great value for money Indian food served in a pleasant modern interior
decorated with ethnic photographs. There are no pork or beef dishes,
making it very popular with Indian guests. Specialities include *roghan josh*
and a wonderful vegetarian selection. The enthusiastic owner will assist in
making your choice. Set menus are a good idea. ● *Nov–Mar lunch.* ¶●¶ &

€  AE DC MC V

---

**WAGAMAMA**, Max Euweplein 10. **Map** 4 E2. [ 528 7778.
Wagamama have expanded their Japanese noodle empire from London to
Amsterdam. Modern, designer canteen-style interior with large shared wooden
tables. The menu is varied and ideal for a quick snack or a full meal. Good
location near museums. One of the very few no-smoking restaurants. & ⊘

€  AE DC MC V JCB

---

**LULU**, Runstraat 8. **Map** 4 E1. [ 624 5090.
Tongue-in-cheek interior of this friendly bistro is complemented by well
cooked regional dishes mainly from France. Favourite dishes are *confit* of
duck and *carpaccio*. Background music by the likes of Edith Piaf and Charles
Aznavour add to the atmosphere. ● *lunch.* ¶●¶

€€  AE DC MC V JCB

---

For key to symbols *see p225*

**Price categories** are for a three-course meal for two, excluding drinks, plus all unavoidable extra charges such as cover, service and tax:

€ up to €25
€€ €26–€30
€€€ €31–€45
€€€€ over €45

**CREDIT CARDS**
Indicates which major credit cards are accepted in those restaurants where the credit card symbol is shown.

**GOOD WINE LIST**
Denotes a wide selection of good wines.

**GARDEN OR TERRACE**
Weather permitting, meals can be served outside.

**ATTRACTIVE SETTING**
Restaurant with a striking interior design, or with a good view or pleasant setting such as an attractive canalside.

| | CREDIT CARDS | GOOD WINE LIST | GARDEN OR TERRACE | ATTRACTIVE SETTING |
|---|---|---|---|---|
| **BLUE PEPPER,** Nassaukade 366. **Map** 3 D1. 489 7039. €€€<br>Creative blue and metal enviroment for authentic Indonesian flavours. *Rendang* (stewed beef), and *ikan pepes* (spicy fish in banana leaf), presented on beautiful plates, retain original taste and quality. Transcends the *rijsttafel* (*see p227*) with exciting menus full of taste and spice. Tradition on a gastronomic level. ● lunch. ♦ | AE MC V | | ■ | ● |
| **DINING ELEVEN,** Reestraat 11. **Map** 1 B5. 620 7968. €€€<br>A friendly restaurant offering value for money, great food and interesting wines. Refined home cooking with a gastronomic touch with roots in Dutch and Flemish cuisine. Concise menu and wine list combines very well; quality is maintained throughout the meal. ● lunch. ♦ ♿ | AE DC MC V JCB | ● | | |
| **DYNASTY,** Reguliersdwarsstraat 30. **Map** 7 B5. 422 6426. €€€<br>Refined South-East Asian cuisine in a colourful up-market restaurant. The menu is a cross-section from Thailand, Vietnam and China. First class wine list complements the herbs and spices in the food. Ask advice from the helpful staff. The garden is perfect for a romantic evening meal. ● lunch; Tue. | AE DC MC V | ● | ■ | ● |
| **GARLIC QUEEN,** Reguliersdwarsstraat 27. **Map** 4 F1. 422 6426. €€€<br>Garlic, garlic and more garlic. The beef stew contains 60 cloves, the confit is a whole bulb and even the ice-cream can have the novelty of garlic. Dishes are available for guests who do not enjoy this essential ingredient. The full enjoyment is the versatility of this fragrant product. ● lunch; Mon & Tues. ♿ | AE DC MC V | | ■ | |
| **SICHUAN FOOD,** Reguliersdwarsstraat 35. **Map** 7 B5. 626 9327. €€€<br>Chinese food with a Michelin star. Despite the name, many dishes come from other regions of China and consist of standards like Peking duck and Cantonese *dim sum*. More adventurous are the Sichuan dishes which rely on chillies and Chinese peppers. Friendly service is always available for guidance. ● lunch. ♦ | AE DC MC V | ● | | |
| **TAKENS,** Runstraat 17d. **Map** 4 E1. 627 0618. €€€<br>The adventurous and individualistic chef cooks interesting, tasty food using a delicious combination of flavours and ingredients. *Tortellini* of white fish with coriander and lemongrass, and baked pigeon with *risotto* of truffle and gravy reveal the ideas behind this restaurant. ● lunch. ♦ | AE DC MC V | ● | | |
| **HET TUYNHUYS,** Reguliersdwarsstraat 28. **Map** 7 B5. 627 6603. €€€<br>A former coach house from Amsterdam's Golden Age has been lovingly renovated in a mixture of Dutch and Mediterranean styles. Interesting combinations influence the excellent food; sweet potato soup with *tempura* of gamba or *lobster a la nage* with mussels, thyme and pasta. Wines are well chosen. The garden is perfect in the summer. ● Sat & Sun lunch. ♦ ♿ | AE DC MC V | ● | | ● |
| **ZOMERS,** Prinsengracht 411. **Map** 4 E1. 638 3398. €€€<br>Individual approach to both the food and décor makes this a good choice to enjoy good food in relaxed surroundings. Menu and interior are sometimes adapted to a special theme. Food combines Italian and French cuisine. The wine list is affordable. ● lunch; Oct–Mar: Mon. ♦ ♿ | AE MC V | ● | | ● |
| **BLAKES,** Keizersgracht 384. **Map** 4 E1. 530 2010. €€€€<br>Blakes radiates taste and style with Anouska Hempels' designer interior and the East-West flavours of the beautifully presented food. Thai-style squid-ink soup and *tortellini* with *foie gras* reveal the eclectic approach. Lunch *bentos* (4 dishes served in a wooden box) are a good introduction to the various menus. ● Sat lunch; Sun all day. | AE DC MC V | ● | | ● |
| **'T SWARTE SCHAEP,** Korte Leidsedwarsstraat 24. **Map** 4 F2. 421 3353. €€€€<br>Housed in a building dating from 1687 and offering enjoyable French based food in a cosy Dutch ambiance. The menu includes a *parfait* of goose liver wrapped in truffles as well as more modern combinations. Service can sometimes be slow, but the wait is worthwhile. ♦ | AE DC MC V | ● | | |

**VOSSIUS,** Hobbemastraat 2. Map 4 E2. 577 4100 €€€€ AE DC MC V
Robert Kranenborg is mentor to many chefs in The Netherlands. In his own sober-chic, star restaurant he insists on the best products for his French cuisine, based on light, contemporary, concentrated sauces in dishes like scallops with *bouillon*, wild mustard fruit and chicory. A no-smoking restaurant. A culinary highlight. ● *Sun; 31 Dec–10 Jan & 29 Jul–15 Aug.*

## EASTERN CANAL RING

**MOKO,** Amstelveld 12. Map 5 A3. 626 1199. € AE DC MC V
Young, hip, trendy modern restaurant surprisingly situated in a 17th century church on a large cobbled square overlooking houseboats, gabled houses and canal bridges. The interior is now ultra modern and attracts a similar public who wish to be seen. Regular DJ provides the required atmosphere.

**ZUSHI,** Amstel 20. Map 7 C5. 330 6882. € AE DC MC V JCB
Eating *sushi* from a revolving conveyor belt may be an unusual concept, but the Japanese have perfected this self-service system. Sitting at the counter awaiting your coloured, price-coded plate heightens the appetite. Modern, minimalist interior further evokes the industrial atmosphere. The best of the *kaiten* (conveyor belt) restaurants.

**LE HOLLANDAIS,** Amsteldijk 41. Map 5 B5. 679 1248. €€ MC V JCB
Country-style French food cooked in Holland with excellent home-made sausages, and choices that exhibit the best regional dishes from oysters to lamb. Excellent list of 80 French wines to complement the food. Relaxed atmosphere. This restaurant is worth finding. ● *lunch; Sun.*

**INDRAPURA,** Rembrandtplein 40-42. Map 7 C5. 623 7329. €€ AE DC MC V JCB
Thousands of Indonesian islands produce an enormous variety of gastronomic styles which go beyond the *rijsttafel*. In the beautiful colonial interior enjoy food from Java (mild, sweet, no pork), Sumatra (spicy, Indian) or Sulawesi (fragrant, fresh and mildly spicy). Well chosen wines. ● *lunch.*

**TEMPO DOELOE,** Utrechtsestraat 75. Map 5 A3. 625 6718. €€ AE DC MC V
For authentic Indonesian food ring the doorbell of Tempo Doeloe. It is good that spicy dishes are clearly marked on the menu: hot means hot. Many other dishes show off the more delicate side of Indonesian cooking. Friendly service will assist you in compiling a meal that suits your taste. ● *lunch; Sun.*

**LE ZINC ... ET LES DAMES,** Prinsengracht 999. Map 5 A3. 622 9044. €€ DC MC V
Rustic interior in a restored canalside warehouse is a perfect setting for home-style French regional cooking that may include fried pike-perch, pheasant and *crème brûlée*. Well chosen selection of wines by the glass, carafe or bottle. The ground floor bar is ideal for drinks. ● *lunch; Sun.*

**BREITNER,** Amstel 212. Map 7 D5. 627 7879. €€€ AE DC MC V
The wonderful location on the Amstel will not distract you from the dishes served in this essential restaurant. Original, modern cooking, including duck glazed with grapefruit and a red pepper sauce will attract those who appreciate delicious food. ● *lunch; Sun; last 2 weeks of Jul.*

**INEZ IPSC,** Amstel 2. Map 7 C5. 639 2899. €€€ DC MC V
The door is easy to miss and the climb up the stairs does not prepare you for this colourful restaurant with a great view over the Munt Tower and the canals. The eccentric interior and relaxed atmosphere reflect modern cooking without restrictions. Experimental but worth trying.

**PUYCK,** Ceintuurbaan 147. Map 4 F4 676 7677. €€€ MC V
French-Asian food with full understanding of both cuisines exhibited by *Rillette* of Peking duck in Chinese pancakes or Thai green curry *sorbet*. Wines have a set corkage added to the cost price. A fantastic opportunity to taste top wines at an attractive price. One of the best. ● *lunch; Sun & Mon.*

**SEGUGIO,** Utrechtsestraat 96. Map 5 A3. 330 1503. €€€ AE MC V
New generation Italian restaurant in a split-level setting with open kitchen. Wild rabbit with *pevarada* sauce is outstanding; scallop dishes are succulent; try the *ravioli* of the day. Main courses have a French touch. Well chosen wine list is divided into light, medium and intense flavours. ● *lunch; Sun.*

**VAN VLAANDEREN,** Weteringschans 175. Map 5 A4. 622 8292. €€€ AE MC V
One of the best star restaurants for chef Marc Philippart to reveal his modern and classic dishes. *Coquilles St Jacques* with Iranian caviar in a *Sauternes* sauce or the *Bresse* pigeon with duck liver are ideal. ● *lunch; Sun, Mon.*

**Price categories** are for a three-course meal for one, excluding drinks, plus all unavoidable extra charges such as cover, service and tax:

€ up to €25
€€ €26–€30
€€€ €31–€45
€€€€ over €45

**CREDIT CARDS**
Major credit cards are accepted in those restaurants where the credit card symbol is shown.

**GOOD WINE LIST**
Denotes a wide selection of good wines.

**GARDEN OR TERRACE**
Weather permitting, meals can be served outside.

**ATTRACTIVE SETTING**
Restaurant with a striking interior design, or with a good view or pleasant setting such as an attractive canalside.

| | CREDIT CARDS | GOOD WINE LIST | GARDEN OR TERRACE | ATTRACTIVE SETTING |
|---|---|---|---|---|
| **UTRECHTSEDWARSTAFEL,** Utrechtsedwarsstraat 107-109. **Map** 5 B3. ( 625 4189.<br>The innovative surprise menus offered, are a great gastronomic adventure. They range from three to five courses and different levels of complexity. Wines are chosen by the glass to complement the daily changing products and individual taste. Fascinating combinations. ● lunch; Sun; Mon. ¶●¶ — €€€ | AE MC V | ● | | |
| **ZUIDLANDE,** Utrechtsedwarsstraat 141. **Map** 5 A3. ( 620 7393. — €€€<br>Seasonal cooking using top-quality ingredients at a very reasonable price. This is the place to go if you enjoy goose liver and truffle *millefeuille* or roast duck with a snail *ragout*. The interior has a sophisticated rustic style and there is occasional live music to enhance the cooking. ● lunch; Sun; Mon. ¶●¶ | AE MC V | ● | ■ | |

## MUSEUM QUARTER

| | CREDIT CARDS | GOOD WINE LIST | GARDEN OR TERRACE | ATTRACTIVE SETTING |
|---|---|---|---|---|
| **AUJOURD'HUI,** Cornelis Krusemanstraat 15. **Map** 3 B5. ( 679 0877. — €€<br>Top quality products and down to earth dishes are the cornerstone of this relaxed restaurant. Cutlets of Bawykow (slowly smoked) salmon with creamed potato and *escalopes* of turbot show the influences from France. Great wine menu with many wines from the New World. ● Sat; Sun. ¶●¶ ⅄ | AE DC MC V JCB | ● | ■ | |
| **DWINGER,** Overtoom 28. **Map** 4 D2. ( 618 0368. — €€<br>Contrasts in the designer interior with rustic accents, continue in the food with Italian influences and traditional Dutch touches. Potato and avocado salad with grilled tuna, cod in parma ham with mashed potatoes, and *panna cotta* with forest fruits sauce are full of pronounced flavours. ● lunch; Mon. ¶●¶ | AE MC V | ● | ■ | |
| **ZABAR'S,** Van Baerlestraat 49. **Map** 4 D4. ( 679 8888. — €€<br>Adventurous Mediterranean-based food makes use of a wide range of exciting ingredients to produce courgette soup, grilled tuna and lamb with sweetbreads. This would not be out of place in Australia or California. Inventive wine list complements the cuisine. ● Mon & Sat lunch; Sun. ⅄ | MC | ● | | |
| **BRASSERIE VAN BAERLE,** van Baerlestraat 158. **Map** 4 E4. ( 679 1532. — €€€<br>Well established brasserie with excellent wine suggestions for every dish; lamb cutlets with coarse mustard and a *Collioure* to goose *confit* with a *Grüner Veltliner Smaragd*; The extensive menu offers a wide selection from traditional to inventive. Worth booking in advance. ¶●¶ | AE DC MC V | ● | ■ | |
| **LE GARAGE,** Ruysdaelstraat 54-56. **Map** 4 E4. ( 679 7176. — €€€<br>Bustling brasserie for the in-crowd lined with red-plush benches and closely packed tables. Owner Joop Braakhekke is well known for his television cookery programmes and his love for food is reflected in the lively French regional menu using fresh ingredients. ● Sat & Sun lunch. ¶●¶ | AE DC MC V JCB | ● | | ● |
| **NEW CADANS,** Roelof Hartstraat 6-8. **Map** 4 E5. ( 676 5201. — €€€<br>A modern, architectural interior is the setting for cooking, using many Dutch products in a contemporary style. The *ravioli* of lobster is delicious. There are dishes with Italian, French and Asian flavours and good vegetarian choices. The lemon meringue pie is a good *finale*. ● lunch; Sun. ¶●¶ | AE MC V | ● | | |
| **RADEN MAS,** Stadhouderskade 6. **Map** 4 D2. ( 685 4041. — €€€<br>After a warm welcome, you are shown into the luxurious restaurant and treated to live piano music and an extensive choice of Indonesian dishes ranging from *rijsttafel* (*see p227*) to whole lobster with a spicy sauce. Great wines to tempt you. The complete evening out. ● lunch. ¶●¶ ⅄ ♪ | AE DC MC V | ● | | |
| **ROBERTO'S/HILTON HOTEL,** Apollolaan 138. **Map** 3 C5. ( 710 6025. — €€€<br>Authentic Italian regional dishes and freshly made pastas appear on the menu in this up-market trattoria. Try starting with the *risotto radicchio* followed by *ossobucco* and finish with the *tiramisu*. Good Italian wines enhance the relaxed atmosphere and service. ¶●¶ ⅄ | AE DC MC V JCB | ● | | |

**SPRING**, Willemsparkweg 177. **Map** 3 C4. 📞 *675 4421.* €€€
Clever use of space in a modern interior shows the attention to detail in the whole restaurant. French-based cooking using fresh, seasonal products: fish, shellfish and offal are favourites. Wines are well chosen. A favourite for many in Amsterdam. ● *Sat lunch; Sun.* 🍴

*AE DC MC V*

## PLANTAGE

**LA RIVE/AMSTEL HOTEL**, Prof. Tulpplein 1. **Map** 5 B4. 📞 *622 6060.* €€€€
Grand restaurant the two star cooking of Edwin Kats. Signature dishes of salted cod croquettes with oysters and caviar, and poached pigeon with maize *crêpes* and goose liver stand out. Menus range from traditional to contemporary. Wines and service are perfectly matched. A gastronomic treat. ● *Sat lunch; Sun.* 🍴

*AE DC MC V JCB*

## FURTHER AFIELD

**AMSTERDAM**, Watertorenplein 6. **Map** 8 D5. 📞 *682 2666.* €
Housed in a former pumping station, this large and popular restaurant has a variety of dishes, mainly from Western Europe. *Merguez* (sausages) with French fries, *chou farci* (stuffed cabbage) and roast quail are served, alongside grilled swordfish, risotto and *peperonata*. Wiener *schnitzel*, Dutch shrimps and oysters are also available. 🍴

*AE DC MC V*

**KAIKO**, Jekerstraat 114. 📞 *662 5641.* €€
The best *sushi* in town. A set menu offers *sushi, miso* soup, salad and dessert. Sit at the bar in order to get the full experience and see the chef at work. Other menus let you discover the full range of Japanese cooking, but the *sushi* is the highlight. ● *lunch; Thu; Sun.* 🍴

*AE DC MC V JCB*

**DE KAS** Kamerlingh Onneslaan 3 📞 *462 4562* €€€
The dream of many chefs worldwide; preparing a culinary set menu from organic products from your own fields and selected suppliers. Set in a designer interior in a period glasshouse. Exceptional location for a very special restaurant where freshness is the key. There should be more places like this. ● *Sat lunch; Sun.* 🍴 &

*AE DC MC V*

**MANGERIE DE KERSENTUIN**, Dijsselhofplantsoen 7. **Map** 4 D5. 📞 *570 5600.* €€€
Enjoyable, informal atmosphere in which to enjoy the pure tastes of the unpretentious food. Try the pickled salmon with cauliflower cream and sorrel or the bourbon vanilla *crème brûlée*. Comprehensive wine list is well chosen. Friendly service. ● *Sat lunch; Sun.* 🍴 &

*AE DC MC V JCB*

**QUARTIER SUD**, Olympiaplein 176. 📞 *675 3990.* €€€
A gastronomic Grande Brasserie open all day offering traditional, classic and modern dishes from Caesar salad to guinea fowl with fennel purée and ginger sauce. Chef Denise Mooy uses her experience from top kitchens in Holland and France to make great dishes appear simple. Easy going flavours match the ambiance. ● *Sat & Sun.*

**LA SIRÈNE/LE MERIDIEN**, Apollolaan 2. **Map** 4 E5. 📞 *570 5724.* €€€
The enticing display of shellfish as you enter the restaurant, the polished nautical interior and the surrounding canals combine to provide a unique experience in Amsterdam. The selection of seafood is mouth-watering; the menu has a good selection of dishes. Very helpful service. &

*AE DC MC V*

**VOORBIJ HET EINDE**, Sumatrakade 613. 📞 *419 1143.* €€€
Glass fronted, modern restaurant on Java Eiland. Interesting designer interior, but the food is the great attraction. Exciting taste combinations; full flavours to subtle infusions; modern to classic with a twist; attention to texture, temperature and quality. A rising star. ● *Sun–Tue, Sat lunch.* 🍴 &

*MC V*

**VIS AAN DE SCHELDE**, Scheldeplein 4. 📞 *675 1583.* €€€
Quality fish and seafood restaurant opposite the RAI exhibition halls. Renovated interior is the ideal setting to enjoy the very best fish and seafood. The Netherlands is well known for oysters, mussels and flatfish; these can be prepared in a simple manner or in more involved culinary creations. ● *Sat & Sun lunch.* 🍴

*AE MC V*

**YAMAZATO/HOTEL OKURA**, Ferdinand Bolstraat 333. **Map** 4 F5. 📞 *678 8351.* €€€
Traditional Japanese cuisine, on a star level offering more than just *sashimi* or *tempura*. Selections served in a *bento* (wooden box) are a good introduction. Seasonal specialities and a *kaiseki* menu will please discerning diners. Sober setting and restrained atmosphere; this is not Nobu. 🍴 &

*AE DC MC V JCB*

# Light Meals and Snacks

IN ADDITION TO the normal assortment of burger joints, pizzerias and the like, most Dutch cafés and bars serve food ranging from simple bar snacks to a three-course meal. Those that offer lunch-time snacks and an evening meal are generally known as *eetcafés*. While the choice of dishes tends to be limited, the quality is generally high and prices are often very reasonable. Some *eetcafés* have started serving more adventurous dishes and generally offer a good vegetarian selection. However, café and bar kitchens close early and it is difficult to get a meal after 9pm. For more information on cafés and bars, including a selection of the top ten in Amsterdam, see pages 46–7.

## BARS AND STREET STALLS

ALMOST ALL BARS serve a range of snacks. The standard selection of nibbles includes olives, chunks of Dutch cheese served with mustard and *borrelnoten* (nuts with a savoury coating). More substantial tapas-like snacks include *bitterballen* (deep-fried meatballs), *vlammetjes* (deep-fried batter envelopes similar to meat and vegetable spring rolls) and *osseworst* (a spicy mince-beef sausage).

Given the maritime tradition of the Netherlands, it is worth trying the fish dishes available in bars and from stalls on the street, such as herring served with onion or gherkins. Pizza, sandwiches and hamburgers are also commonly available from stalls. However, the most popular snack from street stalls is french fries or *patat frites*, which are served with mayonnaise in a plastic tray or a paper cone (*see p226*).

## PANCAKE HOUSES

PANCAKES (*pannekoeken*) are a popular, value-for-money light meal in Amsterdam. The French-style *crêpe* is believed to have been adopted in the Netherlands during the Napoleonic occupation (*see pp28–9*) as a way of using up leftovers.

These days there is nothing penny-pinching about the wide range of sweet and savoury toppings available at most pancake houses in Amsterdam. It is not uncommon to find up to 70 varieties on offer and you can usually combine any of these to create the pancake of your choice. The best places

include **Bredero**, **De Carrousel**, **Boerderij Meerzicht**, **The Pancake Bakery** and **Upstairs**. Portions may seem small, but they are deceptively filling. Pancakes and waffles served with syrup are also available as the staple snack at smoking coffeeshops (*see p49*).

## BROWN CAFÉS AND BARS

THE TERM *eetcafés* is most commonly applied to traditional brown cafés (*see also p48*). These often offer much better value and a more relaxed ambience than many small restaurants. Outstanding brown cafés include **De Prins**, **Het Molenpad**, **Carel's**, **De Reiger** and **Blincker**, which have extensive and appealing menus. Not suprisingly, they often get crowded and it can be hard to find a free table.

The majority of basic *eetcafés* just offer filling homemade fare, such as soup, sandwiches, salads, omelettes and chips. The only unfamiliar dishes you are likely to come across are *uitsmijter* (a large open sandwich with roast beef or ham, topped with fried eggs) and *erwtensoep* (a thick pea soup with pork). Of the cheaper, more down-to-earth varieties of *eetcafés*, **De Doffer** and **Aas van Bokalen** both serve filling food that is excellent value. Aas van Bokalen is widely considered to provide one of the best deals in the city and De Doffer has the attraction of a billiard room. Both places attract a young, lively crowd and are popular with students.

However, an increasing number of Amsterdam's cafés and bars are becoming more

ambitious in the food they offer. **Café Cox**, located in De Stadsschouwburg (*see p111*), is a perfect example of this more adventurous approach. At smart *eetcafés*, the menu is rarely limited to a single style or national cuisine. A notable exception to this rule is **Van Puffelen**, which offers more formal French-style dishes. Meals are served in the back extension of this intimate brown café, which has an impressive 19th-century interior.

## DESIGNER BARS

AN EXTENSIVE RANGE of food is offered in some of the more up-market designer bars (*see p49*). This type of bar is invariably more expensive than other types of cafés and bars in the city and in most cases the quality of the fare does not justify such inflated prices. **Café Schiller**, housed in a beautiful Art Deco building on Rembrandtplein, is an honourable exception. Amid portraits of 1930s cabaret stars painted by Frits Schiller, you can enjoy a value-for-money selection of snacks and meals in an evocative period bar. Both **Het Land van Walem** and **De Balie** also serve tasty food in a stylish setting. **Morlang**, next door to Het Land van Walem, is less chic, but the food is better value, and the trendy **Café Esprit** is popular with Kalverstraat shoppers.

## SPECIALIST CAFÉS

IF YOU FEEL LIKE trying something different, sample the delicious Belgian home cooking at the Flemish cultural centre **De Brakke Grond**, where meals are served in both the café and the restaurant. **De Zotte** also serves down-to-earth Flemish food and stocks a huge variety of Belgian beers. While the quality is not as exceptional, the portions are large enough to soak up the strongest of beers.

Probably the best value meal in town is served at **Terzijde**. One enormous home-cooked dish, which could be anything from chilli con carne to pasta, is served every night at this modern "neighbourhood" café.

## DIRECTORY

### PANCAKE HOUSES

**Bredero**
Oudezijds Voorburgwal
244. **Map** 7 C3.
**(** 622 9461.

**De Carrousel**
Tweede Weteringplantsoen
1.
**Map** 4 F3.
**(** 625 8002.

**Boerderij Meerzicht**
Koenenkade 56.
Amsterdamse Bos.
**(** 679 2744.

**The Pancake
Bakery**
Prinsengracht 191.
**Map** 1 B4.
**(** 625 1333.

**Upstairs**
Grimburgwal 2.
**Map** 7 B4.
**(** 626 5603.

### BROWN CAFÉS AND BARS

**Aas van Bokalen**
Keizersgracht 335.
**Map** 1 B5.
**(** 623 0917.

**Café Carel's**
Voetboogstraat 6.
**Map** 7 B4.
**(** 622 2080.

**Café Cox**
Marnixstraat 429.
**Map** 4 D1.
**(** 620 7222.

**De Doffer**
Runstraat 12–14.
**Map** 4 E1.
**(** 622 6686.

**'t Doktertje**
Rozenboomsteeg 4.
**Map** 7 B4.
**(** 626 4427.

**Blincker**
St Barberenstraat 7.
**Map** 7 B4.
**(** 627 1938.

**Molenpad**
Prinsengracht 653.
**Map** 4 E1.
**(** 625 9680.

**Pieper**
Prinsengracht 424.
**Map** 4 E1.
**(** 626 4775.

**De Prins**
Prinsengracht 124.
**Map** 1 B4.
**(** 624 9382.

**Van Puffelen**
Prinsengracht 375–377.
**Map** 1 B4.
**(** 624 6270.

**De Reiger**
Nieuwe Leliestraat 34.
**Map** 1 B4.
**(** 624 7426.

**De Tuin**
2e Tuindwarsstraat 13
(near Westerstraat).
**Map** 1 B3.
**(** 624 4559.

### PROEFLOKALEN AND MODERN TASTING BARS

**De Drie Fleschjes**
Gravenstraat 18.
**Map** 7 B2.
**(** 624 8443.

**Gollem**
Raamsteeg 4.
**Map** 7 A4.
**(** 330 2890.

**Henri Prouvin**
Gravenstraat 20.
**Map** 7 B2.
**(** 623 9333.

**In De Wildeman**
Kolksteeg 3.
**Map** 7 C1.
**(** 638 2348.

**L&B Limited**
Korte Leidsedwarsstraat
82–84. **Map** 4 E2.
**(** 625 2387.

### GRAND CAFÉS AND DESIGNER BARS

**De Balie**
Kleine Gartman-
plantsoen 10.
**Map** 4 E2.
**(** 553 5130.

**Café Americain**
American Hotel,
Leidsekade 97.
**Map** 4 E2.
**(** 556 3000.

**Caffè Esprit**
Spui 10.
**Map** 7 B4.
**(** 622 1967.

**De Jaren**
Nieuwe Doelenstraat
20–22.
**Map** 7 C4.
**(** 625 5771.

**De Kroon**
Rembrandtplein 17.
**Map** 7 C5.
**(** 625 2011.

**Het Land van
Walem**
Keizersgracht 449.
**Map** 7 A5.
**(** 625 3544.

**Café
Luxembourg**
Spui 22–24.
**Map** 7 B4.
**(** 620 6264.

**Morlang**
Keizersgracht 451.
**Map** 7 A5.
**(** 625 2681.

**Café
Schiller**
Rembrandtplein 26.
**Map** 7 C5.
**(** 624 9846.

**Vertigo**
Nederlands
Filmmuseum,
Vondelpark 3
**Map** 4 D2.
**(** 612 3021.

### SMOKING COFFEESHOPS

**The Bulldog**
Leidseplein 15.
**Map** 4 E2.
**(** 626 5185.

**Caffe Chocolata**
Spuistraat 51.
**Map** 7 D1.
**(** 622 6241.

**The
Grasshopper**
Nieuwezijds Voorburgwal
59.
**Map** 7 A4.
**(** 624 6753.

**Global Chillage**
Kerkstraat 51.
**Map** 4 E1.
**(** 777 9777.

**Rusland**
Rusland 16.
**Map** 7 C4.
**(** 627 9468.

**Siberië**
Brouwersgracht 11.
**Map** 1 C3.
**(** 623 5909.

### COFFEESHOPS AND SALONS DE THÉ

**Arnold Cornelis**
Elandsgracht 78.
**Map** 1 B5.
**(** 625 8585.

**Backstage**
Utrechtsedwarsstraat 67.
**Map** 5 A3.
**(** 622 3638.

**The Coffee
Gallery**
Jodenbreestraat 94.
**Map** 8 E4.
**(** 618 4808.

**Metz & Co**
Leidsestraat 34-36.
**Map** 4 F1.
**(** 520 7020.

**Pompadour**
Huidenstraat 12.
**Map** 7 A4.
**(** 623 9554.

**Reibach**
Brouwersgracht 139.
**Map** 1 B2.
**(** 626 7708.

### SPECIALIST CAFÉS

**De Brakke
Grond**
Nes 43.
**Map** 7 B3.
**(** 626 0044.

**Terzijde**
Kerkstraat 59.
**Map** 4 E1.
**(** 626 2301.

**De Zotte**
Raamstraat 29.
**Map** 4 E1.
**(** 626 8694.

# SHOPS AND MARKETS

AMSTERDAM has a huge range of shops and markets, so if you are present-hunting, you will find no shortage of ideas. Most of the large clothing and department stores are to be found in the Nieuwe Zijde, especially along Kalverstraat *(see p72)*, but there are many other shopping areas to discover. The narrow streets which cross the Canal Ring, such as Herenstraat and Hartenstraat, contain a diverse array of specialist shops selling everything from ethnic fabrics and beads to unusual games and handmade dolls. The best luxury fashion is to be found on the classy PC Hooftstraat and Van Baerlestraat. However, if you are looking for a bargain, take time to explore the street markets and numerous second-hand shops. Here you can pick up recent fashion items and worn leather jackets cheaply.

**Atrium of the Magna Plaza in the former Postkantoor**

## OPENING HOURS

SHOPS ARE usually open from 9am or 10am to 6pm Tuesday to Saturday and from 1pm to 6pm on Monday *(see p256)*. Many shops are now also open on Sundays. In the city centre, shops stay open until 9pm on Thursdays. However, legislation does allow shopkeepers in the city centre to remain open between 7am and 10pm seven days a week. Retailers are most likely to take advantage of this law in the run up to Sinterklaas *(see p53)* and during Christmas.

## HOW TO PAY

CASH IS the most popular method of payment, so if you intend to use a credit card, ask if they are accepted before buying. Although cards are becoming more widely accepted, department stores often require purchases to be paid for at a special till, and smaller shops may only accept them for non-sale items and goods costing more than 45 euros. Eurocheques are accepted in most shops and, if you have a bank account in the Netherlands, direct debits are becoming popular. Some tourist shops take foreign currency, but offer a poor rate of exchange.

## VAT EXEMPTION

MOST DUTCH GOODS are subject to value added tax (BTW) of either 19 per cent for clothes and other goods, or 6 per cent for books. Non-EU residents are entitled to a refund, subject to certain conditions. Shops which stock the relevant forms will have a sign saying "Tax free for tourists". On leaving the country, this form must be stamped by customs who will then send it back to the shop. The shop will eventually refund you the tax paid. Unless your purchase is an expensive one, you may find that it is not worth the effort involved.

**Stoeltie Diamonds *(see p242)***

## SALES

SALES TAKE PLACE mainly in January and July but smaller shops and boutiques may offer discount items at any time. *Uitverkoop* describes anything from a closing-down sale to a stock-clearance sale, while *korting* merely indicates that discounts are being offered.

Towards the end of a sale, further discounts, which will be calculated at the till, are often subtracted from the marked-down price. Beware of clothes rails marked, for example, *VA 40* or *Vanaf 40* as this sign means "From 40" – the items cost 40 euros or more, rather than exactly 40 euros.

## DEPARTMENT STORES AND MALLS

PERHAPS AMSTERDAM'S best-known department store is **De Bijenkorf** on Dam square, often described as the Dutch Harrods. It has a huge perfumery, and stocks a wide range of men's and women's clothing, plus toys, soft furnishings and household goods. At Christmas it devotes a whole floor to decorations. Both **Maison de Bonneterie** and **Metz & Co** are more exclusive. Among the less expensive stores, **Hema** is very popular for household goods, children's clothes and underwear. Also popular for basic items is **Vroom & Dreesman**. The only shopping malls in central Amsterdam are the Kalvertoren (Kalverstraat, near Singel) and Magna Plaza, which is housed in the old Postkantoor building *(see p78)*. The impressive, vaulted interior of this former head post office now contains a huge assortment of upmarket boutiques and shops.

## MARKETS

AMSTERDAMMERS' love of street trading is most graphically illustrated on 30 April during Queen's Day *(see p50)*, when Amsterdam turns into the biggest flea market in the world, as local people crowd the city to sell off all their un-wanted junk. Such is the crush of eager bargain-hunters that the entire city centre is closed to traffic during the festivities.

As Amsterdam still resembles a collection of small villages, every district has its own local market. The best-known of these, because of its size, is the Albert Cuypmarkt (see p122) in the Pijp district, which sells a wide assortment of food, both Dutch and ethnic. This market is also good for cheap clothes and reasonably priced flowers.

Apart from the local markets, Amsterdam has a wide range of specialist markets. Visitors to the city and residents alike are drawn to the excellent array of seasonal flowers on sale at the Bloemenmarkt (see p123). Another market popular with tourists is Waterlooplein flea market (see p63). Despite the crowds, vigilant collectors can still seek out the odd bargain among the bric-a-brac; there is also a selection of new and second-hand clothes for sale.

Browsers will be fascinated by the hundreds of stalls at the Looier Kunst Antiekcentrum (see p113), which sell anything from antique dolls to egg cups. Every Wednesday and Saturday on the Nieuwezijds Voorburg-wal there is a specialist market for stamp and coin collectors. Gourmets should head for the Noordermarkt (see p92), which holds an organic food market on Saturdays. The best prices, however, are to be found about 25 km (16 miles) northwest of Amsterdam in the port town of

**MEXX, a smart boutique on PC Hooftstraat (see p126)**

Beverwijk, where the **Beverwijkse Bazar**, open on Saturdays, is one of Europe's largest indoor flea markets. Next door the market continues with a cross-section of Oriental merchandise, including rugs, carpets, pottery, crafts and food.

**Smoked fish on display at the Albert Cuypmarkt**

## SPECIALIST SHOPS

DOTTED THROUGHOUT Amster-dam are dozens of small specialist shops. One of the more unusual is **Condomerie Het Gulden Vlies**, located in a former squat, which sells con-doms from all over the world. Equally unusual is **Christmas**

**World**, which sells festive adornments all year round, and **Party House**, which has a vast collection of paper decorations. **Capsicum Natuurstoffen** has a huge selection of exotic silks and linens, while **Coppenhagen 1001 Kralen** has more than 1,000 different types of beads. It is also worth making time to explore **Joe's Vliegerwinkel** for its wide range of kites, **Simon Levelt** for tea and coffee, or **Hooy & Co.** for an array of wonderful-smelling herbs.

## BOOKS, NEWSPAPERS AND MAGAZINES

AS BOOKS ARE SUBJECT to value added tax in the Nether-lands, you may find them slightly more expensive than at home. English-language books are generally available, particularly at **The American Book Center** and **Waterstone's**. Holiday reading can be picked up very cheaply at second-hand book-shops, such as **De Slegte**. Collectors of comics should not miss a visit to **Lambiek**. Amsterdam does not have its own English-language newspaper, but most city-centre newsagents stock foreign papers. *Het Financieel Dagblad* has a daily busi-ness update in English and publishes a weekly English-language ed-ition. Both *Time Out Amsterdam* and *What's On* are useful listings magazines (see p256).

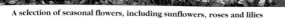

**A selection of seasonal flowers, including sunflowers, roses and lilies**

# What to Buy in Amsterdam

Amsterdam has hundreds of tourist shops selling souvenirs, but those looking for something different will find a better selection of genuine Dutch items in one of the city's specialist shops or even at an ordinary supermarket. Authentic Delftware is only found at a handful of licensed dealers, but there are still many jewellers selling anything from uncut stones to second-hand diamond rings. Dutch cheese, chocolate and locally produced beers and *jenevers* offer a flavour of the city, while a bunch of flowers is always appreciated.

**Traditional wooden clogs**

### Ceramics
*Finely detailed model canal houses can be be bought singly or by the row.*

**Droste chocolate pastilles**

**Sweet and salty varieties of drop liquorice**

### Dutch Sweets
*Handmade Belgian chocolates and Droste pastilles are both delicious, but salty liquorice is an acquired taste.*

**Handmade Belgian chocolates**

### Flowers
*Bulbs and cut flowers are a colourful reminder of the city and, due to greenhouse production, many blooms are available all year round.*

**Tulip bulbs**

**A bunch of fresh tulips**

### Gouda Cheese
*There are many types of Gouda of different maturity (see p242). Any shop will be happy to let you try a slice before making a purchase.*

**Two popular brands of beer**

### Beer in Amsterdam
*A huge variety of imported, bottled beers are sold in Amsterdam as well as many local brews (see p242).*

**Sturdy stone flagons of *jonge* and *oude jenever* (see pp48–9) – also available in flavoured varieties**

Dutch windmill prints

## Old Maps and Prints
*Historically famous for cartography, Amsterdam has a good selection of new and old maps, and many second-hand bookshops stock etchings.*

Reproductions of old maps of Amsterdam and Russia

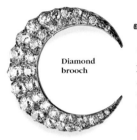
Diamond brooch

Chain-link, diamond-encrusted bracelet

### Diamonds
*Diamond-cutting was first established in Amsterdam during the 16th century. The city is still one of the major diamond centres.*

Different coloured brilliant-cut diamonds

## ROYAL DELFT
In response to the demand for Chinese design, more than 30 factories sprang up in Delft in the 17th century, producing distinctive blue-and-white porcelain *(see p195)*. Today, only De Porceleyne Fles still makes real Delftware. Items from this factory are sold with a certificate of authenticity.

Polychrome jug painted in colours used on 17th-century majolica

Pynaker tobacco jar influenced by Japanese Imari ware

Plate painted in traditional Delft blue

Painter's initials

Year code – DB means 1982

Trademark since 1876

Item number

**Genuine De Porceleyne Fles marks**

**Delft-blue vase**

17th-century plate made for rich family

Decorative 17th-century fireplace tile

### Antique Delft
*Old Delftware is highly sought after and expensive, but Delft fireplace tiles can be picked up more cheaply.*

# Where to Shop in Amsterdam

THE NETHERLANDS IS JUSTLY famous for its flowers, beer and cheese. A wide choice of these indigenous products is available in Amsterdam, which has also long been regarded as the world centre for diamonds. Owing to the large numbers of overseas settlers living in Amsterdam and the cosmopolitan outlook of its residents, it is easy to find a selection of foreign goods in the city. These range from Indonesian beads to French designer wear.

## FASHION AND CLOTHES

VAN BAERLESTRAAT and PC Hooftstraat contain numerous designer boutiques such as **MEXX**, offering top names like Katharine Hamnet and the leading French and Italian designer labels. The smart set from the Canal Ring haunt the stylish **The People of the Labyrinths** and **Pauw** for their timeless clothes and accessories.

Boutiques in the Nieuwe Zijde offer less pricey items. The French designer **Agnès B** has her own shop along Rokin selling classic designer wear. If leather's your thing, try **Robin & Rik** on Runstraat for handmade leather clothes and accessories. Along Kalverstraat, **Sissy Boy** specializes in refined classic suits as well as eye-catching designs.

Fanatics of second-hand clothes will find well-priced and stylish selections at shops such as **Zipper**. For the widest choice of fashionable boots and shoes, **Dr Adams** is almost a Dutch institution.

## ANTIQUES AND FURNISHINGS

WHILE YOU CAN pick up the odd bargain on Waterlooplein (see p63) and at the Noordermarkt (see p92), the best place for antiques is around Spiegelgracht. A wide selection of shops sells everything from 17th-century tiles to icons. The **EH Ariëns Kappers** has a comprehensive collection of old prints, maps and graphic art. It is also interesting to visit an auction house. Both **Sotheby's** and **Christie's** have branches in Amsterdam. Looier Kunst en Antiekcentrum (see p113), has a potpourri of odds and ends, while **De Haas** and **Object Interior** have good collections

of 20th-century furniture and accessories. If you like to barter, **Tut Tut** buys and sells antique toys, silver and glassware.

## FLOWERS AND BULBS

NO DUTCH PERSON would dream of visiting a friend without a bunch of flowers, so Amsterdam is crowded with flower shops. Worth visiting are **Maison Rivièra**, for a vast assortment of colourful domestic blooms and **Gerda's Bloemen en Planten** for its stock of tropical flowers.

Cut flowers are cheapest at Albert Cuypmarkt (see p122), but Bloemenmarkt (see p123) has a better selection, as well as hundreds of bulbs and tubers. It also sells potted plants, but due to customs regulations, these usually can't be exported.

## DIAMONDS

AMSTERDAM has a long tradition of cutting and polishing diamonds (see p30). It is still possible to purchase loose stones and diamonds in a new setting at one of the city's many diamond-cutting centres such as **Stoeltie Diamonds** or Coster Diamonds (see p128). The city is also well stocked with jewellers, several specializing in diamonds. The best second-hand jewellery can be found in the fascinating antique shops around Spiegelgracht.

## CHEESE

AS THE DUTCH are fussy about their cheese, you can buy a good selection from supermarkets such as **Albert Heijn**, street markets and at specialist shops. Instead of buying the red-wax-covered Edam, try one of the many varieties of Gouda. Mature Gouda (overjarige kaas) has a rich, salty taste and crumbly

texture, while young Gouda (meikaas) is fresh and curdy. This cheese is also sold with cummin (leidsekaas) or cloves (nagelkaas) (see p226).

## CHOCOLATES

VERKADE AND DROSTE are the best-known makes of chocolate in the Netherlands. For a treat, visit **Pompadour**, for its delicious hand-made chocolates, or a branch of the up-market Belgian chocolate specialist, **Leonidas**.

## BEERS AND SPIRITS

THE DUTCH ARE knowledgeable beer drinkers. Along with brand-name lagers like Heineken, Grolsch and Amstel, there is also a huge range of bottled beers on offer. Local specialities include Zatte, a rare, bottle-fermented beer and Wieckse Witte, a white beer. Specialist shops like **De Bierkoning** offer the widest choice and best advice.

The Dutch spirit jenever, the "father" of gin, is often sold in stone bottles and flavoured with herbs or fruit (see p48).

## POTTERY AND GLASSWARE

BLUE-AND-WHITE POTTERY is stocked by most tourist shops, but only items with a certificate are real Delftware. **Rinascimento** sells the real thing from De Porceleyne Fles, one of the original Delft potteries.

The Jordaan is the best place to hunt for modern pottery, while **Glasgalerie Kuhler** has a stunning range of modern glass, and **Het Klei Kollektief** offers an ever-changing choice of bright ceramics.

## POSTERS AND PRINTS

THE BEST PLACES to find good reproductions of paintings are in museum shops. **Art Multiples** offers an excellent selection of the less famous Dutch scenes.

A range of old etchings can be found at **Old Prints** and among the stalls at the Oudemanshuispoort (see p61).

## DIRECTORY

### DEPARTMENT STORES

**De Bijenkorf**
Dam 1.
**Map** 7 B2.
( 621 8080.

**Hema**
Kalvertoren, Kalverstraat.
**Map** 7 B4.
( 422 8988.
Nieuwendijk 174–176.
**Map** 7 B2.
( 623 4176.

**Maison de Bonneterie**
Rokin 140–142.
**Map** 7 B4.
( 531 3400.

**Metz & Co**
Leidsestraat 34-36.
**Map** 7 A5.
( 520 7020.

**Vroom & Dreesman**
Kalverstraat 201.
**Map** 7 B5.
( 622 0171.

### MARKETS OUTSIDE THE CITY

**De Beverwijkse Bazar,**
Montageweg 35
Beverwijk

### SPECIALIST SHOPS

**Capsicum Natuurstoffen**
Oude Hoogstraat 1.
**Map** 7 C3.
( 623 1016.

**Christmas World**
Damrak 33.
**Map** 7 B3.
( 622 7047.

**Condomerie Het Gulden Vlies**
Warmoesstraat 141.
**Map** 7 C2.
( 627 41/4.

**Coppenhagen 1001 Kralen**
Rozengracht 54.
**Map** 1 B4.
( 624 3681.

**Jacob Hooy & Co**
Kloveniersburgwal 12.
**Map** 8 D3.
( 624 3041.

**Party House**
Rozengracht 93a/b.
**Map** 1 B4.
( 624 7851.

**Simon Levelt**
Prinsengracht 180.
**Map** 1 B4.
( 624 0823.

**Joe's Vliegerwinkel**
Nieuwe Hoogstraat 19.
**Map** 8 D3.
( 625 0139.

### BOOKS, NEWSPAPERS AND MAGAZINES

**The American Book Center**
Kalverstraat 185.
**Map** 7 B5.
( 625 5537.

**Lambiek**
Kerkstraat 78.
**Map** 7 A5.
( 626 /543.

**De Slegte**
Kalverstraat 48–52.
**Map** 7 B3.
( 622 5933.

**Waterstone's Bookseller**
Kalverstraat 152.
**Map** 7 B4. ( 638 3821.

### FASHION AND CLOTHES

**Agnès B**
Rokin 126.
**Map** 7 B4.
( 627 1465.

**Dr Adams**
Oude Doelenstraat 5–7.
**Map** 7 C3.
( 622 3734.

**The People of the Labyrinths**
Van Baerlestraat 44.
**Map** 4 D3.
( 664 0779.

**MEXX**
PC Hooftstraat 118–120.
**Map** 4 D3.
( 675 0171.

**Pauw**
Leidsestraat 16.
**Map** 7 A5.
( 626 5698.

**Robin & Rik**
Runstraat 30.
**Map** 7 B4.
( 627 8924.

**Sissy Boy**
Kalverstraat 210.
**Map** 7 B4.
( 626 0088.

**Zipper**
Huidenstraat 7.
**Map** 7 A4.
( 623 7302.

### ANTIQUES AND FURNISHINGS

**Christie's**
Cornelis Schuytstraat 57.
**Map** 3 C4.
( 575 5255.

**De Haas**
Kerkstraat 155.
**Map** 4 F2.
( 626 5952.

**EH Ariëns Kappers**
Nieuwe Spiegelstraat 32.
**Map** 4 F2.
( 623 5356.

**Object**
Leliegracht 16.
**Map** 7 A2.
( 627 1622.

**Sotheby's**
De Boelelaan 30.
**Map** 7 B4.
( 550 2200.

**Tut Tut**
Elandsgracht 109, Looier Markt. **Map** 1 A5.
( 627 7960.

### FLOWERS AND BULBS

**Gerda's Bloemen en Planten**
Runstraat 16.
**Map** 4 E1.
( 624 2912.

**Rivièra Maison**
Herenstraat 2–6.
**Map** 7 A1.
( 622 7675.

### DIAMONDS

**Stoeltie Diamonds**
Wagenstraat 13–17.
**Map** 8 D5.
( 623 7601.

### CHEESE

**Albert Heijn**
Nieuwezijds Voorburgwal 226. **Map** 7 B2.
( 421 8344.
Many other branches.

### CHOCOLATES

**Leonidas**
Damstraat 15. **Map** 7 B3.
( 625 3497.

**Pompadour**
Huidenstraat 12.
**Map** 7 A4.
( 623 9554.

### BEERS AND SPIRITS

**De Bierkoning**
Paleisstraat 125.
**Map** 7 B3.
( 625 2336.

### POTTERY AND GLASSWARE

**Fleur de Lys**
Beethovenstraat 41.
**Map** 4 D5. ( 622 1737.

**Galleria d'Arte Rinascimento**
Prinsengracht 170
**Map** 1 B4.
( 622 7509.

**Glasgalerie Kuhler**
Prinsengracht 134.
**Map** 1 B4.
( 638 0230.

**Het Kleikollektief**
Hartenstraat 19.
**Map** 7 A3.
( 622 5727.

### POSTERS AND PRINTS

**Art Multiples**
Keizersgracht 510.
**Map** 7 A5.
( 624 8419.

**Old Prints**
Spiegelgracht 27.
**Map** 4 F2.
( 625 8852.

# ENTERTAINMENT IN AMSTERDAM

AMSTERDAM OFFERS a diverse array of world-class entertainment. A variety of performances are staged in hundreds of venues throughout the city, ranging from the century-old Concertgebouw (see p128) to the 17th-century IJsbreker café on the Amstel (see p248). The Dutch passion for American jazz draws international greats like BB King, Pharaoh Sanders and ex-patriot Nina Simone to annual events such as the Blues Festival and Drum Rhythm Festival (see p50). The city's most popular events take place in the summer, and include the Holland Festival (see p51) and the Amsterdam Roots Festival (see p51). There is a huge choice of multilingual plays and films throughout the year. There is also plenty of free entertainment from the multitude of street performers and live bands in late-night bars and cafés.

## ENTERTAINMENT INFORMATION

ONE OF THE MOST useful sources of entertainment information is Uitkrant, a free listings magazine (see p256). It is printed monthly and available, as are a variety of other Dutch-language listings, from theatres, cafés and bars, libraries and tourist offices. Although written in Dutch, it is easy to follow and offers the most comprehensive daily listings of what's going on.

The **Amsterdam Tourist Board** (see also p256) publishes an English-language listings magazine every two weeks called Day by Day. It can be picked up for a nominal price at Tourist Board offices and some newsagents, or free issues can be found in selected hotels and restaurants. For music listings look out for the Pop & Jazz Uitlijst published by the **AUB** (Amsterdam Uitburo). Daily newspapers including De Volkskrant, Het Parool, NRC Handelsblad and De Telegraaf publish a selection of listings on Thursdays, although they are mainly excerpts from Uitkrant.

**Late-night bar in the Red Light District**

## BOOKING TICKETS

AMSTERDAM'S MAJOR classical music, opera and dance performances, such as those by the Dutch National Ballet, are likely to be sold out weeks ahead of time. It is advisable to book tickets in advance to ensure the day, time and seats of your choice. For most other events, it is possible to buy tickets on the day.

The main reservations office for entertainment and all cultural activities is the AUB, which is located next to the Stadsschouwburg (see p111) in Leidseplein. You can make reservations, pick up tickets in advance (a booking fee is charged) and obtain information in person or over the telephone. You can also make bookings at the venue itself, or through Tourist Board offices or the **Dutch Tourist Service**, which offers a booking service for theatres. Tickets to major rock concerts can be obtained at the Tourist Board, AUB and at some of the large record shops in the city centre. Although some of the most popular club

The Stopera complex, home to the Dutch national opera and ballet companies

The Neo-Classical-style pediment of the Concertgebouw *(see p128)*

dates need to be booked in advance, entrance to night-clubs like the Paradiso and De Melkweg *(see pp110–11)* can usually be bought at the door. Going to the cinema is popular with Amsterdammers, so it is advisable to book tickets in the afternoon for evening performances during a film's opening week. Most multi-screen cinemas provide a Dutch-speaking automated booking service. All booking offices are usually open from Monday to Saturday, between 9am and 6pm, or later. Credit cards are generally not accepted and it is important to collect reserved tickets at least an hour before the show starts, or the tickets may be resold.

**Theatre sign on Nes** *(see p74)*

## REDUCED-PRICE TICKETS

ENTRY TO SOME performances can be obtained at bargain prices for holders of the Cultureel Jongeren Passport (CJP). Valid for one year, it is available to anyone under the age of 26 for nine euros. Some hotels include reduced-price entry to certain events as part of their package deals – check details with your travel agent. Cinemas usually offer a 30 per cent discount from Monday to Thursday. Several venues, such as the Concertgebouw *(see p128)* and the Westerkerk *(see p90)*, have free lunch-time concerts throughout the year.

## FACILITIES FOR THE DISABLED

NEARLY ALL Amsterdam's major theatres, cinemas and concert halls have unrestricted wheelchair access and assistance is always available. A number of the city's smaller venues, however, are housed in old buildings not designed with the disabled in mind. Venues like the IJsbreker *(see p248)* will make special arrangements if they are notified beforehand. Cinemas also provide facilities for the hard of hearing and visually impaired. Always telephone the box office a couple of days before your visit and specify what you require.

## OPEN-AIR ENTERTAINMENT

AS AMSTERDAMMERS are avid supporters of theatre and of all sorts of music, there are plenty of open-air venues operating throughout the summer. In the heart of the city, the Vondelpark

open-air theatre *(see p128)* stages a wide variety of free concerts and theatre performances. The restored turn-of-the-century Nederlands Filmmuseum *(see p129)* is housed in a pavilion in the park. During the summer, free screenings and documentaries are shown, as well as silent films that are sometimes accompanied by live music.

The Prinsengracht classical music concert *(see p51)* is performed in August on a group of canal barges. On the outskirts of the city, the scenic Amsterdamse Bos *(see p155)* is the setting for productions of Shakespeare, Chekhov and other classical dramatists, staged in the open-air theatre. In the south, Amstelpark *(see p154)* is the venue for De Parade at the end of July *(see p246)*. Amsterdammers also enjoy rowing on the Amstel, where rowing clubs operate from a boathouse near Amstelpark.

## USEFUL ADDRESSES

### AUB
Leidseplein 26. **Map** 4 E2.
📞 0900 0191.
🖥 www.uitlijn.nl

### Dutch Tourist Service
Damrak 7. **Map** 7 C2.
📞 520 7000.

### Amsterdam Tourist Board
Stationsplein 10. **Map** 8 D1.
📞 0900 400 4040.
Leidseplein 1. **Map** 4 E2.
📞 0900 400 4040.
🖥 www.visitamsterdam.nl
🖥 www.amsterdamtourist.nl

Customers enjoying café life in the popular Thorbeckeplein

# Theatre, Dance and Film

THEATRE AND DANCE are important aspects of cultural life in Amsterdam, and performances take place throughout the year in dozens of venues all over the city. Experimental theatre can be found in one of the oldest streets in the city, along the Nes (see p74). Theatres on the Nes, such as De Brakke Grond, are also popular venues for radical theatre productions. The city's main locations for dance include the Felix Meritis, Meervaart, Muziektheater, Stadsschouwburg and the Dutch Dance Laboratory, for experimental productions. The Dutch love cinema and, though Amsterdam has only a few large cinema complexes, there is a surprising number of venues that show a variety of films, from first-run, mainstream and art, to foreign-language, revival and gay.

## THEATRE AND CABARET

AMSTERDAM HAS more than 50 theatre venues and boasts a number of English-speaking companies. The Toneelgroep Amsterdam is the resident theatre company at **Westergusfabriek**, and the **Theater Bellevue**, **Stadsschouwburg** and the **Felix Meritis** (see p113) are important venues for touring theatre companies.

Experimental theatre can be found at a range of locations throughout Amsterdam, including the **Westergasfabriek** and the former public bath-house, **Badhuistheater de Bochel** (Hunchback), which is home to a resident theatre cooperative of the same name. De Trust is a small theatre company that was founded in 1988 and specializes in translating and staging Austrian and German plays, while the Orkater musical theatre company often holds performances at Stadsschouwburg and the Theater Bellevue.

The annual Holland Festival (see p51) in June offers a prestigious series of opera, theatre and dance performances. It features international talent such as Peter Brook, Peter Zadek and John Jesurum. The International Theatre School Festival presents innovative performances at **De Brakke Grond**, **Frascati** and other venues on the Nes (see p74) at the end of June. The **Tropentheater** has a packed programme of lively productions from developing countries.

Downriver from the Muziektheater, near the smart Amstel Inter-Continental (see p223), the **Koninklijk Theater Carré** plays host to long-running international musicals such as Les Misérables and Cyrano. The Koninklijk Theater Carré is often the setting for elegant premières attended by members of the Dutch royal family. Closer to the Muziektheater and also facing the Amstel is the charming 17th-century **De Kleine Komedie**. It can seat an audience of up to 500 and offers a perfect setting for cabaret. It also features stand-up comedy and occasionally has English-language theatre productions. Although De Kleine Komedie is closed throughout the summer, such is its reputation throughout Europe, that bookings must be made at least three months in advance.

Summer outdoor theatre can be seen at the **Vondelpark** open-air theatre (see p128) and at the Amsterdamse Bos (see p155), a woodland park on the edge of town. Here, a pathway lined with Classical Greek statuary leads to a 1,800-seat amphitheatre, the venue for performances of Shakespeare and Chekhov plays. In the south of Amsterdam, the Amstelpark (see p154) is the venue for De Parade, a tent city erected each summer in late July and early August where international dance, theatre and circus acts perform before a rapturous audience. Merry-making often carries on into the early morning hours.

## DANCE

THE NETHERLANDS possesses two world-class ballet companies, the Dutch National Ballet and the Nederlands Dans Theater (NDT). The Dutch National Ballet is housed in the 1,600-seat **Muziektheater** (see p63), which provides magnificent views along the Amstel river, and is renowned for its classical and modern repertoire.

The NDT regularly performs in venues throughout the city. Ballets from the Czech artistic director, Jiri Kylian, form the majority of the programming. In addition to the core company, the NDT also has two other companies, NDT2 and NDT3. NDT2 is a younger company made up of dancers aged 18–21 who perform the work of established choreographers such as Hans van Manen. It also performs the works of younger choreographers such as Lionel Hoche and Paul Lightfoot. NDT3 is composed of former members of the original Nederlands Dans Theater. These highly experienced dancers, who are all over the age of 40, perform shows of unparalleled technical expertise and control.

Dance is often performed at Stadsschouwburg and at the Felix Meritis, Amsterdam's 18th-century concert hall and one of its earliest performance venues. Westergasfabriek, the former gasworks, also holds dance performances.

Amsterdam is a laboratory for experimental dance, and many innovative performances can be seen throughout the city. They are not confined to any one venue though, so it is best to check the entertainment listings, such as Uitkrant and Time Out Amsterdam (see p256), for full details. Experimental dance can be enjoyed regularly at top venues like the Stadsschouwburg and the **De Meervaart**. Companies to look out for include Introdans, who combine jazz with flamenco alongside other varieties of ethnic dance, and Opus One, who mix jazz, classical ballet and tap. Needless to say, the Nederlands Dans Theater's repertoire also includes experimental dance routines.

The Holland Festival in June *(see p51)* is used as the principal platform for premières of shows by top choreographers from both the Nederlands Dans Theater and the Dutch National Ballet. The International Theatre School Festival, also in June, focuses increasingly on dance, with performances taking place in the historic street of Nes *(see p74)*, which is one of the very oldest parts of the city.

## FILM

AMSTERDAMMERS love the cinema, and there are more than 45 venues in the city. All films are screened in the original language with subtitles. Movie lovers should not miss the plush Art Deco Tuschinski Theater *(see p123)*. Constructed between 1918 and 1921, this cinema features a luxurious foyer, stained-glass windows, tables, sofas and lamps. First-run films often open at the Tuschinski, and this is often the place to catch public appearances by Dutch and international film stars.

It is easy to find out which films are showing where, as each cinema has a listing at its entrance, and details are also posted in bars and cafés.

Programmes change on a Thursday, and most new film listings, carried in the daily newspapers, are printed on that day. *De Filmkrant* is a highly regarded, free monthly film magazine which carries complete listings, which are written in Dutch but are very easy to understand. The ticket prices vary from five to eight euros, depending on whether it is a matinée or an evening screening, although some longer films can command a slightly higher admission price.

Some of the larger cinema complexes carry afternoon matinées during the week and these usually begin at 2pm. At the weekend the schedule varies. Some of the cinemas, such as the mainstream **City** and the arthouse **Kriterion**, often schedule several showings of children's films at the weekend. For adults, the Kriterion offers a great selection of arthouse and mainstream films, with late-night screenings of cult and erotic movies.

Evening shows usually begin at either 6:30pm or 7pm, and there is a second showing at 9pm or 9:30pm, although a few cinemas also have an 8pm screening. Be prepared for the intermission, which is known as the "pauze". This is a 15-minute obligatory break that is usually scheduled to coincide exactly with the most exciting scene of the film. If you suddenly get the urge to see a film and don't particularly mind what it is, check out Leidseplein *(see p110)*, one of the biggest gathering areas in the city, where cinemas, cafés, restaurants and bars abound.

One first-run and mainstream cinema that can be found within a two-minute walk of Leidseplein is the **Filmmuseum Cinerama**, a fairly glittery complex. There is also the high-profile, seven-screen, 2,094-seater **City** complex.

**The Movies** near Harlemmerpoort *(see p93)* specialises in films with a psychological connection. The theatre also houses a pleasant pub and restaurant. There is also the Cinecenter, situated on a side street just off the main square across from De Melkweg *(see p110)*; and for a real treat, **Filmtheater de Uitkijk**, which is a short walk along Leidsestraat to Prinsengracht. This small, venerable 158-seat venue specializes in movie classics and, best of all, refuses ever to indulge in the dreaded "pauze". Dating from 1913, De Uitkijk is Amsterdam's oldest operational cinema.

## DIRECTORY

### THEATRE AND CABARET

**Badhuistheater de Bochel**
Andreas Bonnstraat 28.
Map 5 C4. 668 5102.

**De Brakke Grond**
Vlaams Cultureel Centrum, Nes 45.
Map 7 C3.
626 6866.

**De Kleine Komedie**
Amstel 56–58.
Map 5 B3.
624 0534.

**Felix Meritis**
Keizersgracht 324.
Map 1 B5.
623 2321.

**Frascati**
Nes 63.
Map 7 B4.
626 6866.

**Koninklijk Theater Carré**
Amstel 115–125.
Map 5 B3.
0900 252 5255.

**KIT/Tropentheater**
Linnaeusstraat 2.
Map 6 E3.
568 8500.

**Stadsschouwburg**
Leidseplein 26.
Map 4 E2.
624 2311.

**Theater Bellevue, Nieuwe de la Mar**
Leidsekade 90. Map 4 D1.
530 5301.

**Westergasfabriek**
Haarlemmerweg 8–10.
Map 1 A1.
586 0710.

**Vondelpark**
Map 4 D3.

### DANCE

**De Meervaart**
Meer en Vaart 300.
410 770.

**Het Muziektheater**
Amstel 3.
Map 7 C5.
625 5455.

*See also under*
**Felix Meritis**
**Stadsschouwburg**
**Westergasfabriek**

### FILM

**The Movies**
Haarlemmerdijk 161.
Map 1 B2.
638 6016.

**Kriterion**
Roetersstraat 170
Map 5 C3
623 1708

**Filmtheater de Uitkijk**
Prinsengracht 452.
Map 4 E2. 623 7460.

**Filmmuseum Cinerama**
Marnixstraat 400–402.
Map 4 D1. 623 7814.

**City Theater**
Kleine Gartmanplantsoen 15–19. Map 4 E2.
0900 1458.

# Classical Music and Opera

AMSTERDAM IS A CITY with a long and rich tradition in classical music and opera. The principal orchestral venues house some of the world's finest musical events. The city has also acquired a reputation as a centre for early music and organ recitals, with performances in traditional settings such as the English Reformed Church or the Oude Kerk. In summer, concerts can be enjoyed as you relax in one of the city's beautiful parks.

## ORCHESTRAL, CHAMBER AND CHORAL MUSIC

AMSTERDAM'S music centrepiece is the **Concertgebouw** (see p268), renowned for its acoustics and home to the celebrated Royal Concertgebouw Orchestra. International orchestras and soloists come here regularly, and each summer it hosts Robeco Groep concerts, which are famous for showcasing young talent. Early music is also performed here, often by the world-famous Amsterdam Baroque Orchestra and the Orchestra of the Eighteenth Century.

The **Beurs van Berlage** (see p79) was originally the city's stock and commodities exchange and is now the residence of the Netherlands Philharmonic Orchestra. Many of the country's better orchestras and chamber choirs perform here. The **RAI** (see p151) is principally a convention centre, but is often the setting for classical music and opera events. The **Tropenmuseum** (see pp152–3) often features traditional music from developing countries. Modern classical music, opera and

choirs can also be heard at De Melkweg (see pp110–11) and the Paradiso (see p251).

Though **Cristofori's** main business is buying, restoring and selling grand pianos, it also organizes orchestral, chamber and choral concerts. Many performers are internationally renowned artists who can often be called upon to talk about their work before or after a performance.

The **IJsbreker**, which overlooks the Amstel, was once a stopping-point for 17th-century ice-breakers. Today, it is the popular venue for innovative modern music.

## MUSIC IN CHURCHES

CHURCHES in Amsterdam offer concerts throughout the year. The city prides itself on its 42 historic church organs, and those in the **Oude Kerk** (see pp68–9) and the **Nieuwe Kerk** (see pp76–7) are particularly magnificent.

Carillon concerts are often held in the Oude Kerk and at lunch time on Tuesdays in the **Westerkerk** (see p90). The 17th-century **English Reformed Church** holds concerts

that range from Baroque to modern. In the summer, free lunch-time concerts are given by new ensembles and young musicians – monthly programmes are available from the church. The **Thomaskerk**, built only a few decades ago, holds a free lunch-time concert every other Tuesday (except in July and August).

## OPERA

BUILT IN 1988, the **Muziektheater** houses the Stadhuis (town hall) and the Dutch National Opera. Its nickname, the Stopera, is a combination of both names (see p63). It is one of Europe's most up-to-date theatres and features an internationally famous repertoire, as well as lesser-known and some experimental works. Opera can also be seen at the Stadsschouwburg (see p111) on Leidseplein. More experimental opera is performed at the **Westergasfabriek** and sometimes at nightclubs such as the Paradiso and De Melkweg (see p251). Also, check the Holland Festival listings for world premières (see p51).

## OPEN-AIR CONCERTS

THE PRINSENGRACHT concert (see p51) takes place in late August. Musicians perform on barges on the canal in front of the Pulitzer Hotel (see p221). In summer, concerts also take place in the Vondelpark open-air theatre and the Amsterdamse Bos (see p155), and at various other parks.

---

# Pop, Rock and Nightclubs

AMSTERDAM is bursting with live music. From the omnipresent street entertainers to a whole variety of music venues and nightclubs, as well as countless music cafés, it is hard to avoid the city's rock and pop and club scene. Concerts and clubs tend to be cheap and relaxed, with few venues having a strict door policy or dress code. Local bands and musicians are encouraged, and many venues receive subsidies from the local council, so tickets, with the exception of the big-name concerts, rarely cost more than eight euros. Some of the best bands can be enjoyed for the price of a drink. Fierce competition means that venues and clubs come and go faster than the city's trams. For the latest information and gig guides, consult the free *Pop & Jazz Uitlijst*, available from the AUB ticket service and Tourist Board offices *(see p245)*; both sell advance tickets for major concerts. The free magazine *Uitkrant* and English-language *Day by Day* also carry concert listings *(see p244)*.

## POP AND ROCK

MANY BIG NAMES tend to by-pass Amsterdam and head for Rotterdam's Ahoy and Utrecht's Vredenburg stadiums instead. However, mainstream pop concerts are occasionally held at the RAI *(see p151)*. Middle-of-the-road artists tend to play in large theatres, such as the Theater Carré *(see p145)* and the Theater Bellevue *(see p247)*. The Marcanti Plaza and Escape nightclubs *(see p251)* host a variety of hot dance and soul acts.

For most Amsterdammers, rock and pop are synony-mous with two venues – **Paradiso** and **De Melkweg**. Paradiso, housed in a con-verted church just off Leidse-plein, is more prestigious. De Melkweg is housed in a former dairy, hence the name, the "Milky Way" *(see pp110– 11)*.

Both the Paradiso and De Melkweg offer an extremely varied programme: rock, pop, dance, rap and world music. The standards range from chart-toppers and cult heroes to local hopefuls trying their luck at one of the regular talent nights. Big-name bands which come to play in Amsterdam invariably turn up at one of these two places.

The brown café **De Korte Golf** opts for guitar rock and attracts a mainly student crowd, while followers of rock'n'roll should visit the **Cruise-Inn**. The **Arena** is part of the well-known hotel *(see p223)*, where young tourists and locals cram in for music from the 1950s to 1990s, jazz and salsa. Another budget hotel, **The Last Waterhole**, found in the Red Light District *(see p60)*, features live rock.

Blues music alternates with rock at the loud and crowded **Malo Meloe**. Smoky, sweaty and beer-soaked, this place may not seem particularly inviting, but the atmosphere is convivial. From May to September, free concerts are held every Sunday afternoon in the Vondelpark open-air theatre *(see pp128–9)*, often featuring some of the country's top pop acts. The Drum Rhythm Festival *(see p50)*, held annually at the end of May, is a high-spirited celebration of the sheer diversity of popular music. Cutting edge musicians from around the world come to Amsterdam for a weekend extravaganza featuring drum-and-bass, asian underground, jungle, hiphop, R&B, soul, triphop, world music and more.

## JAZZ

THERE MAY WELL BE more jazz venues in Amsterdam than anywhere else in the world. The relaxing rhythms of jazz music are perfectly suited to the mood of the brown cafés and bars *(see pp46 – 9)*.

The city's jazz flagship is the **Bimhuis**, a venue that takes its music seriously. Commonly known as the "Bim", it is the best venue for contemporary jazz and has an international reputation.

Café-restaurant **Casablanca**, in the Red Light District on the Zeedijk, offers live jazz three or four times a week (always on Friday, Saturday and Sunday). More traditional than the Bimhuis, the music here is played by both veterans and new-comers alike.

The many jazz cafés dotted around the city are very popular. Most of them are small brown cafés where local bands perform. Late opening and free entry boost their appeal, although drinks cost a little above average. Most cafés hold weekly jam sessions, when anyone can take the stage. An upmarket version of the jazz café is the **B&W Café,** a large airy café next to Artis Zoo, owned by celebrated local trumpeter and bass player, Rene van Beeck. On Sunday afternoons he gathers up some of the best of his fellow jazz musicians to join him for a lively jam session, usually playing American jazz from the 1940s and 50s.

Around Leidseplein are the **Alto Jazz Café**, the **Bourbon Street** and the **Bamboo Bar**. Alto is best on Wednesday evenings when Hans Dulfer, the so-called "father" of the Amsterdam jazz scene, is in residence. His daughter Candy is a regular attraction at the **De Heeren van Aemstel**. **De Engelbe-waarder** has popular jam sessions on Sunday after-noons. The Vondelpark *(see pp128–9)* is also a popular jazz venue in the summer, when free open-air concerts are held here.

The Dutch passion for jazz turns to frenzy in the summer, with a festival in almost every town. In July, the North Sea Jazz Festival *(see p51)*, held in Den Haag, attracts some of the biggest names in jazz.

## WORLD MUSIC AND FOLK

IN THE NETHERLANDS the world-music scene has been heavily influenced by its many immigrant communities. The West Indian, Indonesian, Maghreb, West African; Surinamese and Turkish traditions are thriving, and are actively encouraged by the city's authorities. A high-brow programme of ethnic, classical and popular concerts is on offer at the Soeterijn theatre (see p246). Groups from around the world appear there on a regular basis, with a strong emphasis on Asian music.

The **Akhnaton** is a multi-cultural youth centre. Its main strengths are Caribbean, African and Arabic music. In addition, there are regular performances by reggae, rap, and salsa artists. These styles are also features of the dance nights.

De Melkweg, and to a lesser extent the Paradiso and Arena, also schedule world music – De Melkweg hosts a colourful Amsterdam Roots Festival (see p51) in June. Live salsa and samba is a nightly attraction at the popular **Canecão Brazilian Bar**, where South American locals mingle with the tourists.

The indigenous folk music of the Netherlands is an acquired taste. It sounds like a mix of traditional German folk music, French chanson and old sea shanties. Large cafés around Rembrandtplein, including **Jantjes Verjaardag** and **Hof van Holland**, provide folk music for tourist consumption. For a more authentic experience, head for the Jordaan. In bars like **De Twee Zwaantjes** and **Café Nol** regulars sometimes burst into joyous song.

Many of Amsterdam's Irish pubs feature live music. Some of the best are **Mulligan's**, **The Blarney Stone** and the huge and popular **O'Donnells**, where you can hear authentic fiddle playing almost every weekend.

## CLUBS AND DISCOS

AMSTERDAM is well-known for its lively nightclub scene.

There is little pretension here, and the mood is relaxed and carefree. Most clubs open at 11pm but don't really get going before 1am. They usually close at 4am during the week, and 5am on Friday and Saturday nights. Entrance prices are relatively low and drinks are reasonably priced. Few clubs enforce a strict dress code, but they do reserve the right to refuse admission. It is an established custom to tip the doormen on the way out.

Amsterdam was one of the very first cities to embrace house music during the late 1980s. It still dominates most clubs, but there is now more variety on offer. DJs and music vary from one night to the next, so check listings for details.

**More** is presented as the successor of the exclusive Roxy which, before it burned down, was where the beautiful people of Amsterdam gathered to rub shoulders with which-ever stars were in town. More has a members-only policy, though it often only applies during busy times.

Far more friendly and less pretentious is **Mazzo**. Though small and intimate, it attracts a young and trendy crowd that prefers to enjoy the latest pro-gressive house sounds from the top DJs without having to dress up for the occasion. Also well worth a visit is the **Westergasfabriek** to the north of the Jordaan, a huge former gasworks, now a collection of music and dance spaces. One of these is occupied by the **West Pacific** restaurant and club where a wide selection of tunes, from jungle to trance and triphop, get punters onto the dance-floor once dinner is over.

Amsterdam's students have established their own club, called **Dansen Bij Jansen**. The two sweaty dance floors in this rambling club are always packed at weekends. You will need a student card to get in, but provided you look the part there should not be a problem.

The leading non-house club in town is **The Backdoor Amsterdam**, with its varied and enjoyable menu of soul, funk and jazzdance. For a

varied choice of music, the **Odeon** plays house music on the ground floor, '60s–'80s classic disco upstairs and jazz-dance in the basement. The city's two biggest dance halls are **Escape** and the **Marcanti Plaza**, which attract a young crowd from out-of town each weekend. **Time** is visited by a young, mainly Amsterdam crowd. The atmosphere is uncomplicated and unadorned. The discos around Leidseplein are basically extended bars with small dance floors, catering for tourists and attracting a wide age range. Mainstream and chart music tend to be played.

## GAY AND LESBIAN CLUBS

CLUBBING is at the heart of Amsterdam's gay scene. The best-known venue is **iT**, a large and glitzy disco off Rembrandtplein. The techno sounds and camp floor shows attract a trendy, mainly gay male crowd. Thursdays and Sundays are officially "mixed" nights. This kind of crossover is not unusual, and most gay clubs will rarely turn away women or straight men.

**Exit**, in Reguliers-dwarsstraat, is a smaller, less-camp version of iT. Up the road, the designer café **Reality**, also in the Reguliers-dwarsstraat, opened its doors recently and offers disco with different styles of music.

At weekends, the gay community centre, **COC Amsterdam**, organizes a popular mixed disco. **De Trut** is housed in the basement of a famous former squat and packs in a mainly lesbian crowd on Sunday nights. The decor is seedy, but the dance floor is big and the drinks are cheap.

The newest lesbian disco is **You II**, with music from the Top 40. Details of other events are available from the **Gay and Lesbian Switch-board**. Het Vrouwenhuis provides bridge evenings and occasional parties for lesbians. The decor is imaginative and the atmosphere friendly. **Saareinn II** is frequented by lesbians and gays and offers a friendly, relaxed atmosphere.

## DIRECTORY

### POP AND ROCK

**Arena**
's-Gravesandestraat 51.
**Map** 6 D4.
☎ 850 2400.

**Cruise-Inn**
Zuiderzeeweg 29
(Amsterdam-Noord).
☎ 692 7188.

**Escape**
Rembrandtplein 11–15.
**Map** 7 B5.
☎ 622 1111.

**De Korte Golf**
Reguliersdwarsstraat 41.
**Map** 7 B5.
☎ 626 5435.

**Mazzo Club**
Nieuwe Nieuwestraat 114.
**Map** 1 B2.
☎ 627 3730.

**The Last Waterhole**
Oudezijds Armsteeg 12.
**Map** 8 D2.
☎ 624 4814.

**Maloe Melo**
Lijnbaansgracht 163.
**Map** 4 D1.
☎ 420 4592.

**De Melkweg**
Lijnbaansgracht 234a.
**Map** 4 E2.
☎ 531 8181.

**Paradiso**
Weteringschans 6–8.
**Map** 4 E2.
☎ 626 4521.

### JAZZ

**Alto Jazz Café**
Korte Leidsedwars-
straat 115.
**Map** 4 E2.
☎ 626 3249.

**B & W Café**
Plantage Kerklaan 36.
**Map** 5 C2.
☎ 422 8989.

**Bamboo Bar**
Lange Leidsedwars-
straat 66. **Map** 4 E2.
☎ 624 3993.

**Bimhuis**
Oudeschans 73–77.
**Map** 8 E3.
☎ 623 1361.

**Bourbon Street**
Leidsekruisstraat 6–8.
**Map** 4 E2.
☎ 623 3440.

**Casablanca**
Zeedijk 24/26.
**Map** 8 D2.
☎ 625 5685.

**De Engel-
bewaarder**
Kloveniersburgwal 59.
**Map** 8 D3.
☎ 625 3772.

**De Heeren van
Aemstel**
Thorbeckeplein 5.
**Map** 7 C5.
☎ 620 2173.

### WORLD MUSIC
### AND FOLK

**Akhnaton**
Nieuwezijds Kolk 25.
**Map** 7 C1.
☎ 624 3396.

**The Blarney
Stone**
Nieuwendijk 29.
**Map** 7 C1.
☎ 623 3830.

**Canecão Brazilian
Bar**
Lange Leidsedwars-
straat 70.
**Map** 4 E2.
☎ 638 0611.

**Café Nol**
Westerstraat 109.
**Map** 1 B3.
☎ 624 5380.

**Hof van
Holland**
Rembrandtplein 5.
**Map** 7 C5.
☎ 623 4650.

**Mulligan's**
Amstel 100.
**Map** 7 C5.
☎ 622 1330.

**O' Donnell's**
Ferdinand Bolstraat 5.
**Map** 4 F5.
☎ 676 7786.

**Jantjes Verjaardag**
Reguliersdwarsstraat
108–114. **Map** 6 F4.
☎ 625 1973.

**De Twee Zwaantjes**
Prinsengracht 114.
**Map** 1 C3.
☎ 625 2729.

### CLUBS AND
### DISCOS

**Dansen Bij Jansen**
Handboogstraat 11.
**Map** 7 B4.
☎ 620 1779.

**Escape Theater**
Rembrandtplein 11.
**Map** 7 C5.
☎ 622 1111.

**Marcanti Plaza**
Jan van Galen-
straat 6–8.
**Map** 1 C1.
☎ 682 3456.

**Mazzo Club**
Nieuwe Nieuwestraat 114.
**Map** 1 B2.
☎ 627 3730.

**The Ministry**
Regulierdwardsstraat 12
☎ 623 3981.

**More**
Rozengracht 133.
**Map** 1 A5.
☎ 528 7459.

**Odeon**
Singel 460.
**Map** 7 C5.
☎ 624 9711.

**Sinners in Heaven**
Wagenstraat 3–7.
☎ 620 1375.

**The Backdoor
Amsterdam**
Amstelstraat 32.
**Map** 8 D5.
☎ 620 2333.

**Time**
Nieuwezijds Voorburgwal
163–65. **Map** 7 B3.
☎ (0620) 606 0693.

**Trance Buddha**
Oudezijds Voorburgwal 216
**Map** 1 A1.
☎ 524 4000.

**West Pacific**
Westergasfabriek,
Haarlemmerweg 8–10
**Map** 1 A1.
☎ 488 7778.

### GAY AND LESBIAN
### CLUBS

**COC
Amsterdam**
Rozenstraat 14. **Map** 1 B5.
☎ 626 3087.

**Exit**
Reguliersdwarsstraat 42.
**Map** 7 B5.
☎ 625 8788.

**Gay and Lesbian
Switchboard**
☎ 623 6565.

**iT**
Amstelstraat 24.
**Map** 8 D5
☎ 625 0111.

**De Trut**
Bilderdijkstraat 165.
**Map** 3 C1.
☎ 612 3524.

**Het Vrouwenhuis**
Nieuwe Herengracht 95.
**Map** 8 E5.
☎ 625 2066.

**Reality**
Reguliersdwarsstraat 129.
**Map** 7 C5.
☎ 620 6788.

**Saarein II**
Flandsstraat 119.
**Map** 1 B5.
☎ 623 4901.

**You II**
Amstel 178. **Map** 7 C5.
☎ 421 0900.

# CHILDREN'S AMSTERDAM

A S A LIVELY, cultural city, Amsterdam can be a fascinating place to visit with children. Its network of canals is fun to explore and many of the squares are alive with street musicians and performers. The city's many parks offer a wide range of outdoor activities and the streets are lined with tempting shops, restaurants, cafés and food stalls. Even in summer, there is no guarantee of good weather, but you can always find something to do on wet days. Some theatres and museums are geared for children and there is nearly always an English-language film showing that is suitable for children.

## PRACTICAL ADVICE

I F YOU ARE visiting Amsterdam with a very young child, a baby sling or pouch is essential. While the city centre is small enough to be covered on foot, manoeuvring a heavy pushchair around the cobbled streets can be tough going. Negotiating one of the city's notoriously steep flights of stairs or getting on a crowded tram or canal boat with a push-chair is virtually impossible, and they are actually banned in some of the museums.

For sightseeing, it is worth taking a boat trip. Details of the options available are given on pages 276–7. Most of the operators offer discounts to children under 12 and allow toddlers to travel free. Trams are another entertaining and efficient way to get around (see p272), although they tend to be crowded at peak periods. Like all other forms of public transport in the city, children under four go for free and under-12s travel at half-price.

Children are welcome at the majority of hotels in Amsterdam (see p212). Some of the bigger ones even provide baby-sitting facilities. If your hotel does not offer this, **Babysit Centrale**

**Kriterion** provides reliable, cheap child care. The service is 24-hour, but bookings must be made between 5pm and 7pm.

## BABYSITTING SERVICE

**Babysit Centrale Kriterion**
Roetersstraat 170.
Ⓒ 624 5848.

## THEATRES AND MUSEUMS

M ANY THEATRES, such as the **Circus Elleboog** and **De Krakeling**, hold children's shows on Wednesdays or Sundays and the Vondelpark (see p128) stages weekly open-air shows in summer.

Seasonal attractions include the Christmas circus at the Koninklijk Theater Carré (see p145). The Amsterdam Tourist Board's monthly publication, *Uitkrant*, contains a complete listing, which is easy to understand, despite being written in Dutch (see p256).

A number of Amsterdam's museums have sections which

**Rangda witch from Bali at the Kindermuseum**

are geared for children. Nemo (see p150) is one of the best for older children, with its wide range of hands-on exhibits and buttons to press. The Nationaal Luchtvaartmuseum Aviodome (see p155) is a firm favourite with anyone who is interested in aeroplanes and space travel. Adventurous 6- to 12-year-olds will like the exhibitions at Tropenmuseum's Kinder-museum (see pp152–3), which brings to life the cultures and traditions of the developing world. Would-be pirates love climbing aboard the *Amsterdam*, a full size replica of an 18th-century East Indiaman moored outside the Nederlands Scheepvaart Museum (see pp146–7). The waxworks at Madame Tussauds Scenerama (see p74) are also worth a visit, although small children may be upset by a few of the more grue-some exhibits. Most of Amsterdam's museums offer substantial discounts to children and toddlers under four normally get in free.

## CHILDREN'S THEATRES

**Circus Elleboog**
Passeerdersgracht 32. **Map** 4 E1.
Ⓒ 626 9370.

**De Krakeling**
Nieuwe Passeerdersstraat 1. **Map** 4 D1.
Ⓒ 624 5123.

## ZOOS AND CITY FARMS

A S ARTIS ZOO incorporates both covered and open-air animal pens, along with a

**Crocodiles basking in the Reptile House of Artis zoo** *(see p142–3)*

The full-size replica of the *Amsterdam*, outside the Scheepvaart Museum

Planetarium and the Geologisch Museum, it is a great place to visit whatever the weather *(see pp154–5)*. Cheaper, but less extensive, animal viewing options in and around the city include the animal enclosure in the Amsterdamse Bos *(see p155)*, donkeys and llamas in the Vondelpark *(see p128)* and free-roaming Highland cattle in the Amstelpark *(see p154)*.

## SPORTS AND RECREATION

Amsterdam's parks provide a whole range of activities which children will enjoy. The Vondelpark *(see p128)* has well-maintained playgrounds, free puppet shows and face-painting sessions at the Milk Bar in summer. The Amstelpark and Amsterdamse Bos have a range of activities covered on pages 154 and 155 respectively. The Electrische Museumtramlijn *(see p155)* runs regular round trips to and from the Amsterdamse Bos in vintage trams. You can also camp in designated campsites in this park *(see p213)*.

There are a number of indoor swimming pools on the outskirts of Amsterdam, the best of which is **Miranda Bad**, a tropical paradise with water chutes, a beach and a wave machine. Indoor pools tend to close during the summer holidays and are replaced by the open-air pools, like the municipal pool in Twiske, a rural park north of the IJ. The seaside, which is only 20 minutes away by train, has miles of clean, sandy coastline.

Perhaps the most fun can be had simply exploring Amster-dam's network of canals by hiring canal bikes *(see p277)*. When the canals are frozen during a hard winter, your children will never forget the thrill of skating around the city.

## SWIMMING POOLS

### Miranda Bad
De Mirandalaan 9.
546 4444.

## EATING OUT

Children may not be welcome in some of the more expensive restaurants, but most places are tolerant. Many cafés and cheaper restaurants offer a children's menu such as chicken, chips and *appelmoes* (apple purée). Don't miss weekend tea times at the **Kinderkook Kafé** where the food is cooked and served by children. Advance reservations (at least a month) are essential both for eating

and for children who want to cook. Amsterdam also has a good selection of pan-cake houses *(see p236)*, offering a huge selection of sweet and savoury toppings. Other treats include *poffertjes*, which are tiny pancakes loaded with butter and icing sugar.

If hunger strikes when you are on the move, then there can be few children who do not like chips with mayonnaise, available at numerous street stalls all over town *(see p236)*.

## CHILDREN'S CAFÉS

### Kinderkook Kafé
Oudezijds Achterburgwal 193. **Map** 2 D5. 625 3257 Mon–Fri 1–5pm.

## SHOPPING

Alongside an assortment of large toyshops selling anything from computer games to the latest Barbie accessories, there are also a few small shops that sell traditional wooden and handcrafted toys. Look out for the exquisite dolls'-house furniture at **De Kleine Nicolaas**.

Good children's clothes can be found at most department stores, but for something out of the ordinary go to **Oilily**, an exclusive children's shop.

## SHOPS FOR CHILDREN

### De Kleine Nicolaas
Cornelis Schuytstraat 19. **Map** 3 C1. 676 9661.

### Oilily
PC Hooftstraat 131-133. **Map** 4 D3. 672 3361.

Children resting weary legs outside Kort café and restaurant *(see p225)*

# SURVIVAL GUIDE

# PRACTICAL INFORMATION

A MSTERDAM is a cosmopolitan city and visitors should find its citizens, who are often multilingual, helpful and friendly. The official networks for helping tourists, whether with information about sights or medical attention, are efficient and straightforward. Telephones, parking meters and cash dispensers may seem familiar to European visitors,

**Exploring the city on foot**

but other tourists will need to follow instructions closely. One of the particular pleasures of visiting the city is to enjoy the relatively car-free environment. Trams, water transport, bicycles and pedestrians are all given a much higher priority in the centre than motor vehicles. Indeed, the ideal ways to explore are on foot (*see pp270–71*), or by bicycle (*see pp274–5*).

**The Tourist Board office on Stationsplein, opposite Centraal Station**

## TOURIST INFORMATION

V ERY FEW CITIES are as well-equipped to help the visitor as Amsterdam, and in general the Netherlands has a comprehensive network of tourist information centres. The state-run **Amsterdam Tourist Board (VVV)** is still widely known by its former name VVV, which is pronounced "fay-fay-fay".

Be wary if you use accommodation agencies unrelated to the Tourist Board: the accommodation they offer can often be unnecessarily expensive or of poor quality.

## THE AMSTERDAM TOURIST BOARD (VVV)

T HERE ARE FOUR Tourist Board offices in Amsterdam, and almost 450 throughout the Netherlands. The multilingual staff provide

**The logo of the Amsterdam Tourist Board**

useful information on sights, entertainment, events, transport, walks and tours. They will also change money and book hotels, plays, shows, excursions, and concerts (all for a small fee). Most Tourist Board leaflets and maps are also available from news-agents and museums. If you are seeking information before you travel, the **NBT** (Netherlands Board of Tourism) produces its own brochures, maps and useful leaflets.

## ARENA

T HIS CENTRE, not to be confused with the stadium of the same name, caters for the independent traveller on a tight budget, and welcomes people of all ages. It comprises not only a hotel with about 600 beds (*see p223*), but a pop concert and exhibition venue, café, restaurant and a youth information centre.

## ENTERTAINMENT

P OSTERS AND LISTINGS in the city's bars and cafés are an immediate guide to entertainment in Amsterdam (*see p244*). The free monthly *Uitkrant* has comprehensive listings, and, though in Dutch, is accessible to non-Dutch speakers. The Amsterdam Tourist Board produces the monthly *Day by Day*, which has a useful calender section.

The Tourist Board also produce a number of free English language leaflets providing details of festivals and cultural highlights.

AUB Uitburo (*see p244*) gives information on and sells advance tickets for the city's theatres and concerts, for a small fee. AUB also publish a leaflet listing venues for non-classical music. Libraries and theatres supply entertainment freesheet listings and display cinema programmes.

**Some of the best of Amsterdam listings, in both English and Dutch**

**Museum entrance tickets**

## MUSEUM CARD

THE VERY successful Museum Card (*Museumjaarkaart*) appears expensive, but it does provide admission to more than 400 museums throughout the Netherlands. This includes all the major ones in Amsterdam, though it does not cover their special exhibitions. Valid for a year, and with separate cards for adults and under 18s, you will recoup the cost after about ten visits. The card can be bought from Tourist Board and NBT offices and all the participating museums.

## DISABLED VISITORS

FOR SUCH a forward-looking city, Amsterdam sometimes displays a certain disregard for the needs of disabled people, although there is information available (*see p213*). While museums, galleries, cinemas, theatres and now even churches often have wheelchair access and adapted toilets, getting around from venue to venue can be a real worry. Cobbled streets make life very difficult for wheelchair users, and public toilets with easy access are virtually non-existent.

## OPENING TIMES

OPENING TIMES for retailers in Amsterdam vary enormously, but each shop has its hours of business posted on the door (*see p238*). Shops in the centre of town may be open between 7am and 10pm

all week, including Sundays (*see p238*). Popular opening hours are 11am to 5pm from Monday to Saturday. In central Amsterdam, Thursday is *koopavond* or shopping night, when the shops close at about 9pm. Banks open from 9 or 10am to 4 or 5pm, though many in the centre stay open till 7pm on Thursday. The GWK (*see p260*) now runs a 24-hour service. Many of the state-run museums are closed on Monday, and open from 10am to 5pm, Tuesday to Saturday and from 1 to 5pm on Sunday. Most of the museums also adopt these Sunday hours for all national holidays (*see p53*), apart from New Year's Day, when they are always closed.

**Shoppers on Kalverstraat**

## LANGUAGE AND ETIQUETTE

PEOPLE WHOSE mother tongue is English will not have a language problem in Amsterdam. Nearly all Dutch people speak some English, but it's appreciated if you can handle a few niceties, such as saying *Dag* (Good day) before asking a Dutch person whether they speak English. This guide has a phrase book on pages 311–12. The Dutch are quite liberal in many ways, but they retain a few conventions. Expect your hand to be shaken a lot, and if you are out with a crowd, introduce yourself, or people may think you standoffish. When eating out, the Dutch tend to pay for their own share of the bill.

**Sign for disabled parking**

### DIRECTORY

#### TOURIST INFORMATION

**AUB Uitburo**
Leidseplein 26.
**Map** 4 E2.
📞 0900 0191.
🌐 www.uitlijn.nl

**Amsterdam Tourist Board (VVV) Offices**
🌐 www.visitamsterdam.nl
🌐 www.amsterdamtourist.nl

**Centraal Station**
Platform 2 and in front of station,
Stationsplein 10.
**Map** 8 D1.
📞 0900 400 4040

**Leidseplein**
Leidseplein 1.
**Map** 4 E2.
📞 0900 400 4040.

**Stadionplein**
Argonautenstraat 98.
📞 0900 400 4040.

#### NETHERLANDS BOARD OF TOURISM (NBT) OFFICES WORLDWIDE

**World Wide Web**
🌐 www.nbt.nl/holland

**Canada**
Suite 710, 25 Adelaide Street East,
Toronto,
Ontario M5C 1Y2.
📞 (416) 363-1577.
📠 (416) 363-1470.

**UK**
PO Box 523,
London SW1E 6NT.
📞 0891 717 777.
📠 020-7828 7941.

**USA**
Central: Suite 1854,
225 N. Michigan Avenue,
Chicago, IL 60601.
📞 (312) 464-6552/
888 Go Holland.
📠 (312) 819-1740.

# Personal Security and Health

**Policeman on wheels**

**A**FTER A RECENT CLEAN-UP by the authorities, Amsterdam is now one of the safest cities in Europe. It does have a reputation for crime, most of which is drugs-related, but tourists should not be affected by this provided they act sensibly. It is a good idea, however, to take out travel insurance which should cover any loss of money or personal items. For those who do find themselves in trouble on holiday, the city has efficient emergency services and facilities ranging from an **HIV Positive Line** to a **Legal Advice Centre**.

**Members of the armed Dutch police force**

**Damrak leading to Centraal Station: a place to be wary of pickpockets**

## PERSONAL PROPERTY

**W**HILE AMSTERDAM is safer than most American and European cities, theft is still a cause for concern. Pickpockets work crowded tourist areas and on the trams, especially in summer, so take precautions: don't put wallets and money in back pockets, leave handbags exposed or flash cash about.

Bicycle and car theft, particularly of foreign vehicles, is also a problem. Muggings are

fairly rare, but it is best to avoid parks and poorly lit places at night. Women would also be wise not to frequent bars and cafés late at night. Finally, don't take photographs of prostitutes in the Red Light District, as it causes serious offence.

If you are the victim of theft or assault, report it to the nearest police station. You are anyway obliged to report any personal injury. In serious cases or emergencies, phone the **Emergency Services**.

## MEDICAL TREATMENT AND INSURANCE

**A**LL EU MEMBERS can receive medical and dental treatment in the Netherlands at a reduced charge. Before travelling, British visitors should fill in form E111, obtainable from larger post offices, and seek a refund for any treatment from the DoH on their return home. However, you will never be turned away by a doctor even if you do not have an E111, although you may have to pay more for treatment. It is probably also a good idea to take out private insurance, which should cover the cost of repatriation in an emergency.

Minor problems can be dealt with by a chemist *(drogist)*, who stocks non-prescription drugs. For a medicine on prescription, go to a pharmacy *(apotheek)*, open from 8:30am to 5:30pm Monday to Friday. Details of pharmacies open outside normal hours are

**Fire engine**

417

**Ambulance**

**Police car**

posted in all pharmacy windows and in the afternoon newspaper *Het Parool*. The **Centrale Medical Service** *(Centrale Doktersdienst)* will direct you to the nearest pharmacy open outside normal hours, and can also refer you to a duty GP or supply the name of a dentist.

Minor accidents are treated in hospital outpatient clinics, open 24 hours a day, and the VVV *(see p256)* can advise on these. In an emergency, make your way to a hospital with a casualty unit, or call an ambulance.

## MOSQUITOES

ATTRACTED by the canals, mosquitoes can be a real irritant. Residents and regular summer visitors deal with them in various ways. Burning coils,

ultra-violet tubes, mosquito nets, repellent sprays and anti-histamine creams and tablets are available from large pharmacies or supermarkets.

## DRUGS

THOUGH SOFT DRUGS have not been legalized in the Netherlands, the police tend to ignore the possession of small amounts of cannabis. They also tolerate the sale of small amounts in designated "smoking" coffeeshops *(see p49)*. Hard drugs are a completely different matter. The Zeedijk area has been cleaned up but is still best avoided late at night, and anyone caught with hard drugs will certainly be prosecuted. Never try to take drugs out of the country: penalties are stiff.

**A selection of anti-mosquito preparations**

**Hash Museum sign** *(see p61)*

## LOST PROPERTY

TO HELP with any insurance claim, you must report lost or stolen property as soon as possible, preferably to a police station in the vicinity of the loss. They hold recovered items for a day or so before sending them to the main police lost-property office. If you lose your passport, you must also tell your consulate *(see p265)*. For items lost on public transport, try **Centraal Station** or the GVB head office *(see p273)*.

---

### DIRECTORY

#### PHARMACIES

**Dam**
Damstraat 2.
**Map** 7 C3.
☎ 624 4331.

**Jordaan**
Westerstraat 180.
**Map** 1 B3.
☎ 624 9252.

**Koek, Schaeffer & Van Tijen**
Vijzelgracht 19.
**Map** 4 F3.
☎ 623 5949.

**Medicijnman**
Utrechtsestraat 86.
**Map** 5 A3.
☎ 624 4333.

**Het Witte Kruis**
Rozengracht 57.
**Map** 1 A5.
☎ 623 1051.

#### HOSPITALS

**Academisch Medisch Centrum**
Meibergdreef 9.
☎ 566 9111.

**Sint Andreas Lucas Ziekenhuis**
Jan Tooropstraat 164.
☎ 510 8911.

**Onze Lieve Vrouwe Gasthuis (with casualty unit)**
1e Oosterparkstraat 279.
**Map** 6 D4.
☎ 599 9111.

**VU Medisch Centrum**
De Boelelaan 1117.
☎ 444 4444.
24-hour first aid:
☎ 444 3636.

#### EMERGENCY SERVICES

**Ambulance, Fire & Police**
☎ 112.

#### HELPLINES

**AIDS SOA Helpline**
☎ 0900 204 2040.
🕐 2–10pm Mon–Fri.

**Central Medical Service**
☎ 592 3434.

**SOS Crisis Helpline**
☎ 675 7575.
🕐 24 hours a day.

**HIV Plus Line**
☎ 685 0055.
🕐 1–4pm Mon, Wed & Fri; 8–10:30pm Tue & Thu.

**Legal Advice Centre**
Bureau voor Rechtshulp,
Spuistraat 10.
**Map** 7 B1.
☎ 520 5100 (call in normal office hours for appointment).

#### SEXUAL ABUSE

**De Eerste Lijn**
☎ 613 0245.
🕐 10:30am–11pm Mon–Fri, 4–11pm Sat & Sun (women who have suffered sexual violence and/or ill treatment).

**Stichting Vrouwenoprang**
(Don't Touch My Body House).
☎ 638 7636.
🕐 24 hours a day.

#### POLICE

**Headquarters**
Elandsgracht 117.
**Map** 1 B5.
☎ 559 9111.

**Main Police Stations**
Lijnbaansgracht 219.
**Map** 4 F2.
☎ 559 2310.

Beursstraat 33.
**Map** 7 C2. ☎ 559 3390.

#### LOST PROPERTY

**Centraal Station**
NS Lost Property Information, Stationsplein 15.
**Map** 8 D1.
☎ 030 235 3923.
🕐 8am–8pm Mon–Fri, 8am–5pm Sat. (After 3 days, items found on trains are sent to NS Afdeling Gevonden Voorwerpen, Tweede Daalsedijk 4, 3551 EJ Utrecht.)
☎ 030 235 3923.

**Police**
Stephensonstraat 18.
☎ 559 3005.
🕐 noon–3:30pm.

# Banking and Local Currency

AMSTERDAMMERS are strangely partial to cash transactions and, surprisingly, credit cards are not as universally acceptable in the Netherlands as in many other countries. The larger hotels, shops and most restaurants will, however, accept the major credit cards. Many will also take travellers' cheques as payment.

Amsterdam has an excellent foreign exchange network, and transactions are virtually hassle-free for visitors, particularly English speakers. Most currencies can be exchanged at the airport or ferry terminal. There is no limit to the amount of currency you can bring into the country.

**ABN-AMRO automatic cash dispenser**

**GWK exchange counter at Schiphol Airport**

## TRAVELLERS' CHEQUES

TRAVELLERS' CHEQUES are still a good way to carry the bulk of your money. They are useful for paying hotel bills, but if you use them in a restaurant, for example, the management is not obliged to pay you the change if the cheque is larger than the bill.

Choose a name that is well known, like American Express, and they can be changed for cash in most Dutch banks, and are accepted in many retail outlets.

## CHANGING MONEY

YOU CAN CHANGE currency in banks (see p257), **American Express** offices and post offices. These all charge a small commission. The independent bureaux de change charge an exorbitant commission and give a poor exchange rate, but the official ones, **GWK** *(grenswissel-kantoorbureaux)*, are fair.

If you arrive by ferry, don't change any money on the boat, where you can pay for things in sterling. Wait until you can visit the GWK just after disembarkation. This stays open both for day and night arrivals. Avoid changing your money in hotels, as their charges tend to be very high.

**Rabobank**

**High street bank logo**

## CREDIT CARDS

MOST CREDIT CARDS can be used to obtain money. The exchange rate is slightly better than for currency. Bank automatic cash dispensers most commonly accept Access, American Express, Mastercard, Diner's Club, Banknet, and Visa. Few banks will advance you cash against credit cards. Some restaurants require a minimum purchase to use a credit card. Check you have some cash just in case.

## DIRECTORY

### BANKS AND CASH DISPENSERS

**ABN-AMRO**
Koningsplein/Singel 429–435.
**Map** 7 B4. 527 9700.

**ING-bank**
Damrak 80.
**Map** 7 C1. 550 3100.

**Postkantoor**
Singel 250–256.
**Map** 7 A3. 556 3311.

### AMERICAN EXPRESS

Damrak 66. **Map** 7 C1.
504 8777.

### GWK

Centraal Station.
**Map** 8 D1. 627 2731.
7am–10:30pm daily.

Schiphol Airport Station.
653 5121. midnight–10:30pm daily.

Amstel Station.
693 4545. 8am–8pm
Mon–Sat, 10am–5pm Sun.

### LOST OR STOLEN CARDS AND CHEQUES

**American Express**
504 8000.

**Diner's Club**
654 5511.

**Mastercard**
030-2835555.

**Visa**
660 0611.

**American Express Travellers' Cheques**
0800 022 0100.

## THE EURO

Twelve countries have replaced their traditional currencies, such as the Dutch guilder, with the euro. The Netherlands, Austria, Belgium, Finland, France, Germany, Greece, Ireland, Italy, Luxembourg, Portugal and Spain chose to join the new currency; the UK, Denmark and Sweden have stayed out for the moment. The Euro was introduced on 1 January 1999, but only for banking purposes. Notes and coins came into circulation on 1 January 2002. Each country using the euro produces their own coins, which have one common European side, but these, like the notes which are all uniform in design, can be used anywhere inside the participating member states.

### Bank Notes

*Euro bank notes have seven denom-*
*inations. The 5-euro note (grey in*
*colour) is the smallest, followed by*
*the 10-euro note (pink), 20-euro*
*note (blue), 50-euro note (orange),*
*100-euro note (green), 200-euro*
*note (yellow) and 500-euro note*
*(purple). All notes show the 12 stars*
*of the European Union.*

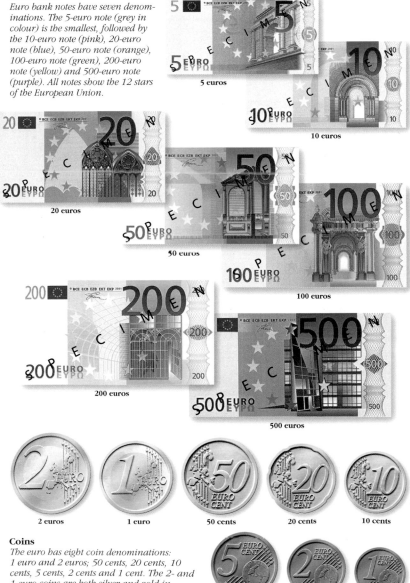

5 euros

10 euros

20 euros

50 euros

100 euros

200 euros

500 euros

2 euros

1 euro

50 cents

20 cents

10 cents

### Coins

*The euro has eight coin denominations:*
*1 euro and 2 euros; 50 cents, 20 cents, 10*
*cents, 5 cents, 2 cents and 1 cent. The 2- and*
*1-euro coins are both silver and gold in*
*colour. The 50-, 20- and 10-cent coins are*
*gold. The 5-, 2- and 1-cent coins are bronze.*

5 cents

2 cents

1 cent

# Communications

**PTT telephone booth at station**

BEFORE 1989, telephone and postal services in the Netherlands were part of the same state-run company, PTT. Both continue to carry the PTT logo, in green and white for telecoms and red and white for postal services, but they are now independent of each other. The telephone network is still state run, while postal services are now privately run. Both services are among the most forward-looking and efficient in Europe.

**ptt telecom**

**PTT telecoms logo**

---

## REACHING THE RIGHT NUMBER

• Internal directory enquiries, dial 118 (one number per call).
• Local operator, dial 0900 8008. International operator, dial 0900 8418.
• To phone the USA or Canada, dial 001 followed by the number.
• To phone the UK, dial 0044 followed by the number, omitting the 0 from the area code.
• To phone Australia, dial 0061 followed by the number.
• To phone New Zealand, dial 0064 followed by the number.
• To phone the Irish Republic, dial 00353 followed by the number.

---

## USING THE TELEPHONE

PUBLIC TELEPHONES in Amsterdam can be found on streets all over the city, at railway stations, in post offices, and in cafés and bars. The city's green-trimmed glass booth payphones take phonecards; some also take credit cards. Phonecards can be bought at post offices, supermarkets, newsagents and railway stations. Instructions for using the telephones are in both English and Dutch. When you phone popular numbers such as airports, you may encounter the electronic voice which tells you, *"er zijn nog een (one)/twee (two) wach-enden voor u"*, "there are one/two people in the queue before you". Most hotels have IDD (International Direct Dialling) units, but be aware that the telephone costs that will appear on your bill are likely to be inflated.

## USING A CARD PHONE

1 Lift the receiver.

2 Insert phone- or credit card. Wait for dialling tone – a low hum.

3 Dial the number. The ringing tone in the Netherlands comprises long medium-pitch tones. The engaged tone is slightly faster. Instructions are also in English.

4 Replace the receiver at the end of the call and withdraw card.

**Colourful selection of pictorial phonecards**

**Pavement terminals provide instant internet access**

## ELECTRONIC COMMUNICATIONS

FASTER THAN A LETTER and cheaper than a phone call, sending and receiving electronic mail is easy and convenient once you have set up a free email account (go to www.hotmail.com for example, and follow the instructions).

**24-hour internet access at the Europe-wide chain easyEverything**

There are several internet cafés in Amsterdam where, for a modest fee, you can check your email account in comfort. They offer a variety of refreshments ranging from alcohol and coffee to light snacks. Most are close to the main attractions and so are easily accessible to visitors. Opening hours vary, but with the arrival of **easyEverything** it is now possible to go online at any time of the day or night.

Also worth a look is the website www.amsterdam.nl. Financed by Amsterdam city council, it offers a wealth of well-designed information about the city in Dutch and English, as well as access to councillors, commercial services and hundreds of local home pages. You can access this information through one of the pavement (sidewalk) terminals, but they may be withdrawn in the future.

## POSTAL SERVICES

A MSTERDAM'S NUMEROUS POST OFFICES are distinguished by the PTT logo. Apart from offering the usual postal services – stamps, telegrams, poste restante – they will also change currency and travellers' cheques, and have telephone, telex and fax services. The main post office also has photocopying facilities and sells commemorative stationery and stamps.

## SENDING A LETTER

W HEN YOU WANT to post letters going abroad or outside Amsterdam, use the *overige bestemmingen* slot in any of the red post boxes to be found throughout the city.

Letters up to 20 g can be sent anywhere in Europe – not just within the EU – for a universal flat rate, while destinations further afield cost slightly more. Postal charges have been increasing at intervals since privatization. There are often long queues for stamps *(postzegels)* at post offices and it can be quicker to purchase them at tobacconists or souvenir shops. Most post offices are open Monday to Friday only, from 9am–5pm.

## POSTE RESTANTE

I F YOU'RE NOT SURE where you'll be staying, you can have your mail sent to **poste restante**, addressed to the Central Post Office. The service is free but you will need some form of photo identification, such as a passport or driving licence when you come to collect your mail.

---

### DIRECTORY

**Postal Information and Lost Mail Enquiries**
(phone enquiries only).
☎ 0800 0417.
🕐 8am–8pm Mon–Fri, 9am–1pm Sat

**Main Post Office**
Hoofdpostkantoor PTT,
Singel 250–256, 1012 SJ.
**Map** 7 A2.
☎ 556 3311. 🕐 9am–6pm Mon–Wed & Fri, 9am–8pm Thu, 10am–1:30pm Sat.
**Poste restante** 🕐 7:30am–7pm Mon–Fri, 9am–noon Sat.

**easyEverything**
Reguliersbreestraat 22.
**Map** 7 C5.
☎ 423 2639. 🕐 24 hours daily.

Damrak 33.
**Map** 7 C1.
☎ 320 8082. 🕐 24 hours daily.

**Internet Café**
Nieuwendijk 30.
**Map** 7 C2.
☎ 620 0902. 🕐 9–1am Sun–Thu, 9–3am Fri & Sat.

**Internet Café**
Martelaarsgracht 11.
**Map** 7 C1.
☎ 627 1052.
🕐 9–1am Sun–Thu, 9–3am Fri & Sat.

---

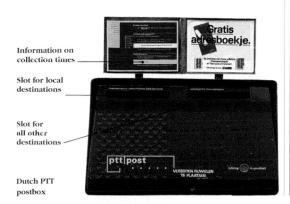

Information on collection times

Slot for local destinations

Slot for all other destinations

Dutch PTT postbox

# Additional Information

**Pre-packed tulip bulbs in Bloemenmarkt**

## VISAS AND CUSTOMS

**Diamond brilliants**

FOR A STAY lasting up to three months, Australian, EU, New Zealand and US nationals need only a valid passport. EU nationals over 17 years of age are entitled to import limitless goods for personal use, except for tobacco and alcohol on which duty has already been paid. The limits are: 800 cigarettes; 400 small cigars; 200 cigars; 1 kg of tobacco; 10 litres of spirits; 20 litres of fortified wine; 90 litres of wine; 110 litres of beer.

**Sign for public conveniences**

Bulbs can be brought into the UK, but the US requires an inoculation certificate. Non-EU members buying diamonds can reclaim VAT on returning home. Phone the free **Customs Information** line for details.

Cats and dogs may be brought in, providing they have a certificate of inoculation against rabies.

## DUTY-FREE GOODS

CITIZENS of non-EU countries must abide by the following restrictions: 200 cigarettes or 50 cigars or 250 g of tobacco; 1 litre of spirits or 2 litres of fortified wine or 2 litres of non-sparkling wine; 50 g of perfume; 500 g of coffee; 100 g of tea; other goods or gifts to the value of €56. Duty–Free goods are no longer available to EU citizens.

## TOILETS

AMSTERDAM IS SHORT on public conveniences, and visitors, especially women, often have to resort to using the facilities situated in hotels, museums and cafés. This is acceptable practice, although a few cafés and bars will charge up to 25c whether you are a patron or not. The large stores also expect 15c or more, while station toilets have attendants who will insist on a tip. Parents will also have to pay 15c for baby-changing facilities in large shops. The only café with toilets for disabled people is 't Nieuwe Café, located in Dam square.

**Browsing among the bottles in the duty-free shop at Schiphol Airport**

## CONVERSION TABLE

**Imperial to Metric**
1 inch = 2.54 centimetres
1 foot = 30 centimetres
1 mile = 1.6 kilometres
1 ounce = 28 grams
1 pound = 454 grams
1 pint = 0.6 litres
1 gallon = 4.6 litres

**Metric to Imperial**
1 centimetre = 0.4 inches
1 metre = 3 feet, 3 inches
1 kilometre = 0.6 miles
1 gram = 0.04 ounces
1 kilogram = 2.2 pounds
1 litre = 1.8 pints

## TIME

LIKE ALL its neighbouring countries, the Netherlands is on Central European Time, 1 hour ahead of Greenwich Mean Time in winter and 2 hours ahead in the summer. Sydney is 9 hours ahead in winter (8 in summer), Johannesburg 2 (1 in summer); New York is 6 hours behind in winter (7 in summer), Los Angeles 9 (10 in summer).

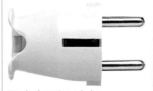

**Standard continental plug**

## ELECTRICITY

THE VOLTAGE in the Netherlands is 220, 50-cycle AC, and compatible with British equipment, but since the Dutch use two-pin continental plugs you will need an adaptor.

American visitors need to convert their equipment or buy a transformer. Dutch wall sockets require a larger plug than those used in the USA.

## TELEVISION

THE FIVE MAIN channels of Dutch TV serve standard European fare, but most hotels and homes have cable TV, with 20 or so channels available, including French, German, Belgian and Italian stations. Other cable channels on offer include BBC1 and BBC2; NBC Superchannel, offering largely American programming and international news; CNN; and the Euroversion of MTV, with pop and rock videos 24 hours a day. All British and American shows are subtitled on the Dutch and Belgian channels, but are dubbed on the French, Italian and German channels.

## RADIO

IN THE NETHERLANDS, news is broadcast on Dutch Radio 1 (747kHz), pop music on Radio 3 (96.8MHz) and classical music on Radio 4 (98.9MHz). It is also possible to pick up BBC Radio 4 on 198kHzAM and the World Service on 648kHzAM. Stations of all kinds are often opening in the city, aimed especially at youth.

## NEWSPAPERS

MOST FOREIGN daily and Sunday newspapers reach the city centre by lunch time on publication day. The widest variety is sold at **Athenaeum Nieuwscentrum** and **Waterstones** in Kalverstraat, and includes the *Wall St Journal*, *International Herald Tribune*, the *Guardian* and other quality newspapers.

## EMBASSIES AND CONSULATES

MOST EMBASSIES are located in Den Haag *(see pp186–7)*, which is a 45-minute train ride from Centraal Station to

**A selection of newspapers available**

the Central Station of The Hague. Some countries, however, also have special consular facilities situated in Amsterdam. These include the UK, USA, France, Germany and Italy.

For a comprehensive list of offices in the city, consult the main Amsterdam telephone directory under *Consulaat*.

---

## DIRECTORY

### EMBASSIES AND CONSULATES

**Australia**
Carnegielaan 4, 2517 KH
Den Haag.
[ (070) 310 8200.
[w] www.australian-embassy.nl  ◯ 8:45am–4:45pm Mon–Fri.

**Canada**
Write to: Sophialaan 7,
2514 JP Den Haag.
[@] info@canadiantourism.nl
◯ 9am–5:30pm Mon–Fri.

**Ireland**
Dr Kuyperstraat 9,
2514 BA Den Haag.
[ (070) 363 0993.
[@] embassy@irish-embassy.demon.nl
◯ 10am–12:30pm,
2:30–5pm Mon–Fri.

**New Zealand**
Carnegielaan 10, 2517KH.
[ (070) 346 9324.
[@] nzemb@bart.nl
◯ 9am–12:30pm,
1:30–5:30pm Mon–Fri.

**South Africa**
Wassenaarseweg 36, 2596
CJ Den Haag.
[ (070) 392 4501.
[@] www.zuidafrika.nl
◯ 9am–noon Mon–Fri,
2–4pm Mon–Fri: phone
only.

**UK Consulate**
Koningslaan 44.
**Map** 3 B4.
General enquiries: [
676 4343. ◯ 9am–noon,
2–3:30pm Mon–Fri.

Visa enquiries: [ 676 4343.
◯ 9am–noon Mon–Fri
(visa collections only).

**UK Embassy**
Lange Voorhout 10,
2514 ED Den Haag.
[ (070) 364 5800.
[w] www.britain.nl

**US Consulate**
Museumplein 19.
**Map** 4 E3.
[ 5755309
[w] www.usemb.nl
◯ 8:30am–noon.

**US Embassy**
Lange Voorhout 102,
2514 EJ Den Haag.
[ (070) 310 9209.
[w] www.usemb.nl

### RELIGIOUS SERVICES

**ANGLICAN**
**Episcopal Christ Church**
Groenburgwal 42.
**Map** 5 A2.
[ 624 8877.
Services in English:
9:15 & 10:30am, 7:30pm
Sun.

**DUTCH REFORMED CHURCH**
**Oude Kerk** (see pp68–9),
Oudekerksplein 1.
**Map** 7 C2.
[ 664 3655.
◯ Mar–Oct: 11am–5pm
Mon–Sat, 1–5pm Sun;
Nov–Feb: 1–5pm daily.
Service: 11am Sun.
**Westerkerk** (see p90),
Prinsengracht 281.
**Map** 1 B4. [ 624 7766.
◯ Apr–Sep: 10am–4pm
Mon–Sat. Service:
10:30am Sun.

**ENGLISH REFORMED PRESBYTERIAN CHURCH**
Begijnhof 48 (see p75).
**Map** 1 C5. [ 624 9665.
◯ Jun–Sep: 2–4pm
Mon–Fri. Service in
English: 10:30am Sun.
Service in Dutch: 7pm Sun.

**JEWISH**
**Orthodox Community Amsterdam**
PO Box 7967, Van der
Boechorststraat 26.
[ 646 0046.
◯ 9am–5pm Mon–Fri
(phone first).

**Liberal Jewish Community Amsterdam**
Jacob Soetendorpstraat 8.
[ 642 3562.
Services: 8pm Fri, 10am Sat.

**MUSLIM**
**THAIBA Islamic Cultural Centre**,
Kraaiennest 125.
[ 698 2526/690 9291.
Prayers: daily.

**QUAKER**
**Religieus Genootschap der Vrienden**,
Vossiusstraat 20.
**Map** 4 D3. [ 679 4238.
Meeting: 10:30am Sun.

**ROMAN CATHOLIC**
**St John & St Ursula**
Begijnhof 30. **Map** 1 C5.
[ 622 1918.
◯ 10am–5pm daily.
Services: 9am & 5pm
Mon–Fri, 9am Sat, 10am
Sun. Service in French:
11:15pm Sun.

### CUSTOMS INFORMATION

[ 0800 0143 (freephone).

### NEWSAGENTS

**Athenaeum Nieuwscentrum**
Spui 14–16. **Map** 7 B4.
[ 624 2972.

**Waterstone's**
Kalverstraat 152.
**Map** 7 B3. [ 638 3821

# GETTING TO AMSTERDAM

O NE OF EUROPE'S most popular tourist destinations, Amsterdam is easily accessible by plane, coach, car, ferry and train. Since the autumn of 1994, travellers from the UK have also been able to reach Amsterdam via the Channel Tunnel. Each method has its own benefits and disadvantages, and the choice will largely depend on whether time, money or comfort is the priority. Whichever you choose, it's always worth making a few enquiries to find the best deal to suit your requirements. Not only is there a wide selection of "packages" and special-interest holidays on offer, but prices can fluctuate widely throughout the year, and new ventures are emerging all the time.

**KLM's hotel bus into the city centre**

**Clear directions from the departures board at Schiphol**

## BY AIR

T HERE IS AN IMMENSE choice of flights to Amsterdam from the UK and the Republic of Ireland, with seven carriers operating direct flights. These include the national airlines **Aer Lingus**, **British Airways** and **KLM**. Cheap trips are advertised in the travel sections of national newspapers and in listings magazines, and are also available through discount agencies. Smaller operators are usually, but not always, less expensive than the national airlines. Flights are very quick – under an hour from London, for example.

There are dozens of inclusive package deals. Organized through a reliable agency, these can be far cheaper than booking a ferry or flight and separate accommodation.

## USING AMSTERDAM AIRPORT SCHIPHOL

*All the airport signs at Schiphol are colour-coded: yellow ones indicate the transfer desks and gates, green ones the amenities such as coffee bars, restaurants, shops, children's play area and well-equipped baby rooms. For business people and those in transit, there is an amazing range of facilities from business centre and conference rooms to sauna and golf and fitness centres.*

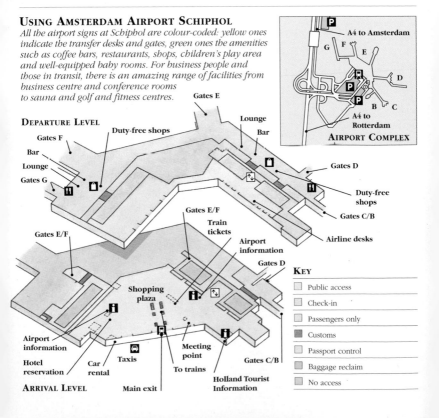

**AIRPORT COMPLEX**

A4 to Amsterdam
A4 to Rotterdam

**DEPARTURE LEVEL**

Gates E
Lounge
Bar
Gates F
Duty-free shops
Bar
Lounge
Gates G
Gates D
Gates E/F
Duty-free shops
Gates E/F
Train tickets
Gates C/B
Airport information
Airline desks
Gates D
Shopping plaza
Airport information
Gates C/B
Hotel reservation
Taxis
Meeting point
Car rental
To trains
Holland Tourist Information

**ARRIVAL LEVEL**

Main exit

**KEY**

| | |
|---|---|
| ☐ | Public access |
| ☐ | Check-in |
| ☐ | Passengers only |
| ■ | Customs |
| ☐ | Passport control |
| ☐ | Baggage reclaim |
| ☐ | No access |

Planes on runway at Amsterdam Airport Schiphol

## LONG-DISTANCE FLIGHTS

AMSTERDAM is a popular staging post for overseas visitors to Europe. You can fly from many US cities to Schiphol, and operators running non-stop services on scheduled flights include the Dutch company **Martinair**, **Delta**, **TWA**, **United Airlines** and **Northwest Airlines**/KLM. These last two also offer free or reduced-price connecting flights. Other operators fly via the major European capital cities, such as Paris and Rome, but London is probably the cheapest transAtlantic destination, with uniquely varied connections. Fare prices vary according to

Travel poster from the 1950s advertising KLM's European flights

season, with APEX the cheapest year-round option. The leader in the field of charter flights from the USA is Martinair which offers mid-range prices on non-stop flights from a number of cities.

Cheaper still are the fares of the "seat consolidators", who buy up unsold seats from the major carriers and sell them off at a huge reduction. For bargain flights, check out the free weeklies and travel sections of newspapers. Several companies offer excellent-value package tours. KLM has the widest range of options, but as always, it's well

**Signs showing departure gates**

worth shopping around. The cheapest route for visitors from Australia and New Zealand is also a London stop-over, as scheduled flights direct to Amsterdam are expensive. **STA Travel**, which has offices in Australia, New Zealand and the USA, is a source of expert advice for independent travellers.

## ARRIVING AT SCHIPHOL

AMSTERDAM AIRPORT Schiphol has maintained its single terminal status and remains one of the world's most modern, efficient, clean and user-friendly airports. In the welcoming arrivals hall, you will find a tourist information desk, a post office, a bureau de change desk and left-luggage facilities.

There are three main ways of getting into the centre of Amsterdam, 18 km (11 miles)

to the northeast. Despite its name, the KLM Hotel Bus Service is open to anyone: you don't have to come by KLM, or be staying at one of the six hotels in the city centre where it stops. These buses leave from outside the main exit every 30 minutes between 6:30am and 3pm and every hour between 3pm and 10pm.

Taxis are plentiful at the rank outside the arrivals hall, but the rule that cabbies stopping here are obliged to wear ties and jackets hardly justifies the high taxi fares. The best method of all for getting to Amsterdam centre is by rail.

Transfer desk at Schiphol

## FROM SCHIPHOL BY RAIL

FOR THE SCHIPHOL AIRPORT rail service, just walk into the shopping plaza, buy a ticket to Amsterdam's Centraal Station and catch the next train. Trolleys, which are free of charge, can be taken right on to the platform.

Trains run 7 times an hour between 5:40am and 1pm, after which they run hourly. The journey takes about 20 minutes, and the fare is cheaper than the bus. There are also rail connections from Schiphol to the majority of stations in the Netherlands.

Railway platform at Schiphol Plaza – destination Amsterdam

Beware of pickpockets at Amsterdam's Centraal Station

## BY FERRY

THE DUTCH RAILWAYS, Neder-lands Spoorwegen, in conjunction with **Stena Sea-link** and **British Rail**, operate a twice-daily boat-train service from London to Amsterdam via Harwich and the Hook of Holland. The total journey time is about 7 hours 30 minutes. **P&O**'s rival twice-daily service from Felixstowe to Zeebrugge has no linked rail ticket. British Rail operates an integrated service from London via Dover and Os-tend, taking a total of 13 hours, and a faster version by Jetfoil, which lasts nine hours. **North Sea Ferries** sail daily from Hull to Rotterdam; the crossing takes 14 hours. The other cross-Channel routes viable for Amsterdam are run by **Sally Lines**, from Ramsgate in England to Ostend in Bel-gium and Dunkirk in France.

The logo of Dutch Railways

## BY TRAIN

EUROSTAR RUNS FROM London via the Channel Tunnel; passengers for Amsterdam must change at Brussels. Journey time is about 7 hours. All trains arrive at Centraal Station, including those from Schiphol Airport. The station has all the amenities of a big terminus. However, it's very crowded and a magnet for pickpockets and drug-pushers. Head for Stationsplein by the main entrance, following signs to the Amsterdam Tourist Board (VVV) (see p256). Avoid

the rear entrance which can be the haunt of prostitutes. On Stationsplein, beware of hotel touts. The tram stops are only a few yards from the entrance, and the bus stops are further across the square on the left. Most tram and bus routes start here (see pp272–3). The Tourist Board office is the white pavilion building found on your left, and the GVB municipal transport authority office is located in the same building. Students and those under 26 can benefit from discount rail travel both to and within the Nether-lands. The Inter-Rail pass and the Freedom pass both allow 3, 5 or 10 days' unlimited travel in the Netherlands. For details, call the **European Information Line**. You don't even have to be a student to qualify for some of the deals.

## BY BUS AND COACH

LONG-DISTANCE bus or coach travel can be a cheap, if sometimes tiresome, option for those visiting Amsterdam. The choice lies between **Eurolines**, crossing by ferry (Dover–Calais or Ramsgate–Ostend), and **Hoverspeed City Sprint** (Dover–Calais) travelling by hovercraft. Both companies run at least two daily services in summer from London to Centraal Station in Amsterdam, and at least one service a day in winter.

With all the various transport permutations available to UK–Amsterdam travellers, it's worth searching out the one that best suits your needs of time, money or comfort.

Comfortable travel by coach

## BY CAR

IN EUROPE ONLY the Irish and northern Scandinavians have to cross the sea to get to Amsterdam. An ever-expanding motorway system makes it easy to reach the Netherlands from most of western, central and southern

Cars parked on Afsluitdijk, between the North Sea and IJsselmeer

**Taking the car and bicycles**

Europe. A valid driver's licence is sufficient for driving in the Netherlands, although many car-hire firms and the motoring organization **ANWB** (Royal Dutch Touring Club) favour an international one. To take your own car into the Netherlands you will need proof of registration, valid insurance documents, a road safety certificate from the country of origin and an international identification disc.

Major roads (marked N) are well-maintained, but Dutch motorways (labelled A) have narrow lanes, traffic lights and sometimes no hard shoulder. European routes are labelled E.

There are four levels of speed limit: 100 km/h (60 mph) or 120 km/h (75 mph) on motorways, 80 km/h (50 mph) outside cities and 50 km/h (30 mph) in urban areas. From the A10 ring road, the S-routes (marked by blue signs) take you to the centre of Amsterdam.

The ANWB provides a break-down service for members of foreign motoring organizations. A non-member can pay for the ANWB's services, or become a temporary ANWB member.

If you have a breakdown on a major road or motorway, use the yellow telephone pillars.

## DRIVING IN AMSTERDAM

BE CAREFUL of cyclists and trams when driving in the city. Trams take precedence and cyclists need ample space. Take care when turning, and allow cyclists priority. Much of the city centre is one-way, and when driving in the canal area, remember that the water should be to your left. Main roads with priority are marked by a white diamond with a yellow centre; otherwise priority is from the right.

**The blue signs guiding you to city centres**

---

# GETTING AROUND AMSTERDAM

THE BEST WAY to see Amsterdam is on foot. Almost everything of interest is within comfortable walking distance. The city's layout is quite simple, with its concentric canals (*grachten*) and interlocking roads, but it can seem confusing at first. The *Street Finder (see pp278–91)* will help you negotiate the maze of narrow streets. The simplest way to orientate

**Street sign indicating district**

yourself is to remember that, starting from the Singel, the main canals are arranged in the alphabetical sequence of Herengracht, Keizersgracht, Prinsengracht and Singel. Houses are numbered starting at Centraal Station and finishing, with the high numbers, at the Amstel. Amsterdam is not a city to drive around and there are limited and expensive facilities for motorists.

**Pedestrian crossing, Dam square**

## WALKING

BEFORE EMBARKING on a walk around the city, make sure that you are wearing sensible shoes – the brick-cobbled streets can be tiring as well as hazardous. Another problem is dog mess, so look down before looking up to admire canalside architecture.

Some people may not be used to trams and bicycles, so remember to look both ways when crossing tram routes (trams can be almost silent), and keep off the cycle paths.

Many pedestrian crossings are regulated by lights. Those without lights only indicate what is thought to be a suitable place to cross the road, and cars are not required to stop for you.

## WALKING TOURS

THE CANAL WALK on pages 94–105 takes in some of the city's grandest canals. The Guided Walk along the Historic Waterfront *(see pp160–61)*

explores Amsterdam's trading history. For a tour of the tranquil Jordaan and the Western Islands, see pages 158–9.

Walks organized by **Yellow Bike Tour** pass many of the important buildings and monuments around the Canal Ring and in the Jordaan. Two contrasting walks by **Let's Go** take you into the famous Red Light District *(see p60)*. A day-time walk concentrates on some of the city's oldest buildings; the night-time walk visits the lesser-known streets. Details are available from the Amsterdam Tourist Board *(see pp256 – 7)*. **Amsterdam Travel & Tours** covers the Red Light District, while guides from **Mee in Mokum** take you around historic Amsterdam. **Archivisie** covers the heart of the city, including examples of Amsterdam School architecture *(see p97)* and medieval areas.

**The penalty for illegal parking**

## CARS IN AMSTERDAM

ALTHOUGH THE CITY is ill-suited to motor traffic, provision is made for those who visit as part of a motoring holiday. However, parking is difficult, clamping prevalent and theft rife, so it is wise to follow some simple rules.

If you're staying in a hotel, book one with secure parking facilities and leave your car there while in the city. If you are coming from outside, park on the outskirts of the city in a "P&R" (park and ride) and use the excellent public transport into the centre. If you do drive into town, use

**Pedestrian zone**

**Pedestrian crossing**

**Right turn only**

**Give way**

**Brug open motor af !**

**Bridge open – turn off engines**

**End of right of way**

a car park rather than a meter or roadside space. Finally, if you do park in a public place, remember to remove your car radio and all other valuables.

Parking space is at a premium in the city, especially on the streets, and meters on main canal banks are rarely free in office hours. Most meters are limited to two hours. They take coins and/or parking cards. Avoid out-of-order meters as you could get fined or clamped. If you use a car park, first put money in the ticket machine, which can be some way from the parking place.

Illegally parked cars get clamped and you will be fined. If you have a credit card, phone the **Stadstoezicht** and a Pay-and-Go car will arrive. You pay on the spot and the clamp is removed. To pay with cash, go to the nearest Stadstoezicht service centre within 24 hours, otherwise your car will be towed away incurring additional charges.

There are now several 24-hour covered car parks, such as **Muziektheater-Parking** and **Byzantium**. Uncovered car parks are free from

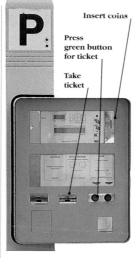

Insert coins

Press green button for ticket

Take ticket

**A pay-and-display ticket machine**

midnight to early morning. All city car parks are denoted by a white P on a square blue background. A three-day parking pass costs around €23 from all Stadstoezicht centres and some hotels.

## CAR RENTAL

YOU MUST BE aged 21 or over to hire a car and possess a licence and passport. Some companies also insist on a minimum of one year's driving experience. Most of the major agencies have offices in the city, and at Schiphol Airport, but local Dutch firms are significantly cheaper. All outlets require a substantial deposit.

## TAXIS

THE BEST WAYS to find a cab are to pick one up at a taxi rank, or phone a rank or **TBA Taxicentrale**, which runs a 24-hour service. You will find that the response is fast, apart from Friday and Saturday nights. Rates are generally high, so only give a small tip, unless your driver has been particularly helpful.

**Taxi drivers waiting patiently for a fare**

---

# Travelling by Public Transport

**A**MSTERDAM'S INTEGRATED public transport system, for which Centraal Station is the focal point, is efficient and inexpensive. The **OVR** gives information on all public transport within the city and the rest of the Netherlands, but does not make reservations. Tickets for travel around Amsterdam can be bought from machines and on trams and buses. The cheapest way to travel is to buy a *strippenkaart*, available from the **GVB**, Tourist Board offices, and at newsagents.

**Watch out for trams**

the driver. This is difficult in the rush hour, as trams can get very crowded. If you have a young child or heavy suitcase, keep one foot on the bottom step when you board, to hold the door open. Trams are awkward for the elderly and people with push-chairs, and impossible for those with a mobility problem.

Tram stops will generally be announced, but if you're not sure where to get off, ask for guidance. Press a button inside the tram to open the doors, and remember that many stops are in the middle of the road, so take care when you get off.

**Tram terminus at Centraal Station**

## TRAMS

**A**MSTERDAM'S TRAM lines, whose routes are shown on a free transport map, obtainable from the GVB, are the most common form of transport in the city. Trams start operating at 6am on weekdays and slightly later at weekends. They finish before midnight, when night buses take over. Blue boards at the tram and bus stops give the name of the stop and the route numbers it serves. Maps in the shelters are helpful and show the routes. You can get on and off by any but the front door. On trams with a conductor, use the rear door only to board and offer your ticket for stamping. When there is no conductor use the stamping machines inside. If you need to buy a ticket, you can board at the front and pay

## BUSES

**L**IKE THE TRAMS, the majority of Amsterdam's buses set out from Centraal Station, but they soon branch out from the city centre and largely complement the tram network.

**No. 35 bus serving the north of the city from Centraal Station**

---

## USEFUL TRAM ROUTES

The most useful tourist routes go south from Centraal Station along Damrak or NZ Voorburgwal, diverging after the Singel. Lines 13, 14 and 17 lead west into the Jordaan.

### KEY

— Line 4
— Line 5
— Line 7
— Line 9
— Line 14
— Line 16

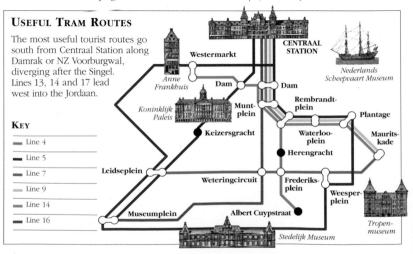

CENTRAAL STATION

Westermarkt

*Anne Frankhuis*

Dam

*Koninklijk Paleis*

Munt-plein

Keizersgracht

Leidseplein

Weteringcircuit

Museumplein

Albert Cuypstraat

*Stedelijk Museum*

Dam

Rembrandt-plein

Plantage

Waterloo-plein

Maurits-kade

Herengracht

Frederiks-plein

Weesper-plein

*Nederlands Scheepvaart Museum*

*Tropen-museum*

## USING THE STRIPPENKAART

Time indicator        Insert *strippen-kaart* here

**1** Starting from the top, fold top strip back and stamp the second one for one person travelling in central Amsterdam for up to one hour. The stamp indicates time and date of travel and zone in which you have boarded.

**2** For a second person travelling in the centre, stamp here as well, to validate two more strips.

**3** For a subsequent journey which crosses into two zones, such as a visit from Dam square to the Olympic Quarter (*see p154*), validate the next three strips by stamping the *strippenkaart* here.

*Strippenkaart* stamping machine

They have the same stops and ticketing system as the trams, but you must board by the front door. A small bus 'de Opstapper' leaves every 10 minutes from Centraal Station (Mon–Sat) along Prinsengracht to Waterlooplein and back. It runs close to many sights, museums and shopping areas. Normal public transport tickets can be used on this.

Night-bus stops feature a black square with a special number on it, running from 71 to 79. Buses run all night but the service is infrequent, so be prepared for a long wait or take a taxi.

## METRO

AMSTERDAM'S underground system comprises only three lines, all terminating at Central Station. Mainly used by commuters, it is of little use to tourists as it only covers four stations in the centre, all on the eastern side – Amsterdam CS, Nieuwmarkt, Waterlooplein and Weesperplein. The Metro runs for around half an hour longer than trams on weekdays, and the ticketing system is the same. Take care at night when stations are popular with drugdealers.

**Checking a train timetable**

## TRAINS

THE DUTCH national railway company, Nederlandse Spoorwegen, runs a busy network, which is considered one of the best in the world. It is reliable, clean and reasonably priced. The OVR (Openbaar Vervoer Reisinformatie) office gives a mass of information on rail trips for tourists, plus details of special fares, such as family rovers, which allow you to stop off en route to your destination. It does not, however, sell tickets, which are sold at the ticket office. Information and bookings for rail travel abroad is available from the **Nederlandse Spoorwegen Internationaal** office, which is located in the hall of Centraal Station.

**Sign for Metro station**

## TRAM AND BUS TICKETS

THE STRIPPENKAART (ticket strip), available in multiples of 15 units, allows you to travel all over the Netherlands. Each unit, or strip, covers one zone, even when changing tram, bus or Metro. Counting from the top, leave blank the number of strips required for your journey by folding them back and stamping the next one in the machine. Most sights are in the central zone, so for most trips you will need to validate only two strips per person travelling Any number of people can travel on a single *strippen-kaart*, providing it still has enough unused strips left

**Three-day dagkaart**

Tickets for one hour's unlimited travel can be purchased on board, but cost proportionally more. The *dagkaart* (day ticket), extendable for up to 9 days, and a season ticket are both on sale from the GVB.

# Getting Around by Bicycle

**Bicycle safety helmet**

T HE BICYCLE is the ideal form of transport in Amsterdam. More than half a million people cycle to school or work, and use a bicycle to do the shopping or go out in the evening. The city's traffic system is biased in favour of bicycles, with an excellent network of integrated cycle lanes (*fietspaden*), dedicated traffic lights and road signs, and special routes linking different parts of the city. More and more tourists are adopting this way of exploring Amsterdam and its environs. You can bring your own bicycle, hire one for just a day or join a cycle tour.

**Promoting the pleasures of biking**

**Cycle tour crossing Nieuwe Herengracht**

## RULES OF THE ROAD

A MSTERDAM'S TRAFFIC can appear to be chaotic at first, so above all remember always to ride on the right. Be aware that motorists, tram drivers and other cyclists will not necessarily recognize you as an inexperienced tourist.

Motorists and other cyclists have priority when entering your road from the right, unless otherwise stated. Trams have priority, if only because they are bigger and can't be steered, so don't argue with them. Always keep a wary ear open for their distinctive rattle and stay clear. If you are not sure who has right of way – or anything else err on the side of caution. You will need to be patient with pedestrians who are clearly tourists and unfamiliar with the local rules of the road. Dutch cyclists are naturally anarchic and often ride through red lights, but don't try to follow their example. Many novices dismount at busy junctions and cross on foot, to be on the safe side.

The part of the road with tramlines should be used only by trams, buses, taxis and emergency services. If you have to move inside the tracks to pass a stationary vehicle, do so at an angle, otherwise your front wheel may get stuck. Also watch out for people emerging from parked cars, and foreign coaches whose drivers may be unsympathetic to cyclists. You may cycle two abreast, but only if you do not block traffic. Don't carry passengers on your bike, or ride on footpaths or pavements – even though the Amsterdammers do.

You are legally obliged to have reflector bands on both wheels and a large reflector at the back, as well as lights. Don't try to copy the Amsterdammers, who tend not to use lights at night. And, although the locals don't bother, it is a wise precaution to wear a helmet.

For a puncture or mechanical problem, head for one of the many bicycle shops (*fietsenmakes*) found around the city.

**Crossing tramlines at a safe angle**

## BUYING A BICYCLE

B E CAREFUL when buying a bicycle. A cheap one for sale on the street will almost certainly have been stolen, and an expensive one from a specialist shop will probably end up being stolen. On the other hand, it's worth buying a second-hand bargain if you are staying for a few weeks and plan to do a fair amount of cycling. There are quite a number of reputable secondhand dealers in Amsterdam, and you'll find that some hire companies also sell bicycles.

**Traffic lights for bicycles**

**Bicycles allowed**

**No entry except to bicycles and mopeds**

uitgezonderd

## HIRING A BICYCLE

BICYCLE HIRE SHOPS abound in Amsterdam. All require a deposit, but some will accept your passport instead of cash. Rental costs start at around five euros a day with deposits varying from €20 to €100. Tandems are more expensive.

The brakes on some Dutch bikes are worked by back-pedalling. This can take some practice, so if you think you'll find it difficult, insist on a cycle with handlebar brakes.

**A selection of bicycles for hire**

## BICYCLE SECURITY

BICYCLE THEFT is rife, so it's essential to secure your cycle even when parking for just a few minutes. Fasten both front wheel and frame to a post or railings with a metal U-shaped lock. Hire shops are happy to advise on security matters, and will normally provide a lock in the rental price.

**A metal U-lock**

**Transporting a bike long-distance**

## TAKING YOUR OWN BICYCLE

TAKING A BICYCLE on the ferry to the Netherlands is free. When you book your ferry ticket, inform the clerk of your plans. If you're travelling to one of the British ferry ports by train, you will need to book the bicycle on British Rail. On your arrival in the Netherlands, if you want the cycle to go with you by train, buy a ticket for it. To take your bicycle by air, you must make a cargo booking with the airline at least a week in advance. It will have to be included in your 20-kg (44-lb) luggage allowance, and you must pay any excess. Remove the wheels and fold down the handlebars ready for transportation.

## BICYCLE TOURS

GUIDED BICYCLE TOURS are increasingly popular as a way of discovering the city and its environs at a sedate pace. The price of the tours usually includes bicycle hire. **Yellow Bike** organizes tours in the city, and you can book tours at their office or at an Amsterdam Tourist Board office *(see p256)* from April to October.

If you want to go it alone, the Tourist Board also provides maps with routes, cycle lanes and refreshment stops. Arena Hotel *(see p223)* produces an excellent folder with suggestions and maps for cycle trips around and outside the city. City tours usually take about 3 hours, country trips rather longer at around 7 hours.

**MacBike's multilingual cycle guide for energetic visitors**

---

# Getting Around by Canal

A MSTERDAM HAS EVOLVED around its network of canals, earning it the name "Venice of the North". Though the canals were built for moving goods rather than people, today they provide a marvellous means of viewing the city's splendid sights, as well as its everyday life. Canal boats offer a huge variety of tours to satisfy the most diverse requirements, and are usually featured in tourist brochures. Boat trips are particularly well-suited to those without the time to explore on foot or by tram, or to the elderly and families with children, who are not able to walk long distances.

**A brightly decorated row boat**

## CANALBUS

T HE CANALBUS SERVICE runs every 30 mins along three routes, with 11 stops located near the major museums, shopping areas and other attractions. The journey takes an hour or 85 minutes and you can embark or alight at any of the stops along the route. It is claimed that the canalbus is the first boat in Europe to run on gas.

A day ticket can be purchased, and the canalbus is also available on Saturday evenings for one-and-a-half-hour jazz cruises which start from ouside the Rijksmuseum at 8pm and 10pm. It is generally advisable to reserve a place on these before-hand at a **Canalbus** kiosk, as they are very popular and can get fully booked, especially in summer.

"Sissi", the **Aan de Wind Water-sport**'s boat, runs on request from the stop next to the Amstel Inter-Continental (see p223) to Centraal Station and back Beware however, as the "Sissi" is extremely expensive.

**Embarkation point for P. Kooij**

## CANAL TOURS

T HERE ARE MANY operators in Amsterdam offering canal tours with foreign-language commentaries. Boats depart from a number of embarkation points, mainly from opposite Centraal Station along Prins Hendrikkade, the Damrak and along the Rokin. Many *rond-vaartboten* (tour boats) have glass tops, some of which can be opened in fine weather. It is not always necessary to book seats for tours, but it is wise to do so for lunch time, evening and dinner cruises, especially during the peak tourist season.

Night cruises can feature cheese-and-wine refreshments, a stop at a pub or a romantic candlelit dinner. **Lovers** offers a comprehensive selection of such cruises in addition to its daytime trips. Beside city-centre tours, **Artis Express** operates a spec-ial service from Centraal Station to Artis (see *pp142– 3)*, the Scheepvaart Museum (see *pp146– 7)*, Tropenmuseum (see *pp152– 3)* and the Hortus Botanicus (see *p142)*. On hot days, try **P. Kooij**, as it has the most open-topped boats.

**Brochures and ticket for canal cruises**

**Canal tour on the Oude Schans, showing the Montelbaanstoren in the background**

The Museum Boat on Singelgracht

## MUSEUM BOAT

A RECENT INNOVATION, the Museum Boat takes in, and stops near, all the major city sights. Tours start every 30 minutes daily, between 10am and 5pm, from opposite Centraal Station. You can buy an ordinary ticket, which gives unlimited use for one day, or a day-ticket and a discount on the museum admission prices. Both can be bought at at the Centraal Station embarkation stage or any landing points. Details of landing stages are on the transport map on the inside back cover of this guide.

Polished interior of a water taxi

## WATER TAXIS

W ATER TAXIS are more convenient than canal boats for sightseeing and parties, and are in fact not used as taxis. They are also expensive – around 90 euros an hour for an 8-seater and double that for a 25-seater. After the first hour, the tariff is €34 and €68

Canal taxi logo

respectively, per half hour. Some boats are old-fashioned, with wooden interiors. Food, drink and guides can also be booked in advance. If you want to use one of these boats you will need to book in advance from **Water Taxi**.

Sightseeing by canal bike

## CANAL BIKES

T HE KEEP-FIT WAY to see the city is by canal bike. These are really two- or four-seater pedal-boats. Propelling them requires considerable energy, but children love them and when you've had enough, you can stop for a drink.

You can pick up or leave a pedal-boat at any of the canal-bike moorings in the city centre: Prinsengracht at the Westerkerk, Keizersgracht near Leidsestraat, Leidseplein between the Marriott and American hotels, and along the Singelgracht just outside the Rijksmuseum. These four locations operate from 9:30am to 7pm every day, and until 10:30pm during July and August.

Between November and March only the mooring at Singelgracht is open. Rain shields are provided in wet weather and included in the price, along with a route-planning map of Amsterdam.

# STREET FINDER

THE PAGE GRID superimposed on the *Area by Area* map below shows which parts of Amsterdam are covered in this *Street Finder*. The map references given for all sights, hotels, restaurants, shopping and entertainment venues described in this guide refer to the maps in this section. A complete index of the street names and places of interest marked on the maps follows on pages 288–91. The key, set out below, indicates the scales of the maps and shows what other features are marked on them, including transport terminals, emergency services and information centres. All the major sights are clearly marked so they are easy to locate.

## KEY TO STREET FINDER

| | |
|---|---|
| | Major sight |
| | Place of interest |
| | Other building |
| M | Metro station |
| 🚆 | Train station |
| 🚌 | Coach station |
| 🚋 | Tram route |
| 🚌 | Bus route |
| | Tour boat boarding point |
| | Canalbus boarding point |
| | Museum boat boarding point |
| 🚕 | Taxi rank |
| P | Parking |
| ℹ | Tourist information office |
| ✚ | Hospital with casualty unit |
| 🚓 | Police station |
| ✝ | Church |
| ✡ | Synagogue |
| C | Mosque |
| ⊠ | Post office |
| = | Railway line |
| | One-way street |
| | Pedestrianized street |

**SCALE OF MAPS 1–6**

0 metres      250
0 yards       250      **1:12,000**

**SCALE OF MAPS 7–8**

0 metres    100
0 yards     100      **1:7,000**

0 metres          500
0 yards           500

*Western Canal Ring*

*Central Canal Ring*

*Museum Quarter*

**Fresh fruit for sale in the Noordermarkt** *(see p92)*

House with an elevated neck gable
*(see p97)* on the Geldersekade

Magere Brug, the
city's most famous
bridge *(see p119)*

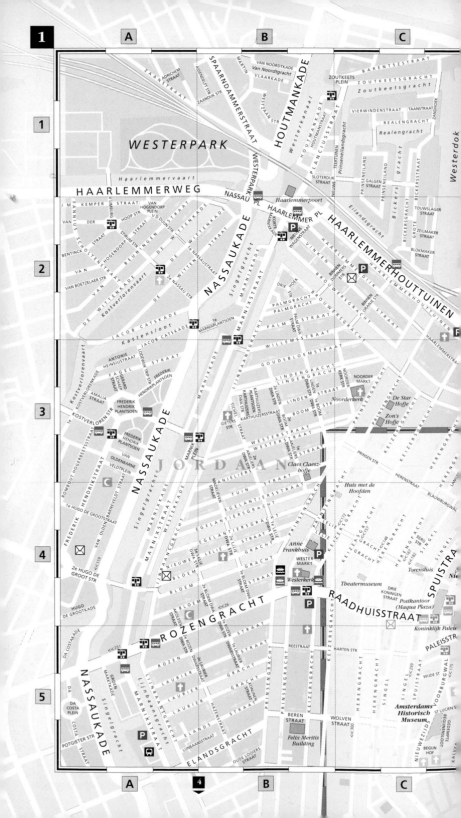

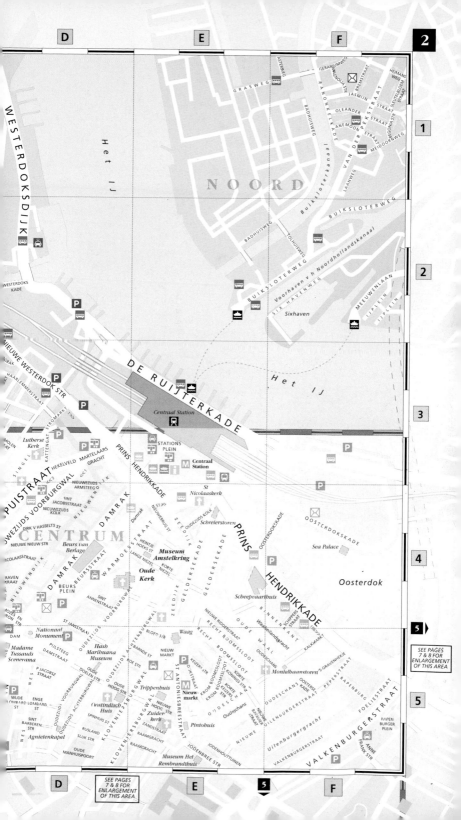

WESTERDOKSDIJK

Het IJ

N O O R D

GRASWEG

ASTERWEG

BADHUISWEG

GERANIUMWEG

RANONKELKADE

JASMIJNSTRAAT

BREMSTRAAT

HEIMANS WEG

SLEUTELBLOEM STR

VAN DER PEKSTRAAT

OLEANDER STRAAT

KANEMOOISTR

BEGONIASTR

MEIDOORNWEG

Buiksloterkanaal

LAANWEG

BUIKSLOTERWEG

Buiksloterweg

BADHUISWEG

TOLHUISWEG

Voorhaven v h Noordhollandskanaal

BIK HAVENWEG

Sixhaven

MEEUWENLAAN

IJPLEIN

IJPLEIN

WESTERDOKS KADE

NIEUWE WESTERDOK STR

HAARLEMMERSTRAAT

MOLEN

DE RUIJTERKADE

Het IJ

Centraal Station

STROMARKT

Lutherse Kerk

Kattengat

SINGEL

HEKELVELD

PUISTRAAT

MARTELAARS GRACHT

PRINS HENDRIKKADE

STATIONS PLEIN

Centraal Station

NIEUWEZIJDS VOORBURGWAL

SINT JACOBSSTRAAT

NIEUWEZIJDS ARMSTEEG

NIEUWEZIJDS KOLK

DIRK V HASSELTS ST

St Nicolaaskerk

NIEUWEBRUG ST

ZEEDIJK

OUDEZIJDS KOLK

Schreierstoren

PRINS HENDRIKKADE

OOSTERDOKSKADE

OOSTERDOKSKADE

Sea Palace

CENTRUM

DAMRAK

NIEUWE NIEUW STR

NICOLAASSTRAAT

Beurs van Berlage

DAMRAK

Damrak

WARMOESSTRAAT

HEINTJE HOEKS ST

LANGE NIEZEL

Museum Amstelkring

KORTE NIEZEL

GELDERSEKADE

OUDEZIJDS VOORBURGWAL

OUDE ZIJDS ACHTERBURGWAL

Oude Kerk

ZEEDIJK

OOSTERDOK

Oosterdok

RAVEN STRAAT

NIEUWENDIJK

DAMRAK

BEURS PLEIN

SINT ANNENSTRAAT

Scheepvaarthuis

NIEUWE RIDDERSTRAAT

OUDE WAAL

BINNENKANT

Waalseilandsgracht

SCHIPPERS STRAAT

KALKMARKT

MOZES EN ARON

ST JANSSTRAAT

Nationaal Monument

DAM

Waag

NIEUWE MARKT

RECHT BOOMSSLOOT

RECHT BOOMSSLOOT

OUDE WAAL

'sGRAVENHEKJE

PEPERSTRAAT

RAPENBURG

RAPEN BURGER PLEIN

Madame Tussauds Scenerama

PULSTEEG

DAMSTRAAT

Hash Marihuana Museum

OUDEZIJDS VOORBURGWAL

OUDEZIJDS ACHTERBURGWAL

ROEI STR

BARNDE ST

KEIZER STR

KROM BOOMSSLOOT

KORTE KONINGS STR

KORTE KONINGSSTR

Montelbaanstoren

OOSTERSE KADE

OUDESCHANS

FOELIESTRAAT

VALKENBURGERSTRAAT

P JACOBSZ STRAAT

Oostindisch Huis

Trippenhuis

SINT ANTONIESBREESTRAAT

Nieuwmarkt

KROM BOOMSSLOOT

OUDESCHANS

NIEUWE UILENBURGERSTRAAT

ANNE FRANK STR

WUDE LOMBARD ST

ENGE LOMBARD STR

OUDE HOOGSTR

SPINHUIS ST

KLOVENIERSBURGWAL

Zuiderkerk

ZANDSTRAAT

Pintohuis

Oudeschans

Uilenburgergracht

SINT BARBEREN STR

Agnietenkapel

OUDEZIJDS ACHTERBURGWAL

SLUK STR

RUSLAND

RAAMGRACHT

RAAMGRACHT

JODENBREE STR

JODENHOUTTUINEN

NIEUWE UILENBURGERGRACHT

VALKENBURGERSTRAAT

OUDE MANHUISPOORT

Museum Het Rembrandthuis

SEE PAGES 7 & 8 FOR ENLARGEMENT OF THIS AREA

SEE PAGES 7 & 8 FOR ENLARGEMENT OF THIS AREA

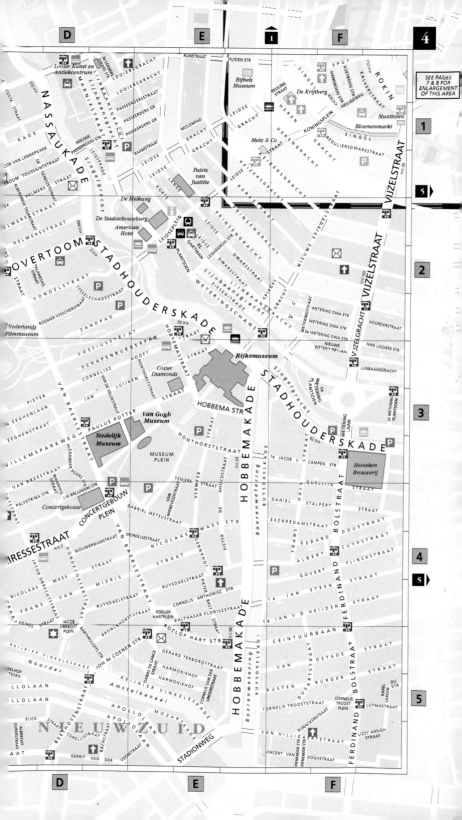

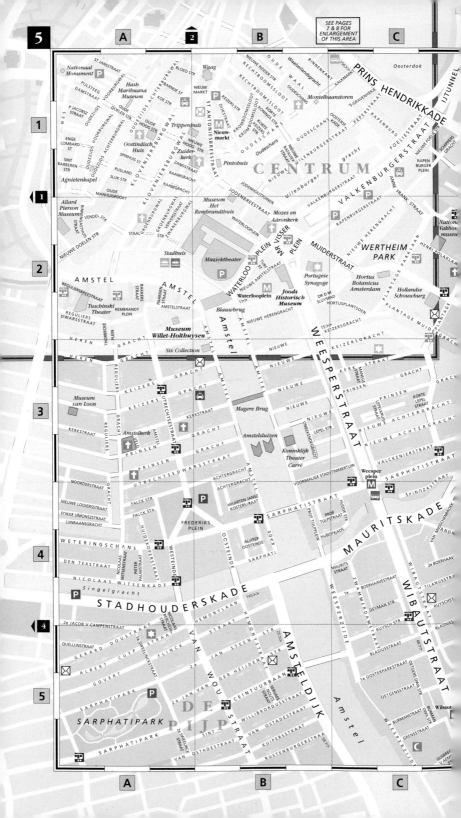

Oosterdok

Nederlands
Scheepvaart
Museum

KATTENBURGER STRAAT

KATTENBURGERKADE

KATTENBURGER KRUISSTRAAT

Kattenburgervaart

2e WITTENBURGER STRAAT

PLEIN

WINDROOS

WINDROOSKADE

BIJLTJESPAD

KATTENBURGERGRACHT

KATTENBURGERGRACHT

WITTENBURGERKADE

WITTENBURGER DWA STR

Wittenburgervaart

**1**

LINDEN STR

WITTENBURGERGRACHT

GROTE WITTENBURGERSTRAAT

K.L. WITTENBURGER

WITTENBURGER POOLSTR

PAREL STR

WAAIGAT

NIEUWE OOSTENBURGERVOORSTRAAT

Oostenburger-Touwbaan

OOSTENBURGER PK

16 ECOHOORN

OOSTENBURGERVAART

CONRAD STRAAT

REER

1e LEEGHWATER STR

2e LEEGHWATER STR

HOOGTE

LAAGTE

NIEUWEVAART

TUSSEN KADIJK

OSTERDOKSKADE

CRUQUIUSSTRAAT

CZAR

Nieuwevaart

OOSTENBURGERGRACHT

COMPAGNIESTRAAT

ADMIRALITEIT STRAAT

BLANKEN

CRUQUIUSKADE

**2**

ENTREPOTDOK

ENTREPOTDOK

Entrepotdok

KADIJK

Verzetsmuseum

ANTAGEKADE

PLANTAGE DOKLAAN

HOOGTE KADIJK

Nieuwevaart

Werf 't Krombout
Museum

ZEEBURGE STR

FUNENKADE

De Gooyer
Windmill

PONTANUSSTRAAT

ZEEBURGERPAD

Lozingskanaal

ZEEBURGERDIJK

Planetarium

Geologisch
Museum

PLANTAGE DOKLAAN

Entrepotdok

MAURITSKADE

SINGELGRACHT

SARPHATISTRAAT

KAZERNE STR

SARPHATISTRAAT

1e LOUISE WENT STRAAT

VON ZESEN STR

PW VLAMING STR

PONTANUSSTRAAT

**ARTIS**

WETTERMANLAAN

PLANTAGE MIDDENLAAN

PLANTAGE KERKLAAN

PLANTAGE BADLAAN

Aquarium

Muidergracht

COMMELIN

STRAAT

DAPPERSTRAAT

STRAAT

**3**

Muiderpoort

ALEXANDER PLEIN

ALEXANDERKADE

WAGENAAR

STRAAT

1e VAN SWINDENSTRAAT

Singelgracht

Muidergracht

Tropenmuseum

LINNAEUSSTRAAT

2e VAN SWINDEN

DAPPER

PLEIN

STRAAT

PIETER NIEUWLAND STRAAT

DAPPERSTRAAT

PONTANUSSTRAAT

**MAURITSKADE**

**OOST**

REINWARDT

WITTENBACH

DOMSELAERSTRAAT

**Muiderpoort**

JOTTEROOR

TER GOUWSTR

**4**

MARY ZELDENRUST STR

2e BOERHAAVE STR

'S GRAVESANDESTRAAT

'S GRAVESANDE PLEIN

**OOSTERPARK**

OOSTERPARK

KASTANJE

STRAAT

KASTANJE

OETEWALERSTRAAT

OETEWALERPAD

LINNAEUSPLANTSOEN

VAN DER VIJVERSTRAAT

RHAAVE

VANSTRAAT

Onze Lieve
Vrouwe
Gasthuis

RUYSCHSTRAAT

OOSTERPARK

BEUKENWEG

2e OOSTER

EIKENWEG

EIKEN

PLEIN

PARK

WEG

VROLIKSTRAAT

POLDERWEG

TILANUSSTRAAT

PARK

STRAAT

BEUKENWEG

2e OOSTER

EIKENWEG

POPULIERENWEG

BEIJERSWEG

WESSELS STRAAT

**5**

STER IEPENWEG

PARK IEPENWEG

3e OOSTER IEPEN WEG

PARK STRAAT

BEUKENWEG

BEUKENWEG

POPULIERENWEG

HEITJOG STRAAT

RETIEFSTRAAT

CILLIERSSTRAAT

PRETORIUS STRAAT

ORANJE

LINNAEUSKADE

BREDEWEG

**MIDDENWEG**

DIAMANTWEG

PLATANENWEG

TUGELAWEG

PRESIDENT

JOUBERT STR

REITZ

BRAND STR

CHRISTIAAN DE WET STR

KRUGERPLEIN

KRUGER STR

MARIT-STRAAT

SPITSKOP STRAAT

KINGS MAGERSFONTEIN STRAAT

TUGELAWEG

TIEFSTRAAT

LAINGS

PRETORIUSSTRAAT

MAJUBASTRAAT

TRANSVAALSTRAAT

STEVE BIKO PLEIN

PAARDEKRAALSTRAAT

NYKSTRAAT

TRANSVAAL PLEIN

TRANSVAALKADE

PRETORIUS STRAAT

RINGDIJK

Ringvaart

WILLEM BEUKELS STRAAT

SIMON STEVIN STR

CORNEL STR

WAKKERSTRAAT

DIBBEL STR

ZACHARIAS JANSZSTRAAT

HOGEWEG

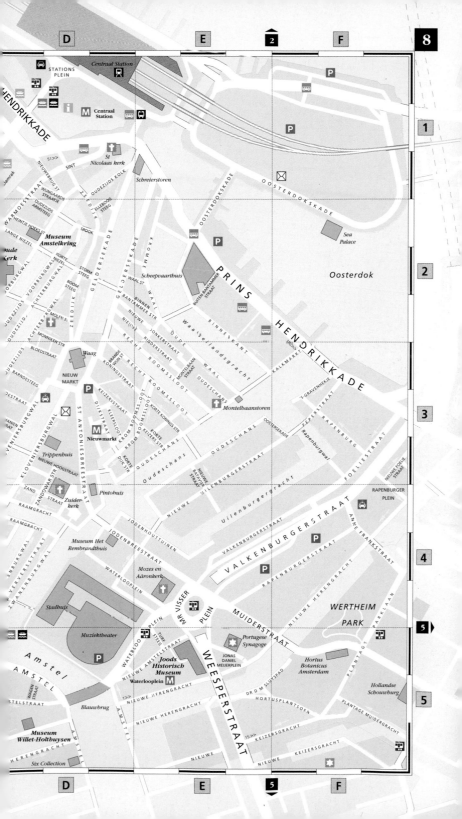

# Street Finder Index

# General Index

# Acknowledgments

DORLING KINDERSLEY would like to thank the following people whose help and assistance contributed to the preparation of this book.

## MAIN CONTRIBUTORS

Robin Pascoe has lived in Amsterdam for the past 15 years. She is a freelance journalist and writes for various Dutch newspapers. She also works for the Dutch national news agency ANP, the international development news agency IPS, and the BBC.

Christopher Catling has been visiting the Netherlands for over ten years, since writing his first guide for business travellers in 1984. He has since written a further four guides to Amsterdam and the Netherlands. Besides this guide, he has contributed to four *Dorling Kindersley Travel Guides:* Florence and Tuscany, Venice and the Veneto, Great Britain and Italy.

## ADDITIONAL PHOTOGRAPHY

Steve Gorton, Clive Streeter

## ADDITIONAL ILLUSTRATIONS

Arcana (Graham Bell), Richard Bonson, Stephen Conlin, Roy Flooks, Mick Gillah, Kevin Goold, Stephen Gyapay, Chris Orr, Ian Henderson, Philip Winton, John Woodcock

## EDITORIAL AND DESIGN

MANAGING EDITORS Vivien Crump, Helen Partington
MANAGING ART EDITOR Steve Knowlden
SENIOR EDITOR Peter Casterton
DEPUTY EDITORIAL DIRECTOR Douglas Amrine
DEPUTY ART DIRECTOR Gaye Allen
PRODUCTION David Proffit
PICTURE RESEARCH Lorna Ainger
DTP DESIGNER Siri Lowe
Johan Blom, Susan Churchill, Lucinda Cooke, Seán O'Connell, Martin Cropper, Karlien van Dam, Russell Davies, Gadi Farfour, Anthea Forlee, Fay Franklin, Annette Jacobs, Gail Jones, Nancy Jones, David Lindsey, Rebecca Milner, Caroline Radula-Scott, Simon Ryder, Debbie Scholes

## INDEX

Hilary Bird

## CARTOGRAPHY

Jane Hanson, Phil Rose,
Jennifer Skelley (Lovell Johns Limited)
MAP CO-ORDINATORS Michael Ellis, David Pugh

## SPECIAL ASSISTANCE

Greet Tuinman, Charlotte van Beurden, Poppy

## PHOTOGRAPHY PERMISSIONS

Dorling Kindersley would like to thank the following for their kind permission to photograph at their establishments:
Airborne Museum, Arnhem; Allard Pierson Museum; Amstelkring Museum; Amsterdams Historisch Museum/Willet-Holthuysen Museum; Artis Zoo; Aviodrome; Beurs van Berlage; Boerhaave Museum, Leiden; Carré Theater; Concertgebouw; Coster Diamonds; Domkerk, Utrecht; Electrische Museumtramlijn; Europoort, Rotterdam; Filmmuseum; Frankendael; Anne Frankhuis; Grote Kerk, Alkmaar; Grote Kerk, Edam; Hash Marihuana Museum; Heineken Museum; Hollandse Schouwburg; Hortus Botanicus, Leiden; Joods Historisch Museum; Justitie Hall; Koninklijk Paleis; Krijtberg; Kröller-Müller Museum and National Park, Otterlo; Nederlands Scheepvaart Museum; Madurodam, Den Haag; Maritime Museum, Rotterdam; Monnickendam; Nieuwe Kerk; Nieuwe Kerk and Oude Kerk, Delft; Oude Kerk; Paleis Het Loo, Apeldoorn; Peace Palace, Den Haag; Portugese Synagoge; Prince William V Gallery, Den Haag; Prinsenhof, Leiden; Prison Gate Museum, Den Haag; RAI International Exhibition Centre; Rijksmuseum; Rijksmuseum, Utrecht; Rijksmuseum van Oudheden, Leiden; Rijksmuseum van Speelklok Tot Pierement, Utrecht; St Bavo, Haarlem; St Nicolaaskerk; SAS Hotel; Scheveningen Sea Life Centre; Sint Janskerk, Gouda; Stadhuis-Muziektheater; Stedelijk Museum; Stedelijk Molenmuseum, Leiden, Technologie Museum; Teylers Museum, Haarlem; Theater Museum; Tropenmuseum; Vakbonds Museum; Van Gogh Museum; Van Loon Museum; Verzetsmuseum; Werf 't Kromhout Museum; Westerkerk; Westfries Museum, Hoorn; Zuiderzee Museum.

## PICTURE CREDITS

t = top; tl = top left; tc = top centre; tr = top right; trc = top right centre; cla = centre left above; ca = centre above; cra = centre right above; cl = centre left; c = centre; cr = centre right; clb = centre left below; cb = centre below; crb = centre right below; bl = bottom left; b = bottom; bc = bottom centre; br = bottom right; (d) = detail.

Every effort has been made to trace the copyright holders, and we apologize in advance for any unintentional omissions. We would be pleased to insert the appropriate acknowledgments in any subsequent edition of this publication.

Works of art have been reproduced with the permission of the following copyright holders:
© ABC/MONDRIAAN ESTATE/HOLTZMAN TRUST, LICENSED BY ILP 1995: 136br; © ADAGP, PARIS AND DACS, LONDON 1995: 136cl, 200t, 204cb; © DACS, LONDON 1995: 38bl, 136bl, 201tl; © JASPER JOHNS/DACS LONDON/VAGA NEW YORK: 137cb.

The Publishers are grateful to the following museums, photographers and picture libraries for permission to reproduce their photographs:

AKG, LONDON: 20clb, 22cl, 23c, 24cl, 26br, 27t, 101tr, 130tc, 185tr, 209c; Niklaus Strauss 137br; MAX ALEXANDER 127bl; AMSTERDAM HISTORISCH MUSEUM: 84bl, 85cr, 85br; AMSTERDAMS HISTORISCH MUSEUM: 16, 21bc, 22–3c, 23tc, 23crb, 23bl, 24–5c, 25clb, 28cl, 29t, 29cb, 30cl, 31cr, 38cl, 81t, 81tr, 81cr, 81br, 82tl, 82b, 83t, 83b, 90b, 94, 120cl, 120c,

120bl, 121cr; ANP Photo: 35tc, 35crb, 35bl.
B&U International Picture Service: 35tl, 35tr,
51cr, 53b, 101bl, 105br, 180cl, 203t; Boymans-van
Beuningen Museum, Rotterdam: 200cl, 200b,
201tc, 201cr, 201br, 200t; Bridgeman Art Library:
Christie's London *The Groote Market Haarlem
with the Church of St Bavo* Gerrit Berckheyde
c.1668 176t; Giraudon/Musée Crozatier Le Puy-en-
Velay France *King Louis XIV* 27br; Kremlin
Museums Moscow 28bl; Private Collection *The
Oude Zijds Voorburgwal in Amsterdam* Cornelius
Springer 44cl; Private Collection *Self-Portrait
Kazimir Malevich* 137cr; Stapleton Collection
Delft tile 19th century 192tl.

Camera Press: Karsh of Ottawa 137tr; Jean-Loup
Charmet: Musée de l'Armée 28br; Colorsport: 34cla.

Jan Derwig: 99tr, 151b, 224b, 266cl, 267cr; Drents
Museum, Assen: 18bl.

Mary Evans Picture Library: 9c, 19cra, 19bc, 21bl,
23br, 24bl, 25br, 27bl, 29br, 30cb, 30bc, 31bl,
33crb 55c, 163c; Louis Raemaehois 32bc; Jean
Veber 31br; Eye Ubiquitous: T Rafferty 263br.
Foto Natura: Fred Hazelhoff 205cb.

Gauguin Restaurant: 224cl; Gemeentearchief,
Amsterdam: 19tl, 21ca, 21cb, 22tl, 22bc, 29cr,
45b, 99tl, 99cl, 100clb, 101br, 102bl, 103tr, 103cr,
104tr, 105tr, 105cr; Gemeentearchief, Kampen: 21tl.

Frans Hals Museum, Haarlem: 25tl, 28–9c, 178t,
178bl, 178br, 179tl, 179tr, 179bl, 179br; Vanessa
Hamilton: 97tl, 101cr, 104cl; Robert Harding
Picture Library: 58tr; Peter Scholey 116t; Adam
Woolfitt 11br; Hulton-Deutsch Collection: 38t.

Iconografisch Bureau: 103tl; The Image Bank:
Bernard van Berg 52cr; Fotoworld 50b; Inter-
national Flower Bulb Centre: 24bc, 180bc, 181tl,
181cla, 181cl, 181clb, 181bl; International
Institute of Social History: 32tl. James Davis
Travel Photography: 225tr; Collection Jewish
Historical Museum, Amsterdam: *My Father at
Morning Prayers* Eduard Frankfort 1886 64cl;
*Mahzor*, Illuminated Manuscript on Parchment,
Cologne area, c. 1250 64crb.

Kröller-Müller Museum: 204tl; Mauritshuis, Den
Haag: 188t, 188c, 188bl, 189t, 189cr, 189br, 189bl,
193tl; MGM Cinemas BV: 33cr; Municipal Museum
de Lakenhal, Leiden: 184b; Museum Huis Lambert
van Meerten, Collection RBK: 195t.

National Fietsmuseum Velorama, Nijmegen: 31tl,
274tr; Netherlands Architecture Institute Archive:
98cl; Isaac Gosschalk 105cl; De Klerk 33t, 97cra;

Nemo Science and Technology Center: 150b.
Picture Box: Lee Auteur 156; © Photo RMN,
Paris: 8–9; Prentenkabinet der Rijksuniversiteit,
Leiden: 30br.

Range Pictures: 26tr; Museum Het Rembrandthuis:
59b; Retrograph Archive Ltd: 267bl; Martin Breese
30tl; Rijksmuseum-Foundation, Amsterdam: 24tl, 26tl,
28cla, 38c, 40b, 130cl, 130b, 131t, 131cl, 131br, 132t,
132b, 133t, 133b; Rijksmuseum Paleis Het Loo,
Apeldoorn: E Boeijinga 206tr, 207tl, R Mulder 206cl;
AAW Meine Jansen 206bl; R Mulder 206clb; Royal
Palace, Amsterdam: Erik Hemsmerg 25tr, 37cr, 70,
74t; Royal Tropical Institute: 152cla, 152cl.

Scheepvart Museum: 17b, 26cr, 27c, 146tl, 146ca,
146cb, 147c; Science Photo Library/Earth Satellite
Corporation: 10cl; Harry Smith Horticultural
Collection: 34b; Spaarnestad Fotoarchief: 33c, 97tr,
99cb; Stedelijk Museum, Alkmaar: 32c; Stedelijk
Museum, Amsterdam: 136tr, 137tl, 137tc; ©
ABC/Mondriaan Estate/Holtzmann Trust, licenced
by ILP 1995 *Composition in Red, Black, Blue, Yellow
and Grey* Piet Mondriaan 1920 136br; © ADAGP
Paris and DACS London 1995 *Portrait of Artist with
Seven Fingers* Marc Chagall 1912–13 136cl; © DACS
London 1995 *Red Blue Chair* Gerrit Rietveld 1918
136bl; © DACS London 1995 *Steltman Chair* Gerrit
Rietveld 1963 38bl; © Jasper Johns/DACS
London/VAGA New York 1995 *Untitled* Jasper Johns
1965 137cb; Stedelijk Museum De Lakenhal, Leiden:
104br; Tony Stone Images: 173cl, 268bl; Kim
Blaxland 181tr; David Hanson 208–9; John Lamb
2–3; Manfred Mehlig 162–3; Rohan 100t.

Hans Tulleners: 99cr, 100cr, 102c.

Universiteitsbibliotheek van Amsterdam: 96tr;
Vincent Van Gogh (Foundation), Van Gogh
Museum, Amsterdam: 38br, 134t, 134c, 134bl,
134br, 135t, 135cr, 135crb.

Western Australian Maritime Museum: 26ca;
World Pictures: 95cr. ZEFA: CPA 52b; Steenmans
53c; Streichan 45t.

Front Endpaper: All special photography except
Royal Palace Amsterdam Erik Hemsmerg trc.

Jacket
Front – Alamy com: Charlie Newham main image;
DK Picture Library bl; Max Alexander cb; Steve
Gorton cr. Back – DK Picture Library b, t. Spine –
Alamy com: Charlie Newham.

All other images © Dorling Kindersley.
For further information see: www.dkimages.com

# Phrase Book

## IN EMERGENCY

| | | |
|---|---|---|
| Help! | **Help!** | Help |
| Stop! | **Stop!** | Stop |
| Call a doctor | **Haal een dokter** | Haal uhn **dok**-tur |
| Call an ambulance | **Bel een ambulance** | Bell uhn ahm-bew-**luhns**-uh |
| Call the police | **Roep de politie** | Roop duh poe-**leet**-see |
| Call the fire brigade | **Roep de brandweer** | Roop duh **brahnt**-vheer |
| Where is the nearest telephone? | **Waar is de dichtstbijzijnde telefoon?** | Vhaar iss duh **dikhst**-baiy-zaiyn-duh tay-luh-**foan** |
| Where is the nearest hospital? | **Waar is het dichtstbijzijnde ziekenhuis?** | Vhaar iss het **dikhst**-baiy-zaiyn-duh **zee**-kuh-houws |

## COMMUNICATION ESSENTIALS

| | | |
|---|---|---|
| Yes | **Ja** | Yaa |
| No | **Nee** | Nay |
| Please | **Alstublieft** | Ahls-tew-**bleeft** |
| Thank you | **Dank u** | Dahnk-ew |
| Excuse me | **Pardon** | Pahr-**don** |
| Hello | **Hallo** | Hallo |
| Goodbye | **Dag** | Dahgh |
| Good night | **Slaap lekker** | Slaap **lek**-kah |
| morning | **Morgen** | **Mor**-ghuh |
| afternoon | **Middag** | **Mid**-dahgh |
| evening | **Avond** | **Ah**-vohnd |
| yesterday | **Gisteren** | **Ghis**-tern |
| today | **Vandaag** | Vahn-**daagh** |
| tomorrow | **Morgen** | **Mor**-ghuh |
| here | **Hier** | Heer |
| there | **Daar** | Daar |
| What? | **Wat?** | Vhat |
| When? | **Wanneer?** | Vhan-**eer** |
| Why? | **Waarom?** | Vhaar-**om** |
| Where? | **Waar?** | Vhaar |
| How? | **Hoe?** | Hoo |

## USEFUL PHRASES

| | | |
|---|---|---|
| How are you? | **Hoe gaat het ermee?** | Hoo ghaat het er-**may** |
| Very well, thank you | **Heel goed, dank u** | Hayl ghoot, dahnk ew |
| How do you do? | **Hoe maakt u het?** | Hoo maakt ew het |
| See you soon | **Tot ziens** | Tot zeens |
| That's fine | **Prima** | **Pree**-mah |
| Where is/are? | **Waar is/zijn?** | Vhaar iss/zayn... |
| How far is it to...? | **Hoe ver is het naar...?** | Hoo vehr iss het naar |
| How do I get to ...? | **Hoe kom ik naar...?** | Hoo kom ik naar... |
| Do you speak English? | **Spreekt u engels?** | Spraykt ew **eng**-uhls |
| I don't understand | **Ik snap het niet** | Ik snahp het neet |
| Could you speak slowly? | **Kunt u langzamer praten?** | Kuhnt ew **lahng**-zahmer praa-tuh |
| I'm sorry | **Sorry** | Sorry |

## USEFUL WORDS

| | | |
|---|---|---|
| big | **groot** | ghroaht |
| small | **klein** | klaiyn |
| hot | **warm** | vharm |
| cold | **koud** | khowt |
| good | **goed** | ghoot |
| bad | **slecht** | slekht |
| enough | **genoeg** | ghuh-**noohkh** |
| well | **goed** | ghoot |
| open | **open** | open |
| closed | **gesloten** | ghuh-**slow**-tuh |
| left | **links** | links |
| right | **rechts** | rekhts |
| straight on | **rechtdoor** | rehkht dohr |
| near | **dichtbij** | dikht baiy |
| far | **ver weg** | vehr vhekh |
| up | **omhoog** | om-**hoakh** |
| down | **naar beneden** | naar buh-**nay**-duh |
| early | **vroeg** | vrookhh |
| late | **laat** | laat |
| entrance | **ingang** | **in**-ghahng |
| exit | **uitgang** | **ouht**-ghang |
| toilet | **wc** | vhay say |
| occupied | **bezet** | buh-**zett** |
| free (unoccupied) | **vrij** | vraiy |
| free (no charge) | **gratis** | **ghraah**-tiss |

## MAKING A TELEPHONE CALL

| | | |
|---|---|---|
| I'd like to place a long distance call | **Ik wil graag interlokaal telefoneren** | Ik vhil ghraakh **inter**-loh-kaahl tay-luh-foe-**neh**-ruh |
| I'd like to call collect | **Ik wil 'collect call' bellen** | Ik vhil 'collect call' **bel**-luh |
| I'll try again later | **Ik probeer het later nog wel eens** | Ik pro-**beer** het laater nokh vhel ayns |
| Can I leave a message? | **Kunt u een boodschap doorgeven?** | Kuhnt ew uhn **boat**-skhahp **dohr**-ghay-vuh |
| Could you speak up a little please? | **Wilt u wat harder praten?** | Vhilt ew vhat **hahr**-der **praah**-tuh |
| Local call | **Lokaal gesprek** | Low-**kaahl** ghuh-**sprek** |

## SHOPPING

| | | |
|---|---|---|
| How much does this cost? | **Hoeveel kost dit?** | Hoo-**vayl** kost dit |
| I would like | **Ik wil graag** | Ik vhil ghraakh |
| Do you have...? | **Heeft u...?** | Hayft ew... |
| I'm just looking | **Ik kijk alleen even** | Ik kaiyk alleyn **ay**-vuh |
| Do you take credit cards? | **Neemt u credit cards aan?** | Naymt ew credit cards aan |
| Do you take traveller's cheques? | **Neemt u reischeques aan?** | Naymt ew **raiys**-sheks aan |
| What time do you open? | **Hoe laat gaat u open?** | Hoo laat ghaat ew opuh |
| What time do you close? | **Hoe laat gaat u dicht?** | Hoo laat ghaat ew dikht |
| This one | **Deze** | **Day**-zuh |
| That one | **Die** | Dee |
| expensive | **duur** | dewr |
| cheap | **goedkoop** | ghoot-**koap** |
| size | **maat** | maat |
| white | **wit** | vhit |
| black | **zwart** | zvhahrt |
| red | **rood** | roat |
| yellow | **geel** | ghayl |
| green | **groen** | ghroon |
| blue | **blauw** | blah-ew |

## TYPES OF SHOPS

| | | |
|---|---|---|
| antique shop | **antiekwinkel** | ahn-**teek**-vhin-kul |
| bakery | **bakker** | **bah**-ker |
| bank | **bank** | bahnk |
| bookshop | **boekwinkel** | **book**-vhin-kul |
| butcher | **slager** | slaakh-err |
| cake shop | **banketbakkerij** | bahnk-**et**-bahk-er-aiy |
| cheese shop | **kaaswinkel** | **kaas**-vhin-kul |
| chip shop | **patatzaak** | pah-**taht**-zaak |
| chemist (dispensing) | **apotheek** | ah-poe-**taiyk** |
| delicatessen | **delicatessen** | daylee-kah-**tes**-suh |
| department store | **warenhuis** | **vhaar**-uh-houws |
| fishmonger | **viswinkel** | **viss**-vhin-kul |
| greengrocer | **groenteboer** | **ghroon**-tuh-boor |
| hairdresser | **kapper** | **kah**-per |
| market | **markt** | mahrkt |
| newsagent | **krantenwinkel** | **krahn**-tuh-vhin-kul |
| post office | **postkantoor** | **pohst**-kahn-tor |
| shoe shop | **schoenwinkel** | **sghoo**-nuh-vhin-kul |
| supermarket | **supermarkt** | **sew**-per-mahrkt |
| tobacconist | **sigarenwinkel** | see-**ghaa**-ruh-vhin-kul |
| travel agent | **reisburo** | **raiys**-bew-roa |

## SIGHTSEEING

| | | |
|---|---|---|
| art gallery | **gallerie** | ghaller-ee |
| bus station | **busstation** | **buhs**-stah-shown |
| bus ticket | **strippenkaart** | **strip**-puh-kaahrt |
| cathedral | **kathedraal** | kah-tuh-**draal** |
| church | **kerk** | kehrk |
| closed on public holidays | **op feestdagen gesloten** | op **fayst**-daa-ghuh ghuh-**slow**-tuh |
| day return | **dagretour** | **dahgh**-ruh-tour |
| garden | **tuin** | touwn |
| library | **bibliotheek** | bee-bee-yo-**tayk** |
| museum | **museum** | mew-**zay**-uhm |
| railway station | **station** | stah-**shown** |
| return ticket | **retourtje** | ruh-**tour**-tyuh |
| single journey | **enkeltje** | **eng**-kuhl-tyuh |
| tourist information | **VVV** | fay fay fay |
| town hall | **stadhuis** | staht-**houws** |
| train | **trein** | traiyn |

## Staying in a Hotel

| | | |
|---|---|---|
| Do you have a vacant room? | Zijn er nog kamers vrij? | Zaiyn er nokh **kaa**-mers vray |
| double room with double bed | een twees persoonskamer met een twee persoonsbed | uhn **tvhay**-per **soans**-kaa-mer met uhn **tvhay**-per-**soans** beht |
| twin room | een kamer met een lits-jumeaux | uhn **kaa-mer** met uhn lee-zjoo-**moh** |
| single room | eenpersoons-kamer | ayn-per-**soans-kaa**-mer |
| room with a bath | kamer met bad | **kaa**-mer met baht |
| shower | douche | doosh |
| porter | kruier | **krouw**-yuh |
| I have a reservation | Ik heb gereserveerd | Ik hehp ghuh-ray-sehr-**veert** |

## Eating Out

| | | |
|---|---|---|
| Have you got a table? | Is er een tafel vrij? | Iss ehr uhn **tah**-fuhl vraiy |
| I want to reserve a table | Ik wil een tafel reserveren | Ik vhil uhn **tah**-fuhl ray-sehr-**veer**-uh |
| The bill, please | Mag ik afrekenen | Mukh ik **ahf**-ray-kuh-nuh |
| I am a vegetarian | Ik ben vegetariër | Ik ben fay-ghuh-**taahr**-ee-er |
| waitress/waiter | serveerster/ober | Sehr-**veer**-ster/**oh**-ber |
| menu | de kaart | duh kaahrt |
| cover charge | het couvert | het koo-**vehr** |
| wine list | de wijnkaart | duh **vhaiyn**-kaart |
| glass | het glas | het ghlahss |
| bottle | de fles | duh fless |
| knife | het mes | het mess |
| fork | de vork | duh fork |
| spoon | de lepel | duh **lay**-pul |
| breakfast | het ontbijt | het ont-**baiyt** |
| lunch | de lunch | duh lernsh |
| dinner | het diner | het dee-**nay** |
| main course | het hoofdgerecht | het **hoaft**-ghuh-rekht |
| starter, first course | het voorgerecht | het **vohr**-ghuh-rekht |
| dessert | het nagerecht | het **naa**-ghuh-rekht |
| dish of the day | het dagmenu | het **dahgh**-munh-ew |
| bar | het cafe | het kaa-**fay** |
| café | het eetcafe | het **ayt**-kaa-**fay** |
| rare | rare | 'rare' |
| medium | medium | 'medium' |
| well done | doorbakken | dohr-**bah**-kuh |

## Menu Decoder

| | | |
|---|---|---|
| **aardappels** | **aard**-uppuhls | potatoes |
| **azijn** | aah-**zaiyn** | vinegar |
| **biefstuk** | **beef**-stuhk | steak |
| **bier, pils** | beer, pilss | beer |
| **boter** | boater | butter |
| **brood/broodje** | broat/**broat**-yuh | bread/roll |
| **cake, taart, gebak** | 'cake', taahrt, ghuh-**bahk** | cake, pastry |
| **carbonade** | kahr-bow-**naa**-duh | pork chop |
| **chocola** | show-coa-**laa** | chocolate |
| **citroen** | see-**troon** | lemon |
| **cocktail** | cocktail | cocktail |
| **droog** | droakh | dry |
| **eend** | aynt | duck |
| **ei** | aiy | egg |
| **garnalen** | ghahr-**naah**-luh | prawns |
| **gebakken** | ghuh-**bah**-ken | fried |
| **gegrild** | ghuh-**ghrillt** | grilled |
| **gekookt** | ghuh-**kuakt** | boiled |
| **gepocheerd** | ghuh-posh-**eert** | poached |
| **gerookt** | ghuh-**roakt** | smoked |
| **geroosterd brood** | ghuh-**roas**-tert broat | toast |
| **groenten** | **ghroon**-tuh | vegetables |
| **ham** | hahm | ham |
| **haring** | **haa**-ring | herring |
| **hutspot** | **huht**-spot | hot pot |
| **ijs** | aiyss | ice, ice cream |
| **jenever** | yuh-**nay**-vhur | gin |
| **kaas** | kaas | cheese |
| **kabeljauw** | kah-buhl-**youw** | cod |
| **kip** | kip | chicken |
| **knoflook** | **knoff**-loak | garlic |
| **koffie** | coffee | coffee |
| **kool, rode of witte** | coal, **roe**-duh off **vhit**-uh | cabbage, red or white |
| **kreeft** | krayft | lobster |
| **kroket** | crow-**ket** | ragout in bread-crumbs, deep fried |
| **lamsvlees** | **lahms**-flayss | lamb |

| | | |
|---|---|---|
| **lekkerbekje** | **lek**-kah-bek-yuh | fried fillet of haddock |
| **mineraalwater** | meener-**aahl**-vhaater | mineral water |
| **mosterd** | **moss**-tehrt | mustard |
| **niet scherp** | neet skehrp | mild |
| **olie** | **oh**-lee | oil |
| **paling** | **paa**-ling | eel |
| **pannekoek** | **pah**-nuh-kook | pancake |
| **patat frites** | pah-**taht** freet | chips |
| **peper** | **pay**-per | pepper |
| **poffertjes** | **poffer**-tyuhs | tiny buckwheat pancakes |
| **rijst** | raiyst | rice |
| **rijsttafel** | **raiys**-tah-ful | Indonesian meal |
| **rode wijn** | **roe**-duh vhaiyn | red wine |
| **rookworst** | **roak**-vhorst | smoked sausage |
| **rundvlees** | **ruhnt**-flayss | beef |
| **saus** | souwss | sauce |
| **schaaldieren** | **skaahl**-deeh-ruh | shellfish |
| **scherp** | skehrp | hot (spicy) |
| **schol** | sghol | plaice |
| **soep** | soop | soup |
| **stamppot** | **stahm**-pot | sausage stew |
| **suiker** | **souw**-ker | sugar |
| **thee** | tay | tea |
| **tosti** | **toss**-tee | cheese on toast |
| **uien** | **ouw**-yuh | onions |
| **uitsmijter** | **ouht**-smaiy-ter | fried egg on bread with ham |
| **varkensvlees** | **vahr**-kuhns-flayss | pork |
| **vers fruit** | fehrss frouwt | fresh fruit |
| **verse jus** | **vehr**-suh zjhew | fresh orange juice |
| **vis** | fiss | fish/seafood |
| **vlees** | flayss | meat |
| **water** | **vhaa**-ter | water |
| **witte wijn** | **vhih**-tuh vhaiyn | white wine |
| **worst** | vhorst | sausage |
| **zout** | zouwt | salt |

## Numbers

| | | |
|---|---|---|
| 1 | **een** | ayn |
| 2 | **twee** | tvhay |
| 3 | **drie** | dree |
| 4 | **vier** | feer |
| 5 | **vijf** | faiyf |
| 6 | **zes** | zess |
| 7 | **zeven** | **zay**-vuh |
| 8 | **acht** | ahkht |
| 9 | **negen** | **nay**-guh |
| 10 | **tien** | teen |
| 11 | **elf** | elf |
| 12 | **twaalf** | tvhaalf |
| 13 | **dertien** | **dehr**-teen |
| 14 | **veertien** | **feer**-teen |
| 15 | **vijftien** | **faiyf**-teen |
| 16 | **zestien** | **zess**-teen |
| 17 | **zeventien** | **zayvuh**-teen |
| 18 | **achtien** | **ahkh**-teen |
| 19 | **negentien** | **nay-ghuh**-teen |
| 20 | **twintig** | **tvhin**-tukh |
| 21 | **eenentwintig** | **aynuh**-tvhin-tukh |
| 30 | **dertig** | **dehr**-tukh |
| 40 | **veertig** | **feer**-tukh |
| 50 | **vijftig** | **faiyf**-tukh |
| 60 | **zestig** | **zess**-tukh |
| 70 | **zeventig** | **zay**-vuh-tukh |
| 80 | **tachtig** | **tahkh**-tukh |
| 90 | **negentig** | **nayguh**-tukh |
| 100 | **honderd** | **hohn**-durt |
| 1000 | **duizend** | **douw**-zuhnt |
| 1,000,000 | **miljoen** | mill-**yoon** |

## Time

| | | |
|---|---|---|
| one minute | **een minuut** | uhn meen-**ewt** |
| one hour | **een uur** | uhn ewr |
| half an hour | **een half uur** | uhn hahlf ewr |
| half past one | **half twee** | hahlf tvhay |
| a day | **een dag** | uhn dahgh |
| a week | **een week** | uhn vhayk |
| a month | **een maand** | uhn maant |
| a year | **een jaar** | uhn jaar |
| Monday | **maandag** | **maan**-dahgh |
| Tuesday | **dinsdag** | **dins**-dahgh |
| Wednesday | **woensdag** | **vhoons**-dahgh |
| Thursday | **donderdag** | **donder**-dahgh |
| Friday | **vrijdag** | **vraiy**-dahgh |
| Saturday | **zaterdag** | **zaater**-dahgh |
| Sunday | **zondag** | **zon**-dahgh |

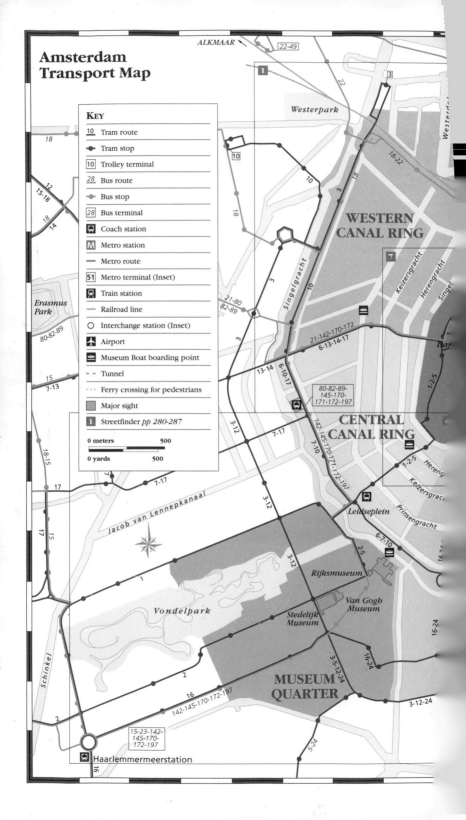

# Amsterdam
# Transport Map

ALKMAAR

22-49

Westerpark

**KEY**

| | |
|---|---|
| 10 | Tram route |
| •—• | Tram stop |
| 10 | Trolley terminal |
| 28 | Bus route |
| •—• | Bus stop |
| 28 | Bus terminal |
| 🚍 | Coach station |
| M | Metro station |
| — | Metro route |
| 51 | Metro terminal (Inset) |
| 🚆 | Train station |
| — | Railroad line |
| ○ | Interchange station (Inset) |
| ✈ | Airport |
| 〓 | Museum Boat boarding point |
| - - | Tunnel |
| ⋯ | Ferry crossing for pedestrians |
| ▨ | Major sight |
| 1 | Streetfinder *pp 280-287* |

| 0 meters | 500 |
|---|---|
| 0 yards | 500 |

Erasmus
Park

80-82-89

15

7-13

18-15

17

17

15

WESTERN
CANAL RING

Keizersgracht
Herengracht
Singel

21-142-170-172
6-13-14-17

13-14

6-10-17

80-82-89-
145-170-
171-172-197

CENTRAL
CANAL RING

142-145-170-171-172-197

7-10

7-17

Leidseplein

6-7-10

Prinsengracht

3-12

Jacob van Lennepkanaal

7-17

3-12

3-12

Rijksmuseum

2-5

Vondelpark

Stedelijk
Museum

Van Gogh
Museum

16-24

2

16

142-145-170-172-197

MUSEUM
QUARTER

3-5-12-24

16-24

3-12-24

5-24

15-23-142-
145-170-
172-197

🚆 Haarlemmermeerstation

16

Schinkel

18
15-18
12
18
14

18

10

10

3

21-80
82-89

3

Singelgracht

18

Westerpark

22

1

3

7

18-22

1-2-5

Heren

Keizersgrac

1-2-5